GW00712281

The Ladies of Londonderry

For Martin

The Ladies of Londonderry

Women and political patronage

DIANE URQUHART

I.B. TAURIS
LONDON · NEW YORK

Published in 2007 by I.B.Tauris & Co Ltd
6 Salem Road, London W2 4BU
175 Fifth Avenue, New York NY 10010
www.ibtauris.com

In the United States of America and Canada distributed by
Palgrave Macmillan a division of St. Martin's Press
175 Fifth Avenue, New York NY 10010

International Library of Historical Studies 50

ISBN: 978 1 84511 410 7

A full CIP record for this book is available from the British Library
A full CIP record for this book is available from the Library of Congress

Library of Congress catalog card: available

Printed and bound in India by Replika Press Pvt Ltd
From camera-ready copy edited and supplied by the author

I am glad to see that in Ireland, as well as in this Isle, you are fulfilling, in a manner worthy of you, the duties of your high station. You set a great example, and one, which, while it pleases all, does not astonish me, who have known you so long.

Benjamin Disraeli to Frances Anne, third Marchioness of Londonderry, 16 September 1857.[1]

You have seen unique things, and have seen them with firm and brilliant eyes… You want to tell them the things that no newspaper, nor even any common diarist knows or can know, the intimate, vivid, private things…You will be working for the next age, for the historian still unborn…

Edmund Gosse to Theresa, sixth Marchioness of Londonderry, 27 March 1915.[2]

You have played a full part in contemporary history with humour, fortitude and courage…

Telegram to Edith, seventh Marchioness of Londonderry on her eightieth birthday from Harry and Eleanor Nathan, 3 December 1958.[3]

Contents

List of Illustrations

Acknowledgements

I wish to express my sincere thanks to the Research Development Fund and Research Leave Scheme of the University of Liverpool, the Eoin O'Mahony Bursary of the Royal Irish Academy and the Institute of Irish Studies of the Queen's University of Belfast. I am most grateful to Prof. Mary O'Dowd for her support in the early stages of the work and for suggesting the title of the introduction. I would like to thank my colleagues at the Institute of Irish Studies of the University of Liverpool for their support and good humour, especially Marianne Elliott, Linda Christiansen, Dorothy Lynch, Pat Nugent, Frank Shovlin and Kevin Bean. Very special thanks are also due to Ian McKeane whose skilful translations of nineteenth-century French made the material come to life, Maria Power who read the whole manuscript and Mark Wells for indexing. At I.B.Tauris thanks to Lester Crook who shared my enthusiasm for the topic from the outset, Liz Friend-Smith and Nicola Denny. I would also like to thank Lady Bury, the Marquess of Londonderry, H. E. Dáithí O'Ceallaigh, David Cannadine and Anthony Malcolmson.

I am most grateful to the following for granting permission to publish from the manuscripts in their care: the Syndics of Cambridge University Library; the Centre for Kentish Studies; Hertfordshire Archives and Local Studies; Parliamentary Archives at the House of Lords; Leeds University Library; the Public Record Office; the National Portrait Gallery and the Deputy Keeper of the Records of the Public Record Office of Northern Ireland. Extracts from the Ramsay MacDonald papers are reproduced by courtesy of the University Librarian and Director of The John Rylands Library, The University of Manchester. Extracts from the Londonderry Archive are reproduced by permission of the Durham Record Office. Extracts from the Chamberlain papers are reproduced by kind permission of Special Collections, Information Services, University of Birmingham. Staff at the above-named repositories have been unfailing helpful but special thanks are due to those at the Public Record Office of Northern Ireland, especially Anne McVeigh, and Durham County Record Office where the bulk of this research was conducted. I am also grateful to the following individuals and organisations for granting permission to publish material: Viscount Craigavon, Robert Lowry, H. Montgomery Hyde, the Ulster Women's Unionist Council, *Country Life*, *Newcastle Evening Chronicle* and the *Evening Standard*.

On a more personal note, I would like to thank my family, in particular, Betty and Eric Urquhart, my sister, Alyson, and my grandmother, Elizabeth Rooney as well as my friends, Gill McIntosh, Caroline Calvert, Gail McMullen, Ciara Gallagher and Joe Braden whose encouragement over the past years meant more than they knew.

Introduction

Peeresses, patronage and power

The three lives that form the backbone of this study encapsulate a century and a half of tumult: the rise of democracy and the associated popularisation of politics, the dual processes of industrialisation and urbanisation that resulted in wholesale social transformation, demands for national and individual self-determination and war on a previously unimagined scale. On a personal level, these were also turbulent years for the Marchionesses of Londonderry with exacting standards of class and gender-based acceptability, miscarriage, childbirth and death, widowhood and activism within the most male-defined social landscape - politics - all featuring in their lives. The lineation between the private and public aspects of these women's lives, however, should not be too firmly drawn. There is no question that the marchionesses formed part of a small coterie of political confidantes and hostesses who worked by distinctly personal means in high society to promote their family, direct careers and impart change while marriage and widowhood would respectively facilitate and impede their political influence. Indeed, the idea of the personal being political, brought to the public's attention by the second-wave feminism of 1960s America, can be applied to a different place and a different time: in this instance to nineteenth and early twentieth-century Britain and Ireland.

Of the Londonderry trio, my first encounter was with Theresa, sixth Marchioness. While researching women's entry into Ulster politics in the late nineteenth and early twentieth centuries, her clarity of thought and determined leadership of the first formal organisation of Unionist women in Ireland propagated it into the largest female political association in the country's history. Next came the realisation that her daughter-in-law, Edith, seventh Marchioness fronted an obscure organisation to muster women in an emergency situation in the early years of the newly established Northern Irish state. Soon, in consequence of her association with the first Labour Prime Minister, Ramsay MacDonald, Edith would be branded the *via media* of the British cabinet: quite a journey to make in the space of a few years. With the discovery that before these two women, in the early nineteenth century, another Lady Londonderry, Frances Anne, third Marchioness lionised the young Benjamin Disraeli and bolstered the family's political and financial fortunes, remarkable similarities began to emerge.

The generational mirroring between these three women, connected not by ties of blood but by marriage, is unique. The norm in other aristocratic families was for one, or at most two, brilliant political hostess to emerge to the fore. Although Lady Emily, the wife of Robert, Viscount Castlereagh, later the second Marquess of Londonderry, partook in some political entertaining in the early nineteenth century this was neither wholly successful nor on the scale of her successor, Frances Anne who came to prominence in the 1820s.[1] Her establishment of Holdernesse House, later re-branded Londonderry House just in case there should be any mistake of its ownership, as one of the twenty great aristocratic London houses placed the family firmly in the ranks of the political elite.[2] As a hostess, Frances Anne was succeeded by Theresa who, from the 1880s, was patron to the Tory leader, Andrew Bonar Law and two Unionist Party leaders, Walter Long and Edward Carson. By the time of Theresa's death in 1919, she not only passed a title to her female successor, Edith, who is widely accepted as the last great British political hostess, but a responsibility to continue the political work begun a century earlier: a clear example of Burke's idea of a familial partnership 'not only between those who are living, but between those who are living, those who are dead, and those who are to be born.'[3]

But these women were not recorded in mainstream histories of the nineteenth and early twentieth centuries, nor were their names writ large, or often writ at all, in histories of conservatism, unionism or the aristocracy. Nor was this an isolated omission: aristocratic women have not featured prominently in histories of high politics or their class. The recent approach to writing upper-class women into the past has been twofold: firstly, biographical, indivualisitic and familial as evidenced by the work of Tillyard and Foreman and secondly, a more collective approach adopted by Lewis, Jalland, Jupp, Reynolds, Shkolnik and Williams.[4] As a result of this work, the dynamism, import and creative genius of many of these women is emerging. But undoubtedly there are many more significant life stories to be told from the ranks of the aristocratic female, doing exactly what a biography should: illuminate life beyond its subject.

Montgomery's Hyde fine, if sympathetic, familial study, *The Londonderrys* and de Courcy's popular biography of Edith, seventh Marchioness threw some light on the women on the Londonderry family. Hyde's work also won the Ladies Londonderry an unlikely promoter in Enoch Powell who, reviewing the book in 1979, opined that 'leaving aside for a moment the wives, there are really only two persons of any true distinction in the whole gallery', Castlereagh and the seventh Marquess.[5] Historically 'the wives' were largely left aside but there has been a recent revival of interest in the Londonderrys both from within the family circle and without. Two studies of the seventh Marquess have been produced in the same number of years along with the autobiography of Annabel Goldsmith, daughter of the eighth Marquess, but this is the first collective, gender-based study.[6]

The contemporary standing of the Marchionesses of Londonderry was very different from their relative historical neglect as they featured in autobiographies, the press and diaries of the nineteenth and early twentieth centuries. The hauteur of some family members, coupled with a penchant for wealthy display, caused some backbiting but the Londonderry name was certainly popularly known. The marchionesses were seemingly aware that they were taking a part in the making of history or, at the very least, that their lives were worth recording for future generations. There was an element of circularity to their notion of history: producing family biographies and memoirs as well as carefully preserving their own papers for posterity. Frances Anne wrote travelogues and an account of her paternal family, elaborately gilt bound her letters from Tsar Alexander I and hand copied her husband's Peninsular War letters and dispatches as well as authoring some startlingly frank memoirs in middle age.[7] Theresa kept a political diary, published a short biography of her famed predecessor, Lord Castlereagh in 1904 and intricately boxed her correspondence in an alphabetical system that is still maintained by the Public Record Office of Northern Ireland.[8] By comparison, Edith's recording of her life and that of her forebears was more public. Her autobiography, *Retrospect* was published in 1938 and she also sought to bring her predecessor, Frances Anne to prominence, publishing both a biography and her correspondence with Disraeli. Edith was encouraged in the 1950s to write another biography, this time of her mother-in-law, Theresa, a woman who 'inspired alarm' even amongst those who knew her well, but declined: 'I suppose it is too soon. The ladies of her time spoke their minds in no uncertain terms, and I doubt whether anyone to-day is so ruthless - a good thing, but not for the writer of biographies.'[9] The marchionesses were also vociferous correspondents and literally thousands of letters survive: Theresa's correspondence eventually took over several rooms of Londonderry House and the seventh Marquess and Marchioness amassed in the region of 10,000 letters.

Although the approach deployed here is biographical, this is also a book about politics: conservatism, unionism and a democratic rise. Yet in consequence of the indirect way that aristocratic women exerted political power, few acknowledged their influence and when they did it was usually in derogatory terms. There is certainly eighteenth and early nineteenth-century evidence to suggest women's political activity at elections, at Westminster and at court. For some women the scope and impact of this influence was sporadic and specific, assisting, for instance, in the election of a family member. The level of female participation in this area was remarkably similar in both Britain and Ireland: twenty-nine per cent of Irish counties saw the participation of upper-class women in post-union elections from 1801-20 while the comparable figure for Britain stands at twenty-eight per cent for the period 1790-1820.[10] More unusual and, as a consequence, controversial was support for non-relatives such as Georgiana, Duchess of Devonshire's now infamous foray into Fox's election campaign in 1784 and more specifically her close contact with canvassers and voters. This prompted an outpouring of gendered disapproval and hostility with her actions branded unfeminine and socially compromising. This pattern of short-term involvement and then retreat was more commonplace than any sustained political interest on the part of aristocratic women. The early nineteenth century, however, fuelled by more political coverage in a flourishing press and more frequent Commons' attendance, saw female aristocratic interest in politics augment. But the means to exert influence, through personal means and through men, changed little.

Indeed, in the nineteenth and early twentieth centuries, just as in the eighteenth century, aristocratic women's position in society essentially revolved around men. In childhood and adolescence fathers or male guardians held ultimate control and on marriage this passed to husbands. But marriage into a politically prominent family could facilitate a woman's, and sometimes a man's, entry to the political elite. Once access to political society was attained, an individual woman's influence was effectively shaped by the strength of her own personal ambition and ability. This heady combination of opportunity and predestination placed Frances Anne, Theresa and Edith Londonderry in a position where they could exert considerable influence. Marrying into the Londonderrys, they joined one of the leading Tory families of the period who were regularly listed amongst the fifteen wealthiest families in Britain and Ireland with six large country houses, a London mansion and landed holdings of over 27,000 acres in counties Down, Antrim and Donegal and close to 23,000 acres in England and Wales. Their gross annual revenue amounted to £100,000-110,000 in the 1880s and to put this into some historical and contemporary context, until 1914 an estimated £10,000 per annum was needed to maintain an upper-class standard of living and this yearly income would be equivalent to approximately £7-£7.7 million in today's values.[11] The Down property covered the most acreage but Durham, brought into the family by Frances Anne's marriage to Charles Stewart in 1819, at half its size, soon realised the highest return due to its profitable coalmines. As a result of these extensive and valuable landed holdings, the family controlled two parliamentary seats in Down and Durham in the pre-reform years of the early 1800s.

Despite their prosperity, the Londonderrys were relative newcomers to the aristocracy. From Scots Presbyterian planter stock, they came to Ireland in the early 1600s. The middle decades of the eighteenth century saw their standing grow from that of relatively modest landholders on the Ballylawn estate, near Moville in Co. Donegal, granted in the time of James I, to prosperity and political rank. This process was hastened by Alexander Stewart's fortuitous marriage to his cousin, Mary Cowan in 1737. Seven years later, she inherited a fortune from her brother, Sir Robert Cowan, the Governor of Bombay and, following family advice, invested in the purchase of some sixty townlands in Newtownards and Comber in Co. Down. The Newtownards estate, formerly called Mount Pleasant, became known as Mount Stewart and remained the Londonderrys' Irish base for the coming centuries.[12] The family sat in the Irish parliament from 1769, but it was Robert Stewart's marriage into politically prominent families not just once but twice that hastened the family's rise from the Dublin parliament to Westminster. Stewart's first wife, Lady Susan Seymour-Conway was a daughter of the first Marquess of Hertford, a former Irish Viceroy while his second wife, Lady Frances Pratt was a daughter of the Whig Lord Chancellor, the Earl of Camden.[13] In 1786 Stewart was appointed a Privy Councillor of Ireland and three years later was raised to the Irish peerage, albeit to its lowest rank, as Baron Londonderry. In 1795 his brother-in-law, the first Marquess of Camden became Irish Lord Lieutenant and in the same year Stewart was again promoted, created Viscount Castlereagh and in 1796, Earl of Londonderry. The latter entitled his eldest son, Robert to the courtesy title of Castlereagh and he served as Chief Secretary to Camden during his lieutenancy.

As the first earl was a representative peer at the time of the Act of Union, he was granted a lifetime's seat in the Lords but he rarely availed of the opportunity, preferring instead to pass most of his time in Down. Soon, however, Castlereagh's outstanding abilities earned the family further advancement. Aged twenty-one, he was elected to Westminster as MP for Down but not before waging one of the costliest electoral contests on record. Although estimates range from £60,000, in all likelihood in excess of £30,000 was expended in a poll that lasted sixty-nine days. This hit the family's finances hard: work on the neo-classical Mount Stewart was delayed and a Dublin house and art collection were sold to finance the election. But, thereafter, Castlereagh's political promotion was rapid: serving as President of the India Board of Control and, from 1802, as Secretary of State for War with responsibility for sending a young Sir Arthur Wellesley, later the first Duke of Wellington, to command the expeditionary force during the Peninsular War. In 1812 Castlereagh was appointed Foreign Secretary and leader of the House of Commons and his solicitous negotiations at the 1814 Congress of Vienna and the stress he laid on peace between the great powers put him *en route* to greatness. It was in recognition of his services that, in 1816, the family's greatest elevation to the peerage came, with his father's creation as Marquess of Londonderry. But the new marquess did not undergo any political rejuvenation and remained content to let Castlereagh, his only surviving child from his first marriage, take centre stage. This obviously impacted on the first Marchioness of Londonderry's opportunity to exert influence as did a 'melancholy adventure' when visiting one of the Camden estates in Kent when she alleged to have been robbed and returned home 'quite naked'. This prompted rumours as to her mental stability and although her family and the Down estate provided some solace, she did not partake of society thereafter.[14] The 1816 promotion, however, clearly signalled social acceptance but the Londonderrys were, and would remain, essentially Anglo-Irish and over the next 150 years there were both pros and cons to such a label.

The Londonderrys' Anglo-Irishness would place them in a key brokering position between the Unionist and Tory parties when the question of Irish home rule dominated politics from the 1880s. At the same time, the term 'Anglo-Irish' came into more popular usage, used to identify one part of the populace as less deserving of the title 'Irish' than the rest.[15] The idiom has been denounced, perhaps rightly, as a historical construct, yet it still possesses some validity; often deployed by those it was originally designed to alienate. The Londonderrys clearly considered themselves integral to the privileged class both in Ireland and England, part of an aristocratic elite whose common bonds of marriage, religion, education, language, landed wealth and sense of obligation crossed any racial considerations. Yet, the duality enshrined in Anglo-Irishness also set them apart. At certain times, most obviously during the home rule debates, they easily transplanted their innate belief in their right to lead to Ireland and the various bodies established to give unionism a portent and a basis from which to oppose any form of Irish self-

government. At other times, however, a sense of otherness can be determined, as
in 1822-23 when the third Marquess and Marchioness waged an audacious campaign to attain a UK peerage that scandalised their compeers.

The prominence of the Londonderrys' politicking, the scale of their hostessing
and the lo evity of their bastion at Londonderry House was distinctive amongst
t⎯   ⎯ rish kin, rivalled only by the fifth Marquess of Lansdowne's leader-
s⎯   ⎯ ⎯nists in the House of Lords and his associated entertaining at Lans-
⎯   ⎯ ⎯use in London's Berkeley Square from 1903-16. More commonplace
was transient Anglo-Irish contact with London society and the series of events
known as the season. Here they were social participants rather than leaders, normally travelling to London to partake in the tail end of entertainments from May
to July after the close of the Dublin season that ran from Christmas to St. Patrick's Day. That this Anglo-Irish set remained distinct from London society is
evidenced by *The Queen*'s 'Society in Ireland' column which continued into the
interwar period. Differences between Dublin and London society were also manifest. As the Countess of Fingall remarked, 'Irish society was too small to have the
circles and cliques of London.'[16] And political hostessing, although not a complete unknown in Ireland, was never widespread amongst the indigenous aristocracy. Indeed, by the early twentieth century Lady Fingall's entertainments for Sir
Horace Plunkett at Kilteragh Lodge and Sarah Purser's monthly, and more artistic, salons at Mespil House were exceptions rather than the norm.

However, political hostesses, although never large in number, remained 'a
dominant factor in English politics' at least until the First World War:

> They had vast resources, had been trained almost from birth in the art of en-
> tertainment, and were excellent judges of character. They provided…a rendez-
> vous where men of all shades of opinion - provided the shades were not too
> deep or discordant - might meet to discuss the affairs of the session and the
> day…to be on their list was to have a certain cachet[.][17]

In addition to this hostessing role, women like Ladies Bradford and Waldergrave
and Harriet, Duchess of Sutherland were aristocratic confidantes to Disraeli, the
Duke of Newcastle and Gladstone respectively. Other women adopted a stricter
party mantle: Ladies Spencer and Marjoribanks worked for the Liberals while
Ladies Lansdowne and Ellesmere, the Duchesses of Downshire and Buccleuch
and the Marchioness of Salisbury all sheltered under a Conservative and Unionist
banner. Indeed, the latter party used 'the mixture of private friendship, kinship
and social activity as a party device for a good deal longer' than the Liberals with
the Labour Party never, officially at any rate, endorsing such informal means.[18]

Regardless of personal or party affiliation, political hostesses and confidantes
required charm, intelligence, wealth, venues for entertaining, the discretion only
to pass the information given openly at their tables to those for whom it was intended and, most importantly, a desire to carry out the role.[19] High society was
the domain of the political hostess with the London season, dating from the reign
of Charles I, providing the timetable for their lives. The season ran from January
to July or August, although until the 1830s much of the entertaining only began in

April. By this time, society's revolution round the royal court had waned becoming instead focussed on a group of aristocratic families. A lack of space at Westminster for large entertainments from the 1830s to the 1850s also gave function to private houses. Hostesses were, therefore, required to hold London-based entertainments when parliament was in session from February; host weekend house parties; interact in the series of events held during the season as well as organise extended country house parties during the parliamentary recess from October to January. Given this, it is unsurprising that society women were acknowledged as quasi-leaders, exerting political sway and embroiling themselves in an elaborate code of etiquette. And, although often trivialised as a 'Strange hocus-pocus that juggles certain figures into prominence', high society had a definite and important position in the workings of late nineteenth and early twentieth-century politics.[20]

High society was frequently depicted as akin to a large family, held together by ties of blood, marriage and personal acquaintance. It was, therefore, 'extremely difficult…for a stranger to obtain a place until credentials had been carefully examined and discussed. Mere wealth was no passport.' And the chief society examiners were women. Without their endorsement progress for those deemed outsiders was doomed as society ostracised 'anything like unwarranted familiarity… resents peremptorily and punishes pitilessly any act of intrusion or presumption on the part of those who have not made their social footing good, or who are not furnished with the due credentials.'[21] Yet not everyone delighted in such exclusivity. To Arthur Balfour's secretary, Jack Sandars, the season amounted only to 'London liabilities' while Escott, writing in the 1880s, bemoaned its monotony, 'perpetually in the company of the same persons and one's ears will be full of the discussion of the same topics'.[22] But this was one of high society's primary functions: it was here that friends were cultivated for political means, politics was discussed freely amongst politicians, their wives and confidantes and patronage could be both distributed and won.

Political patronage is often represented as reaching its zenith in the eighteenth century but its continued existence and potency can be found in the nineteenth century and beyond.[23] Pensions and sinecures were largely defunct by the 1840s but promotions, safe seats at elections, salaried posts in local government or an unpaid title with honours, for instance, were still in the hands of only a few during the nineteenth century and provided ideal political starters for the younger sons of the aristocracy. Patronage essentially embraced the idea of an uneven friendship, one based in 'inequality, reciprocity and intimacy…a relationship between individuals of unequal status, wealth and influence'.[24] While such inequity reigned neither political patronage nor those who distributed it or benefited from it were a spent force. For aristocratic women, however, there was a more varied pattern of patronage. This was less linked to formal appointments, although undeniably the Ladies Londonderry and other women of their class were often approached for assistance in this direction, but introductions to society, or persons who could help fulfil ambition, were more common.[25]

With the trust of the political elite and controlling access to high society, it was little wonder that aristocratic women were deigned 'the only being who elects without voting, governs without law, and decides without appeal.'[26] But these were not wholly unbounded lives. They were constrained by etiquette and social acceptability although, unlike the common law that governed most women's lives, aristocratic women had some input into the unwritten rulebook. They were also affected by changes in the traditional position of their class, but did the gradual extinction of aristocratic government also terminate the influence and activism of the political confidante and hostess? Or, by virtue of her personal means of exercising influence, was she in possession of power for longer than many of her male counterparts?

1

Frances Anne, third Marchioness of Londonderry and the creation of tradition: 'They ought to make you Queen'[1]

With family at the very heart of both the existence and transmittal of aristocratic power, it should come as no surprise that the benefits and advance of that power were neither individually nor gender based.[2] This familial base also impacted on the vistas of its members. Aristocratic women were not restricted to a private realm of domesticity and social nicety. Instead, like their male compeers, they functioned on a dual plane of public and private actuality.[3] This merger was perhaps nowhere more apparent than in the aristocratic approach to governance: politicking was 'simply part of family life'.[4] Thus to find upper-class women actively involved in maintaining political position by electioneering, identifying candidates, organising voters and, at times, elections or seeking to attain political advance by hostessing and liaising with those who could assist in these ends was not seen as an anathema to their family, their class or their sex. Furthermore, aristocratic women, like Frances Anne Vane-Tempest, later the third Marchioness of Londonderry, in possession of a determination of spirit, vast wealth and landed resources, were persons of import in their own right and such standing survived the marital contract.[5]

Of the three Londonderry confidantes, Frances Anne was undoubtedly the wealthiest and her marriage the most controversial. Her parentage was characteristically Anglo-Irish: the only child of Sir Henry Vane-Tempest, MP and Baronet of Wynyard and Long Newton in Durham and Anne Catherine, Countess of Antrim in her own right.[6] In 1618, in reward for serving the English interest in Ireland, James I raised Frances Anne's maternal family to a viscountcy and two years later to the Earldom of Antrim. Late in the next century, a hereditary marquessate was granted with Frances Anne's maternal grandfather the first recipient and in 1790, in the absence of male heirs, he obtained a new patent allowing him remainder to his daughters.[7] Therefore, on his death in the following year, in line with the strictures of primogeniture, his eldest daughter, Anne Catherine became Countess of Antrim and Viscountess Dunluce in her own right attaining the Glenarm estate, including the castle, whilst her sister, Charlotte received Dunluce and the remainder of land in Kilconway. Some two decades of litigation ensued but, in the absence of reversionary clause in the patent, the marquessate was effectively extinct.[8]

The merger of this Irish title and estate with an English equivalent came in April 1799 when Anne Catherine, then aged eighteen, married Sir Henry Vane-Tempest, a less than conscientious Tory MP. Although he held his seat for Durham city without interruption from 1794-1800 and again from 1807-12 for Co. Durham, with the intervening gap of his own choosing, he 'probably never spoke in parliament, and was certainly an irregular attender' at the Commons.[9] Their only child, Frances Anne was born on 17 January 1800 at Lord Litchfield's House in London's St. James' Square with Lord Darlington and the first Duke of Cleveland as godfathers, Mrs. Frances Taylor, wife of Michael Angelo Taylor, the lawyer and sometimes MP for Durham city, whom the child was named after and Lady Rachel Sandford, a sister of Lord Antrim, as godmothers. A coveted childhood might have been expected but Frances Anne's upbringing was far from conventional and, by her own admission, happy.

With relatively few of Frances Anne's early letters surviving, the memoir she composed in middle age for her children provides an intimate glimpse of her young life. That she wrote these in such a brutally honest vein, with little romanticism or gloss of a lost youth, for family consumption is remarkable. Indeed, in these reminiscences she alleged that her parents, though 'To all outward appearance...were well suited, both young, gay and rich, each the greatest Partí going' they were, in reality, 'an ill assorted pair. She with a domestic quiet sensible man might have made a good wife and mother, while he with a strong minded amiable woman had been another being. As it was, they encouraged each other's follies and rushed into every species of extravagance.' Her father was 'violent' and neglectful of his wife, 'leaving her for weeks' and the noted *bon viveur* 'drank and spent mints on his theatres, Hounds, Races' and yet he was 'universally beloved. My mother was very fond of him altho' she trembled at the sound of his voice.' Frances Anne claimed to have been made chronically insecure by her parents' ill-disguised desire for a son and heir but this, 'whether from the odd life my mother led, up at night, in bed all day, racketting, hunting', never occurred. At the age of six, a governess was appointed for her and although in position for less than a year, her charge alleged that she had done 'little else but box my ears and rap my knuckles. Never was any child so harshly treated as I was by Father, Mother and Governess. I met with nothing but cuffs and abuse.' The impact of this was momentous. Frances Anne sought solace with the household staff with the result that her 'affections were blighted': 'I grew sly. I made friends with the servants who used to tell me who I was and what I should be. All this I listened to till one day I was overheard saying "Papa has no business to cut down a tree here, everything is mine".' Such insolence was not ignored. Frances Anne was beaten and a toy taken from her to prove a point: she possessed nothing by right. But her unchecked association with servants, particularly her maid, continued, giving her an inflated sense of self and 'visions of futurity before my eyes.'[10] She remained demanding and ill content, writing, aged seven, to her mother with the opening lament, 'I did expect my Papa would have answered my letter'. This child was clearly already attuned to the idea that hers was a life of import: a tenet that would shape her whole life.

Hints of the familial discord that would later lead Frances Anne to the Chancery Court were also evident in her early letters as she expressed the hope that her parents would 'not disapprove' of her 'writing to [her godmother] Aunt Taylor'.[11] The latter was the only relative she regarded with any affection and whose visits were 'a perfect Jubilee'. Taylor 'took pains' with her niece, nursing her through childhood illnesses like smallpox and scarlet fever and counselling her as she fast veered into adolescence. Aged twelve Frances Anne was mature beyond her years, declaring herself 'a woman in size, thoughts and feelings.' Yet, although aware of her status in life and the fortune that lay before her, she harboured no high opinion of her physical merits: 'I was singularly ugly, broad, fat, awkwardly made, with immense feet, huge purple hands, greasy stubborn hair and a fixed redness in my face.'

The death of Frances Anne's father in August 1813, when she was aged thirteen, greatly affected her. Even though a remote presence in her life, he had been the more affectionate parent: 'He never beat or scolded me but at her [mother's] instigation.' Frances Anne felt the loss but frankly admitted, 'at 13 sorrow is not lasting and I soon began to find the difference in my situation'. Her father's death made her one of the richest heiresses of the early nineteenth century and, in a reversal of the usual child-parent support role, with responsibility for paying her mother's jointure: 'I was mistress of all around me. The Cuffed Child whose mother had grudged her dresses and pocket money was now an immense Heiress.'[12] Her demeanour, like everyone's surrounding her, quickly transformed and the 'smothered flame of discord' between her joint guardians, her mother and aunt Taylor, now broke forth. The Taylors did not try to suppress Frances Anne's youthful arrogance; instead they pledged to protect her and respect both who and what she was. But, with the benefit of mature reflection, Frances Anne felt they ill-judged her situation, further fuelling the self-importance that encouraged her 'open rebellion to my mother…my whole nature revolted, and urged by my Governess and my own violent feelings I wrote to Mrs. Taylor imploring her to protect me against such a parent.' This letter resulted in Frances Anne being made a ward of the Chancery Court in 1814. She continued to reside with her mother but the living arrangements were far from orthodox: 'I had my liberty and my will. I took no master, had my pocket money [of £2,000 per annum] and lived in the Drawing-room.'

The next few months of this teenage life were even more extraordinary. Her mother's preoccupation during an alleged liaison with Mr. Beckett, the Under-Secretary of State for the Home Department, led to Frances Anne's involvement with his younger brother, Edmund. Although eleven years her senior and betrothed to another, a four-month relationship ensued: 'we were together all day… *on n'est pas deux impunément mais l'amour vient en troisième*' (*in translation*, 'our relationship is innocent but add love and then we shall pay'). In hindsight she found it inconceivable that the relationship was neither suspected nor discovered. That the strictures of chaperonage were breached in such a young girl, especially an aristocratic heiress whose relations were anxious to protect the family reputation and

fortune, seems remarkable as is the fact that Frances Anne saw the events as fitting for inclusion in what was essentially a family memoir. At the same time, a
decision was taken on the grounds that she had shown 'such specimens [of] vio-
lence of temper that all feared to take charge' that, aged fifteen, she should move
into her own establishment. A house and servants were subsequently rented in
London's Cadogan Place and with an allowance of £5,000 per year, equivalent to
some £300,000 in today's values, Frances Anne was placed under the supervision
of Mrs. Cade, a respectable widow and a governess. It was only Cade's discovery
of correspondence between her new charge and Edmund Beckett that brought
the surreptitious relationship to light. Her mother and Mr. Beckett were duly informed and Frances Anne was forced to burn his letters and return his ring, 'they
got my scrawls back but my hair [ring] did not accompany them, nor was it ever
returned.'

Frances Anne revelled in the feeling of having been freed from her mother but
this was short lived. Cadogan Place offered her little excitement and she soon
found life 'sad dull'. She was also aware, certainly from the age of fifteen, that her
marriage was being brokered. Lords O'Neill, Lowther and Beauchamp as well as
the Duke of Leinster were early possibilities. The former proposed in 1816 but
Frances Anne's reaction was one of shock: 'Never was I more thunderstruck
[than]…at this abrupt proposal'. Again, given that both legally and in terms of
social convention she was still in minority, a lack of control from either mother or
guardians was evident: perhaps understandably Frances Anne considered herself
'without an adviser.' She declined the offer, believing O'Neill saw her solely as an
enticing financial prospect. Next came the Duke of Leinster who travelled to
England 'for the express purpose of being introduced' but his grandfather was
already attempting to broker a match with her guardians and again the variance
between aunt Taylor and Frances Anne's mother emerged. The former believed
this would be nothing but 'a mercenary marriage…and said I was too young to
marry for a Year. My mother tormented me'. And Frances Anne felt increasingly
adrift: 'I am quite at a loss to conjecture what plan is in contemplation for the
future care of me…[and provide] all the protection necessary to guard me from
the malignant attacks of an envious world'.[13]

Although due to be presented by her mother at the royal court in the spring of
1817, heralding her formal entry to the marriage market, this was delayed for a
year due to the upset caused by her mother's own nuptials to singer, Edmund
Phelps. Any union with a countess just a month after their first meeting would
have caused society gossip but the fact that, to use Frances Anne's words, 'His
birth was as low as possible', moved this 'degrading marriage' into the realms of
scandal.[14] Frances Anne refused to attend the wedding or their house for the best
part of a year, but her coming out in 1818 was also a coming of age. Freed from
governesses for the first time in her life, she now embraced society. With a new
house in New Norfolk Street in London's Park Lane, the relationship with her
mother was gradually rebuilt. As Frances Anne wrote to her in March 1818: 'I am
extremely flattered by your telling me you have missed me. It is a pleasure to
know I have been thought, although I fear it is a selfish feeling.'[15] She also lost
much of her earlier physical gaucherie, growing into a tall and striking figure. Her

beauty was occasionally remarked upon but references to her temperament and hauteur were more prevalent as she matured into a woman 'with a fascination of manner which few could withstand; and an energy of character and loftiness of mind which eminently qualified her to take part in great undertakings'.[16]

Like much of her earlier life, Frances Anne's marriage was unconventional. She first met Lord Charles Stewart, British Ambassador to Austria from 1814 and half-brother of the illustrious Foreign Secretary, Robert Stewart, Lord Castlereagh, at her mother's London residence on 3 February 1817. Stewart was an old acquaintance of the countess and thus to find him dining without other company was not unusual. This first meeting between future husband and wife was, however, far from encouraging; when asked what she thought of him, Frances Anne replied 'not much...he seemed finniken and looked as if he had false teeth'. But this first impression was fleeting. She later reminisced that she soon found 'his manner pleasing' and became both flattered by his attentions and increasingly reassured by his presence: '[he] took care of me at Court, and talked to me a great deal.' Initially she scoffed at the idea that this was a courtship, but her mother's 'eulogisms' contrasted with her aunt's 'abuse' of Stewart, who was twenty years her senior and a widower with a son just five years her junior, made her 'first think of it. I continued to meet him constantly. He daily won upon me...I began to feel restless and discontented and more interested ab[ou]t him.' Her aunt's objections were so severe that Frances Anne concealed her growing feelings for Stewart and agreed to leave town for Tunbridge Wells, with Mrs. Cade in tow. Contrary to Taylor's motive to cool her ardour, this gave Frances Anne time for reflection and the result of her cogitations 'was a determination to accept Lord S.'[17] She accepted his proposal of marriage on 9 April 1817.

Romanticised claims that it was the 'distinction of Lord Stewart's character, the elegance of his manners and his chivalrous bearing' that overcame all obstacles to this marriage, 'like the knights of old he won a principality, and the princess who ruled it', can be easily dispelled.[18] There was nothing sentimental about the highly publicised Chancery Court proceedings that accompanied this match. Frances Anne's mother's application to this court for advice on the marriage settlement resulted in a counter move from Taylor, which Stewart decried 'political[ly] Machiavellian' in spirit, to obstruct the marriage.[19] Chancery proceedings, presided over by Lord Chancellor Eldon, began two days after Stewart's proposal. A three-month hearing ensued when Frances Anne was prohibited from seeing her mother alone and Stewart suffered the ignominy of being restrained from meeting or corresponding with her. In court the intentions of Frances Anne's mother and step-father were called into question as were the wishes of her late father whose determination by will that his only child and heir should reside with her aunt if his wife remarried had been ignored. Taylor's recounting of Stewart's courtship of Frances Anne was even more damning. She claimed that by late February 1817 reports were 'universally prevalent' that they were to marry and an anonymous letter sent to her confirmed this. Three further letters followed and Taylor averred that the countess instigated meetings between the two with the effect that these 'constant attentions effectually prevented other persons from being ac-

quainted' with Frances Anne. Taylor thus laid the accusation of scheming firmly
at the feet of the countess.

Even stronger charges were levied against Stewart and the Londonderry dynasty: Taylor believed him to be a fortune-seeking philanderer, 'in embarrassed
circumstance' with 'dissipated and irregular...habits' and deriving monies only
from military and public appointments.[20] In Taylor's opine, his attraction to her
niece lay only in 'a desire to possess the fortune'. The final blow came in her im-
putation that 'insanity prevails in some branch from which His Lordship is immediately descended - that such insanity has shewn itself in a manner to have rendered coercion necessary in more than one member of the family.'[21] Similar allegations had provided the grounds for another, ultimately unsuccessful, protest in
1813 when Lord and Lady Ellenborough tried to prevent their son marrying Lady
Catherine Stewart. Chancery thus considered new medical and familial testimony,
as well as that presented in the Ellenborough-Stewart case when three physicians
categorically denied 'Scrophula or what is called Evil in the family of Lord or
Lady Londonderry'. Any possibility of inherited insanity was also denied, with
one doctor writing at length, 'I never observed anything in the constitution of the
ladies in mind or body that had any resemblance to hereditary affection or that
could be rationally supposed to have descended to them from their parents or
could be propagated by them or their children.'[22]

Most of Taylor's claims were refuted, but there can be little doubt that the
countess encouraged the relationship, arranging meetings for the pair throughout
March and April 1817 and extolling Stewart's merits 'stating him to be the best
match in England for her Daughter'.[23] A marriage settlement to keep the estates
intact and provide for the family beyond the lifetime of the familial head and the
eldest son's inheritance was drafted in Chancery in 1817 with discussions beginning the day after Frances Anne accepted Stewart's proposal. A jointure, in essence a widow's annuity, of £10,000 was fixed for Frances Anne, but this sum
was hugely disproportionate to both her fortune and the nineteenth-century aristocratic norm of ten per cent of the monies a woman brought into a marriage
being returned in widowhood.[24] Moreover, Taylor's charge of an arranged and
hastily considered match was not wholly unfounded, but her claims of financial
insolvency were less well supported. Frances Anne's wealth easily outstripped that
of her prospective groom, but he was far from impoverished as heir to the Londonderry estates with a fairly distinguished military career and ambassadorial and
royal household appointments behind him. He showed early promise as Under-
Secretary for War whilst his half-brother, Castlereagh, was Secretary of State but
he disliked the minutiae of administration and preferred soldering: commanding
the Hussars in Portugal and serving as Adjutant-General of the British forces
under Wellesley during the Peninsular War. Aged thirty-two he was appointed
Major-General, serving until he was invalided in 1812. Two years later he was
appointed British Ambassador to Austria, Europe's political and social centre,
with an annual salary of £12,000. In the same year he was promoted to the UK
peerage as Baron Stewart. He was also Colonel of the twenty-fifth Regiment of
the Light Dragoons; Governor of Fort Charles in Jamaica and Lord of His Majesty's Bedchamber; collectively these appointments produced a yearly income of

£3,700. Rental from the family's Irish estates, of which Stewart received a portion, produced an additional £12,000 per annum and his personal property amounted to £26,000. To Chancery he denied both the charge of conspiracy and the lure of the heiress. Instead he claimed the attraction lay in 'her peculiar character of mind, her excellent understanding and the personal qualities with which she is gifted'. Their courtship, albeit brief, had, in his view, been 'marked by the most delicate and respectful attention to her situation and Rank…as becomes a man of Honor…always in the company of others and…[he] never had the intention of secretly or unduly influencing the mind and conduct of Lady Frances or of inducing her to marry'.[25]

Castlereagh's advice to his half-brother was that the whole Chancery affair needed careful management, imploring him to avoid 'misrepresentations and possibly fresh mortifications'. He and his father, the first Marquess, mediated with the Countess of Antrim but the counsel of Tory premier, Lord Liverpool amid fears of the political ramifications if this be 'made a party question by the opposition', underlined the merger of the private and public spheres. Liverpool urged both Castlereagh and Stewart to distance themselves from the Chancery fray and not attend the hearing in person.[26] And unsurprisingly this controversial union attracted public and press interest as well as inspiring Tom Moore's satire:

And 'tis plain when a wealthy young lady so mad is,
Or any young lady can go astray
As to marry old dandies that might be their daddies,
The *stars* are in fault, my Lord Stewart, not they.[27]

The Countess of Antrim's *affidavit* was predictably defensive, highlighting her 'most anxious solicitude for the just and Honorable introduction into life and the protection of her Dau[ghte]r…which becomes a Mother and w[hi]ch…a Mother alone can justly appreciate and feel'. She also reiterated her belief that Stewart was an ideal suitor and the 'alleged objections against him were not founded in truth.'[28] That her first marriage to Harry Vane-Tempest was regarded as 'a match of her own making' and her second union was not universally approved perhaps made her even more sympathetic towards her only child, now under fire and public scrutiny for accepting Stewart.[29]

Frances Anne's own memory of the case highlights how difficult she found the proceedings that excited more that usual public curiosity, drawing crowds to the Chancery Court and reports in both *The New Times* and *The Courier.* 'harassed to death by all the painful histories which were daily put before me respecting him… I was committed before the world'. With her hand shaking, she wrote to her mother and her aunt of the strain the hearing placed on her constitution and the futility of trying to prevent 'an alliance which sooner or later (if I live) must take place'. The constant presence of Mrs. Cade, even in her mother's company, was 'insufferable' yet Frances Anne also showed considerable fortitude, acknowledging 'no resource remained but to go thro' the trial patiently.'[30] Days later, at Lord Eldon's request, she put her own case in writing, adopting a similar approach to the dispatch of 1814 that convinced her guardian aunt she was in need of Chancery's safeguard: 'I cannot find one objection to proscribe my marriage…your Lordship will I trust give your immediate sanction to the Union which I am convinced will give me a suitable and I may, my Lord, add a necessary protection.'[31] Even though permission was granted for the marriage, the Chancellor questioned the reliability of Frances Anne's declared income with the main Durham colliery only held on lease and deemed the claims of Stewart's dissipation and fortune hunting 'unworthy'.[32] Eldon ultimately considered the proposed marriage not as eligible as Frances Anne might be entitled to but 'he did not finally consider the objections so fatal to the proposal that he ought to withhold the Court's consent.'[33]

Taylor's threat of appealing to the Lords both delayed and overshadowed the marriage but the ceremony finally took place on 3 April 1819 with a 10 o'clock evening service at the Countess of Antrim's London home with eighty guests present. Presided over by the Bishop of Exeter, the bride was given away by the Duke of Wellington rather than her stepfather. On marriage Charles changed his patronymic to Vane; a construct to show pride in the family dynasty and marital union and following 'the tradition that a family's name went with its property.'[34] And, as one of over four thousand such name changes between 1760 and 1879, this was not uncommon. The agreed marriage settlement of 1819 saw three trustees appointed to safeguard Frances Anne's interests and the Vane-Tempest wealth. This gave Charles a somewhat unusual and unstately legal position as he became, in essence, a life tenant on his wife's estates, prohibited from selling property unless he purchased land or government stocks of an equal value.[35] Stewart also had to provide for Frances Anne's mother, aunt and any future children of the union, whilst a portion of debts were to be repaid annually and he had to pledge to improve the much neglected Durham collieries.

For Frances Anne the marriage was cathartic: distanced from her formerly favourite aunt by her protestations about Stewart, disgusted by the manner in which her mother had looked after her financial affairs whilst a minor and finally free of Mrs. Cade's care, her pleasure at leaving London is not difficult to comprehend: 'I was glad to go abroad and there was no one I cared to leave.'[36] On the way to Vienna she was presented at the court of Louis XVIII and feted by the Orleans in Paris before being thrust into the diplomatic limelight as the wife of the British Ambassador to Austria in July 1819. The 'cuffed child' was now an assured young woman whose inherent belief in her own importance eased her into her new station. As Castlereagh remarked to his father, she was 'not a beauty, but she is extremely well looking, mild, and intelligent and innocent…and for her time of life, she seems to have a great deal of decision and character. The situation in which she is placed will require a large scale of both.'[37]

Privately, however, references to her predecessor, the first Lady Stewart, vexed her: 'I knew I was not his first love and this reflecting has always been a corroding one. Besides he had a son, not mine'. Quickly producing an heir, therefore, became a priority and in her familial memoirs she not only recounted her joy at becoming pregnant but also her 'wretched health and worse spirits' after miscarrying in Vienna in early October 1819: 'I found no friends, nor anyone I cared associate with…months I spent in discontent and idleness.' Lonely and depressed, diplo-

matic receptions held little excitement for her and even hostessing dinners for
thirty or forty bored her 'to death.' By December she was holding reception days
in Vienna attended by Princess Rannitz, the Pope's Nuncio and Princess Ca-
honey, sister-in-law to Prince Leopold. Although the spectacle was brilliant, by
her third reception she confided to her mother, 'I think I have had enough of it.'[38]

The letters of one attendee, Martha Wilmot, wife of the chaplain to the Viennese embassy, provide a window into their ambassadorial lives. Originally impressed by Frances Anne's 'unaffected ease and dignified manner...with uncommon grace', Wilmot's views soon altered. By early December 1819, the new wife
and 'chieftainess' of Charles Stewart, in her view, was 'not free from caprice, and
tis equally plain that she is a compleat [sic] spoilt child, with fine natural qualities
and excellent abilities, and with a quickness of perception and a sense of the ridiculous which makes her at once entertaining to a degree and perhaps a little
dangerous'.[39] With Charles obliged to attend Congress at Troppau, Frances
Anne's mood was only lifted by the arrival of Mrs. Cade's daughter to care for
her. Although an employee, this gave her what she previously lacked, a friend of
her own age.[40] But if her sense of isolation diminished, Wilmot's already scant
regard for her lessened as she became 'rather more enlightened on the reverse
side of her L[ad]yship's character...if his family think her a fool, they are mistaken, and will find it out too!' Soon she was even more forthright: 'she is one of
those most uninteresting persons, who seem both to exact and receive universal
homage to her face, which the public repays with *rare* back biting when she is out
of hearing.'[41]

Frances Anne not only quickly fell foul of Wilmot, but of Viennese society at
large. Frustrated by the lack of control she could exercise, even over her own
functions, she noted, 'One thing that bones me very much here is the strict etiquette that is observed. Every thing I propose the old beast the Master of Ceremonies says is not decorum.'[42] Cutting short her own ball because she was taken
ill in the summer of 1820 was certainly not in line with protocol, either in Vienna
or London, and resulted in the Austrian imperial family snubbing the Stewarts. So
scandalous was the event that news spread to England where the always well-
informed Tory confidante, Mrs. Arbuthnot, retold the tale in her diary, noting 'it
is difficult to account for the extraordinary impertinence and ill breeding of such
conduct'.[43] Nor did the situation improve. Soon Wilmot was recording that the
Stewarts 'whom Fate has unfortunately connected us...gave pleasure to nobody':

their united Vanity and Selfishness amounts almost to madness...Their sympathy on those two points is *perfect*...they will not be permitted to return as
Ambassador and Ambassadin from Eng[lan]d...Their pride renders their very
kindness an insult...when they give an entertainment...'tis an ostentatious
display of *their* Superiour [sic] riches and grandeur. She, decked out like the
Queen of Golconda seated on a Sofa, receives you with *freezing* pomp and the
atmosphere which surrounds her is *awful* and *chilling*. He is *her* most humble
slave[.][44]

Princess Lieven's correspondence also reveals Frances Anne's augmenting taste for ostentation both in her personal dress, 'like one of those effigies you see in Greek churches, with no colour or shading but loaded with jewels. She was wearing enough to buy a small German principality', and the internal decoration of her Viennese home: 'I should lose my taste for luxury in that house: it is displayed in such a vulgar way.'[45]

The birth of Frances Anne's first child, a son and heir named George Henry Robert Charles William on 26 April 1821, delighted her: 'the moment when I found myself the mother of a Boy was the happiest I ever experienced before or since.' Yet in celebration, her emerging penchant for extravagance was further apparent: Paris, Brussels, London and Vienna were, by her own admission, 'ransacked' for the layette 'which was magnificent and cost near 2000£. 3 nurses were sent f[ro]m England, a monthly nurse, a wet nurse and a head nurse.'[46] Those witness to the three-day Viennese welcome for the child claimed it caused both 'riot' and 'offence…beyond expression':

> The people declared that such pretension was more than their Archdutchesses allowed themselves, and the same that was practised alone by the Empress… they have acted King and Queen till they forget that they are subjects…our mock Royals…so well do both L[or]d and L[ad]y Stewart understand effect that they ought to have been managers of Drury Lane!!!!
> That[']s all the compliment I pay their Vain[,] Glorious, heartless Lordiness.[47]

Wilmot was not the only one left open-mouthed at the display. Princess Lieven also attended the christening and recorded its 'vulgar ostentation' alongside the 'whole town [who] came to see the farce'.[48]

Frances Anne, although suffering from milk fever, was soon pregnant again but she was well enough to travel to England not only for her confinement in April 1822 but also to begin to realise ambitions in the north-east of the country: refashioning the Durham mansion of Wynyard and purchasing an additional estate on the coast at Seaham with plans to develop a harbour. This was essentially a social statement, a display of position, wealth and intent. The Vane-Tempests' claim on Durham's parliamentary heritage was considerable, having stood in the first Durham election of 1678. In the next century they linked Wynyard to high toryism and established a tradition of political domination in Durham. This was not, therefore, a new territory that needed conquered. Instead Charles and Frances Anne's endeavours amounted to a dynastic continuum, seeking a safe transmittal of power and reputation to their progeny.

The time spent in England also occasioned another reconciliation between Frances Anne and her mother; after a two-year absence, the countess stayed at Wynyard for two months from January 1822. With concerns that Frances Anne was suffering from plethora, a supposed excess of blood in pregnancy that could lead to fever and miscarriage, she was bled repeatedly and treated with laudanum. But, amidst fears that she could lose another baby, her first daughter was born on 15 May 1822. This child was named Frances Anne, after the Dowager Lady Londonderry and Emily, after Castlereagh's wife.[49] The christening was held four weeks after the birth and although the gathering was relatively small, especially by comparison to the fiesta that greeted her first born, with just thirty-four guests, the invite list provides an insight into the Londonderrys' social standing at this juncture: Hungarian Prince Paul Esterhazy, the Hanoverian Minister Munster, the Duke of Wellington, the Lievens as well as the Camdens were all present.

The summer of 1822 also witnessed Frances Anne's first foray into London society entertaining, hosting a dinner for the Duke of York and the officers of the tenth Hussars with the Prince and Princess of Denmark and sixty guests in attendance. Frances Anne's apprehension was palpable but, in a letter to her mother, she recorded: 'It all went off very well which after all one's torment, trouble, etc. is pleasant…it was no trifle to have 60 people to dinner. It was a fine sight, but I am glad now it is over as there was so much fear it might not succeed'. However, it was not only the skills of hostessing that she was learning but also the invidious nature of high society: 'the *Tracassené*, Intrigue and Party Spirit is very tiresome, beside so many military people envy Charles having the King's own Reg[imen]t and there are always plenty to make illnatured remarks.' In spite of this, she enjoyed London society much more than its Viennese counterpart: attending court, Ascot, Eton, Almack's and numerous private dinners.

Frances Anne's early years of marriage certainly shaped her ambition. The faith in her own station, so evident from childhood, was undiminished and, if anything, was bolstered by her contact with Europe's political and royal elite. But Vienna was only a stopgap for her and she already hankered a return to England where her aspirations might be realised. She, therefore, sought a permanent London base and was 'beyond delighted with' their 1822 purchase of Holdernesse House and the adjacent house on the corner of Park Lane and Hertford Street.[50] In time, Holdernesse would stand alongside the whiggish Holland House and Stafford House as one of the grandest London mansions, with a staircase 'designed not only to parade upon, but to be watched doing so…inspired by the room in which the Congress of Vienna met', but in the middle of 1822 at Castlereagh's prompt, they, reluctantly in Frances Anne's case, returned to Vienna.[51]

A month later Castlereagh was dead by his own hand and his suicide brought dramatic changes in its wake. Charles, now the third Marquess of Londonderry, was so subsumed by grief that Frances Anne initially did not tell him of the circumstances of his half-brother's death, a man whom he regarded with 'perfect admiration and entire devotion'. By comparison, the ever candid Frances Anne noted he 'was a mild amiable being, tho' too cold ever to have been a favourite of mine.'[52] Certainly Castlereagh's death raised questions in Charles' mind about the tenure of his own office. Writing to Lord Liverpool of his 'painful and precarious' position and his wife's desire to return to England, he aired the possibility that he 'would not wish to remain more than two years longer abroad'. But outraged at Canning's succeeding Castlereagh as Foreign Secretary, Charles tendered a hasty resignation and openly vented his feelings. The latter was one of his most distinguishing traits and his vehement opposition to Canning led to clashes with the king.[53] Indeed, some believed the new marquess had alienated himself to such an extent that he would be wise to concentrate on his son's, as opposed to his own, career. Similarly characteristic was that fact that such counsel was ignored. The manner of Charles' withdrawal from office also caused offence. His resignation was not made to Canning as convention dictated, but to premier, Lord Liverpool.

The Londonderrys also had another private loss to mourn as Frances Anne suffered her second miscarriage in the space of three years in the middle of 1822, leaving her greatly weakened and again in 'a wretched state of Health and Spirits'. To her mother alone she admitted that she had not felt well since leaving England but the shock and 'attended agitation' of having to inform both her husband and Castlereagh's family of his suicide finally took its toll.[54]

How 'little of the criminal was contained in our conversations?'[55]

September 1822 marked both the start of the Congress of Verona and an intriguing chapter in Frances Anne's life that is told with candor in her memoirs. Congress led to the new Marchioness of Londonderry's second meeting with Tsar Alexander I of Russia whom she first met in Vienna in 1820. This, as well as his amiable and often informal manner and wish to pay his respects to the late Castlereagh, laid the basis for a new familiarity in 1822. Thus the tsar's courtesy visits to the Londonderrys in Vienna in early September were not unusual and nor was Frances Anne's invitation for him to dine. But what followed was extraordinary. Twelve letters from Alexander to Frances Anne, written in French as he did to the majority of his correspondents, survive. The fact that she bound these letters in a red velvet, gilt embossed and imperial crested volume show that they were treasured. Writing at length in her memoir of this association, in the first person, some twenty-six years after the event certainly raises suspicions of middle-aged romanticism but signifies that she never forgot this relationship. Moreover, neither the content of Alexander's remarkable outpourings, nor the fact that Frances Anne saw this as an important point in her life, can be doubted.

Their initial correspondence was mundane, using formulaic nineteenth-century French forms of expression, address and closure. The only hints that this could develop into a more fond alliance are found in the fact that the letters are warm in tone and perhaps unexpectedly so given Frances Anne's young age and Alexander's standing and in that she, unconventionally, wrote to him in the second, as opposed to the third, person. But her letters, beginning in September 1822, display both humility and respect to Alexander's position and by the time of her third letter, written towards the close of that month, she included a gift of a portfolio in recognition of the fact that she was:

> deeply impressed with Your goodness to her Husband and her family and penetrated by the kindness Your Majesty has displayed towards herself…If I have presumed too much in giving this impulse to my wishes Your Imperial Majesty must consider the fault Your own in having so graciously honoured my Husband and myself with the marks of Your condescension.[56]

The tsar was happy to accept both her gift, 'Coming from yourself it is infinitely precious and from this moment it will be my inseparable travelling companion', and her hospitality, 'Be persuaded that if in any way I may have the opportunity of approaching you and enjoying your company - without being bothersome to you - then I would be entirely honoured to rush to seize it.' In his next letter he asked for permission to visit, although it is not entirely clear whether he also wanted to see Lord Londonderry. Her reply, thanking him for deigning 'to think of me and hasten to assure you that it will always be the greatest pleasure for me to receive you', suggests that she would receive him alone.[57] This is reinforced in her memoir as she recorded that at the time of the above exchange, Charles was awaiting Wellington's arrival at congress and:

> for the first time [I] saw the Emperor alone. He sat with me above 2 hours. He certainly is a very fine looking man. If not positively handsome, his countenance remarkably pleasing, his manners…affable and agreeable become when he addresses a woman captivating. His conversation is perfectly beautiful. …He is like a beneficent Genius…During this Interview we had a long exploration, and he gave me to understand the extent of his feelings of attachment [*attachement*] for me, and the strong impression I had made upon him.[58]

The word *attachement* that both used to describe this relationship through all of its stages needs to be understood in its French context, where it implies a combination of affection, fidelity and friendship. Thus, those who quickly labelled this an adulterous liaison were, in fact, mistaken. With her next letter she sent him some English books, one by Lady Caroline Lamb and an undisclosed volume of poetry, but again she was cautious, apologising for any undue familiarity on her part but arraigning him: 'if your excessive generosity has rendered me too forward and deign to accept the assurance of my sincere attachment and of my most respectful devotion.' He took no umbrage and instead appeared touched by her generosity:

> the hand from which I received them will render their perusal even more engaging…how much pleasure I feel knowing that I have the hope of seeing you again in Verona.
> Please keep a place for me in your memory until then and receive the assurance of the sincere and respectful attachment that I have devoted to you.

As congress moved to Verona, although Frances Anne's tone still verged on the apologetic, she felt sufficiently emboldened to inform the tsar of her arrival:

> Forgive me, Sire, if believing that the arrival of a person of as little consequence as myself, could be unknown to Your Majesty, I take the liberty of announcing it to you. Please excuse me if the hope that I have of enjoying the happiness of seeing you makes me take a step perhaps too bold, but encouraged by your excessive benevolence [*text missing but possibly reads* I dare address myself to you. It is] not only with the respect and the veneration due to the greatest of Sovereigns but also with open friendship ordered by the most perfect and sincere admiration and attachment.[59]

He was not so tentative, declaring himself 'eager' to see her and asking for permission to visit the following afternoon. And it was in Verona that their *attache-*

ment grew stronger. Alexander sought her company, as the following undated dispatch makes clear, 'each time that I could have the honour of seeing you, would be a real pleasure for me...and be persuaded that I am too desirous of accepting not to present myself at your door each time that I believed that I could so do without indiscretion.'[60] Through September and October 1822 he dined with the Londonderrys on several occasions in small parties of ten or twelve and took tea at their lodgings but Frances Anne 'never saw the Emperor alone or *chez moi.*' But she grew so accustomed to his company and 'long *tête à tête* visits that he is no *gêne* whatever'.[61] There was also an unusual twist to their association as Alexander revealed that he had seen her portrait by Sir Thomas Lawrence whilst he was sitting for the same, accompanied by Lord Stewart, at Aix-la-Chapelle in 1818 and, in line with his reputation for superstition, 'he had felt a sort of foreboding that the Person whose picture was before him was fated to have an influence over his Destiny, and cause him disquiet'. He was led to believe the picture was of a Miss Stephenson but when he met Frances Anne in Vienna in December 1820:

he imm[ediatel]y felt he was then opposite the original of his Picture and all his Former impressions returned to him with redoubled force, and now the predictions of his imagination were realized.

He told me that for 10 Years he had lived like a Hermit without the least feeling for any woman until his attachment for me. This conversation was romantic, enthusiastic and beautiful, and religious sentiments seemed to dictate his every feeling.[62]

Several meetings and letters followed with France Anne, although keen 'to enjoy' his company, still urging him not to consider her 'indiscreet...Do not find me forward either...since it is unnecessary to let you know that the more one has the advantage of knowing you the more the wish to approach you grows.'[63] Certainly the tsar possessed an easy manner that many found disconcerting for a man of his station. To Madame La Comtesse de Choiseul-Gouffier he was 'too amiable, making one forget his rank too easily. I could not accustom myself to those exaggerated expressions of politeness, respect, and homage which he employed with ladies'.[64] Frances Anne, by comparison, revelled in them. That their association grew closer was evident in Alexander's appointment of Prince Walchowsky as her 'ambassador' in November 1822. Walchowsky subsequently arranged times for meetings between the two but, despite their combined efforts, congress, divided into cliques around Wellington, Madame Lieven and the Londonderrys, began to prate and Alexander informed Frances Anne that their association was 'talked of and that the Empress had questioned him'.[65] The brilliant and infamous Madame Lieven was particularly irritated by Frances Anne being singled out for the tsar's attentions, alleging an 'affaire' and on one occasion putting 'out her thin red paw to snap at' a note Alexander had written to her rival.[66] Frances Anne, for a time, delighted in the talk and pique that she caused amongst the other congressional women. And it was not just congress that was talking of a possible affair. The news reached London, with Thomas Creevey passing on gossip from Whig hostess, Lady Holland, that the young Lady Londonderry had transferred her affections to 'persons of a somewhat higher rank, viz., the Emperor of Russia, and that she is now following the latter lover to Petersburgh.'[67] But it was directly from Verona that Lord Clanwilliam brought the matter to the attention of Castlereagh's widow and Frances Anne's sister-in-law, scorning her for believing 'that the Emperor of Russia is in love with her…however ridiculous it may appear, the Emperor and she, are positively *occupés c'un de l'autre*; and she is likely to make a great fool of herself.'[68]

More seriously, Alexander was under constant surveillance from the Austrian police who monitored his movements, including his visits to Frances Anne. This revelation led to two weeks without contact until December 1822 when Frances Anne, for the first time, conspired to see him alone. Feigning sickness in the early stages of another pregnancy as an excuse for not attending a formal dinner with her spouse, she was clearly relaxed in the tsar's company:

> I had given up dressing for him as he had told me not to mind being *en negligée* and used to come himself in boots and a great coat. When he came his manner was melancholy but as kind…as ever…assuring me his attachment was as fervent and devoted as ever, and that he had suffered much since he had seen me[.][69]

He then read her an extraordinary missive, running to three pages in length and leaving no question as to the depth of his emotion:

> Every time that I find myself in your presence, *Madame*, the effect that you have upon me removes the necessary calm required…to express to you that which in my quarters I resolve to say to you…I therefore take the option of writing it down, persuaded as I am that it is my duty as a man of honour to appraise you of it. …This talk and all these circumstances together have saddened me. I felt my conscience reprove me, a fact all the more humiliating in that at my age I ought to have had enough sense and self control, to have conducted myself in a way which did not draw upon you speculations which are like dagger blows to me. As a friend for so long of your husband and his whole family, what despicable role have I played in all this. To what complications and to what dangers to him, to whom I have the most sweet and most respectful affection, has he not been exposed by the situation into which I have placed him and myself?

> What use the purity, the innocence of the relationship in which we both found ourselves. Apart from the Eternal Judge who knows all things, who can know how little of the criminal was contained in our conversations? Who could believe it to be so? If even those who know you more particularly, *Madame*, will be convinced that the respect that you have so inspired is such that no-one will ever dare speak ill of it. There will be many such, a large number indeed -

that the world could not remain with malicious rather than indulgent conclusions - especially in a country which is not your own and where you cannot be so well known in society?
And it is I who have drawn down upon you all these so wearisome results. I am the guilty party who has placed you in such a position.

These thoughts are cruel for me, they have so affected my mind that I have not had the strength to silence them and to come to call upon you at home as we agreed. I hesitated as much to write to you since our correspondence has been noticed. ...What I can assure you of, as a man of honour, is that no-one in my establishment has noticed your letters and I have not discussed them with anyone.

All I can say, *Madame*, together with the heartfelt (and at the same time, so respectful) affection that I have for you, I shall be obliged to redouble the precautions I take as far as my relations with you are concerned. I have been too long in the world not to have had the time to realise that the immutable laws of the Divine Religion that we share must be faithfully followed. Inner contentment, without which there is no happiness, is based on their scrupulous observation. Your angelic soul is fit more than any other, to enjoy that contentment which is superior to anything that we may enjoy here below - my heart desires above all to see you in possession of this above any other happiness.[70]

The meeting lasted close to three hours and although Alexander agreed to godparent her next child, mindful of her modesty and his own reputation, he was reluctant to leave a dispatch that he wanted destroyed, avowing to Frances Anne '*Nous sommes tous mortel.*' He only left it on condition that it was returned within two hours, giving Frances Anne just time to transcribe the letter and return it with the following enclosure:

I think that the best course of action is for me to return immediately your written lines, since to keep them longer would cause me an even greater effort to separate myself from them...to return a text so flattering and so seductive for a young woman, but also I do my best to do my duty although my route in this world is very limited.

This will be surely, in this life one of the happiest and dearest events, above all since I will always think with enchantment of the right and noble sentiments of the best of men and the greatest of sovereigns...with all the courage of my soul I ask (and I hope with justice on my side) that Your Majesty should not leave Verona without allowing me to see you once more. I trust the more to your generosity in this respect since it is only God himself alone who can know if ever we shall meet again on this earth. But, I am convinced that, after having deigned to express such sentiments towards me that you will always keep a place for me in your memory. This will always be a source of happiness, of inexpressible pleasure for me even during a long absence since it is impossible ever to forget the Emperor Alexander[.]

It thus transpired that the vigilance of Austria's police was not the sole inhibitor to their continued collusion. Alexander's reference to criminal conversation, the nineteenth-century idiom for adultery, leaves little doubt that this *attachement* could have strayed into romance. Indeed, many in congress and London society already believed that it had. This, however, was the affair that never was.

That Frances Anne saw her own future as 'very limited' raises the question of how content she was in the early stages of her marriage. In attracting the attention of the tsar was she regretting her decision to marry a man who would never lead a political party never mind a country? Though her marriage was not dented by this relationship, there is an identifiable and disarming sense of loss in her memoirs: 'my feelings in solitude...brooding over melancholy thoughts - the fickleness of man, the blank anxiety that follows violent excitement and the possibility of never seeing the Emperor again'. They met just once more before Alexander took his leave of Verona: 'He again and again assured me of his affection for me, and that while life should last my image should rest in his heart. I was to write to him, and he promised to let me hear from him constantly.' This time it was she who was subject to the emotional outpourings and her 'agitation quite unmanned him. He shed tears and endeavoured to soothe me, imploring me to be calm for his sake, for my own, and above all he entreated me to consider the wickedness of endangering the Infant within my bosom'. Having 'this too highly gifted and all perfect being at my feet, kneeling before covering my hands as he was his wont with kisses, so far f[ro]m wondering at my weakness' Frances Anne could 'only rejoice and wonder we came out of the ordeal innocent of guilt.' Writing of this parting in 1848, decades after the event, she likened it to 'a faded dream', but there can be no miscomprehension of her feelings:

> In truth I loved him, and though my affection for Charles was unshaken and my admiration and gratitude increased by the unbounded confidence he placed in me, I was engrossed by a new and overpowering feeling. Indeed it was hardly possible to learn oneself loved by such a man as the Emperor Alexander who combined every thing that could please the eye, fascinate the ear, flatter the vanity and captivate the heart...
> I loved what not to love and see
> Was more or less than mortal or than me.

Just as she found it incredulous that no one knew of her earlier girlhood liaison with Edmund Beckett, she now struggled to believe that her husband was 'blind to my feelings or ignorant of my thoughts'. Her mood was certainly greatly affected by Alexander's departure and she remained 'depressed, chilled and languid' but 'Charles bore with this gloom and the feverishness produced by my suffering and never reproached or upbraided me.'[71] He was, instead, attentive and kind but her melancholy persisted, finding Vienna too silent after the congressional round of fêtes, balls, courts, theatres and dinners. It was to her mother that she confided both her separate audience with Alexander and her feelings, sending her one of his letters but, understandably, pleading for secrecy. To her she also admitted, with a more characteristic realism, that the promises of each to visit were 'All *Chateaux en Espagne* - I fear'.[72]

Neither Rome nor Florence could lift her spirits and in the latter stages of pregnancy and anxious to return to England, she abandoned a trip to Naples. The Londonderrys took their leave of Vienna, but even those who had scorned their ostentation missed the extravagant ceremony that earmarked the years 1819-23. As Martha Wilmot, one of their most scathing critics, grudgingly admitted, she missed the pomp of the Londonderry display, 'as far as pleasantness and amusing qualities go she [Frances Anne] *beats* our present Ambassadress all to nothing. *They* gave their first ball last Friday…like a ghost of one of L[ad]y Stewart's splendid parties, dim, pale and rather shabby genteel.'[73]

Frances Anne's despondency persisted in England. The birth a second daughter, named Alexandrina for her godfather, the tsar, in July, greatly disappointed her, 'having wished for and flattered' herself she 'was sure of a Boy.'[74] Post-natal depression, another pregnancy, house renovations, visits to Wynyard, Seaham, Mount Stewart and Glenarm as well as attempts to attain a place for Charles preoccupied her through the remainder of the year, but she wrote at least twice to Alexander. These missives, however, were much less charged than those of December 1822, although in reply, Alexander reminisced:

> Your long silence made me fear that you had erased me from your memory and you can judge yourself how much the proof to the contrary rightly enchanted me. …At the moment that you receive these lines you will be near the end of your second confinement. I shall await news with great impatience. My best wishes go with you without reservation and for everything - if you permit - also that nothing may lack for your (safe) delivery. …Please keep for me, *Madame*, a place in your memory and recall from time to time the sentiments of most respectful attachment that I have vouchsafed to you for all time.

His next and final letter was written in February 1824, opening with an apology for the 'obstacles' delaying his correspondence but expressing a profound 'hope not to be removed from your thoughts - mine often return to the moments when I had the happiness to come to see you in Vienna and in Verona. It is probable that some long time will yet pass before we shall meet again!'[75]

This close association was of little consequence to the tsar, but it was of considerable import to Frances Anne. This is evident not only in her detailed and emotional account of the relationship, but also in the fact that she bound his letters in chronological order, with two notable exceptions. It is Alexander's declaration of December 1822 and her reply that she bound last - thus marking the climax of their intimacy. Alexander kept no diary and his notebooks and personal letters were destroyed by his successor, Nicholas I with the result that we have little beyond Frances Anne's treasured collection of letters and her middle-aged recollections to rely upon. Some contend that this was 'the most romantic episode' in her life; others claim the tsar counted 'among her conquests'.[76] The truth is less sensational. Alexander's flirtatious reputation was deserved: 'He attended all the receptions, flitted about in all the salons, laid himself out to the charm of all the pretty women.' The Austrian secret police observations also record his movements amongst the women attendant at congress, claiming Princess Esterhazy and Sophie Zichy believed 'that they have caught him in their nets...for Alexander, here, as in Frankfurt and elsewhere, it is purely a flirtation.'[77] One of the few biographers to mention his interest in Frances Anne alleged that this simply helped 'dispel the mist of gloom in his mind, enabling him to radiate some of the gaiety and charm which had made his reputation in happier times. But these occasions were rare indeed.'[78] Thus, the attention he paid to her was characteristic; he was probably seeking nothing more than a distraction, especially at Verona where, from October to December 1822, his spirits were deflated by the realisation that European stability was by no means secure.

Although there is clear evidence that governments previously exploited social connections between aristocratic women and foreign dignitaries as a key element in their diplomatic affairs (such as Lady Atkyns with the false Royalist Jean-Pantaléon de Butler in 1793 and Mesdames Gay and de Bonneuil in 1800-02) it is unlikely that Lord Londonderry with his minimal congressional role, still less so his new young wife, would be entrusted with even a minor diplomatic mission to glean information from the tsar. Instead what we can ascertain is the evolving *attachement* between the two protagonists. The mutual respect and affection so evident in their dispatches of late 1822 was a preserver of modesty and halted this 'affair' in its tracks. But what this relationship typifies best is how far Frances Anne had come in the space of just three years. By 1822 she was an intimate of the man perceived as Europe's saviour, liaising with the most powerful diplomats and politicians and causing such talk that by the time she returned to London in 1823 everyone, in high society at least, knew her name. Establishing herself as a political hostess in order to promote her husband and sons thus held few terrors for her.

'A very bold game'[79]

From 1822, in preparation for the family's return from diplomatic employ, the Londonderrys began a campaign for a peerage promotion that both offended and bemused society. The abundance of peerage creations from 1776-1830 caused a reverie with rank that led many already titled aristocrats to seek further advancement. This was especially true for Irish and Scottish peers and the Londonderrys were one of fifty-nine Irish and twenty-three Scottish nobles to gain UK titles at this time. In essence, to be in possession of a regional title was to be elevated but only to the middle ground. In the Londonderry case, the pursuit of a higher, and more importantly, a UK title, reflected their Anglo-Irish political and business interests, their landed holdings and their naked ambition. There were, however, additional pragmatic reasons for seeking greater rank as though Charles, from 1814, possessed a UK barony, taking a second wife whose wealth far outstripped his own raised difficult questions of inheritance. Moreover, both he and Frances Anne wanted to make their presence felt in reaction to losing control of the

Derry militia, one of three stipends held by the late Castlereagh in 1822. The others, Governor of Co. Derry and *Custos Rotulorum* of Co. Down, passed to Charles with little comment and Wellington, one of their most allegiant and untiring supporters, hoped these appointments would buffer any growing sense of grievance and thus 'manage him [Londonderry] as to give him no cause for complaint. He is certainly looking to the establishment of himself as the head of a party.'[80] But the duke hoped in vain. Londonderry petitioned both Wellington and the king in an attempt to regain control of the militia and his new wife, in a portent of her future hands-on approach to familial affairs, wrote directly to Peel.[81] Both were unsuccessful. This was an exception to the near wholesale 'nepotism and patronage among aristocratic families, particularly those with links to the Tory party'.[82] Such exception prompted Frances Anne to censure the government and, although by late November 1822 she knew there was little possibility of the militia decision being reversed in their favour, she believed that it would raise the stakes for their promotion: 'I dare say it cannot now be done, but I am sure we shall have our wants and objects more attended to *now* than formerly'. The subsequent campaign for promotion in the UK peerage marked her political debut and her use of the word 'we' in the above dispatch left no doubt that she was mindful to be at the hub of the campaign.

From late 1822 Frances Anne encouraged her husband towards political independence, advising him to give up his Bedchamber posting, a companionate royal household appointment worth £500 per annum. As she wrote to her mother, 'while he holds that they know he cannot vote in opposition, and nothing but fear will made them attend to him. As soon as he arrives in England he must collect all his friends around him, and endeavour to form a formidable party.'[83] Despite her clear guidance, Londonderry retained the Bedchamber post for some years but, as Wellington predicted and Frances Anne encouraged, he threatened to go into opposition, beginning a trend that lasted for the duration of his political life. In consequence, the Londonderrys again found themselves the fount of society rumour. Princess Lieven mused on the likelihood of Lord Londonderry crossing into the Whig camp, 'I fancy *they* [*author's emphasis*] intend openly to join the ranks of the Opposition. It is obvious that Londonderry is only looking for an excuse. He has just asked for his pension. But it is given only in cases of necessity, and he has been refused; he complains bitterly of injustice and ingratitude.'[84] Lieven pluralizing the decision to be made alludes to the fact that she was of the opinion that this was one resolution that Charles would not be making alone. Mrs. Arbuthnot, although, less convinced of Londonderry's sincerity about siding with the opposition, would in time be proved brilliantly astute in her inference that he 'only acted upon a detestable principle which I now know he has, of always asking and insisting upon having more than he expects to get, in order to get as much as possible, and of pushing every point to extremity.'[85]

Charles publicly aspired to both the Irish lord lieutenancy and the Paris embassy, but those who could realise these ambitions doubted his credentials and his caste. As Liverpool, explaining both his own and Londonderry's position to Wellington, remarked, 'he is very much mistaken if he supposes that he can ever make himself a man of much consequence in this country. He is not sufficiently an Englishman *even for the Continent* and still less so for the franchise of Great Britain and Ireland.'[86] As a potential viceroy, Charles' Irish landed holdings were considered too extensive and his Anglo-Irish background too controversial for this still sensitive posting. But how unusual was Londonderry's conditional loyalty to the Tory party? Certainly there was some fluidity in the two-party system and non-party support from the backbenches of the Commons was neither unknown nor should its existence be taken as indicative of a lack of party loyalty. But the longitude and nature of Londonderry's criticism was in an altogether different league from his contemporaries, making him very difficult to favour and even harder to place both politically and in the ranks of the UK peerage.

Peerage promotion was not only claimed as compensation for the loss of the Derry regiment, but also on the basis of a turn of the century promise made to the Stewart family by the Duke of Portland at the time of the Act of Union. More controversially, Charles' military and diplomatic record was called in for favour, along with that of his late half-brother, Castlereagh. Such ladder climbing so soon after Castlereagh's death was disdained by society, but this claim was not based solely on self-promotion. The Londonderrys' Down estates were not as valuable as the coal ripe acres in Durham that passed down Frances Anne's line and this opened the possibility that the next Marquess of Londonderry would not hold the lion's share of land. With Charles' uncle, Lord Camden as mediator, assisted by Wellington and Londonderry's brother-in-law, Henry Hardinge, the campaign for promotion began in earnest in 1822.[87] And, as Princess Lieven suggested, Frances Anne was determined to air her views: corresponding with both Camden and Liverpool. This was certainly unconventional. Frances Anne was a relative newcomer to the family and, aged twenty-two, she was also a young woman, but her motivation lay in her deep-seated belief in her own station, displayed so vividly in the memoir of her early life, and the situation whereby her husband was legally only a life tenant on her sizeable and profitable estates. As a result, her spouse's position as family head was not as absolute as might be expected in other aristocratic families. Such an implication is reinforced by a consideration of the promotion that was sought: the ideal was for Frances Anne to be made a countess in her own right with remainder to her progeny.[88]

On all fronts such an advance was problematic. Camden was concerned that Portland's union promise of 1800 related only to the line by which the Stewart estates and title descended, effectively excluding Frances Anne and her offspring. There was also a lack of precedent in promoting the female line with remainder, especially to any rank beyond that of baroness. In the Londonderry case, justification for such a 'Departure from the General Rule' simply could not be found.[89] The idea of a reward being given for Castlereagh's services to his half-brother was also unpalatable to many, believing that the former's family should benefit directly from the dedication and distinction of their forebear. But the doggedness that characterised much of Londonderry's political career, ably spurred on by his wife, was very apparent. For most of 1822 they would entertain nothing less than the title of countess. Only occasionally did Londonderry display a realism that was so often lacking in his judgements, acknowledging that his own services were, in truth, incomparable to those of his late brother and only his wife's 'great possessions and great wealth' made him 'ten times more important in the Country than I should otherwise be'.

Despite this, he claimed that his primary motivation was to prove devotion to his wife and, in a Burkian display of family obligation, attain surety for their children:

> It may be the only moment of my life, when, I may be able to prove to her the immense debt of gratitude I owe her…[and] because, taking the Difference in our ages, and the chances of this Mortal life, I should like to place her in the surest possible line of giving the Title with the immense property she will accumulate to posterity.

Worthy as the sentiment might be, one enduring undercurrent of Londonderry's political approach emerged - the threat to side with the opposition. Creation of his wife as a countess would see Londonderry promise Liverpool 'the most fair and manly support in my power', yet any lesser offer would not suffice to 'sacrifice the Independence of action which I think the properties can acquire'.[90] Such a broker's approach, going against the aristocratic grain whereby aggrandisement was usually sought for past services and familial glories rather than as a pact for future loyalty, won Londonderry few admirers and even fewer imitators. By late 1822 even those working to secure the promotion were frustrated. Camden and Hardinge now ventured on a programme of damage limitation, encouraging Charles to remain in his diplomatic posting in Vienna and not return to England to oversee the proceedings and aggravate Lord Liverpool still further, while Hardinge took the more drastic measure of censoring Londonderry's letters to the premier.

Their concerns proved well founded. Against his better judgement, Liverpool personally presented the case to the king in late November 1822 but the monarch declared the creation of Frances Anne as countess in her own right not only 'very unreasonable' but against protocol, deigning 'it was not for the Party to debate upon the Degree and the mode' of promotion.[91] The idea of granting an earldom to Henry, Charles' eldest son by Frances Anne, was also denounced as it would effectively give him greater rank than that of his elder half-brother, Frederick. The only advancement deemed possible was to create Lord Londonderry an English viscount with remainder to his son by Frances Anne. Certainly this fell short of what was coveted, but an English viscountcy was the highest step given at once to a second family with a different name and similar promotions had only been given sparingly to families such as the Percys, Talbots and Montagus.

Charles reacted as a man whose mind, by his own admission, was 'too apt to speak and write what it feels', registering his 'mortification…extreme Discomfort and Disunion' at the 'ungenerous and unjust…measured out grant' to Camden.[92] Frances Anne similarly scorned the offer as an affront and writing directly to Camden she made no attempt to conceal her contempt for the 'miserable offer… my own decided feeling is distinctly to refuse it, to separate from the Gov-[ernmen]t and for the future act with Independence…my son is really not in so poor or miserable a position' to accept.[93] The impact of her intervention was nominal. Indeed, nothing could change the eventuality of the result, yet by adding her voice she displayed a flagrant disregard for convention as well as an inherent belief that hers was a family of import that did not need royal favour to exert influence. Most clear of all, however, was the fact that she would never take a backroom role in its promotion. Camden and Hardinge urged reconsideration and, amidst further threats of opposition, were successful. Ultimately concern for their son, Henry and a sense of personal loyalty to Wellington persuaded the Londonderrys to accept the offer. By December 1822 Frances Anne knew that there was no possibility of her being elevated to the rank of countess, alleging 'that I don't care about as provided Henry is to be a Peer it little signifies about my being a Peeresses, and whether he inherits a title from his father or his mother *revient au même.*'[94] This was, however, a wholly selective interpretation, recording the attainment of a title for her son as her 'favourite object' and solely as a guerdon for her husband's services.[95] Nor did her retelling proffer any hint of the complexity or trial of the proceedings or of the potential for political damage.

Early in July 1823, largely due to Wellington's exertions, Charles was made English Earl Vane and Viscount Seaham with remainder to his second, and Frances Anne's eldest, son, Henry. This created the unusual situation whereby Frederick, Charles' only child from his first union, had the courtesy title of Viscount Castlereagh and entitlement the Irish marquessate and UK barony but as the marquessate was an Irish creation it did not entitle the holder to a seat in the Lords. By comparison, his younger half-brother, Henry now held the title of Viscount Seaham for his father's lifetime with the promise of a UK earldom and a Lord's seat. The choice of titles was also revealing: Vane being one half of Frances Anne's maiden name which Charles had adopted on marriage and Seaham, the site of the Londonderrys' new harbour creation that would allow the Vane-Tempest coal industry to profit and, like Frances Anne's name, survive into the next century.

Clearly the Londonderrys' ambitions were not fulfilled by this promotion; nor were they ever to be fully satisfied. Charles did not hold political office again following the resignation of his diplomatic posting in 1822. Even before this he had attracted negative commentary, with one newspaper report epitomising much of criticism: 'If his Lordship ever merits the name of an able negotiator, we believe it will be at the hands of foreigners - never at the hands of his own countrymen.'[96] In Vienna his vainglory earned him the nickname of Lord Pumpernickel and his performance, especially at Troppau, disappointed Wellington not only because he travelled back and forth to Vienna to attend to his pregnant wife but also as he openly lacked influence with the congressional ministers as well as the triumvirate of Austrian, Russian and Prussian sovereigns. Castlereagh's death also impacted on his political standing; after 1822 he could no longer bask in his half-brother's reflected glory nor rely on him for advice or position. Charles' lack of appointment, however, was always more due to circumstance and ability than desire. Both constituents of the Londonderry pairing were keen for political office, exerting huge effort and expense in pursuit of political gain not just over several years, but decades. It was here that Frances Anne came to the fore. From the early 1820s, examples of letters addressed solely to her can be found alluding to her husband and sons' chances for placement. As one correspondent of June 1822 expressed, no 'arrangement has been proposed' for Charles but Wellington had 'favourable intentions' toward placing her stepson, Frederick.[97] But the position Charles assumed on his return from Vienna as an ultra Tory at the vanguard of opposition to reform and an unwelcome critic of his own party won him few promoters. Frances Anne's role in continually pushing him to central stage was, therefore, crucial, but it was far from easy.

Charles made no attempt to hide his political aspirations but he remained in possession of an over-inflated sense of self and the influence that others could exercise on his behalf. Such ambition sat uneasily beside his parliamentary practices which frustrated even those who held him in high regard. Wellington frequently despaired of him: 'He thinks I can make him an ambassador to-morrow. I could do no such thing.'[98] Londonderry was, therefore, fated to remain in the House of Lords, where his parliamentary performance was often a source of derision, even amongst his party colleagues. In 1827, some five years after Frances Anne's suggestion, he resigned the Bedchamber, siding with a body of 'Old Tories', including Eldon and Rutland, united in opposition to a partial Whig fusion with Canning's Tory ministry. Wellington and Peel also resigned but Londonderry's behaviour was more outlandish than the rest, prompting the former to stay out of town to avoid being drawn into his 'foolish Mischief'.[99] Given his growing reputation, Charles was unlikely to be appointed under Liverpool's premiership and he stood even less chance under his old antagonist, Canning. The latter's death in 1827, however, raised Charles' hopes, especially after Lord Goderich's brief time as premier ended in January 1828 and Wellington succeeded to the post. But Londonderry's restless ambition remained as neither he nor his eldest son were appointed. Charles believed he had been 'passed over by one's best and most powerful friends [which] entails not only personal mortification, but it depreciates the estimation in which one is held in the world, and where friends do not uphold, enemies become more vindictive'. The realisation that his brother-in-law and former Durham nominee, Hardinge was to replace Palmerston at the War Office was, therefore, almost insufferable for him: 'all but me, civil and military friends, have been noticed, it is under-valuing myself if I do not feel the disappointment'.[100]

His search for position was unrelenting and eventually alienated royal favour. As early as 1823, the king was greatly pleased at the opportunity 'of giving L[or]d L[ondonderry] a sharp answer' in refusing his approach to be Master of the Buckhounds.[101] The Londonderrys' relationship with the king remained problematic, standing in stark contrast to the cordiality and preferment enjoyed by their successors. 1828 saw them cut from royal balls, again in reaction to Charles' behaviour, but he was beginning, at last, to discern that he was the source of the problem. Writing to Wellington in January 1828 he opined, 'I suspect too strongly that my name is an interdict, and is of little moment what course I steer. …I am not without heavy embarrassment and little prospect of friendship'.[102] Wellington tried to make amends for Londonderry's behaviour but it was the Duke of Cumberland who successfully laid the basis for a royal entente, if only of a temporary nature.[103] Londonderry remained, however, depressed and despondent as to his future prospects. It was perhaps then no coincidence that the same year, 1828, marked the beginning of the lavish entertainments at Holdernesse House that would continue for decades and prevent Charles and the Londonderry name from wholly languishing in the political backwaters.

By this juncture Holdernesse was one of four Londonderry houses and although aristocratic advancement in the peerage was often accompanied by house renovation to match the newly elevated standing of their owners, the Londonderrys took this to an extreme. The purchase of Holdernesse House and an adjoining mansion in London's fashionable Park Lane at a cost of £43,000 with £200,000 spent on enlargement and refashioning by the Wyatts and the rebuilding and refurbishing of Frances Anne's former Flemish-style house, Wynyard in Co. Durham into a neo-classical mansion, again by Philip Wyatt, at a cost of £102,000 with an additional £27,000 expended on furnishing and £18,000 on landscaping, represented a serious social statement.[104] This was accompanied by heavy, and often speculative, investment in creating a harbour at Seaham, an idea that was mooted prior to Frances Anne's marriage. The London property formally opened in 1828 with a ball and fête for 300 and the Duke of Gloucester, the Lievens and the Wellingtons in attendance. Although it took a few more years for the house to acquire a real political *foci* and number amongst the great London houses, like those belonging to the Marquess of Stafford and the Duke of Northumberland, with these lavish receptions Frances Anne came into her own and whilst her hostessing continued, her spouse's hope of preferment lived on.

Although never universally loved, the scale and opulence of Frances Anne's entertainments earned her notoriety. Society scrambled to gain entry to her house, often to backbite, alleging, for instance, that she imitated the Whig hostess, Lady Holland, or to display a resigned jealous admiration.[105] Familial forerunners in this hostessing role can be found in both her guardian aunt, Frances Taylor who ran a London salon and in her sister-in-law, Lady Emily Castlereagh, the second Marchioness of Londonderry from 1821, who, assisted by Tory hostess Lady Jersey, hijacked Almack's Club in London's King Street 'and began to apply strict criteria for entry and behaviour'.[106] Emily was certainly supportive of her spouse and accompanied him on his first foreign engagement in 1813 but she was not a resounding social success and some questioned the likelihood of the match. Her dress sense veered towards the eccentric, never more famously than wearing her husband's Garter in her hair, and, prone to jealously, she could also be cloying: the Comtesse de Boigne found her 'persevering attendance' on Castlereagh 'slightly ridiculous…She never left her husband at any time…While he worked she was beside his desk. She followed him to the town and to the country, and accompanied him upon every journey'.[107] Indeed, some believed Emily to be insincere and Lady Bessborough was disconcerted by her 'look of contented disregard of the cares of life'.[108] Princess Charlotte refused to have her as a lady-in-waiting and a well-publicised quarrel with Lady Conyngham proved socially compromising in 1820. Thus, although Castlereagh's renown and his appointment as Foreign Secretary in 1812 opened opportunities for political hostessing, such as the number of dances and assemblies that Emily held for political and diplomatic purpose in London as well as less formal entertainments at Cray Farm in Kent, she lacked the personal merits of a great hostess. Indeed, in Paris during 1814 her nightly suppers were branded by Lady Shelley as 'extremely stupid' and four years later at Aix-la-Chapelle the parties were 'of such inconceivable boredom that everyone fled.'[109] Castlereagh's premature death in 1822 also meant that Emily had less than a year as marchioness and although as a dowager she re-entered society after eighteen months in mourning, her constitution never fully recovered: she died in 1829.

None of Emily's receptions were comparable to the grandeur of France Anne's events. Contemporary descriptions abound of the latter's gatherings, such as the summer fancy dress ball of 1828 that saw the hostess resplendent as Elizabeth I, holding a mock court with herself, somewhat predictably, installed on a throne. As in Vienna, considerable comment was excited by her lofty manner: 'polite and high-bred but stately and frigid…such as invariably inspired awe into those who were introduced to or had occasion to pass her'.[110] The composition of her gatherings also recalled a formalisation common to earlier *salonieres* with set arrangements for salutations and the hostess in a commanding position. This, however, did not always have the desired effect:

> the Marchioness had taken her seat near one of the doors by which the company were intended to go out to bow to them in passing, the whole people the moment they saw her seated in her grandeur turned about and went back the way they came rather than pass through the perilous straits.[111]

At her self-styled Holdernesse 'court', Frances Anne's hauteur intensified with age, paying 'little notice of her guests as a rule…[becoming] so rigidly condescending at her parties that people used to say, 'Are you going to see Lady ____ insult her guests to-night?''[112] It was Lady Londonderry who was referred to but such condescension earned her considerable repute.

Holdernesse became a great London house in the late 1820s and its hostess, although never a famed beauty as is attested by Creevey's slight on her as a 'dumpy, rum-shaped and rum-faced article', became a frontrunner of London fashion.[113] Mrs. Arbuthnot heralded her, 'covered with emeralds and diamonds', as the best dressed at the king's drawing room in 1825 while to Earl Grey she was 'a most extraordinary personage…She seems chiefly occupied with her jewels, which I found her one evening displaying to a circle of ladies, as a peddler does his wares - from an immense box, which the page had some difficulty in carrying.'[114] It was not surprising that she attracted regular press commentary for costumes that almost defied description, exceeding in magnificence 'any thing of the kind ever seen':

> a diamond bandeau…a brilliant diamond tiara; the necklace and ear-rings were emeralds and diamonds; the waist was encircled by a diamond cestus, over a gown which was magnificently looped in numerous parts with unrivalled coloured stones. The front of the gown was formed in the shape of an apron, and was crossed alternately with rows of topazes, pink and yellow turquoise, emeralds, amethysts, rubies and diamonds, until they reached the waist, where they were met by a brilliant diamond stomacher.[115]

The extensively modified Wynyard Hall also began to be put to political ends in the 1820s. Walpole laid new aristocratic ground by bringing many of his government to Houghton in Norfolk in the 1720s and 1730s, inaugurating a trend that became commonplace by the end of the century. Unlike Walpole's exclusively male assemblages, increasingly these country house parties were attended by both sexes. September 1827 saw the Londonderrys entertain Wellington at Wynyard for a week and to great local aplomb, although some of the duke's closest allies thought such close association with a wildcard like Londonderry could be detrimental. With thirty-seven house guests, including Whig leader, Lord Grey, the Ravensworths, Hardinges, Gresleys, society portrait painter, Sir Thomas Lawrence and local notables such as the Bishop of Durham and Lord Bathhurst, and a classic mix of civic and private receptions, this was something of a coup. Yet not all of Frances Anne's early events were an unqualified success. One fête of July 1828 could only secure the commendation of 'splendid but dull' with a 'want of ease and vivacity.' Society gossip may help explain the less than convivial atmosphere as, in light of escalating debts caused by low coal prices, a glut in the market and investment in Seaham, the Londonderrys were borrowing to pay wages and executors had seized horses and carriages just two days earlier.[116]

Politically Charles was also in trouble. Hardinge remained allegiant throughout the 1820s whilst trying to curb Londonderry's excesses, informing him, at length, that, encouraged in his folly by Frances Anne, he was the architect of his own misfortune and that he jeopardised Castlereagh's chances of promotion by declaring he would not consider his son's employment as compensation for his own abandonment:

> L[or]d Castlereagh was present at this and not well pleased to find out for the first time that his father was chiefly the cause of his not being employed. The real truth is, L[or]d L[ondonderry] is so strange, so flighty, so intensely selfish and so governed by his absurd wife that he is not fit to be trusted in any high office, besides which [as]…the possessor of 80,000£ a year…it w[oul]d be most unfair to prefer him.[117]

1829 saw him still without government appointment but now with aspirations to be Lord Privy Seal. And the Londonderry interest had not been totally cast aside as Wellington, ignoring Charles' sentiments, named Castlereagh a Lord of the Admiralty. Charles vented his displeasure at being overlooked by seeking a way to oust his former champion, Wellington and form a ministry. He also approached Whig leader, Grey on the possibility of forming a coalition but the latter refused to be drawn in this direction. Further signs of desperation emerged when, in a reversal to the usual nomination process, Castlereagh sought to secure a position for his father from Wellington. The response, however, was forthright and the message unmistakable:

> By God, your father has not behaved well to me…he has considered me…in a political view as his enemy, but he has treated me with private hostility. …He is undoubtedly a very able man and has power to make himself felt. At the

same time, there was no scheme or cabal of any sort, or any party opposed to
the Government, that your father was not mixed up in or at the bottom of.[118]

The accumulated political snipes and thwarted ambitions for promotion hit Londonderry hard but he continued to blame society rumour and a flawed reading of
his loyalties:

The stories that the malicious propagate are too numerous and are generally
too successful...I am to be pitied, and no one need shew warmth to me. My
friends throw me off, considering me *not worth having* Devoted as a friend or
bitter as an enemy, I feel I am not of a passive nature for those I love; I would
sacrifice all I possess, in weal or in woe, so long as they are kind to me...But
that same warmth of character makes me susceptible, and neglected and forgotten, and standing alone, bereft of all former intimacies...But it is best to be
silent and keep one's mortification to oneself, doing the best one can, for
those who only care for one...I should be very sorry you were ever so unhappy, as the person you deem the most fortunate of men has been this last
year.[119]

That this was written to Wellington's confidante, Mrs. Arbuthnot forces one to
question the idea of Londonderry suffering in silence, but by 1830 the duke certainly found him impossible to place and too partisan for statesmanship: 'He forgets his own situation and all antecedent circumstance; and he likewise forgets
that a man who is charged with the government of a country is not in a situation
in which he has only to please himself and his friends.'[120] The difficulty of promoting Charles led to increasingly strained relations with Wellington. Frances
Anne's reaction to her spouse's frustration was personal: she refused to speak to
the duke for some months during 1830-31 and, as a consequence, faced social
estrangement. This was most apparent early in 1831 at a party to mark the Duke
of Rutland's birthday. There the assemblage of about forty persons 'voted her
ladyship [Frances Anne] a bore and, for the first three days, when there happened
to be a vacant place at the dinner table she had no one to sit near her and...the
vacant chairs...pursued her'. Such was her isolation and vexation that she was
reportedly close to tears, highlighting the import of social convention as well as
the less savoury side of high society.[121]
   During 1831 Charles again entertained the thought of a coalition with Grey only
to be rebuffed for a second time. In spite of the slights and Londonderry's push
for independence, Wellington remained loyal and, like Hardinge, became an important restraining force, advising him against pushing for a Lords' motion questioning the king's right to create peers during strained debates over the first reform of the electorate in close to 150 years. Indeed, Charles' fervent opposition
to this reform caused more widespread vilification than ever and the criticism was
now close to *en masse*. His parliamentary style of bombarding questions to ministers, opposition members, party colleagues and even, on occasion, the monarch
opened him to the charge that he was unable to curb his oratory to suit his audience. Venting his rage at reform to the king was inadvisable, but growing 'so vio-

lent and frantick [sic] with reform Ministry and politicks [sic] foreign and domestick [sic] that the King, who had borne all in patient silence, said at length, 'And now My Lord you had better go and see your Mother" was simply imprudent. This reckless policy elicited few answers and served more to alienate than console. Yet Charles persisted, determined in his duty 'to ask questions and comment on publick [sic] events whether he was answered or not or whatever the Government might suppose to be the motive or effect of his conduct.'[122] This led some privately, and others more publicly, to question his state of mind. Mrs. Arbuthnot certainly thought him 'mad...the most wrong-headed person in the world' while Lord Ellenborough, husband to Charles' half-sister, Octavia, was not alone in entrusting to his diary the 'fear' that he was 'half mad. The House seems to treat him so.'[123]

Subject to considerable press ridicule, Charles was soon branded 'The Noble Buffoon' and when he did make a point worthy of merit, the response was cutting: Londonderry 'said a good thing the other day, which, if only on account of its rarity deserves to be chronicled.'[124] To much of the press, Londonderry was a fool: his speeches were exhibitionist; his voice was deemed harsh and monotonous and led one paper to quip: 'Tis doubtful in the speeches that you make, Which most prevail - the pains you give or take.'[125] The contrast to the late Castlereagh could hardly have been more marked. As the reform debates continued in the early 1830s, Londonderry's opposition became even more extreme, on one occasion having to be physically restrained in the upper house, when 'four or five Lords held him down by the tail of his coat to prevent his flying at somebody.'[126] Charles was a man much maligned and sometimes unfairly so but he was his own worst enemy. The threatened move to the opposition benches was much boasted of but never done, causing some to brand his conduct 'abominable' and 'furiously violent', a deliberate construct 'to make himself formidable, which...his gross folly and madness will always prevent'.[127] And, despite his misguided exertions, he was powerless to impede the passage of the 1832 Reform Act that revised enfranchised boroughs and increased the electorate from 435,000 to 652,000.

Post-reform, Londonderry ranked alongside Roden and the Duke of Cumberland as one of the most die-hard, ultra Tory peers, with a growing and deserved reputation for seeking alliances with whoever would promise him position. Holdernesse was used for ultra meetings and in 1833, this time in league with Cumberland and Buckingham, discussions of forming a party, again separate from Wellington, were uncovered, astoundingly by Londonderry showing the damning letters to the duke. The latter believed this to be yet more proof, were it needed, of Londonderry's 'madness' and 'disgusted' him 'more than ever with Party Politicks':

I will take my own course and pitch them all [to] the Devil...I am no longer *their* Leader. Am I to become their follower?...Ultra Tory peers on the one side, and the House of Commons and Sir Robert Peel and the Real Interests of the Country on the other[.][128]

Although Londonderry struggled to attain political office, the family was still provincially dominant: Frederick remained ensconced in the Down seat and, alongside the Earl of Durham, the Londonderrys continued to nominate candidates to Durham city. Indeed, throughout the early and mid nineteenth century their sense of proprietorship over both Down and Durham was over-riding and unchanging. Complaints regarding outright peerage interference in elections dated to 1641 and from the time of the Irish Act of Union a Commons' sessional order was in existence to prevent Lords, peers or prelates interfering in elections to the lower house. But aristocratic influence was alive, if not always well, in both the pre and post-reform era. However, from the start of the nineteenth century problems began to emerge with the Durham candidature, suggesting that aristocratic deference in this part of the country was on the wane. In 1800, Frances Anne's father stood down in favour of his brother-in-law, Michael Angelo Taylor who had the inauspicious claim of being called the 'most ridiculous man in the world'.[129] Durham Tories might have coped with this but Taylor's whiggish leanings were too much and they ran an alternative candidate. This early challenge was unsuccessful, but it was the forerunner of many future clashes. Londonderry nominees were defeated in 1802 and 1804 and in 1819, the year of Frances Anne's marriage into the Londonderry family, a desire for local political control was quickly apparent. The Durham seat, again in the caretaking of Angelo Taylor, riled Charles to such an extent that he pledged to 'be a thorn in…[Taylor's] side, and spend his last guinea' ridding Durham of him.[130] Taylor's Whig propensities did little to endear him to Charles, but the bitter Chancery proceedings instigated by Taylor's wife in an attempt to prevent his marriage made his continued election unbearable. Hardinge was persuaded to stand, but the settling of old scores through any 'electioneering tryal' [sic] made him nervous, fearing critics would accuse 'the Wynyard family of treating the Independent City of Durham as a Close Borough'. The freemen of Durham, therefore, drew up a requisitior 'expressive of their wish that a formidable connection with the *old interest* may stand' and printed notices were distributed to electors in the sizeable towns of the locale to foster support for Hardinge as a candidate of the Londonderrys' choosing.[131] That the city of Durham's pre-reform electorate distinguished between an 'old' landed interest and a growing independence of thought on who could best represent them was highly significant: to these freemen the aristocracy no longer possessed an automatic right to rule. That Hardinge aired his concerns to Frances Anne was similarly important: she was at the crux of the proceedings, immersed in everything that impacted on her familial rank.

The 1820 stand was effective and the Londonderrys controlled half of the city's parliamentary representation from 1820-31 and again from 1831-32, but nominations were often problematic. Though representing different parties, with the Earl of Durham leaning towards whiggism and reform in comparison to the Londonderrys' high toryism, a local co-operative spirit, inspired by a steadfast belief in aristocratic predetermination to rule, prevailed. Durham and Londonderry returned one of the two candidates for the city and if, as in 1826, 1828 and 1831, this was challenged they would support one another. To cite Charles' own words, even if his wife 'married a commoner, he must have been a member for the

County or City from the property and influence in Durham.'[132] And to maintain this influence, especially for an electorate increasingly at odds with these magnates' view, bribes and promises of employment were frequently offered as recompense for supporting the Londonderry cause.[133]

The 1832 Reform Act dented, but did not completely overhaul, the Londonderry influence in Durham. This is not to suggest that this much-contested legislation, so hated by Londonderry, changed nothing. Post-1832 Durham was divided into two divisions, one southern, which continued under the control of the county's largest landowner, the Duke of Cleveland and the other, northern, that became the post-reform domain of the Londonderrys and the Earls of Durham. Both divisions benefited from a lack of minor county gentry to challenge the two-pronged dominance, but this was not uncontested territory. As previously, the electoral return of Londonderry candidates was by no means automatic and in the first post-reform election none of their candidates were elected, leaving a lone Castlereagh in the Commons to represent Down and his family's interest in the lower house. This poor showing was undoubtedly a backlash against Londonderry's vehement and much publicised anti-reformist stance. Indeed, on the very eve of the 1832 reform, the freemen of Durham city called on voters to 'not submit to the dictation' of the Marquess of Londonderry.[134] This independent stand, although not sustained, was sufficient to goad a reaction from Londonderry: he established the first county Conservative association in the following year. With headquarters in Durham city and a Sunderland branch, this body, outwardly, appeared both progressive and democratic. But by design it was a means to formalise the local control that the Londonderrys claimed as a right and an attempt to be free from growing party centralisation. In consequence, Londonderry continued to dominate nominations on the basis of the Vane-Tempest political tradition but as the 1830s drew on there was much local concern about his intransigence and reluctance to accept any advice from the locale, either from prominent clergy or party supporters.

In the wider political environ Charles was unable to exert the same sway and increasingly his first-born was being placed *in lieu* of him. The 1834 Tory ministry, headed by Peel, saw Castlereagh appointed Vice Chamberlain of the king's household and sworn in as a Privy Councillor. By comparison, his father was still in the political cold and although, in a move that was symbolic of growing party allegiance, he now acknowledged Peel as party head, another embarrassment loomed. Peel, prompted by Wellington and supported by Palmerston and the Russian Emperor, informed Londonderry that he would be appointed Ambassador to St. Petersburg in March 1835. This was possibly a means to rid the Lords of Londonderry but the Commons' outcry at the appointment, headed by Tipperary MP and former Catholic Association organiser *par excellence*, Richard Sheil, resulted in Londonderry resigning before he was even *in situ*. The opposition to this posting was so furious that it essentially deprived Londonderry 'of the power of efficiently performing' and, with an uncharacteristic sensitivity, he expressed a desire of 'not embarrassing the King's Government'.[135] Contemporaries, such as Charles Arbuthnot, believed the opposition formed part of a wider political calculation to damage Wellington, but much of the attack was personal to Londonderry. Princess Lieven again feared him 'mad' but she was 'truly sorry' for him: 'he is a most good-natured creature, and he has been very badly treated.'[136] Peel also felt Londonderry deserved some compensation and his discomfort was evidenced by him failing to appoint another to this post for the duration of his ministry.

Throughout the late 1820s and early 1830s, both locally and in the metropolis, therefore, there was much work to be done in preserving and promoting the Londonderrys' political standing. Voters, especially in Durham, increasingly needed to be convinced that their nominees were worthy of support and Frances Anne's political receptions, balls, banquets, house parties and receptions were often the only means by which to counter the growing criticism of her spouse. Little wonder that by the mid 1830s she was actively seeking another to push and one, who in time, would be able to return the favour.

'There is nothing like female friendship - the only thing worth having.'[137]
Benjamin Disraeli, the Tory statesman whose dependence on women and aristocratic patronage was notorious, played an important part in the Londonderrys' lives from 1835. Indeed, Disraeli, a man who, by his own admission, disliked clubs and male society, never lacked female correspondents, ranging from his sister to various aristocratic women, who included Frances Anne amongst their number. Later in life and after Frances Anne's death, he corralled this female faithful into a mythical 'Order of the Bee'. Though Frances Anne missed out on this distinction, she was his patron, his friend and his confidante. Throughout his life Disraeli was a vociferous correspondent and some 10,000 of his letters survive, including hundreds written to Frances Anne. The quality of his letters is also remarkable: he was an open and, at times, conspiratorial correspondent and his letters to his female confidantes, particularly to Frances Anne, are blessed with a familiarity not found elsewhere.[138]

The timing of his meeting with Frances Anne is crucial in understanding the import of her influence. Disraeli was something of a wildcard by the standards demanded of politicians in the mid nineteenth century. With the exception of Wellington, he was the only non-university educated British Prime Minister of the nineteenth century and unlike other non-aristocratic premiers, such as Gladstone whose rise rested on a combination of talent, patronage, money and education, Disraeli owed more to the former two.[139] In the early 1830s, aged thirty and still outside the Commons' domain, he was disappointed by his political progress. He thus turned to high society, domineered by a cluster of women, as a gateway to political promotion and the Sheridan sisters, Lady Cork and then Lady Londonderry effectively launched him.[140]

Disraeli's first encounter with Frances Anne came in the summer of 1835 when, although still a relatively young man, he was not a complete unknown, having published three novels and stood several times, unsuccessfully, for election. He had made some in-roads into high society following an initial introduction by fellow dandy and novelist, Edward Lytton Bulwer and already counted Lady Blessington, Count D'Orsay and Frances Anne's stepson, Castlereagh amongst his intimates. Indeed, he confidently reported a steady social climb to his sister in 1834: 'I have had great success in society this year. ...I make my way amused.'[141]

It was an unrivalled combination of intelligence, wit, charm and extravagant dress that 'made him well known, if not always well liked' amongst this set. He also made no attempt to hide his raw ambition, shocking Melbourne with a 1833 declaration that he would be Prime Minister, which earned him the reply: 'You must put all these foolish notions out of your head; they won't do at all.'[142] This mettle, rather than any attachment to party or divining political principle, was Disraeli's driving force. For him London society was something to be conquered *en route* to political greatness and he was opportunistic, actively seeking promotion and favour. He was also aware that he stood more chance of social adoption in Tory, rather than Whig, circles, due to the latter's reputation as 'a family party, so that it was said that whereas a gentleman might become a Tory, he had to be born a Whig.'[143]

Disraeli's desire for social acceptance as a stratagem for political backing has been much discussed, but Frances Anne's rapid adoption of him has attracted less attention. She is acknowledged as one of a close circle of Disraelian female correspondents but how important was she and, as his political stature grew to realise even his own lofty ambitions, how much influence was he able to expend advancing and defending the Londonderry interest? Moreover, did this friendship enable Frances Anne to uphold her position as a Tory hostess when her husband's career was, at best, static and, at worst, the butt of society quips? Initially it seems that she, always aware of the sway of her own title and wealth, was intrigued by the reputation Disraeli was establishing for himself. It was she who sought him out, asking Castlereagh for an introduction in June 1835. The meeting, however, verged on the farcical. The venue was a London fancy dress benefit ball for the Royal Academy of Music that saw Frances Anne resplendent, if somewhat audacious, as Cleopatra. Disraeli's wit and dandyism amused her but he was less impressed, describing her costume as 'literally embroidered with emeralds and diamonds from head to toe. It looked like armor [sic] and she like a Rhinoceros. Cas[tlereagh] introduced me most particularly to her by her desire' and he added, 'I was with her a great deal.'[144] Disraeli, of course, realised the potential of lionisation by one of the wealthiest and best connected Tory women and he seized the opportunity by asking for permission to write.

Frances Anne's subsequent patronage of Disraeli certainly fitted the society norm whereby those with a belief in the duty of their class to govern were also in possession of an innate responsibility to help those of merit who lacked their position of privilege. Disraeli's first surviving letter to her dates from August 1837 when he had just entered the 'regular bear-garden' of the Commons, but it is evident from his reference to her 'sparking and gay' letters that much had already passed between them and they were already close as he apologetically declined an invitation to visit her in Ireland.[145] Indeed, from mid 1835 she quickly introduced him to her most exclusive social set and for Disraeli a 'threshold was crossed'.[146] This was of considerable significance to him, augmenting a process of aristocratic acceptance already begun. Indeed, it is hard to overestimate the importance of introductions within the strictly controlled confines of high society where admission to the private functions of the aristocracy was especially coveted. The introduction represented of a form of social endorsement with patrons being responsible for those they backed. Patronage was thus rarely hastily or ill considered. Given this, the speed of Disraeli's acceptance into the Londonderry circle was remarkable. The day after their initial meeting in June 1835, he called to Holdernesse and within four days he was dining at Rosebank, the Londonderrys' 'babyhouse' thatched cottage near Richmond on Thames, where he 'sat by my hostess with the Marquis of Camden, Thomas Liddell, Lord Mazarine [sic Massereene], Lady Selina Keir [sic Kerr] and the Ravensworths also present'.[147] Disraeli's misspelling of names accentuates the gaucheness of society's newcomer, but within weeks he was undoubtedly a Londonderry intimate, invited to their public and private functions: London receptions and dinner parties, both formal and *en famille*, such as that of June 1837 when he dined alone with the Londonderrys in the company of an unspecified Russian prince. He also attended the event that possessed the highest social cache, the country house party. Frances Anne was, therefore, responsible for introducing him to a wider social set than he was previously privy to, including the Strangfords, Lady Salisbury and Lords Eglinton and Hardwicke. Such introductions meant that his political rise was well underway. Indeed, it was Strangford, along with Lord Chandos, who backed Disraeli's election to the emergent Tory bastion, the Carlton Club in 1836.[148]

Frances Anne and Disraeli's early association was mismatched in terms of title and social prestige, but it was not wholly disparate. She was just four years his senior so the two were near contemporaries and they quickly became friends. Disraeli was advantageous to her in that he read through her articles, pointing out, with her permission, 'egregious blunders in grammar and orthography' and freely passing on socio-political news, or bulletins as he labelled them, in return for her lionisation.[149] He was also aware of the potency of flattery when courting her favour, informing her of his 'whereabouts, in case you will continue to condescend occasionally to notify your existence to Your faithful Sevt.' and declaring he had nothing 'to offer worthy of your delicate ear, fed, I doubt not, by all the secret histories of the cabinets and saloons of Europe'.[150] Throughout their relationship he also regularly assured her of his devotion, claiming his 'greatest pleasure' was to write to her. But in the late 1830s Frances Anne was undoubtedly of more profit to Disraeli than he was to her.[151] This was very apparent at a July 1838 banquet and ball to mark the review of the Londonderry regiment, the tenth Hussars, in Hyde Park, where Disraeli not only recorded his growing familiarity with Frances Anne but also the exposure that invites to her events could bring:

> There were only 150 asked all sat down. Fanny was faithful and asked me, and I feature in the M[orning] Post accordingly. It was the finest thing of the season. The banquet was in the gallery of Sculpture; it was so magnificent that everybody lost their presence of mind...I think it was the kindest thing possible of Fanny asking me[.]

Less convincingly, he added, 'it was not to be expected in any way.'[152]

By 1837 it was clear that trust was another keynote of this relationship. Indeed, that year saw the Londonderrys again battling against the emergent spirit of independent toryism in Durham and it was to Disraeli that Frances Anne confided her concerns about securing the return of their candidates: Liddell in the northern Durham division, who, if successful, would be the first victorious Tory there in two decades, and Fitzroy in the borough of Durham. Issuing a joint letter, the so-called 'Wyndham Edict', to their employees, tenants and agents 'to come forward with the utmost zeal and ardent exertions…to rescue the County from Radical Domination' the Londonderrys promised 'that the sense of the obligation to us personally will be for ever registered in our memories.' This stood in stark contrast to a thinly veiled threat to those who were 'unmindful and indifferent' to their 'earnest wishes.'[153] That Frances Anne's name appeared alongside that of her husband in this electoral appeal shows that she felt no inclination to disguise her interest either in politics or in the locale that she still regarded as under her family's dynastic control. Travelling 270 miles between Friday morning and Saturday night, without her husband's knowledge for fear that he would advise against the exertions of such a journey, to be present for 'the scratch' further highlights her resolve not to be sidelined. Confiding to Disraeli her 'hope [that] Liddell will head the poll which I think would disgust the proud Earl [of Durham] here in his county as he calls it', she revealed her unconditional trust in him as well as the dissolution of the earlier spirit of landed co-operation.[154] Her hopes were met as 'Bedlam broke loose' in celebration of Fitzroy's return but more especially at Liddell's overwhelming electoral success. Predictably she shared the 'glorious victory' with Disraeli, believing the election of the first Conservative county representative in Durham for twenty years signified a more deferential electorate: 'It used to be the most Radical place in the world but yesterday we were 3 to 1. They dragged my carriage in and all the respectable people of the Co. followed in cavalcade. You never saw such a gathering'. The celebration also afforded the chance for her eldest son, Seaham, although aged sixteen and still in minority, to lend a voice to his family's interest. Frances Anne acknowledged this was a 'trial' for the son she was 'always abusing' but really thought was 'perfection', however, in terms of his own future political advancement, it was invaluable and 'gained him great credit'.[155]

Disraeli was equally jubilant with his own 1837 entry to parliament, returned for the safe Tory seat of Maidstone after five years of effort and three unsuccessful attempts: 'I believe I am the only *new* candidate of our side who had not an opposition. It was thought impossible in these times that a man could enter Parliament for the first time and for a borough in such a manner.'[156] His first object was achieved but his subsequent parliamentary progress was slower than he had anticipated. He was disappointed not to gain office under Peel in 1841 and his dalliance with Young England, the loose and short-lived inter-party association he established in 1842, gave him a taste of leadership but persuaded some, such as Sir James Graham, that the Tories would be better off without him. He was, therefore, still in need of patrons and Frances Anne was pleased to oblige. She continued to introduce him to those she believed could help him progress, winning him invites to parties other than her own, such as Lady Salisbury's reception of February 1838 to which Disraeli found he owed 'the invit[ati]on to Lady Lond-[onderry] at least to her mention of me.' And he had progressed considerably in the space of three years: he now 'knew almost every man there.'[157] In the summer of the same year, his patron was again active as he attended both a Londonderry dinner with the express purpose of meeting the Lyndhursts, of whom Lady Lyndhurst was a skilled, if manipulative, hostess, and a 'very brilliant' ball at which he was introduced to Lord Brougham.[158]

With Disraeli in the Commons, his relationship with Frances Anne gradually developed into a more reciprocal association and their correspondence subsequently changed. This became a less trivial epistolary: he sent her news of political developments, cabinet appointments and inter-party wranglings. That he trusted her discretion was evident in the confidential, or as he described it 'under the rose', information he shared with her, meaning that it was only to be passed onto her husband.[159] This trade in information was 'one of the most important privileges of being in Society', but for the exchange to be truly effective, information needed to be swiftly passed.[160] Here Disraeli was in a league of his own, often writing her the hurried lines that he called torso letters, from the floor of the Commons, under the guise of making notes for a speech so that 'news, received this morning from the fountain-head, may not be stale.'[161] Thus, it was from his pen that Frances Anne learnt of the resignation of Melbourne, whilst his successor, Peel was still with the queen.[162]

By 1839 Disraeli was more closely acquainted with the Londonderry circle than ever. He now counted himself amongst friends at their functions, declaring 'Nothing cd. be more delightful' than being in the company of the Salisburys, Lyndhurts, George Bentinck and Henry Liddell.[163] The Londonderry receptions also brought him into contact with the royals, as in July 1839 at a Rosebank 'petite ball' that he likened to a 'festa in one of George Sand's novels' to mark the Duchess of Cambridge's birthday.[164] As the wife of George III's seventh son, guests included the Queen Dowager, the Duchesses of Kent and Gloucester and the Duke of Sussex and with 'only 150 asked really the very perfume of the land, all brilliants of the first water' Disraeli believed, with justification, that 'the Londonderrys [were] more than kind.'[165]

This friendship was not, however, free from controversy: an aspect of political hostessing that would also try later Lady Londonderrys. In May 1838 Disraeli was forced on the defensive by his future fiancée, Mary Anne Wyndham Lewis' accusing charge: 'I am glad you pass so much of your time with Lady L[ondonderry]… because the more you go there or to any other married lady the less likely you are to think of marrying yourself'. Disappointed by her jealous supposition, his reply was curt, 'I do not know what you mean by passing 'so much' of my time with Lady Londonderry. I do not pass any more time with her than Lady anybody else.'[166] But Disraeli's growing relationship with Mary Anne clearly distanced him from his early patron and to such an extent that, in January 1839, after five months silence and 'leaving her letter unnoticed', he informed his now fiancée, 'I wrote at last today to Lady Londonderry', using her eldest son's 'successful debut at a political dinner' to get him 'out of the scrape. You approve?'[167] This gradual withdrawal from Frances Anne's society did not immediately impact on their friendship: she informed him of her arrival in London for the start of the 1839 season and they were certainly corresponding again by May of that year. In same month he attended her court dress state banquet for the Hereditary Grand Duke of Russia at Holdernesse but, less than two months later, a curious note to his fiancée hinted at a further estrangement, again at Disraeli's instigation. In ill health he called to see Frances Anne but 'refused again, persisting in my error if it be one' her invitation to dine, this time at Rosebank with Lady Jersey. His correspondence does not allude to any earlier refusals but the inference is clear. This is reinforced by another letter, written two days later, again to his fiancée, recording his relief at not being sufficiently well to attend Frances Anne's series of fêtes held in the same day at Rosebank and culminating with an evening ball at Holdernesse, 'without health there is no pleasure in these things, and without you, they afford me nothing at the best but a little distraction.'[168] With no guest list surviving it is impossible to gauge whether Mary Anne was being excluded from the Londonderry set, but there was evidently unease. And herein may lie the explanation of why there is no record of Disraeli notifying his early patron and confidante of his impending nuptials in late August 1839. She, however, wrote to him twice in that month, wishing him well in both missives but with a distinct sense of exclusion:

> Now I suppose your marriage is near at hand and you have no time to write to, or wish to hear from your friends. Nevertheless I trouble you with a line firstly to thank you for all your kindness and secondly to enquire after you and your plans - thirdly to wish you all the happiness and comfort in your new situation and fourthly to tell you about myself that you may now and then, should you be charitably inclined send me a few lines to enliven my exile [at Wynyard].[169]

After his marriage the correspondence and contact between Disraeli and Frances Anne came to an abrupt halt. Jealously on the part of his new wife could be to blame. Certainly Mary Anne was uncomfortable with the close relationship Disraeli shared with his sister, Sarah who after his marriage bypassed sending letters to his London home, instead addressing them to the Carlton Club. It is also possible that the final break was on the part of Frances Anne who, in line with the stand adopted by Lady Jersey, deemed the new Mrs. Disraeli simply too bourgeois to entertain. But this was a desultory removal and the process began, at Disraeli's inclination, as early as 1838.[170] That the distancing was more on his part is perhaps nowhere more apparent, after a six-year lull in their correspondence, than in him seeking to make amends. Sending her a copy of his new, and soon to be much-acclaimed, novel, *Sybil or the two nations* in 1845, Frances Anne featured in its pages, in a classic act of Disraelian flattery, as the Marchioness of Deloraine, 'the only good woman the Tories have...She keeps their men together wonderfully; makes her house agreeable; and then her manner, it certainly is perfect; natural, and yet refined.'[171]

'I do not like to be silent, at least not to you.'[172]

Frances Anne passed no comment on her estrangement from Disraeli in the years 1839-45. Instead, she was preoccupied by coming to terms with a post-reform electorate where, with one in seven men now entitled to vote, it soon transpired that aristocratic deference could never again be taken for granted. As Ireland was excluded from the terms of the 1832 reform, the Down seat caused fewer problems, but in Durham the Londonderry influence was often in peril and elections became increasingly contested. Lord Harry Vane was forced to expend £14,000 on the South Durham election in 1841 and two years later in the Durham city by-election the Londonderrys adopted a selective approach, refusing to trade with pro-Whig businesses and seeking a guarantee of support from those with an uncertain political pedigree. However, the impact of the 1843 strategy was, at best, limited. Not only did they fail to pay a share of the election expenses, but their candidate was unseated for distributing head money amongst voters, a practice outlawed in the previous year. The local Tory response was to again rail against the Londonderry interest, running Thomas Purvis as an independent nominee. Londonderry then cast toryism aside and, in an assertion of the family's dynastic right, backed radical free trader and anti-Corn Law champion, John Bright in the belief that, 'Had Purvis been returned the seat was lost to my family and myself forever. Now I have shown my power and nothing can prevent my regaining it.'[173] And, for a time, it seemed as if Charles was right. Durham Tories asked Peel to intervene, but he refused.

Although this election was declared void on petition, it remained hugely controversial and the *Morning Post*'s commentary was scathing: 'injury has been done to the Conservative cause…[by] a little knot of politicians…whose predominance is as unaccountable as it is mischievous.'[174] Disraeli, although still estranged from Frances Anne, keenly observed the Durham developments and confided to his sister, 'Londonderry's flare-up has cut the Government in the wind; they could not believe it possible. He had threatened to hold aloof, but at a certain hour, finding Purvis would possibly be returned, he made all his men vote for Bright! Oh for fifty Durhams.'[175] The local impact of Londonderry's fleeting support for Bright was also far-reaching. Lord Ravensworth established a rival Tory association, refusing to support Londonderry nominated candidates and causing Charles the ignominy of appointing his former solicitor as the new organisation's secretary. But the Londonderrys rarely backed down and Bright's election was in many ways symbolic of the transitional nature of a partially reformed electorate.

Politics continued to try the Londonderrys and Charles' aspirations for office remained thwarted. With Peel's 1841 accession to the premiership, Disraeli and, as ever, Londonderry, hoped for office. Peel, in an attempt to compensate Londonderry for the St. Petersburg debacle, offered him the Viennese embassy, the post he had held two decades previously. But Londonderry's conditional approach again proved difficult to accommodate, pledging only to accept the ordnance if it came with a cabinet place and predictably threatening to go into opposition if his demands were not met. Following discussion with Frances Anne, he declined the post instead accepting the honorary appointments of Lord Lieutenant of Durham and Colonel of the second Life Guards with the latter giving him an official place at court as Gold Stick in Waiting. Taking such a high-handed approach to office should have convinced even Londonderry that the chances of another appointment were nil. But the next year saw him again seeking in vain an ambassadorial appointment to Paris. For a time, he blamed the English embassy, the French government and even Princess Lieven for his non-appointment and the latter, writing to Palmerston, was clearly exasperated, 'One must be as mad as Londonderry to invent a thing like that'. Three years later she was still out of favour:

> for some time now they [the Londonderrys] have taken offence at me, and I no longer see them…I do not know if he would have made a good ambassador, but at any rate it is certain that he would have been a ridiculous figure, and no doubt the Tories in England considered that it was a drawback for an Ambassador to be ridiculous.[176]

At the same time, Ladies Jersey and Londonderry were competitively pitched against one another vying for the King of Hanover's presence. Frances Anne was ultimately victorious, 'L[ad]y L. carried it by the *substantial* charm of the dinner' but 'the tongue has been very active with both ladies against each other.'[177] Even with the king as the prize at her table, Frances Anne shared her husband's penchant for openly displaying feelings, even to those of the highest rank. The king's praise of Londonderry's first wife led Frances Anne to 'burst forth; [she] would not speak to His Majesty; [she] turned her back upon him.'[178] The notoriety that surrounded Frances Anne in the 1820s therefore remained and little wonder that to Disraeli, characterising her as the Marchioness of Deloraine in *Sybil*, she was 'the grandest dame' with:

> a great knowledge of society and some acquaintance with human nature, which she fancied she had fathomed to its centre; she piqued herself upon her tact, and indeed she was very quick, but she was so energetic that her art did not always conceal itself; very worldly, she was nevertheless not devoid of impulse; she was animated, and would have been extremely agreeable, if she had not restlessly aspired to wit; and would certainly have exercised much more influence in society, if she had not been so anxious to show it.[179]

Though the compliment was double-edged, his accompanying letter was both sincere and reflective:

> It often occasions me great unhappiness, that the personage to whose condescending kindness I am most indebted, and that, too, at a period of my life when it was doubly precious, should be the only one to whom, as it were by some fatal spell, it seems, I never can have an opportunity of expressing my sense of her graciousness.
> Yet life is not so long, and these feelings not so common, that I would willingly let them die. …the often recurring feeling of regret having at this moment domination of my heart, I cannot resist its expression. I will not apolo-

gise for it, for I feel you can comprehend me, since I know, from experience, that you have not only a great station, but that cultivated mind that prompts to sympathy.

Though you may welcome this with silence, deign at least, therefore, dear Lady, not to receive it with unkindness; but permit me to take this occasion, tho' it may be my only one, of assuring you, that I am ever your grateful, and, I will add, tho with profound respect, Your attached Servant[.][180]

Disraeli was not convinced that this overture would be well received but Frances Anne permitted him, once again, 'to lay' his 'pen at…[her] feet' and expressed a hope that they would meet.[181] Disraeli's relief was apparent in his effusions of being 'delighted…flattered…gratified' at their re-acquaintance and Frances Anne shared the sentiment: 'I have often regretted the breach in my acquaintance with one so talented and agreeable as yourself and can only hope that this will not continue and that I shall have the pleasure of seeing you sometime and expressing all the respect and admiration I feel for genius such as yours.'[182]

Just as their first meeting rapidly developed into close friendship, so too their re-association.[183] After a six-year gap, they met on 19 July 1845, significantly with Disraeli's wife in attendance. Was an acceptance of his wife the price of their re-acquaintance? If so, it seems that Frances Anne was willing to acquiesce; after the meeting, Disraeli noted, 'Fanny most friendly to me and suff[icient]ly courteous to MA [Mary Anne]', providing another hint that relations between the two women had pre-empted the earlier strife.[184]

Disraeli and Frances Anne's friendship and correspondence was subsequently renewed and they grew closer during the 1840s as she became his only female confidante outside his family circle. His letters of 1846 are indicative of a relationship being re-built, re-assuring Frances Anne of a place in his life, promising that she would be the recipient of the 'earliest and only copy' of his new novel, *Tancred* and expressing his gratitude 'if I may *occasionally*, I dare not say *often*, hear from you, being as you well know, now, as I have ever been, Your devoted servant'.[185] Flattery re-emerged as a watermark of his dispatches, epitomising Frances Anne at 'the soul and centre of diplomacy'. And in the 1840s he produced some of his most acclaimed missives to her: writing 'in a way that he does to no one else - the calibre of his writing to her is matched only by that of his novels.'[186] Their passing of information was also quickly reinstated: in response to her forthright questioning, he shared his doubts that a parliamentary dissolution would occur in September 1846; passed on details given to him 'in confidence' by the Duke of Richmond and commented on continued Tory disunity: 'the Peelites do not in any way rally, and the Tory rancour flourishes in all its primal virulence and vigor [sic]'.[187] But Disraeli's political repute was growing. Indeed, in an undated letter, most probably written in the mid 1840s, Frances Anne could now pass him a compliment that was circulating through society, '*Le talent règne en Angleterre et ne gouverne pas*' (*in translation*, 'Talent reigns in England and (yet) does not govern').[188] But Disraeli was also self-promoting, angling to oust Peel from the party's head to open the way for his own advance and soon he would be in a position to politically assist her stepson, Frederick and her sons, Henry and Adolphus.

But it was not only her family's political standing that preoccupied Frances Anne in the 1840s. The appearance of 'a strong disease hitherto unknown to agriculturalists' on her Antrim estate, as across much of Ireland in 1845, was to 'the poor tenantry on the mountain farms…a source of great alarm and anxiety'.[189] The Antrim agent reported directly to Frances Anne and this, coupled with her hand-written annotations to his reports, prove her control of the minutiae of estate management. Both prior and subsequent to the famine she financially assisted tenants to improve their holdings: allowances were granted for permanent improvements to tenant dwellings whilst annual monetary prizes were given in an array of competitions, including best cultivation, best kept dwelling, best preservation of milk and butter, best ventilation and the honour of being in possession of the best situated manure heap.[190] A recent re-valuation, however, increased rents and by 1844 arrears in the poorest parts of the estate were commonplace. Ignoring the advice of the Antrim agent, Frances Anne and Charles visited the estate in 1846 and instead of a hostile tenantry, they met with distress and pleas for assistance. An address from the tenants of Ballymacaldrick, an area of some 1,300 acres and the least developed and remotest part of the estate, was indicative of many others: the blighted potato crop was 'the staff of our life - the sole substance of ourselves…and how we shall pass though the coming season or make up our rents is only known to God…we commit ourselves to your benevolent consideration.'[191] An Estate Relief Committee subsequently co-ordinated the efforts of distributing soup and blankets to those in acute need; seed corn was given to those who consumed their grain whilst, in an attempt to encourage crop diversification, turnip and parsnip seeds were made available to all tenants. Fertiliser, such as guano and lime, was supplied and Indian meal was sold cut price according to the number in each family. Frances Anne also let lands hit by blight be free of rent, although some three-quarters of rentals, amounting to £2,100, were received in 1847. In addition, she organised a bazaar, with Queen Victoria and the Duchess of Kent as patrons, which raised several thousand pounds for famine relief in 1847. In that year there were hints at an emergent recovery as the estate's tenant-run assisted Clothing Society began to sell garments at cut price instead of gratis distribution.

At Frances Anne's command, an inscription on a limestone rock at Antrim's Garron Point commemorated the famine:

France Anne Vane, Marchioness of Londonderry, being connected with this province by the double ties of birth or marriage and being desirous to hand down to prosperity an imperishable memorial to Ireland's affliction and England's generosity [*author's note*, this section has since been vandalised] in the year 1846-7, unparalleled in the annals of human suffering, hath engraved this stone.
Fair tablet, fashioned by the Almighty's hand
To guard these confines of the sea and land
No longer shalt thou meet the stranger's sight,
A polished surface of unmeaning white:

But bid him ponder on the days of yore
When plague and famine stalked along the shore.[192]

The vandalised inscription illuminates the bitter legacy of the famine, but Frances Anne's sense of propriety is striking: this was her land, these were her tenants and the famine was her concern.

Politics were similarly trying with further controversy over Londonderry nominations in Durham emerging in 1847. With Seaham now of age and eligible to stand for election, the familial basis to aristocratic candidature and the fact that the former Londonderry nominee in North Durham, Henry Liddell was only a caretaker for the seat became very clear when he was forced to stand down. The provincial and national press, as well as Durham Tories, complained of Londonderry dominance but Seaham was returned unopposed, holding the seat until 1854 when he was succeeded by his younger brother, Adolphus. Elsewhere in Durham, however, their control was ebbing away: their candidate came last in the city poll of 1847.

Disraeli was equally frustrated by his own progress. In an attempt to further his career and secure promotion, he adopted an independent party stance and as such had much in common with Lord Londonderry throughout the late 1840s. This position was confirmed in 1846 with Disraeli's alignment to the protectionist wing of the Tory Party which counted Lord Londonderry amongst its most vocal supporters. Peel's resignation opened the way for Lord John Russell's Whig ministry and the protectionists' independent line was reinforced by the fact that they did not cross the house, instead retaining their seats on the government benches. Although Disraeli was a political star in the ascendant, he was still demanding of Frances Anne, irked by her belief that Peel would return to power and informing her that the only hope for her new 'favourite' was her own backing and sympathy, 'but if you w[oul]d only condescend to be our Duchess de Longueville, I really think we have a better chance of governing the country than the late Cabinet. But we sadly lack feminine inspiration.'[193] Similar sentiments were again apparent with Peel's attendance at the wedding of Frances Anne's second daughter, Alexandrina to the Earl of Portarlington in 1847 when Disraeli bemoaned, 'the only thing I envy him is your patronage.'[194]

But as the leading protectionist voice in the Commons, the demands on Disraeli's time grew to such an extent that he was 'almost obliged to forswear society'. To Frances Anne, however, he pledged that he would 'certainly never pay another morning visit except to you' and he continued to regularly assure her of his devotion, sending her gifts like the turtle he had delivered to Holdernesse in 1848.[195] Their letters also became more relaxed in tone as Disraeli abandoned many of the apologetics which marked the start of their renewed friendship and, in a reversal of the earlier association, a shift in power was emergent: Disraeli was now in a position to introduce the Londonderrys to Lord George Bentinck as well as the recently resigned French Prime Minister François Guizot. The latter was a particularly enticing prospect for an ambitious and competitive hostess like Frances Anne as he was not embracing general society.[196] Disraeli seemed especially anxious for them to accede to this request, writing to Frances Anne from the Commons' front benches 'on the back of a red box amid cries of 'question" avouching that he would 'ask no one but those who, I think wd. interest you, or, at least, not displease you.' He also went a step further, suggesting that this would be 'an easy way' for Lord Londonderry to meet Bentinck.[197] Clearly Disraeli was now in a position to seek favours for his early patron. Indeed, in the wake of the European risings and with the King of France exiled in Surrey, Metternich in Hanover Square and Prince William of Prussia at Lady Palmerston's, Frances Anne, once *au fait* with the majority of Europe's ruling elite, felt in the cold. Disraeli intervened on her behalf, speaking 'to the Queen, very naturally, on the subject you hinted at', inviting the Joinvilles and Aumales to Wynyard. The offer was declined with Disraeli, despite some tempered reasoning, venturing 'to observe that there was a great difference between being the guests of a country house and mixing in the miscellaneous crowds of London saloons, and that there were occasions when the Princes might create sympathies and make friends, whose gold feeling and influence might thereafter be useful.' Although this 'view of the case was not without effect', he was unable to attain a reversal of the decision.[198]

Meanwhile the scale and opulence of Frances Anne's entertaining continued to attract attention. In July 1848 she hosted a historical fancy dress ball for 1,000 guests at Holdernesse and, although the offer of Wynyard hospitality was refused, the French monarchy was in attendance. Her ball following the military review in Hyde Park was now an annual event, frequently attended by 1,500 guests including the Dukes and Duchesses of Norfolk, Cleveland and Sutherland, Wellington, the Peels, Hardinges, Baron and Baroness Brunnow, Prince George and Prince Edward of Saxe-Weimar.[199] By the next month, however, the Young Irish rising and Palmerston's political gesturing over Prussian and Danish ambitions in Schleswig-Holstein came to dominate Disraeli's letters to Frances Anne. To his annoyance, 'I have waited to the last moment to give you the last news - but can say nothing', although, 'after a morning of toil and a night of battle impending, it will prove my greatest pleasure is to write to you.'[200] Three days later, after a meeting with Metternich, Disraeli was able to comment on Palmerston's 'false position' and, on the following day, his 'awful mess'.[201] This was a fitting squaring of the circle as it was Lord Londonderry who had introduced Disraeli to Metternich in May 1848.

Disraeli was now a key Londonderry ally and Frances Anne undoubtedly saw him as 'political hot property', but it has been suggested that her reluctance to accept his wife, 'who in her eyes was irremediably common', remained.[202] However, the rift caused by Disraeli's marriage was, at least superficially, healed. There was cordial, if intermittent, correspondence between these two women from the 1840s and both Disraeli and his wife planned to visit Frances Anne at Wynyard once parliament prorogued in September 1848. The intervening days, however, were critical for Disraeli. Although 'wearied and occupied', he divulged 'quite between ourselves', Lord Stanley's invitation to him to sum up the Commons' session to Frances Anne, and his hope that 'the performance' would be 'a final ceremony, the dropping of a curtain - the last flavour, which is to give a tone to public opinion and an impulse to public discontent for some months.'[203] His dispatch to her on the eve of this speech highlighted its watershed significance. Disraeli believed this to be his personal 'Waterloo, but whether for triumph or dis-comfiture, I dare not now foresee'. Although 'utterly exhausted and dispirited', the fact that he wrote to his early patron before delivering the speech that could make his political career, underscores the strength of their renewed bond.[204]

By early 1849, Disraeli was more assured of his own political rise and although he denied to Frances Anne that he held the party reins, the ensuing parliamentary session essentially saw him accepted as the leader of the opposition. But he did not abandon Frances Anne. Instead, after their former drift, a sense of duty to maintain regular contact crept into his letters. He would now write to her even when he had little or no firm news or when he had a political prediction:

This is a souvenir: it can neither instruct or amuse…you are, and you are among, as good and better judges than any here.

As to the political position in this country…There will be a hot, and perhaps eventful, campaign betn. this and Whitsun. Under ordinary circumstances, the Whigs ought to go out, and, perhaps, even under the present, wish it. But what then? The agricultural distress is so great, and the general prosperity is so doubtful, that, even if we were inclined, fusion under the Standard of Peel, or with his adherents even, seems impossible.

This is dull, dry stuff for your fair ears: but I preferred sending it to si-lence…When shall you return?

He also 'watched' Frances Anne's movements, hoping her 'hours had been as brilliant as they deserve, and as charming as I wish them to be.'[205] And, after the ill-fated Young Ireland rising of 1848, with Frances Anne 'a true Lady Chatelaine' and 'feudal Princess in the Tower of Garron', her new castelled Antrim man-sion, hosting parties for local gentry, clerics like the Deans of Connor and Ross and visitors such as Lords Canterbury, Castleross, Annesley, the Earl of Carlisle, Lord and Lady Bateson and on two occasions, the Irish Lord Lieutenant, the Earl of Clarendon and the Earl of Eglinton, Disraeli could not fail to admire her spirit: 'you have the courage to seize the chance of being shot in Ireland. You exist only in danger, strikes on railroads and storms at sea do not satisfy you, and you keep a bear!'[206] Indeed, although the location of the entertainments and receptions moved from London to country seats, the demands of the summer social calen-dar were considerable. Frances Anne's 'great labours and undertakings' at Wyn-yard included 'the civil', that is receiving local magistrates, clergy, neighbours and judges before the scene of the entertainments moved to the Irish estates where tenants and their children and local charitable events had to be hosted both at Mount Stewart and Garron Tower. To Disraeli Frances Anne complained, 'It was like setting up shop'. Though 'expecting lots of people which is presumptuous-ness in this humble abode, but the air and scenery fascinates people,' she still encouraged the Disraelis to visit as 'I know [it] would inspire you…You owe me something for the North'.[207]

A return from Antrim also marked a renewed search for political place. The Whig association of the protectionists was temporary, abandoned in favour of a Tory regrouping with Londonderry in a broker's role by 1850. But with the

Peelite faction gradually moving towards the evolutionary Liberals, neither Londonderry nor Disraeli could win their support. The wrangling continued with Disraeli using Frances Anne as a conduit, asking her to inform Lord Londonderry, 'under the rose that the fusion' between Aberdeen, Gladstone, Stanley *et al* 'ripens rapidly and assumes in every phasis an encouraging aspect'. He also confided that Londonderry's friend, Sir James Graham's independent line baffled 'all conjecture':

> *Private.* I am told that Peel said to Aberdeen, that even he could not make out what Graham was after...Some say that, if the Whigs can get their Irish Reform Bill well thro' this year, they mean to try their hand next session at an English measure, that Graham has an understanding with them on this subject, and is to lead the new revolution. A pleasant prospect!

Although their reunion had occurred some five years earlier, Disraeli still expressed an occasional insecurity, sending Frances Anne 'not a letter, but a notelette to remind you of my existence, and to pray a line respecting yr. movements' in early 1850.[208] A more relaxed tone was, however, renewed by April with his praise for her 'charming letter...its interesting details and their brilliant expression':

> Here we have only two subjects, and both gloomy ones - Religion and Rents. Schisms in the Church, and the ruin of the landed proprietors are our only themes. ...what I tell you all comes from the Whigs. It is however too late for those, who voted for the Repeal of the Corn Laws to repent or to complain. As long as the great body of the people are well employed at a good rate of wages, all the proprietors, and all the farmers, too, may be ruined without redress. If the evil goes deeper, then we shall have a change.
> As for Parliamentary politics, it is impossible for an Opposition to do more than we have done without turning out a Government. We have had a pitched battle nearly every night since we reassembled, and in some of them the Government have received ignominious defeats[.]

He completed this dispatch on the following day, returning to the idea of party fusion: 'I heard from a high quarter, that the Government a few days back, expressed a strong personal wish to retire, and that Graham is the favorite [sic] to form the new ministry'. He personally doubted the latter and this was reinforced by Graham's reaction to the news: he turned 'quite pale, and bolted.' Disraeli also favourably reported on Frances Anne's son-in-law, John, Marquess of Blandford's maiden speech to the Commons: 'His voice is very good, his manner engaging, his style fluent...he might do very well indeed...and left an impression on the cognoscenti highly favourable.'[209] Frances Anne, meanwhile, taxed by a tenant campaign in Ireland, left Disraeli to meet with Charles several times in May 1850 as they liaised to arrange a meeting between '*Les grands* of the old party.'[210]

In this year, however, the influence which friendship could have on political decision making became most apparent. Disraeli's opposition to the Inspection of the Mines Bill was less on a matter of principle, as he supported previous protective legislation such as the Ten Hours Act of 1847, and more on the basis of his association with the Londonderrys. The Whig-backed bill proposed the regular inspection of mines by government officials and unsurprisingly, given Lord Londonderry's earlier public pronouncements of distaste for protective legislation that he deigned government interference, such as his opposition to the 1829 Coal Bill that delayed the prorogation of parliament as well as the 1840 renewal of the Chimney Sweeps Act (1834) and the Mines and Collieries Bill of 1842, he was one of the most vocal critics of the 1850 bill, declaring 'that he would not allow any inspector to go down his pits, or that if any inspector did go down he might stay there!'[211] Disraeli supported Londonderry's stance, proclaiming the bill hastily and ill considered and interfering with the rights of property. He could, however, only manage to delay the 'infernal' bill's passage, believing Grey tricked him over the timing of the proceedings.[212] As he wrote to France Anne in early August:

I have prevented the 2nd Reading of the Mines bill on two occasions, but I fear I shall not succeed in obtaining further delay to night [sic]. Delay is our only chance, as there is no hope for opposition…the philanthropists on our own side and the political economists on the other, being, strange to say, united in favor [sic] of it.

And, in this private dispatch, he made no attempt to hide his limited knowledge of this particular issue: 'I have given notice of opposing it in principle, but I know nothing about it!'[213] Ultimately, for Disraeli and the Londonderrys this united, if limited, opposition would not bear fruit.

But Disraeli was also emerging as a stabilising influence on at least some of Lord Londonderry's extravagances, encouraging him away from protection in early 1850 and plotting with Graham and Stanley to form a stable ministry as an alternative to the chaotic disunity of the Tory Party. But Graham again balked at the idea, thwarting the Londonderry-Disraeli plan and damaging his own career in the process. Indeed, towards the end of 1850 Disraeli felt that trying to rid themselves of the current administration was pointless without a 'strong and enduring' alternative.[214] Yet he was also becoming increasingly frustrated by Londonderry's continual political manoeuvrings, as he expressed to Lord Stanley in January 1851, 'You know that he [Lord Londonderry] always maintains a political correspondence with me, under the guise of social'.[215] That he had adopted an almost identical approach in the 1830s seems not to have concerned Disraeli.

The downfall of the Russell administration, that Disraeli previously warned Frances Anne of, came in February 1851. Stanley was unable to form a cabinet and, despite renewed mediations with Graham that involved both Disraeli and Londonderry, the Whigs returned to office. In this turbulent political atmosphere Disraeli could often 'only write a hurried line' to Frances Anne and the position of the Whigs came to dominate their correspondence.[216] He also delighted in detailing his own parliamentary manoeuvrings to her, having taken 'advantage of the Chancellor of the Exchequer in the reconstruction of the Budget' due to an omission of an earlier promise to offer some relief to those with landed holdings. In this dispatch there was also a reminder that Disraeli was still a relative political newcomer and a young man, boasting that he had 'forced' the Whigs on this point 'to a trial of strength. I did it entirely on my own responsibility.' Furthermore, his pleasure in reporting to her that the government majority was 'a bare one' was palatable. But the frustration of the truly ambitious was also evident, as was proof that their former rift was well healed. Disraeli complained bitterly about the absence of 'enough of our good men…to have gained the victory!', including Frances Anne's stepson, Frederick, Viscount Castlereagh and her eldest son, Henry, Viscount Seaham in his charge. The absence of Seaham was especially galling for Disraeli, but he deigned, 'we must forget it.'[217] After this brief chastisement, he moved on to consider the political potential of such a close vote: 'the Whigs are as weak as before…the clamor [sic] of a very weak movement party, at the present moment is preposterous, Yet, if Ld. John [Russell] proposes anything temperate, the movement party will spring at him like hands. In short, he ought to resign.'[218]

Although it has been claimed that none of Disraeli's letters to Frances Anne from 1852-53 have survived, there is correspondence from this period. She thanked him, for instance, for keeping her abreast of European developments whilst she wintered at Wynyard in early 1852: 'Louis Napoleon's cover is wonderful. I hope he will not go too fast, but it is all very imperial', although she had only domestic affairs to record in return.[219] He responded by sending her some work made by cottagers on his Hughenden estate and, more importantly, sympathising with her spouse's continued exclusion from political office. This was especially poignant as Disraeli was finally placed on the front bench, appointed Chancellor of the Exchequer and leader of the Commons, in Derby's 1852 ministry. He also reassured her that her son, Seaham was not appointed 'as a sop' but was 'in the first list for parliamentary office.'[220] And, for a time in the summer of 1852, it looked as if the Londonderrys' political lot could change: Charles was under consideration for the position of Commander-in-Chief of Her Majesty's Forces but Peel finally recommended Wellington to Victoria. Just two weeks later the subject of filling the vacant Garter, the most prestigious of all the honours, preoccupied the queen and Londonderry was again in the running. But too much controversy surrounded him to win Victoria's favour: she was 'of opinion that it would not be advisable on the whole to give it to Lord Londonderry'.[221] Ironically, it was only the death of Wellington, one of their most faithful and patient supporters, that freed numerous posts and distinctions and Londonderry was one of those to benefit: he was awarded the Garter in September 1852.[222]

As early as 1850, Disraeli had predicted that power could be slipping from 'the hands of the aristocracy for ever' and there was no shortage of controversy over the Londonderrys' electoral fortunes to prove his point. Although the Tory's dire 1847 Durham city poll led to some rapprochement with the Londonderry interest and resulted in Frances Anne's favourite son, Adolphus being returned for the city in 1852, the contest was marked by corruption and the purchase of votes. Similar tactics in the Down election of the same year led some to recommend transportation for life for the Londonderrys.[223] Disraeli assisted in Adolphus' return, but could do little to help when he was petitioned for bribery six months post-election. Frances Anne, writing from Hamburg where she was 'picking up health', was so vexed by the situation that she described herself as 'stupider than 50 pests and full of venom and ill humour. Under such circumstances I ought to keep myself to myself but a friend will have charity and patience and by writing return good for evil.'[224] When the 'hateful' petition proved successful, although feeling both frustrated and betrayed, she was grateful for Disraeli's support:

> We heard the news last night and all has ended as everything in this world does in disappointment, treachery, the betrayal of those you employ and the imbecility, cowardice and stupidity, not to say the deceit of those you trust in…why Ld. March should have helped to unseat Adolphus passes my comprehension…However, while I indulge in venom and bitterness against idiots who know not how to uphold their own cause, I am not less grateful to a friend who supports and aids under difficulty and if the expression of my gratitude has been delayed, believe it is not the less sincere.

Disraeli tried to reassure her that parliament would be prorogued and dissolved at the end of June thus giving Adolphus another opportunity to stand, but he was also realistic, acknowledging that he faced 'a hard fight at Durham'. He actively worked to secure Adolphus' return, 'I have done all I could for him in giving, or promising places to his future constituents', but remained worried that the Durham city result was indicative of a wider change. Indeed, returning to the idea of an aristocratic decline, he noted this class was 'not only divided, but dispersed.'[225]

Frances Anne shared his fears about Adolphus' chances of election especially in 'such a nasty, treacherous…place *entre nous*' as Durham, but she did not pick up on his intimation that these provincial difficulties could signal a change in landed power.[226] Through 1852-53 Disraeli remained on side, writing 'as strong a letter as I could devise about Adolphus, whose interests I have always endeavoured to uphold', and assured Frances Anne that he would 'lose no opportunity of assisting' him:

> It should be some consolation, that he has shown in his brief career, no inconsiderable promise, that he has gained some experience of his future scene of action which no theoretical acquaintance with it could give; and that he need not lose his time in the interval, but stone himself with that knowledge, which he will, ere, long, avail himself of with effect.[227]

Disraeli's promise that he would not 'lose sight' of her son, 'both for his own sake, and for that one still dearer to me. …I shall always endeavour to foster his taste for public life, and assist him as far as I can' was, therefore, long-lived and although he described this dispatch as 'not a letter, but a dull morning visit', he promised to 'call again very soon.'[228]

But Disraeli's own position was far from secure: he was only chancellor for ten months; his budget rejected by a combination of Whigs and Peelites. With Lord Aberdeen, a Peelite in political persuasion, acceding to the premiership Disraeli's chances for promotion were ruined. To Frances Anne he confided his growing disillusion with the parliamentary arena: 'It is a place-hunting cabal and they were so rapacious after their prey that they forgot in their chase after office to settle their policy.'[229] By the summer of 1853, although passing on 'alarming intelligence' of the 'most warlike speeches' emanating from the cabinet, the electoral prospects for the Londonderrys looked more promising.[230] Their nominee, John Mowbray was elected to Durham and, in the following year, 1854, Adolphus succeeded his older brother as MP for the northern division of the county, retaining the seat for a decade. Disraeli's gloomy prophecies of an aristocratic decline, for a time, therefore, rang hollow.

Yet there was little respite either politically or privately for the Londonderrys. Disraeli was also increasingly despondent and his letters to Frances Anne became less frequent than had been the norm over the past few years, believing that she deserved 'a happier subject and a brighter pen'.[231] February 1854 saw the resumption of regular letters although, with the dual prospect of war with Russia and another reform bill looming, he struggled to throw 'any light on the confusion and chaos that surround us.' The unity of opposition to resist Russian aggression was not echoed in opinions of reform and events were so fast moving that, unusually, he called Frances Anne to London: 'you see, affairs are so critical and capricious that unless you come to town, it will be impossible to convey any accurate idea of them to you.'[232] Impending personal tragedy would, however, preclude her attendance in town for some time.

A 'new and sad era'[233]

The influenza epidemic that swept Europe cost Lord Londonderry, along with some 50 million others, his life on 6 March 1854. The Disraelis were among the first to offer Frances Anne solace in widowhood and invited her to Hughenden. But a sense of commitment to her children, 'who would feel hurt if I had been tempted to look for Sympathy and Consolation with any but them', prevailed. Although she was invited to live with her daughter, Alexandrina and spend time with her son, Harry in Wales, she had 'neither the energy or the courage' to leave her 'own hearth, sad and lonely as it is.'[234] Frances Anne publicly and privately commemorated Charles: she built an elaborate mausoleum next to the house chapel at Wynyard, displaying his uniforms, swords, insignia and trophies and inscribing a list of his twenty-five battles in gold on a marble wall-mounted tablet as well as building Christ Church in Seaham as a more public memorial to him in 1855.

Disraeli delayed writing again until April, admitting that he had been 'often tempted to write...but have been deterred equally by the fear of premature sympathy, and the pain.' But he now tried to console her: 'your life is yet before you and you have so many sources of happiness and duty, that the past must be cherished and not brooded over' and urged, 'Your excellent abilities and strength of character will support you in the difficulties you will have to encounter, while, capable of deep affection, the cares of life will in your case be mitigated by the heart.'[235] But widowhood and her new dowager status brought significant changes to her life and she struggled to come to terms with the loss. Unsurprisingly, she confided her sense of desolation to Disraeli:

You have no idea of the agony I have endured...It seems as if there was only ½ myself left - the friend and partner of 35 years (a life itself) and we had lived out of the world and more for each other. For me there is no future on earth...no human creature can enter into my feelings or understand the extent of my distress...It is no common loss - it is like no other.

Yet, ironically, this, the most stable of the three Lady Londonderrys' marriages, was in some ways less devastating than it would prove for her successors. Frances Anne was the sole executor of Charles' will and inheritrix to her Durham and Antrim estates and so she deigned to 'drag on life with the sole gratification (and...privilege) of carrying out all his plans and objects.'[236] This was by her husband's design; shortly after his wife came of age in 1821 he arranged to bequeath everything to her 'absolute disposal' after his own demise with the aim of making 'her more powerful and a free agent in every future contingency.'[237] In widowhood, the sense of proprietorship, so evident in her early life and in the estate records, now came to the fore. She began to run the family estates in Durham and took sole command of Holdernesse, Wynyard and Seaham Hall for the rest of her life as well as assuming complete control over the collieries and Garron Tower. Thus, only the Irish estates passed to her stepson, Frederick, now the fourth Marquess of Londonderry. Initially she was overwhelmed by the magnitude of the task, writing to Disraeli: 'I am turned into a clerk...I silently suck everybody's brain and go home and digest it all. I think I could manage any one subject but I have so many to go for Estates to Docks, from draining to Railways, quarries to timber and so on till I get hopelessly bewildered.'[238] This was, however, a position of her own choosing: agents or one of her sons could have taken over. Nor was she nominally in control: in 1854 she revived her former surname of Tempest; demanded full agent's reports, suggesting a desire for information on the real state of what were now, once again, her concerns; sacked at least two agents who tried to take advantage of a woman in such an unusual position in the mid nineteenth century; further expanded the Seaham works at a cost of £100,000, establishing four blast furnaces and connecting the Seaham and Sunderland Railway to the London and North-Western line; completing Carnlough limestone railway and harbour as well as building a town hall, the Londonderry Arms hotel and inaugurating a bank, reading room, library and temperance and clothing societies. And, in 1855, in another clear example of her taking stock and regaining control of her business interests, she paid off the remaining £20,000 mortgage on Seaham. But the woman whom Disraeli once depicted as living 'so much in scenes of "cloth of gold"' was increasingly isolated from the niceties of high society. Instead it was collieries, miners and the devotion of the rest of her life to the realisation of her husband's plans that were her priority.

Her workers' entertainments, as opposed to Holdernesse's opulence and extravagance, now caused press attention. Embracing the paternalistic entertainments that became fashionable amongst the aristocracy in the early nineteenth century she fêted, fed and, although her eldest son and future inheritor of the Londonderry title, Earl Vane was present, addressed 2,000 of her Durham pitmen in March 1856. The scale of this event and the gender of its host attracted much comment. It also provided Disraeli with an unusual opportunity to praise France Anne's, as opposed to her sons' or her late husband's, oratory: 'I thought your address very telling, and, both in spirit and expression, without a fault.'[239] The Duke of Rutland was similarly roused to write, musing on the significance of her address: 'A new Era seems coming on and Women's Empire is I think wholly to come back in all its glory'. Another aristocratic woman in business, Lady Charlotte Guest, although by this time remarried with her son in control of the familial iron works, was reminded of her 'old days in power'. The speech, in Guest's opine, was 'most excellent and sensible':

> No man could have done better...It is a move in the right direction and as coming from a woman is deserving of greater consideration. If our aristocracy will avail themselves of such occasions to mingle with, and advise the people, they will do much good for both classes.[240]

The Times' matter of fact coverage similarly commended Frances Anne's assurances:

> that she should always take a deep interest in their welfare. The Marchioness adverted to the bond of union that had existed between her ancestors and the pitmen, and exhorted them to frequent reading rooms, mechanics' institutions, and temperance societies; to avoid public houses, and to be orderly, industrious, and religious. This address was received with vociferous cheering[.][241]

That the paper made no comment on the acceptability of a woman addressing such an assemblage was also illuminating - Frances Anne was acknowledged as the head of a vast and successful industrial concern, managing the north's most extensive and profitable coalfield that extended some 12,000 acres with annual miners' wages amounting to £135,000 in 1856. In the following year, presiding over the annual dinner to 3,000 colliery and works employees in Seaham, an undertaking that saw the consumption of thirty-two sheep, eight cows and 500 five-pound plum puddings as well as sixty barrels of beer, she addressed the huge assemblage in 'gracious' yet 'motherly' terms, calling on her workforce to 'be careful and prudent. You do not know how much this effects my peace...It makes my blood run cold to dwell on these fearful risks, and I think any great calamity among you would break my heart...I pray you remember how deeply I am identified with you.'[242] She also addressed an annual tenants' dinner in Antrim, expounding the need for crop rotation, drainage improvements and flax cultivation and noting: 'the land is like a person's banking account...The more you put in, the more you will be able to draw out. ...Thus for your own sakes I would advise you to avail yourselves of every attainable improvement...you will ere long reap the advantage of your perseverance and industry.'[243]

There is evidence dating to the late 1850s, however, to suggest that Frances Anne was disconcerted by bank accounts closer to home, specifically the extent of her late husband's borrowing. Undeniably the considerable colliery investment made during Charles' lifetime produced long-term gains: their annual coal profits amounted to £33,400 in the decade 1844-54. The extent of inherited debts would also have been far more damning had not the Londonderry trustees, with Seaham's coming of age in 1845, redrafted Frances Anne's marriage settlement to ensure that she 'would inherit a virtually unencumbered estate.'[244] This was a less than popular move: over a thirteen-year period Londonderry was forced to pay close to £185,000 of debts and set aside money for his younger children. Despite this, 1858 saw Frances Anne paying an annual interest of £23,500 on outstanding loans even after clearing £150,000 of her husband's debts. By the time of her death, however, the Londonderry estates and accounts were free of arrears.

But even those who knew her best, Disraeli and her eldest son, were surprised at her business acumen. The former visited her at Seaham in December 1861 and recorded:

This is a remarkable place, and our hostess a remarkable woman. Twenty miles hence she has a palace [Wynyard] in a vast park, with forest rides and antlered deer, and all the splendid accessories of feudal life. But she prefers living in a hall on the shores of the German Ocean [North Sea], surrounded by her collieries, and her blast-furnaces, and her railroads, and unceasing telegraphs, with a port hewn out of the solid rock, screw steamers and four thousand pitmen under her control. One day she dined the whole 4,000 in one of the factories. In the town of Seaham Harbour, a mile off, she has a regular office, a fine stone building with her name and arms in front, and her flag flying above; and here she transacts, with innumerable agents, immense business - and I remember her five-and twenty years ago, a mere fine lady; nay, the finest in London! But one must find excitement if one has brains[.][245]

Her stepson, Frederick, writing from Ireland, reiterated Disraeli's incredulity:

I wish I had your energy and activity - I wonder at your work for you never seemed as if you would rouse yourself to great exertion. I am sure it suits you for you look better and younger by many years than I have ever seen you before all this weight was on you[.][246]

To Frances Anne, however, there was nothing unusual in her business interests: she was simply protecting the inheritance and, in the absence of a spouse, providing for those who would succeed her and continue in the name of Londonderry.

Despite her new business focus, Disraeli continued to correspond, complaining, in a strictly confidential dispatch, of political isolation in 1854: 'I have never yet been fairly backed in life. All the great personages I have known even when what is called "ambitious", by courtesy, have been quite unequal to a grand game. This has been my fate, and I never felt it more keenly than at the present moment':

I already feel, in the position I now occupy, the want of sufficient fortune. There are a thousand things which ought to be done which are elements of power, and which I am obliged to decline doing, or ought to do at great sacrifice. Whether it be influence with the Press, or organisation throughout the country, everyone comes to me, and everything is expected from me. Tho' so many notables and magnificoes belong to the party, there never was an aggregation of human beings who exercised less social influence. ...As for our chief [Palmerston], we never see him. His house is always closed; he subscribes to nothing, tho' his fortune is very large, and expects, nevertheless, everything to be done.[247]

That he expressed these most private concerns to Frances Anne again underlines her continued role of confidante, but she was also seeking solace from Disraeli.

Her favourite son, Adolphus' 1854 call up for active service in the Crimea was devastating for Frances Anne. Disraeli tried to bolster her spirits but could do little to alleviate a mother's anguish:

What you suffer from, is want of sympathy. It is not merely the emotions of the heart, that are the source of happiness, but also that identity of sentiment and taste on all the pursuits and objects of life, which similarity of disposition may give, but which only the friendship, and confidence, and habit, of long years can maturely and completely develop.

You have had, too, after a youth of great prosperity, many sorrows suddenly to darken your life. But the firmness of your character, and your excellent sense, will bear up against all this; and tho' the past cannot be restored, it will, in time, be dwelt upon with solace, or, at least, a softened pang.[248]

Despite his reassurances, she remained troubled, worried by both Adolphus' personal wellbeing and government policy. She vented her increasing sense of frustration to Disraeli:

Surely there must be an hour of reckoning for this hateful Government who go to war without providing an army. It is actual murder to let this heroic wreck of any army fight those hordes and masses of barbarians who reinforce by tens of thousands while we hardly do so with hundreds. And that wintering in the Crimea, without comforts, habitations, hardy provisions...it is all heartbreaking...I think of nothing else even in my sleep...It seems so dreadful to sit at home and do nothing.[249]

Soon Disraeli was lost for words of consolation, 'my heart is with you at this trying moment...I really could only write [to] you'.[250] And, by December, Frances Anne was totally despondent:

I have deplorable accounts - floating encampments on mud, no fresh meat even for the officers...horses dying all round, and none to be got even to bring up the supplies taken out. There seems neither care nor thought, and a total indifference as to what becomes of the wreck of this fine army, and the brave spirits who seem tasked beyond human endurance.[251]

Disraeli's first letter of the new year of 1855 was to his old patron, wishing her 'all that happiness of which, in the present state of affairs, you must be ever dreaming.'[252] His wife also sent Frances Anne a bust for her classical sculpture gallery at Holdernesse and for this, 'and the justice you have done me in appreciating my friendship', she was grateful.[253] Happiness was, however, far distant for her. With 'wretched' spirits, 'upset and absorbed and oppressed', she struggled to 'look forward to what is to become of me - The shock and change has been so quick and the weight of affairs and business etc. that has come upon me is almost more than I can manage.'[254] Disraeli's visits to her at Wynyard now became 'a pilgrimage of friendship' and, despite her grief, he continued to correspond in the old vein. Again, aggravated by Palmerston, he confided, 'our chief has again bolted!':

This is the third time that, in the course of six years during which I have had the lead of the Opposition in the House of Commons, I have stormed the Treasury Benches...You cannot, therefore, be surprised, that I am a little wearied of these barren victories...What is most annoying is that, this time, we had actually the Court with us, for the two Court favorites [sic], Aberdeen (of the Queen) was extinct, and Newcastle (of the Prince) in a hopeless condition: and our rivals were Johnny in disgrace, and Palmerston, ever detested.

But Palmerston was not yet defeated and Disraeli could ill-disguise his disgust: 'he is really an impostor, utterly exhausted, and at the best, only ginger beer, and not champagne, and now an old painted pantaloon, very deaf, very blind, and with false teeth, which would fall out of his mouth when speaking'.[255] By reply, Frances Anne sought to reassure him, but she also levelled a charge that he had ignored her earlier advice regarding Palmerston:

You are now admitting that you would not listen to from me in former years of the man who would sacrifice his dearest friend to his joke or bon mot - the most important object to the whim or fancy of the hour - who only cares for his party because it flatters his vanity to have a long tail...Your brilliant talent, unwearied perseverance and indomitable energy are every day more deeply and highly appreciated, and must at last be successful - that "magic of the mind" must command mankind...on the other hand you are an old man having vegetated for years[.]

She also drew parallels between their financial predicaments, but was sensitive enough to acknowledge that her own trials were not on a par with his:

How sad it is that the thought or want of money creeps into everything and... I wish I could coin, for in my own small way here I want about half a million to carry out all the schemes and projects and really do justice to the charge confided to me. However, my matters must look like the affairs of ants compared to those that occupy your mind.[256]

With Disraeli drawing attention to the government's deficiencies and Frances Anne lamenting the national condition, 'England without an Army, the Country without a Government', their letters of 1854-58 display a pessimism not seen elsewhere in their correspondence.[257] Despite the gloom, Disraeli remained an important purveyor of information; from him Frances Anne learnt of the fall of Sebastopol and, by March 1856, that peace was certain in the Crimea.

The 1857 election saw Disraeli returned unopposed, but the Tory Party was seriously dented. With the government outvoted and a dissolution pending, he faced a second campaign 'with little relish' but hoped to see Frances Anne 'and may I find you as well looking, as when I last kissed your hand by your gracious permission.' But he soon became once more apologetic as he struggled to find time to write and convey events or even his thoughts to her in writing. Such was the pace of events that he became frustrated that he could not talk to her in person, complaining from the Carlton Club: 'I have many things I could say, if we were in your boudoir'. Still, he managed to note, 'The season is over, but the Parliament will last a long time'. And, despite his rushed tone, it is still possible to glean a sense of pleasure at his upward political journey, hoping to impress his early patron by dining with the Comte de Paris and the Duc d'Aumale and asking, 'What do you think of that?'[258]

Wrangles over the Divorce Bill and the outbreak of the Indian Mutiny meant that, as Disraeli had indicated, parliament continued long after the end of the 1857 season. In consequence, he was again forced to pass on an August visit to Frances Anne in Antrim and the pressure of work was unrelenting. The fall of Palmerston's administration in February 1858 opened the doors for the third Derby-led Tory government and for Disraeli at the Treasury. To Frances Anne he confided, 'I am so tired that I can scarcely guide my pen, and would write to no one but you', but they were gradually growing apart. He certainly looked to her for comfort on the death of his sister, Sarah in 1859 and he and his wife dined with Frances Anne in the same year, but their correspondence became more sporadic. This was clear in Disraeli's letter of early November 1861 which noted, 'I generally know where the Marchioness of Londonderry is, by the school of oratory which she inspires. I read with great satisfaction, as all the world did, your own address in Ireland'.[259] However, he remained mindful of the Londonderry interest, especially of Adolphus who, returned from the Crimea and in the Commons, he encouraged to contribute to debates on the India Bill and the ill-fated Reform Bill.[260] But Frances Anne's second, and favourite, son was fighting a more personal battle with war neurosis. The state of his health became well-publicised and his marriage to Lady Susan, the only daughter of the fifth Duke of Newcastle, in 1860 was, therefore, hugely controversial. The Duchess of Manchester aired her concerns directly to Frances Anne only to be rebuffed: 'The hard old devil announced she was convinced that the marriage would promote the happiness of her son, which was all she had to do with.'[261] The subsequent marriage ceremony was predictably understated, without even family in attendance, and Adolphus' mental state was such that he often had to be removed from the house.[262]

Of Disraeli's annual round of autumnal visits in 1861 he deemed 'the most important' was to his old friend at her Seaham 'shop' who now openly admitted that

she liked 'so few people' and was 'too old to make new friends' that she clung
'more to the few that are left.' The return of an unopened letter she had written
to Disraeli in November 1861 revealed the true extent of her sadness and gave
her 'such a feeling of insecurity in everything and that in the midst of life we are
in death.'[263] In the next month, another fire broke out at Wynyard destroying the
chapel, west wing and six rooms and Frances Anne could only conclude, 'What
an ill-fated place and what a doomed family.'[264] In short, her life 'had gone very
sour' in widowhood and coping with Adolphus who was now thought too ill to
ever recover.[265] He was still a sitting MP but his mother correctly believed that it
was only a matter of time before his seat was contested. This co-joined her with
Disraeli in another fight to retain Londonderry control of Durham. With a parliamentary dissolution imminent in late 1861, the news that a Tory candidate other
than Adolphus would be run in Durham spurred Disraeli into action. In a confidential dispatch he stepped into the fray as a mediator, reviving the old Londonderry caveat of opposition:

> The conspiracy you foresaw has already partially exploded. I have written to
> Taylor to say, that if he, or any one connected with the party, either directly or
> indirectly, interfere with the county, or the City of Durham, you will withdraw
> your influence from the party, and probably, will ultimately, throw it into the
> other scale - that without you the Conservatives can do nothing, either in
> County or City, and, therefore, it is no use kicking against the pricks[.]

But he also issued a warning to the notoriously headstrong Frances Anne:

> for the sake of all concerned, the utmost quiet is desirable, and, that as a disso-
> lution of Parliament is highly deplorable, they need not alarm themselves…
> This peremptory dispatch…will, I hope, keep things tranquil. But great tact
> and temper on your part are necessary. It is best to know nothing of all this.
> He who gains time, gains everything - We shall gain time, and the rest depends
> on Adolphus.

With Disraeli's intervention, this issue was settled in Frances Anne's favour but,
although delighted by the result, her faith in Durham's deference to her familial
interest was badly shaken:

> There is a nasty undercurrent of malignants in the county but I hope we shall
> defeat them and am greatly obliged by your firm expression, because altho'
> they can do nothing the buzzing is very disagreeable.
> I think they can hardly be such idiots as not to know that only my son could
> sit as a Conservative for this Liberal Division[.][266]

Her justification for this control had, however, changed. No longer was the political pedigree of the family being highlighted, now homage was due because she
was 'so largely embark'd in trade and commerce'.[267] Such an appeal was temporarily successful. In the last years of Frances Anne's life, Tory, and occasionally Lib-

eral, candidates standing in the locale would notify her of their intentions or formally seek her approval to stand for election. A letter from W. Lindsay, a Liberal standing in Tynemouth and North Shields, exemplified many others:

> When I consider your great influence in this quarter, and the high esteem in which your Ladyship is deservedly held by all whom you employ, and those who really know you, I consider it my duty to advise your Ladyship of the step I have taken. I think my return is certain but if I could be favoured with any support from you, it would be placed beyond all doubt.

This deference continued throughout the early 1860s, with Lord Loughborough, for example, asking whether she wished him to stand in the city of Durham in a seat vacated by the death of the sitting member in 1864 or if 'your wishes and intentions have undergone any change since you were good enough to select me as a proper candidate and to furnish me with letters to several of the principal electors'.[268]

Despite this apparent reverence, the tussle for control of Durham continued. In 1863 Frances Anne again had to appeal to Disraeli to intervene against centralised toryism and the Carlton Club 'at their old tricks meddling here'. The candidate, Mr. Spofforth, was advised by all concerned that 'all must depend' on Frances Anne, but he put himself forward as a candidate without her consent. Although convinced that the affair 'can only end in complete failure…[and] an infinite deal of mischief is done so producing very bad policy', she was still greatly offended by his 'mischievous attempts', his 'folly and impudence of this meddling after being told nothing could be done without me'. And, as in 1861, she hinted to Disraeli that her financial support for the Durham Conservatives could be withdrawn:

> I write you this line because if they go on meddling they will repent it and I will not be answerable for the results.
> I consider it would be the worst policy in the world to provoke a contest and I don't believe any one wishes it but a few drunken freemen who of course would like the uproar.
> It is very provoking.[269]

With this threat and Disraeli's tempered reasoning, there was no electoral contest in Durham in that year. These events, however, show not only the import, especially pertinent in widowhood, of Disraeli's continued support but also illuminate that Frances Anne was the accepted family head and that her belief in aristocratic predestination to rule was unaltered.

To Disraeli in these last years of Frances Anne's life, fighting to protect her family and embroiled in business, she was 'The Tyrant…half ruffian - half great lady'.[270] He visited her, with Mary Anne, in December 1862 to unveil the infamous equestrian stature of the third Marquess that still stands in Durham's market square: notorious because the very man it commemorated threatened to sink a pit in the square if permission was not granted for its erection. But Frances

Anne's own health, like that of her favourite son, was failing. She complained of feeling old to Disraeli as early as 1853: 'Alas my eyes are going, and I who was prepared to compete with a lynx can only see the small print of these pink and green books by daylight with glasses.'[271] Her poor constitution eventually impacted on her activities and her public addresses became rarer. She continued, however, to run both the estates and the mines but deemed it 'a peculiar disagreeable existence - quite alone in this huge home teased out of life with things I don't understand - draining, farming and such like - sulky, worried and tormented.'[272] A telegram breaking the news that Adolphus had suffered a severe relapse and been removed from the house for his wife's safety in 1863, by Frances Anne's own admission, nearly killed her. Adolphus died in June of the next year and this bereavement hastened his mother's withdrawal from public life. Her last address was to her Antrim tenantry in 1864 and her final business venture came later in the same year with the purchase of Seaton Colliery to amalgamate it with neighbouring Seaham in order to comply with protective legislation that demanded a mine needed two outlets from each seam.

Disraeli's last surviving letter to Frances Anne was written in October 1863 but further letters may have followed, especially as one of Frances Anne's final dispatches, dated July 1864, was not written to Disraeli but to his wife. The letter was marked by a now characteristic despondency, 'between illhealth [sic] and sorrow', Frances Anne deigned, 'I have been well nigh crushed'.[273] On the way to summer at Garron in 1864, she suffered a heart attack and heart and liver disease eventually gave way to dropsy. In October Disraeli was informed that she was 'very ill, and there has been a great prostration of strength.'[274] She died at Seaham Hall on 20 January 1865.

'A woman of exceptional capacity, energy and decision'.[275]

Frances Anne referred to her own life as a 'long brilliant existence'.[276] She certainly broke social convention with her active business involvement - running homes in England and Ireland, eleven pits, two railways, lime quarries, blast furnaces, a steamer and managing 12,000 acres in Durham and Ireland. Overseeing the annual shipment of 700,000 tons as the north's largest producer of coal and delivering annual public addresses to both her tenants and employees, at a time when a woman even mounting the platform at a public gathering was controversial, went against Victoria's dictate that 'women are not *made* for governing - and if we are good women, we must dislike these masculine occupations'.[277] Conversely, Frances Anne's role as political wife and confidante aroused little contemporary comment. Such activities were seen, it seems, as part of an aristocratic woman's lot. And Lady Dorothy Nevill, writing in 1919, summed up the position of women like Frances Anne in the mid nineteenth century:

> The social power wielded by great ladies…seems almost inconceivable today, their easy leisured arrogance was taken more or less as a matter of course, and they would have been very much astonished had it aroused any criticism; small wonder, when they were brought up to think they were they very salt of the earth.[278]

Although such surety meant that Frances Anne was never universally beloved, under her reign invitations to Holdernesse were coveted. Her famed love of opulence was also unvarying. Indeed, May 1851 saw her attend a play at Whig peer, the Duke of Devonshire's home, 'in a gown trimmed with green birds, small ones round the body and down the sides, and large ones down the centre. The beak of one of the birds caught in [the] Queen's dress and was some time before it could be disentangled. Lady Londonderry [was] very proud of the episode.'279

Frances Anne's early patronage of Disraeli was certainly significant in accelerating his acceptance into high society and introducing him to those whom could help satisfy even his grand ambition. She championed him when he faced prejudice as a society outsider and they became sufficiently close for Disraeli to jest about their social differences, 'What you, great personages, do, and how you contrive to manage, with so many seats, I am at a loss to conceive! But perhaps you need not know so much as we, little persons, are obliged to become acquainted with.'280 He also classified her as a demon, equal in calibre to his own grandmother as well as Sarah, Duchess of Marlborough and Catherine the Great.

Disraeli's reliance on female confidantes was a constant of his adult life, influencing both his political advance and his fiction: his last novel, *Endymion*, published in the year of his death, took women's beneficent political role as its central theme. Still, in 1873 he was amazed not only to find a hundred letters from Frances Anne at Hughenden but also their detailed content: 'Nothing seems to have escaped her'.281 His gratitude inspired him to award the Order of St. Patrick to her son in the same year, in recognition of 'a *grande dame* who was kind to me when a youth, though she was a tyrant in her way. But one remembers only the good in the departed.'282 Five years later he was again able to proffer some reward, writing to Frances Anne's eldest son, Henry, by then the fifth Marquess, 'If agreeable to yourself, I shd. like to submit, to her Majesty, the name of a very old friend, to whom I am addressing these lines' as his nominee for the Lord Lieutenancy of Durham.283

This was more than an association of convenience: their friendship continued when it transpired that there were restrictions as to what Disraeli could do to assist the Londonderry interest - he could not get Charles high office nor could he alone defeat legislation with the weighty support of the house and popular opinion behind it. Moreover, they continued to correspond and meet in Frances Anne's later years when her political interest was more that of an onlooker than that of an active participant and when Disraeli was of more use to his former promoter than she was to him. In essence, Frances Anne was one of his closest friends and one who never doubted his genius. She predicted that he would become Prime Minister, but died before her prophecy was born out by reality in 1868 and again from 1874-80. Meeting the Russian diplomat, Prince Gortchakoff, at the 1878 Congress of Berlin, Disraeli finally realised the extent of her faith in him: 'Frances Anne...having always mentioned me in her letters [to Gortchakoff], said she thought I should be Minister, and if so, hoped we should be friends.'284 Although this friendship lacked the romantic infatuation that characterised some of Disraeli's relationships with women, especially in the latter years of his life, theirs was an association that outlasted the varying political fortunes that impacted on them both.

On Frances Anne's death some overstated her importance, alleging that she ruled London society. In reality, there were limitations on what she could do to promote her less than blessed spouse whose ambition for high political office was effectively bedded by Queen Victoria's mandate 'that Lord Londonderry should not be employed in any post of importance, as this would, in her opinion, be detrimental to the interests of the country.'[285] One of Frances Anne's obituarists also echoed remarks made some three decades earlier of the Tory confidante, Mrs. Arbuthnot, claiming that she too was 'remarkable for an almost masculine strength of mind'.[286] Although in middle age Frances Anne described herself as having 'rather a matter of fact prosaic mind', she was opinionated, intelligent and determined, with a love of satire, like the fictional 'Wynyard Post' paper that Sir Henry Browne wrote for her amusement in the 1840s.[287] On her marriage in 1819 she became one half of a partnership that was dedicated to dynastic surety and the longevity of the Londonderry line both in terms of heirs and societal standing. Undeniably, however, Frances Anne was the dominant constituent of this alliance. All her activities were directed towards the familial good and the desire 'to survive mortality and live beyond the grave...which when achieved under the evening of life was as brilliant as its morning.'[288] She was never party motivated or party minded. In essence, she was a political wife and confidante rather than a Tory hostess, although many of her contemporaries used the latter appellation. The bitter debates over franchise reform, Catholic emancipation and the Corn Laws divided society, heightening the party basis of political entertaining, but Frances Anne sought only to promote her spouse, her sons and those she believed could assist in this cause.

From Frances Anne's life, it is clear that personal acquaintance, correspondence and entertaining were beneficial political tools in the mid 1800s but after her death in 1865 the political profile of the Londonderrys waned. Frederick, later the fourth Marquess, sat in the Commons for three decades before moving to the Lords on his succession in 1854. He showed some political promise and was appointed to several junior ministerial posts under Peel and Wellington but his 1846 marriage to Elizabeth, widow of the sixth Viscount of Powerscourt, meant that he spent much time at her Wicklow estate. She seems to have possessed scant political interest and this did not alter on becoming the fourth Marchioness of Londonderry. Frederick was effectively removed from the political running in the 1860s as, suffering from syphilis, most probably neurosyphillis common in the tertiary stages of the disease, he was eventually certified. His half-brother and Frances Anne's eldest son, Henry inherited the Durham estates on his mother's death and succeeded to the marquessate in 1872 but, accurately described by Hyde as 'the least conspicuous member of the family', he and Mary, fifth Marchioness, possessed few political aspirations, preferring to live in 'comparative obscurity' on her Welsh estate, Plâs Machynlleth in Merioneth. They travelled to London but only on invite as in 1877 when they dined with Disraeli and the Russian Special Envoy, Count Ignatiev at Downing Street. They also occasionally entertained at Wynyard: for Prince Christian of Schleswig-Holstein with the Marlboroughs in attendance in 1870 and for German Chancellor, Bismarck and the Prince and Princess of Wales in 1883. However, this never developed into a more sustained social interaction, effectively highlighting the fact that personal ambition underpinned political activism. But it was not only the fortunes of the Londonderrys that were subject to flux at this time. The next Lady Londonderry to assume the mantle of aristocratic confidante would have to face the challenge of a greatly augmented electorate and claims that her class no longer possessed a right to rule.

i.   Etching of Wynyard Park, Co. Durham, c. 1885 (private collection).

ii.   Photograph of Mount Stewart, Co. Down, c. 1890 taken either by Theresa, sixth Marchioness or her son, Reginald (*Londonderry Album*, p. 38).

iii.   Photograph of Londonderry House,
Park Lane, London, undated
(*Londonderry House*, plate I).

iv.   Time of engagement portrait of
Frances Anne, later third Marchioness
of Londonderry by Sir Thomas
Lawrence, 1818 (private collection).

v.   Lithograph of Frances Anne, third Marchioness of Londonderry by Richard James Lane after Sir William Charles Ross, 1843, © National Portrait Gallery, London.

vi.   Lithograph of Charles, third Marquess of Londonderry by M. Guaci, 1822 (N. Chater and Co., London) (private collection).

vii.   Portrait of Theresa, sixth Marchioness
of Londonderry by John Sargent,
1912 (private collection).

viii.   Photograph of Charles, sixth Marquess
of Londonderry, undated (private
collection).

ix. House party at Mount Stewart during the Marquess of Salisbury's visit to Belfast, *The Graphic*, 1893. Top row: Mr. Brownlow, H. Foster, MP, Hon. S. McDonnell, Lord Ashbourne, sixth Marquess of Londonderry, Col. Montgomery, Edward Carson, MP, W. S. Macartney, MP, Lord Morris, Lord E. Cecil, John Ross, MP, Lord H. Cecil. Bottom row: Mrs. Foster, the Bishop of Derry, Lord de Ros, sixth Marchioness of Londonderry, the Marquess of Salisbury, Lady Gwendonline Cecil, the Duke of Abercorn, the Marchioness of Salisbury, Sir Horace Farquar.

'This is a place in history': Theresa, sixth Marchioness of Londonderry and the popularisation of politics[1]

Politically the period encompassed by the life of Theresa, sixth Marchioness of Londonderry matched the turbulence of the widespread industrial unrest, agricultural depression and social transformation that pervaded the late Victorian and Edwardian era. Controversy on a constitutional scale over Irish home rule and the power of the House of Lords pitched former convivial opponents and even allies against one another while increased rivalry between Arthur Balfour and Austen Chamberlain further dislodged any sense of unity in the Unionist Party from 1902.[2] As these debates came to dominate parliament, the press and the popular imagination from the 1880s onwards, one society woman emerged to the fore. Theresa Londonderry was the only woman in a position to be active within all facets of unionism in late nineteenth and early twentieth centuries. She continued in the tradition of the third Marchioness as a political hostess and confidante, but she was also one of the first generation of women to take to the political platform, eventually heading the largest female political association in Ireland's history. And, unlike her predecessor, not all of her actions were solely prompted by a desire to promote and protect the Londonderry interest. Instead this was a woman with real political convictions, a doughty defender of the legislative union between Britain and Ireland with an overarching belief 'in causes and not in persons'.[3]

Theresa possessed no pretensions of style as a letter writer, and her self-proclaimed 'scrawl' alludes to the pace at which she lived her life. In 1915 her son, after years of patient deciphering, persuaded her to use a typewriter but even then when proofing her letters she never considered her dictated epitaphs 'strong enough, so bolder expletives' were added by hand.[4] Her carefully boxed collection of correspondence, bound in green and gilt embossed files, amounted to some 5,000 letters and eventually filled four rooms of Londonderry (formerly Holdernesse) House. This indicates how well known she was in her day and suggests that she believed these missives of her life were worth preserving for prosperity. Her surviving correspondence includes letters instructed by the sender to be burnt and those, presumably accidentally, torn in half. However, the majority of Theresa's letters to her favourite politician and ally, Sir Edward Carson are lost, most probably destroyed, like many of the Unionist leader's papers, in the bombing of his London home during the First World War. Her diary, written prior and during the war, was co-bequeathed with her letters and papers to her nephew, Gervase Beckett and Balfour's secretary, Jack Sandars who briefly considered writing a biography of her husband. They were instructed by will 'to publish such as are of "real public interest"' but failed to obey Theresa's command and only extracts of her diary now remain.[5]

Theresa never documented her early life in any detail but a short memoir, begun two months after being widowed in April 1915, survives and she added sporadically to this over the remaining four years of her life. At the same time, following her great friend, Michael Hicks-Beach's suggestion, she also wrote her political recollections.[6] To compliment this, however, only a few letters written both to and by her in her youth remain. Even with this limited evidence, it is clear that in the mid to late nineteenth century, a combination of favourable birth and marriage continued to give women access to the political elite but a woman's influence was still effectively controlled by the strength of her own personal ambition and ability. Theresa lacked neither. Born on 6 June 1856, Lady Theresa Susey Helen Chetwynd Talbot was the eldest daughter of Theresa Anne Cockrell from a London business family and Charles Talbot, Viscount Ingestre and later the nineteenth Earl of Shrewsbury, a Conservative MP and Staffordshire landowner. By comparison to Frances Anne's troubled early years, Theresa's childhood was halcyon. Reared in 'a natural manner - I mean not in the prim and proper manner my Mother and the generation between her and us had been subjected to', Theresa and her three younger siblings 'spent four[,] five and six hours a day out of doors till School room began'. Educated at home by 'decayed' governesses, she was also daily instructed in Latin by a neighbouring clergyman and later by her brother's tutor. More important in the long-term, however, was what can only be described as a political education. From the age of four Theresa was her parents' 'companion...[they] always talked sense to me and explained everything to me of a public and private nature.' Though she reminisced more freely about her father's influence in shaping her beliefs, her mother was active in political society, most famously entertaining Disraeli who was an intermittent visitor to the family homes of Ingestre and Alton Towers.[7] But it was her father who instilled Theresa's lifelong interest in the political. This staunch Tory 'talked politics all the time and always treated us children as though we were grown up'. Theresa recounted, aged nine, being taken to Lord Palmerston's funeral when her father gave her 'a short sketch of what he was like and his politics...Also I remember... his taking me to Stafford House to see Garibaldi, the Italian patriot, and explaining to me about the states in Italy, the oppression and the wish of Italy to be a free and a separate Kingdom.'[8] Her real enthusiasm for politicking began in the next year, when the affairs of the Crimea pre-occupied her and by the age of fifteen she claimed, with some justification, to have heard all the best political orators. Her father took her to the Lords and the Commons and at the latter let her 'peep in...at the door, and see Mr. Gladstone and Mr. Disraeli sitting opposite one another. What fun it will be when the sides are changed.' Aged sixteen she thus coveted a Conservative return to office, but her rationale showed her youth: 'because I'm afraid we shall only be asked to one Court Ball now'.[9] Guests often commented on this unwonted young woman, none more famously than Disraeli who remarked upon her bold ambition and in later life Theresa admitted 'though I was only 13 at the time, he was not far wrong.'[10]

A rare glimpse of a less assured Theresa came in 1873 when she was presented at court. Her account of this event highlighted its symbolic importance in young aristocratic lives: 'I got though the Court very well…it was a very frightening moment when my train was taken away from me, and I followed Mother into the Throne Room. The Queen was so gracious, and kissed me so nicely, that I forgot my fright.' She also put all of her not inconsiderable will into persuading her parents to let her attend her first ball at Stafford House with the monarch, government ministers, the opposition and 'all the people Father has told us about' present. Writing to her sisters, she noted the event surpassed her teenage anticipation: 'though we have often imagined what a dance would be like in our games and the ball suppers on the bath top, the reality far exceeded the expectation…I was shivering with excitement and my bare shoulders which made me feel very awkward.'[11]

Presentation at court and entry, although strictly chaperoned, to the entertainments of high society essentially marked the end of aristocratic childhood. Marriage was now the objective and Theresa's union at the age of nineteen to Charles Vane-Tempest-Stewart, Viscount Castlereagh, the son of Henry, fifth Marquess of Londonderry and Mary Cornelia, the daughter of Sir John Edwards, in 1875 was arranged in the sense that both families approved the match.[12] Her intended, however, was not the realisation of Theresa's childhood ambition: 'It is the one position to have in England. If you cannot be the P.M. then…be his wife'.[13] Charles was not, nor ever likely to be, premier. He was elected to parliament, after two unsuccessful attempts, as MP for Down in May 1878 and with a healthy majority of 1,375 some wits claimed for Liberal leader, Gladstone this was 'the County Down in the Mouth election'. But standing on a Conservative platform of tenant right, intermediate education and abolition of the county cess produced a mixed reception from press. Whilst some praised his moderate line, avoiding any defiant Orange tocsin, others reported the post-election celebratory entertainment of 1,200 Down tenants as having political intent and, more damningly, as 'Mountstewart [sic] Vulgarities'.[14]

It was not only this entry into electoral politics that proved controversial. The 1883 Corrupt and Illegal Practices Act limited the money that a candidate could legally lavish on an electoral contest, aiming to impede the voter bribery that was commonplace to 1880 and to encourage party, as opposed to individual, expense. In 1883, petitions alleging corrupt electoral practices unseated sixteen MPs and Charles was caught in the fray as complaints were levelled against the non-secrecy of the Down ballot. He was not recalled, nor was the election nullified, but his time in the Commons was short-lived; he succeeded to the Londonderry marquessate in the following year. But just as in the lower house, sitting in the Lords as Earl Vane, Charles was modest to the point of diffidence. Never acclaimed as a political innovator, his oratory was too hastily delivered to command much presence, but he resolutely believed in his duty and right to serve at the head of a family rich in political tradition. From Theresa, therefore, came the push and the ambition to further the Londonderrys' political stature or, as she expounded, using more delicate phraseology, 'I flew higher'.[15]

From the mid to late 1880s Theresa emerged as a political force. Indeed, although marriage helped win respectability and secure access to high society this did not automatically weight power in favour of husbands. Contemporaries quickly branded her 'the "strong man" of her family.'[16] In terms of personality, she grew into an undeniably forceful woman, wonderfully described as going 'for life, hammer and tongs, she collared it, and scragged it and rooked it like a highwaywoman in a tiara, trampling on her enemies, as if they had been a bed of nettles - and occasionally getting stung about the ankles in the process'.[17] Forthright and determined, for Sir Alfred Fripp she was 'one of the few great ladies to whom I have always looked up with absolute confidence' whilst Henry Stracey doubted, with due course, whether he had '*ever* seen *anybody* have the slightest influence or power' over her.[18] Theresa also revelled in personal splendour and loved grandeur: 'standing at the head of her stairs when some big party was in progress, with the 'family fender', as she called that nice diamond crown gleaming…hugging the fact that this was her house, and that she was a marchioness from top to toe, and was playing the part to perfection'.[19]

A well read and skilled conversationalist, her household accounts show a reading diet of *Punch, The Spectator, The Times, The Daily Mail, The Northern Star,* the *Daily Northern Whig* and the *Gentlewoman*. She counted Thomas Hardy and Edmund Gosse amongst her intimates and to friends like these she was known as 'Nellie', but offend her, intentionally or otherwise, and she would quickly revert to being Theresa, Marchioness of Londonderry.[20] Indeed, Tory MP George Wyndham was on the look out 'for squalls' after receiving a letter signed with the latter closure.[21] She could also be caustic and a classic example came in the midst of a Commons' Home Rule Bill, when Theresa, resplendent in furs and pearls, strained to hear the debate from the Ladies' Gallery over Mrs. McKenna and Mrs. Churchill's conversation, so 'puffing herself out to her maximum' she demanded, 'Silence, badly dressed children!'"[22]

Behind a sometimes hard public façade, however, lay a staunchly loyal friend. As she said of herself, 'I am a good friend and a bad enemy. No kiss-and-make-up about me, my dear!'; 'It is second nature for me to do anything I can for my own. I have the proclivities of the game hen or the tigress when anyone interferes with her young.'[23] Some, like the second wife of the Unionist leader, Edward Carson, found the strength of Theresa's personality overbearing and confided to her diary that, 'Lady Londonderry…tried to manage everyone…She laid down the law…very bombastic. If she wasn't Lady L. no one would stand her for two minutes'.[24] To others she was 'a born dictator…[who] loved to encounter opposition, so that she might crush it'.[25] The terminology that many contemporaries employed for her certainly emphasised her strong, masculine qualities, claiming she possessed 'the mind of a man with the temperament of a woman.'[62] And her nickname in later life of 'Guy' also raises interesting questions as to how society perceived her as a woman who, although an avowed conservative in every sense of the word, pushed the boundaries of aristocratic female acceptability. She clearly enjoyed and courted male company, especially 'familiar conversation with the men who counted in the direction of the causes in which she believed - the Union with Ireland and the Unionist party', but she was also frustrated that as a result of her sex she was condemned to play an ancillary political part.[27] Though Theresa never approved of first-wave feminism, it transpired during a discussion on the male and female lot in life that she did not hesitate 'in pronouncing for the advantages offered a man', endorsing Lady Mary Wortley Montagu's declaration that the only good of being a woman was that you could not marry one: 'she would have vastly preferred to play a man's part rather than have devoted her talents to the tasks which lie before a woman.'[28]

By the time of this pronouncement Theresa had already fulfilled the maternal requirement of aristocratic wifery, bearing three children, including an all important heir: Helen Mary Theresa (but always known as Birdie); Charles Stewart Henry (later the seventh Marquess) and Charles Stewart Reginald, born in 1876, 1878 and 1879 respectively.[29] Given her own politically induced upbringing, it was not surprising that Theresa instilled in her eldest son a strong commitment both to unionism and the Londonderry name. As he recalled:

It was not going too far to say that our House stood for the Union of Ireland and England...That was to be the raison d'être of my going into the political world. ...As I grew up, my mother used actively press me to take an interest in politics. My father on the other hand was more tacitly, but not less burningly anxious that I should be interested in the political world...My mother talked to me too, about the great Lord Castlereagh, whose name...I bore at the time. In her and my father's talk, as well as that of members of the party who came to our house, conversation always turned to the Union[.][30]

Correspondence with her granddaughter, Maureen who looked to Theresa as her 'first friend as well as my Grandmother and Godmother', also revealed politics at the kernel of Londonderry life: aged sixteen, Maureen wrote in pursuit of information on the Irish question and Lord Kitchener's likely successor. Politics was such a preoccupation that Theresa even suggested to Thomas Hardy that he divine literary inspiration from 'a woman of strong character influencing a man for good, through his affections.'[31] Soon her life would imitate art.

From the 1880s Theresa was considering her husband's long-term career. Whilst her spouse aspired to a court appointment such as Master of the Horse, Theresa, anxious to avoid tokenism, was angling in a different direction. She believed an under-secretaryship would be more fitting and place him in a more advantageous position for future preferment, but Salisbury's 1886 conviction that the post of Irish Lord Lieutenant should be held by an Irishman for the first time provided an ideal opportunity for promotion. Charles' subsequent appointment to the post that was always coveted by his predecessor, the third Marquess, was a significant step forward in fulfilling Theresa's political ambition:

After the Crimes Act was dropped and Lord Salisbury formed his Government, the Unionists of the "Black North" as it is called, were up in arms and said they had been sold to the Home Rulers. They suggested that Lord Londonderry should be asked to be Lord Lieutenant as the name Castlereagh... would reassure the Ulster Party that the Government intended to preserve the Union...I have always considered it much pleasanter to be oneself than to represent any one else, but as I had always been most ambitious for Lord L., I was delighted on his account. He told me if I did not wish it, he would not go to Ireland, but I, of course, begged him to go.[32]

That Theresa exerted some influence in securing this post for her husband is certainly possible; it has been suggested that Charles 'was widely considered to owe his elevation as Irish Viceroy in 1886 to his formidable wife rather than to his own slight talents, though his readiness to spend freely in Dublin was probably the decisive factor.'[33] The specifics of her role are unrecorded, but she had known Salisbury since childhood and the existence of a familial connection on her side to the post, with her great grandfather, Charles Chetwynd-Talbot, second Earl Talbot, Viceroy from 1817-21 and her maternal grandmother, Countess Eglinton, Vicereine in 1852 and again from 1858-59, may have increased her determination that her husband should hold this position.[34] The proposition that she was involved was also the first of many comments to be made on her emergent influence.

What is unquestionable is that in Dublin from 1886-89 the Londonderrys emerged as brilliant political hosts, bolstering the festivities of the Dublin season which contemporaries recalled occurred with 'even more animation than usual, owing to the popularity of the Lord Lieutenant and Lady Londonderry, who was...a perfect hostess'.[35] The Anglo-Irish season, although more contained than its London counterpart, revolved around house parties and six to seven weeks of Dublin Castle receptions from February to March, leaving sufficient time from May to July for participation in the London season. Under Londonderry auspices, the castle drawing rooms were soon depicted as a court, attracting fuller attendances than previously, a fact that Victoria considered a sanction of both herself and her lieutenant during a tumultuous time as the first Home Rule Bill and then its creator, Gladstone, met their defeat.

The viceroyalty also brought the Londonderrys into contact with politicians like their Irish chief secretaries, Sir Michael Hicks-Beach and his successor, Arthur Balfour who became life-long friends and would later impact on Charles' chances for political promotion. Theresa professed that they were asked to retain the viceroyalty in 1889 and this is reinforced by a near contemporary account of Dublin where 'a general belief...that Lord Londonderry would again be Viceroy' was noted.[36] This was a notoriously expensive post, normally costing twice the £20,000 salary and, as such, caused Lord Newton to muse, 'It is always a mystery that anyone could be found voluntarily to accept the Irish Viceroyalty.'[37] Indeed, Londonderry spent £32,675 over his salary during his three years but whether this or a desire to return the political mainstream was the primary consideration in his resignation in April 1889 remains unclear.[38] Although their tenure in Dublin was remembered as brilliant, there was no post for Charles on his return to London. This made his refusal of the Privy Seal in 1895 even more surprising. This sinecure was unlikely to win Theresa's support, but Salisbury offered it with an accompanying cabinet seat. Given this, Londonderry's rebuff was much to Salisbury's chagrin: 'it has been held by many men who have made a high political position...I was not proposing to you an office politically unworthy of you. Of course I can quite sympathise with your desire for work but the Cabinet places giving work in the House of peers is very limited.'[39]

It was 1900 before Charles again held office, this time as Postmaster General. Two years into this post, the opportunity for cabinet rank re-emerged as he accepted the presidency of the Board of Education. He retained this position until 1905 and, from 1902, held it in conjunction with the office of Lord President of the Council. That political society viewed the latter not only as a promotion for Charles but also for his wife was very apparent in the collective terminology deployed by Earl Grey conveying, in a letter to Theresa, his congratulations 'to you and C[harles] on your entrance to the Cabinet':

> I am so glad, for nobody has worked harder, infused more energy and cheerfulness into the party or deserved it more. I always feel a little sorry it was refused before - but now you have what you want - the headship of a big working department and the satisfaction of being in the Cabinet and of having refused it![40]

The press, despite much speculation that Londonderry would be offered a cabinet place from 1900, were less welcoming, sniping at the continuation of 'rank and splendour' in securing 'places without any regard to qualification'. Their contention that this would 'always' be the case would not, however, be born out by reality, but the rising criticism of continued aristocratic patronage was a portent for the future.[41]

In the interim, with both appointments, Theresa made her presence felt. This was not only in an auxiliary sense, becoming *au fait* with post office and board practices, but also more publicly. In November 1903 she broke convention by chairing in all but name a departmental meeting at the Board of Education and questioning the Permanent Secretary and his staff. Had she been deputising for Lord Londonderry this event would perhaps have been less exceptional and certainly more easily understood, but ,with her spouse sitting in 'isolated dignity' at the head of the table throughout the two-hour consultation, this was remarkable. Almeric Fitzroy, present to witness the 'curious scene' at first hand, remarked upon her 'quickness and mastery of detail in handling the subject, and a power of appreciation of principles' that astonished those present: 'It is certainly a new departure when a Minister's wife undertakes to look into matters of departmental administration in the very seat of her husband's authority, and leaves him to the simple functions of an interested listener.'[42] Nor was this an isolated occurrence. During the next year Sir Robert Morant was, somewhat uncomfortably, mulling over Theresa's education suggestions:

what I wrote for you yesterday, I am very dissatisfied with it. I think I have got in all the points that you named: but I fear you will find it not precise enough, not definite enough, not hard-hitting enough. It will bring all the *teachers* to your side...what you want, if I rightly understand you, is to improve the plain common sense daily teaching of the children[.][43]

Just two months later Theresa addressed public meetings with 'rigorous and masculine words' on the import of religious education and church schools.[44] But the removal of the Conservative administration in December 1905 saw Londonderry out of office and Theresa made no attempt to disguise her regret, squarely blaming Balfourian weakness for the downfall.

While Theresa steered her husband's early years in office, the family estate of Wynyard, which of all the Londonderry houses she regarded as home, as well as Mount Stewart, were again being put to political purpose. From the 1880s the Londonderrys were favourites, amongst a small social set of thirty to forty individuals, of the Prince and Princess of Wales, later Edward VII and Queen Alexandra. They were formally entertained by the Londonderrys eight times, mostly at Wynyard but occasionally at Seaham, Plâs Machynlleth and Mount Stewart, between 1890-1903. Edward was particularly close to Theresa, sharing her love of racing and informally calling to take tea with her at Londonderry House which he regarded as the finest mansion in the metropolis. He also asked her to host a banquet on Kaiser Wilhelm II's first visit to England in 1891. A Mount Stewart house party in 1903, with the king, queen and Princess Victoria present, provided a classic example of the tripartite worlds of the Londonderrys. Along with the royals and extended family, such as the Churchills, Staverdales and Shrewsburys, were members of Anglo-Irish aristocracy, including the Earl and Countess of Gosford, the Countess of Erne and the Duke and Duchess of Abercorn who mingled with English peers such as the Earl and Countess of Dudley and Earl Selbourne. In the same year, with the question of army reform under review, Edward assembled the Privy Council at another Londonderry house party, this time at Wynyard. This was symbolically important: although Charles II held several councils in London houses and Victoria held a drawing room at Dalkeith Palace during her visit to Scotland in 1842, the Wynyard assembly represented the first meeting of the council at a country house since Wilton in 1625. Edward used the occasion to formally appoint Charles Lord President of the Council and, as if this was not sufficient delight for Theresa, 'desired the documents connected with the Council to be headed 'At the Court at Wynyard,' which is indeed the old style.'[45]

The Londonderrys were also close to the Duke and Duchess of York, later George V and Queen Mary, who visited Wynyard in 1902 and 1908. Like Theresa's relationship with Edward VII, an easy familiarity developed and Mary, in particular, revelled in the mixed society that Theresa was becoming renown for assembling: accepting an invitation to dine at Londonderry House, 'the Queen says she knows you would ask a few interesting people of the sort she is not in the general way of meeting...and she could talk to them while the King plays bridge!'[46] A trust in Theresa's skill as a hostess was also evident in the royal acceptance her offer to entertain guests on their behalf at the time of the coronation. Theresa was also personally acquainted with the whole cabinet, working as one of a handful of political hostesses including, on Tory side, the Duchesses of Devonshire, Lady Lansdowne, the Marchioness of Salisbury, Lady Dorothy Nevill and the Countess of Jersey and in the Liberal camp, Ladies Palmerston, Waldergrave, Molesworth, Tweedmouth, Beaumont, Cowper, Marjoribanks and Spencer as well as Mrs. Gladstone and Mrs. Asquith.[47] Beneath the generic title of political hostess, however, lay an array of interests.

Mrs. Gladstone, although Theresa's political nemesis from the mid 1880s as a consequence of her husband's controversial conversion to home rule, shared her approach to political life. Her ambition, her spearheading of popular politics as inaugural president of the Women's Liberal Federation from 1887-92 and her disregard for convention were traits common to Theresa. Indeed, Mrs. Gladstone's attendance at a 1885 cabinet meeting, similar to Theresa's later appearance at the Board of Education, led it to be decried a 'Lady's Cabinet' and her groundbreaking cross-county canvass in support of her husband established new ground.[48] Mrs. Gladstone was never, however, a political hostess in the mould of Theresa, Mrs. Palmerston or Mrs. Asquith, nor was she an effective orator or confidante. The Duchess of Manchester, later the Duchess of Devonshire, also held a range of entertainments and receptions with political purpose at both Chatsworth and Devonshire House and her protégés included Lord Hartington, who would later become her second husband, as well as Foster and Dilke. Her 'at homes' at the start of the parliamentary session were certainly important society functions but she was always less party inspired than Theresa, inviting both Conservatives and Liberals to dine. Another contemporary was the Liberal, Lady Tweedmouth, a daughter of the seventh Duke of Marlborough. Her entertainments at Brook House in London's Park Lane earned her a reputation for being privy to political information and she supported her spouse by canvassing in 1890 as well as becoming active in the Women's Liberal Federation. Her invites, however, shared the Duchess of Manchester's cross-party complexion although she later sought to build unity amongst the Liberal Party. By comparison, Margot Asquith was fixated on the Liberals and, in particular, keeping her husband in power. Asquith may have confided in her, but he was impossible to influence and disliked her penchant for interference. Thus, while Margot became a lavish hostess, her deserved reputation for indiscretion ultimately impacted on her power. Theresa, therefore, had most in common with Lady Derby, wife of the first Marquess of Salisbury and later the fourteenth Earl of Derby, who, with an array of confidantes, gained a worthy reputation for seeking promotion for those she favoured.

But amongst this coterie of political hostesses, it was Theresa who was in the ascent. However, it was her marriage, rather than her growing political reputation, that aroused society calumny in the 1880s. Claims that she escaped domestic unhappiness and spousal 'Coventry' for three decades by political activity are not strictly accurate, but this is one of the few 'facts' about Theresa that continues to perpetuate.[49] Her husband's discovery of an affair, due to Lady de Grey sending him letters written by Theresa to Harry Cust, barrister, Conservative MP, editor of the *Pall Mall Gazette* and society Lothario, undoubtedly caused marital strain in 1884. Cust's few surviving letters to Theresa show he was, momentarily at least, enraptured by her. After their first meeting he wrote, 'I wanted to tell you, in front of all, how immensely I enjoyed making…your acquaintance, and, I humbly hope your friendship (mine w[oul]d be unwise) and how amused and interested and fascinated I was, in the best sense, by both.'[50] However, the suggestion that after this infidelity Charles never conversed with Theresa again, except in public, arriving and leaving events in separate carriages and shunning her even on his deathbed, have been greatly exaggerated. The myth of the non-speaking Londonderrys may have provided years of society gossip and inspiration for Vita Sackville-West's literary creation of the Roehamptons in her 1930 novel, *The Edwardians*, but this marriage was far from over.

Theresa's early relationship with her husband was close; they corresponded daily when separated and if Charles was to spend a day travelling he would write twice on the day prior to his departure, 'though I have nothing more to say, as I fear I shall not be able to write tomorrow'; 'I write you another short note, that you may get something every day'. From the time of their courtship he called her 'My darling' and he continued to do so, using the same affectionate address as late as 1912. In reply she signed herself as 'loving wife' or 'little thing'. News of any illness, as in 1908, when Charles was in Belfast, caused alarm, telegrams and offers to return to his wife at Wynyard, 'remember I can run over any time if you would like it.' He, in return, was grateful for the attention she lavished on him, 'Thanks, dearest, *so* much for taking such care of me.'[51] Their correspondence, although partially undated, provides a sufficient chronological spread of letters through the 1880s and into the early decades of the twentieth century to suggest that there was no serious break in their written contact. This pair would also come to front several of the various Unionist organisations established to popularise protestations against Irish home rule in the early twentieth century. In this work, neither worked in isolation, either voluntary or enforced, from one another: 1911 saw Charles not only attend the inaugural meeting of the Ulster Women's Unionist Council with Theresa but she cancelled a later address to the same body to care for him, telling members, 'I preferred to do it myself…just as any of you who are married would'.[52] In the following January, Charles returned the favour, delivering a resolution to the council on Theresa's behalf when she was incapacitated by illness. By this time, they were acknowledged as the aristocratic heads of unionism: using Londonderry House as well as Wynyard and Mount Stewart as hubs for deliberations over the defeat of home rule and lending respectability to popular unionism. Theresa also revived the confidante tradition established by Frances Anne in the second and third decades of the nineteenth century and such associations were still of considerable import within late nineteenth and early twentieth-century politics.

The 'Queen of Toryism'[53]

With mounting opposition to home rule from the mid 1880s, Theresa began to run Londonderry House as a Unionist salon; contemporaries were certainly using this term to describe her receptions from the middle of the 1890s. Londonderry

House may have lacked the external architectural presence of other London society mansions, such as those belonging to the Devonshires, Lansdownes, Lancasters or Derbys, but its early nineteenth-century reputation for brilliance was restored under Theresa's lead. The grandeur of her entertainments as well as the blend of guests became renowned. As Lord Morley recollected, a 1891 lunch for fifty included Balfour, Lecky and the German Emperor'[54] and, with Theresa as the 'presiding genius', her reception rooms became 'the rendezvous of a thousand strivers.'[55] Normally hosting two or three political dinners for Unionists during the parliamentary session, in 1909 Theresa stood in for Lady Lansdowne to host the eve of parliament reception and eventually eclipsed her as the foremost Tory hostess, as she, like her spouse, became less politically active in the 1910s.

By the early twentieth century, the popularity of Londonderry House receptions meant, at times, Theresa was a victim of her own success. One celebration to mark the king's birthday in June 1903, an event more usually held in recent past by the Secretary of State for Foreign Affairs, was literally thronged:

> The crowd…was the densest I had ever seen at a London party; the rooms upstairs were never full because a large section of the company had to remain in the hall, and still a large body was collected in Park Lane, and never entered the House…One girl fainted in the street and had to be laid out on the pavement, and one or two others collapsed inside the building.[56]

These receptions could be attended by 2,000 guests, but smaller events were also being held, like a 1904 dinner for sheriffs, the Prime Minister and twelve cabinet members, which, more effectively than the larger entertainments, lent themselves to the exchange of information and the building of contacts and confidences. For Theresa, dinners like these were 'a parade, and you must not be late for it.' And at Wynyard a footman, known as the 'Whipper-in', was employed to round up the guests so that they would not insult their hostess.[57]

Unlike Margot Asquith, Theresa was gaining a reputation for discretion. As the outpourings of Rosebury, the First Lord of the Treasury, in a letter marked 'most confidential', reveal, he entrusted her with his controversial view of their party leader, Balfour as an 'oppressive and bloodthirsty miscreant'.[58] Moreover, many politicians echoed the 'longing' that George Wyndham expressed to see Theresa 'to talk over all the exciting events'. Wyndham was a regular at both Mount Stewart and Wynyard where they talked 'about everything and everybody'. By 1905 he held her in particular regard and, in a letter marked 'private', agreed to assist both the Unionist Party and, in contrast to Rosebury, rally support around Balfour:

> [to] do all in my power to help the Party and stop any nonsense about A. J. B [Balfour]. I resigned in order to help the Party…*You* may write and say anything to me. But I am not in the mood to stand much from anybody else… you are my friend.
>
> In the rank and file of the Party in the House I do not seem to have any friends.[59]

Though Wyndham complained of isolation, he became one of a small band of political informants who were faithful to Theresa, passing her political information and proffering advice.

To courtier Lord Esher, Theresa was 'the most splendid of women. Nothing seems to come amiss to you', whilst Edmund Gosse recorded his 'great delight... to see you more and more taking so prominent a part in affairs, for I truly think that no woman now living is your equal in capacity for direct political energy... you just dash in..."full of disdainful wrath" because of the intensity of your convictions.'[60] Austen Chamberlain even came to gauge his own political standing by the number of fingers, ranging from two to ten, which Theresa outstretched to him in greeting.[62] Treasury official, Sir George Murray, 'whether in sunshine or in rain', was another 'devoted servant and friend' and, from the early twentieth century, was an important fount of political news: informing her of the Prime Minister's resignation in a 'very private' letter on the day of the event, 3 April 1908; of numerous cabinet reshuffles as well as the likelihood and date of elections.[62] Like Murray, Lord Knollys, private secretary and a key adviser to Edward VII and, from 1910, joint private secretary to George V, passed on information. From the first decade of the twentieth century, Knollys also brought interesting men to meet Theresa and, in return, asked her to quietly advise Mrs. Asquith on her conduct. One of Theresa's most candid correspondents was Reginald Lucas who teased her when her 'judgement of men and things' proved correct that she was a political prophet. He was entertained at Mount Stewart and Wynyard, promising his hostess, 'If I hear any news when I go out, I will report it'. He duly obliged: 'I dined with Lady Derby two nights ago. She said nothing: but I am going to Lady Ampthill on Saturday, and shall doubtless hear something.'[63] Lucas would also pass on rumour and, like Disraeli, often wrote from the Carlton Club, gathering the latest radical, as well as Conservative, opinion and, most importantly for an astute political hostess, differentiating between first and second-hand information. One of her most effusive admirers, however, was Schomberg McDonnell to whom Theresa was, 'Most unique, energetic, elastic hearted and wholly adorable Lady!...bless the beneficent Deity...who was pleased to place you on Earth as an enchantment to our sex and an example to your own.' Beneath the gloss of his adulation, lay serious political content and a faith in her ability that allowed her to exert considerable influence: in 1910 he sent her the rules of the Board of Works that many had not yet been privy to and invited her comment, 'if you have anything to add you can tell me when I come to Wynyard.'[64]

As in the early and mid nineteenth century, an essential part of the rationale for adopting the mantle of hostess was familial promotion and Theresa was no exception to this dictate. She remained very close to her eldest son, Charley and their letters reveal a warmth which was not often apparent in his more muted and, at times, strained relationship with his father.[65] Despite her best efforts to inculcate a sense of Conservative conviction, Charley was a reluctant politician. His reaction to his mother vouching to come to Maidstone to lend her weight to his 1906 electoral campaign was, therefore, one of delight: 'I am sure your presence will do me no end of good; of course I will make out no programme for you but the fact of your being here and driving about, in fact giving the Maidstone people a show, will assist me a great deal'.[66] Charley won this safe Liberal seat by a margin of just 132 votes amid unsuccessful petitions and accusations of irregular electoral practices including bribery, treating voters and the now illegal practice of conveying voters to the poll. In reaction, correspondents like Lewis Harcourt could not resist quipping to Theresa, 'May I come and see you…? I should like a chat before you go to prison for personal corruption at Maidstone!!'[67]

Theresa's contacts were also of key import in securing a timely Commons' debut for her son. It was Wyndham who altered Theresa to the fact that an anti-home rule amendment would be brought before the Commons on 21 February 1906, believing that this presented a prime opportunity for Charley's maiden speech. Theresa acted on Wyndham's hint and Charley subsequently made his first address to the house on a topic his family and he, in time, held dear. But Theresa's political interest was not only rooted in family promotion; it was grounded in conservatism and unionism. The admission of the Liberal Unionists to the Tory fold in 1886 worried her greatly, as did the growing influence of this grouping under Austen Chamberlain's lead. She was also unconvinced by the admittedly lax leadership of Liberal Unionist, the fifth Marquess of Lansdowne in the Lords from 1903, and she subsequently encouraged the emergent leader of southern unionism, the first Earl of Midleton to assume this mantle. He, however, saw no opportunity whilst Lansdowne remained *in situ*: 'there will never be any question of my leading the Irish party in the H[ouse] of Lords so long as he [Lansdowne] is to the fore. His position; standing and influence altogether preclude it.'[68]

Establishing herself as the foremost Tory hostess, Theresa needed to be politically well versed and patronise both central figures and rising stars in the party. Her benefaction of F. E. Smith, later Lord Birkenhead, certainly fell into the latter category. She early prophesied success for Smith, deeming him 'a flyer' after she heard his maiden speech: 'When I met him later at dinner, I found he had not only brains but push, and a jaw, also!'[69] Though a relative newcomer to the Commons, Smith came to champion the die-hard cause and this, coupled with his anti-suffragism, endeared him to Theresa. Smith, however, did not need a wholesale conversion to unionism: as early as 1892 he was haranguing home rulers on numerous Lancashire election platforms. But in the early twentieth century he sought Theresa's company, relishing their political talks and, on occasion, acting on what he deemed her 'heretical influence' as in 1909 when he responded to her prompt to write a letter to the press in support of Bob Cecil. Smith's association with Theresa was not only political, attending Londonderry House receptions and promoting the Unionist cause, it was also personal: holidaying with them in 1907 and asking Theresa to be godmother to his daughter in 1914.[70] For her support and friendship, Smith 'repaid her fully…placing his powers of advocacy unreservedly at Ulster's disposal' and becoming the principal Unionist spokesman in the Conservative Party.[71]

Walter Long was another key contact. Politically more established than Smith and, for a time, in the running as party leader, Long's association with Theresa dated from 1905 when he was Irish Chief Secretary. This appointment, although brief in tenure, raised both Long's personal reputation and the importance of the

Irish question in his political rationale. His early letters to Theresa fall into the typical confidante mode: apprising her of political intrigue; applauding her public addresses and passing on letters of mutual interest. In return, she appraised his speeches, sending him copies of her own, and other's, public addresses, as well as quotations. Their correspondence maintained its formality but became tempered with political banter and the myriad of considerations behind Unionist and Conservative responsive strategies to political developments in the early twentieth century. That Long was central to the formulation of these responses is no longer in doubt. He became a crucial bridge between English and Irish Unionists, rebuilding connections dented by Wyndham's land legislation and the devolution scare of 1905. Indeed, he was established as 'the party's weather-vane on the Anglo-Irish relationship' by 1906 but what was the impact and import of his relationship with Theresa?[72] As Long's health failed, along with his faith in Balfour as party leader, Theresa tried to temper his criticism and exhorted him to remain in parliament. And for this he was grateful: thanking her after a 1907 visit to Wynyard for 'all the help and encouragement…in my Political fight, if it was not for this I really think sometimes I should chuck it all up'. Later in the same year he was even more expressive: 'There can surely be no greater satisfaction for a real friend than to know that they are doing invaluable services to their friend? And this knowledge you ought to have in abundance.'[73]

Long and Theresa agreed on the need for heightened co-operation between English and Irish Unionists and worried about Balfour's continued leadership of the party. At Long's behest, Theresa brought concerns about Balfour's capabilities and the rising influence of Chamberlain within the party to the king's attention in late 1907. And Long was again indebted to her: 'I can't tell you how much I appreciate what you have done in bringing things to H.M.'s notice - it must do good all round.'[74] She also reconciled Long with pro-union journalist, J. L. Garvin by lunching with the latter in 1908. But, as in the relationship between Disraeli and Theresa's predecessor, Frances Anne, this was a dual exchange. Long, especially as Saunderson's successor to the chair of the Irish Unionist Alliance, chairman of the Ulster Unionist Council and working towards the establishment of the Union Defence League in 1907, became increasingly important to her. Health problems led him to resign as chair of the Irish Unionist Party in 1908 and abandon his marginal seat in south Dublin for a safer seat closer to home in London, but his influence and interest in Irish affairs was far from over. In time, Long would prove more politically flexible than Theresa, advocating solution over steadfastness in relation to the Irish question, but he remained one of her closest and most useful confidantes, canvassing for her son and addressing her before approaching either her spouse or son: 'I do not however like to write to him or C. till I have consulted you'.[75] Given this, it is difficult to see Theresa anywhere but at the head of the Londonderry familial interest.

Clearly one consequence of Theresa's Unionist convictions was that she patronised men, like Smith and Long, whom she thought could benefit that cause. Edward Carson, however, 'the horse…[she] backed for 30 years', was always her preferred politician.[76] From the late 1880s Theresa was a constant in Carson's life and he claimed that she was 'always more than kind…you are always the same and you know how I appreciate it'. Teasingly addressing her as 'My dear General', he freely admitted that she was his 'best and kindest friend'.[77] Meeting during the Londonderrys' lieutenancy in Dublin when Carson was Crown Prosecutor, Theresa's correspondence suggests a deliberate cultivation of this 'clever lawyer... whom C. [Charles] thinks may be useful.' The Londonderrys early recognised Carson's potential for leadership and he was consequently courted as their, and unionism's, ally. The Countess of Fingall even claimed it was due to Londonderry influence that Carson was appointed Solicitor General and that Theresa personally informed him of this appointment.[78] By 1903 they were certainly sufficiently close for Carson to enquire whether Lord Londonderry's appointment as Lord President of the Council would be followed by an appointment as leader of the Lords. A less familiar acquaintance would undoubtedly have been rebuked, but Carson was already one of Theresa's favourites. She bolstered his political ambitions when his first wife, Annette was incapacitated through illness and when his second wife, Ruby lacked political experience. But such lionisation caused matrimonial tension for Carson: 'One day there was a great row about a letter from the Dowager Lady Londonderry'. Carson, in pursuit of a quiet life, followed Disraeli's suit and, 'After that...had his letters sent to the [Carlton] Club.'[79]

Much of Carson's limited social life came to revolve around the Londonderrys. From 1893 onwards, his visits to their Durham and Down homes were a welcome respite from work and responsibility: 'it is a dog's life...and I am worn out...I feel very low and depressed and even all the hero worship does not seem to tonic me. I want rest and peace which I will never get! Gloomy old man! I was very happy at Wynyard.'[80] He further confided, 'I believe I was born to lounge and enjoy myself and be at Mount Stewart for long periods of time!':

> I am sure the most interesting chapter in my biography will be one headed "Visits to Wynyard and Mount Stewart" - but how will the biographer ever really understand how delightful these visits have been and why you and his Lordship have always been so kind to me...no one is ever more helpful than yourself and you have indeed been a kind and affectionate friend.[81]

Unlike Theresa, however, Carson was not a society animal and he did not revel in parties, dinners and balls: 'I am always trying to imagine I enjoy myself on these occasions but I don't really and it is all only an artificial respiration.'[82]

The basis of this friendship essentially lay in a shared political vista: alarmed by Irish Nationalists holding the balance of power in the lower house from 1905, both Carson and Theresa feared that 'the real head of the Government will be Redmond. Poor Ireland! But it is long since hopeless and greatly through Unionist weakness.' Towards the end of 1905 Carson shared Long and Theresa's concerns about Balfour's ability to lead the Conservatives and Chamberlain's influence. But, despite much common ground, Carson was never easy to lionise. In the same year that he assumed the mantle of Unionist leader, for instance, he was clearly frustrated by the lack of political progress and flouting the idea of a federal solution, even before the start of the third home rule crisis, he proclaimed himself 'sick to death of the Home Rule tragedy...what I hate most is the number of our people who are apparently quite willing to fall in with the idea.'[83] This was also the man who depicted himself as 'a worn out legislator…[and a] dyspeptic pessimist', 'who always walked up hill with the collar hurting'.[84] To Carson, often despondent and depressed, Theresa was, therefore, a source of consolation, sympathy and reassurance: 'you always understand which is a great deal.'[85] Furthermore, the Londonderrys were amongst only a few from whom Carson accepted comfort following his first wife's death in 1913, asking if he could visit Wynyard and if they would see him in London to alleviate his loneliness, 'Thanks to both of you for all your kindness…for you and his Lordship I would do anything'.[86]

Yet, this was never a sycophantic relationship. Theresa wanted Carson to abandon the bar for full-time politicking, but he resisted her push in this direction for years. He also enjoyed a political tussle, as he wrote in 1911, 'it will be very nice to see you and talk it all over and agree or disagree'.[87] She, in turn, doubted his frequent complaints 'that when you have got to the top there is no satisfaction in it'.[88] She was also perturbed by his complaints about the state of his health and his lack of ambition and self-promotion, famously likening him to a 'Derby favourite, who, when you have him saddled and bridled and ready to be lead out of the paddock, won't run.'[89] Carson would not have disagreed. By his own admission, he possessed 'no ambition and on the whole it is a rotten party!', but he implored Theresa, 'Don't be angry.'[90] He was, therefore, a man in need of some persuasion to lead the fight against home rule and Theresa was evidently unrepentant about coercing him to honour his political obligations:

> I suspect you thought me very brutal in forcing Sir E. C. to come here [to Wynyard] - he looked ill when he arrived and very well when he went away… his absence would have upset the party…I also pointed out that if he was too ill to make a speech…he was too ill to speak Tuesday following[.][91]

Their correspondence was often marked by Carsonite gloom and 'the rottenness of *nearly* everything', but politics provided the backbone of their discussions. Carson sanctioned her political involvement, commending her 'fine feeling of wanting to take a part - just as I do' and commenting on the press coverage of her activities, 'I see by the papers this morning you are campaigning with you usual vigour and ability'.[92] With Carson's move to full-time politics, he was soon in a position to pass on party information and, with her husband in the Lords and her son cutting his political teeth as a Commons' newcomer, this was significant. Often he would write to her every other day and a sense of emergent partnership also evolved between Carson and Lord Londonderry in relation to political organisation in the north of Ireland as, with the former tied up with 1910 pre-election speaking engagements in England, Londonderry was relied on to smooth over any Ulster difficulties. Even with a Conservative and Unionist gain of a hundred seats, the results of the 1910 election disappointed. With Commons' equilibrium and the Irish Parliamentary Party holding the balance of power, Carson was convinced that 'the Irish will simply do as they are told and will act solidly with the Government, so they will have a big majority'.[93] The dynamism of some younger members of the party gave Carson scant reassurance and could do nothing to stave the tumultuous events of the next year. Firstly, F. E. Smith raised the question of payment for MPs which rankled Carson, who not only opposed this in principle but predicted a party split over the issue. Though Smith was another of Theresa's allies, Carson questioned his loyalty, privately alerting her that he believed, wrongly at this stage, that F. E. approved of the emergent home rule proposals. Secondly, Balfour's leadership and his reluctance to allow Irish Unionist rhetoric to dominate the political debate became increasingly problematic. As Walter Long lamented to Theresa: 'I never knew so much discontent. But what can we do? I am in despair. We want a big strong policy and really efficient organisation - and we have got neither'; 'AJB is impossible...I have come to the end of my tether'.[94]

Carson was similarly troubled by Balfour's inclination for indecision as well as moves to rid the Lords of its power of veto and these dual crises soon overshadowed all others:

> I am sure we have made many mistakes and it all comes of hastily pronouncing with a view to the moment and having nothing definitely laid down after full consideration and discussion. Now I believe there are the usual disagreements and no one knows where we stand or what we are going to do and no doubt this will all be fully considered after the veto is abolished. ...I fear the truth is there is no leader on either side...a fight for everything we believe in would not only command respect and in time power but would certainly get us better terms in the long run.[95]

As early as 1894 Lord Rosebury had inferred to Theresa that a solution to the power of the House of Lords' question needed to be found but the answer when it came in 1911 was far from welcome in many quarters, including Londonderry House. Yet, in many ways, the Lords was heading for trouble. In 1809 and again in 1871 Army Regulation Bills had been a cause of contention between the upper and lower houses and in 1832 an *en masse* creation of peers was suggested as a means to pass the Reform Bill. Gladstonian Liberals tried to suppress the Lords over the extent of their alterations to the 1869 Irish Church Bill that disestablished and disendowed the Church of Ireland and the upper house not only rejected the 1906 Plural Voting Bill but also unravelled the Education Bill of the following year as well as ousting two Scottish land bills. This prompted a scathing oratorical attack from Campbell-Bannerman on the undesirability of the Lords' power but the case for reform was not, as yet, overwhelming. The 1909 budget, however, brought the issue to a head, producing a controversy on a par with that which so embroiled the third Marquess of Londonderry, the Reform Act of 1832 and changing the political landscape forever.

Theresa, as usual, was being fed information. Lord Knollys had earlier sought to stem the impending crisis, advising her that the Lords should try to avoid rejecting the 1908 Licensing Bill. Carson also believed this bill might go to a second reading rather than be defeated outright and consequently told Theresa of 'a wavering section - so there you have a field to exercise all your powers of persuasion upon.'[96] The bill was defeated in the Lords but no information survives to suggest that Theresa played a part in its downfall. She was, however, heavily involved in the defence of the Lords' power. In consequence of a December 1908 letter from Sandars, she was also aware that the next budget was 'to contain a proposal for a tax of a halfpenny in the pound on the *capital* value of all land in the country! I hear many owners are making calculations'.[97] Lord Burham, in a private letter, also informed her of the tenor of the proposed legislation and its impact on landed incomes:

> I was wrong in what I told you yesterday about the Budget, I now hear indirectly from the Government that taxation of land value in some form will be embodied in the Budget, and that the valuation of land necessary will be included in the Bill. How that can be done passes my comprehension but so it is likely to be.[98]

Many Unionists in both houses disliked what they perceived to be socialistic notions in the seven new taxes proposed in 1909 budget, four of which were on land and site values, increasing the death duties of 1894 in addition to augmenting the direct tax on incomes of over £3,000 per annum and those with unearned incomes. By May, opening a Conservative fundraiser in Sunderland, Theresa let her opposition be known: 'The Budget proposals were an endeavour to level down, and not up. It penalised success, and would punish those who by their brain, energy, industry and enterprise had raised themselves. Mr Lloyd George would tax expectation.'[99] She went as far to challenge the validity of the popular label attached to this measure: 'It is not right for the Government to call this Budget a "People's Budget" and to boast that its principle is to tax the rich for the benefit of the poor.'[100]

Journalist James Thursfield's prediction to Theresa that the budget would prompt a constitutional struggle, 'probably ending in a dissolution', proved correct: the non-interference that normally characterised the Lords' treatment of the annual budget was broken in October 1909 when they withheld assent until it was put to the electorate.[101] Theresa verbally defended this rejection of the budget at a meeting of Stockton Women's Unionist Association. Taking prejudicial government as a starting point, she claimed, 'a particular class has been singled out… Did they want the second Chamber to be a real Second Chamber or a sham one?'[102] The press reaction to her open criticism of the government was mixed. The *Daily Chronicle* reported the speech under the headline, 'A Wild Peeress', a clear inference that they believed Theresa had overstepped the female aristocratic mark. The charge that she lent heavily on Lord Lansdowne for inspiration was also made and, although his Liberal Unionist credentials disqualified him from ever becoming one of her favourites, she certainly echoed remarks he had made in the Lords' just days earlier. As well as making headlines, Theresa was seen as part of the emergent anti-Lords' reform campaign and was so well versed that Lord Newton, visiting Wynyard in 1909, doubted whether he had anything, bar his own opine, to add to her considerations: 'an omniscient person like you always hears everything at once and I can't add anything to your information.' He, however, referred to a lack of organisation, especially amongst Irish members of the upper house:

> the place is full of Irish magnates, and with all due respect, they appear to me very prolix and diffuse: perhaps it requires your presence to infuse them with the necessary fire. ...The air is full of Omens...It seems to be thought that, for some reason or other, the Govt. want to delay things; and of course it is assumed that the King wants to meddle and prevent a constitutional crisis. ... Even now I don't believe that anyone knows in the least whether we shall pass the budget or not...the one thing on which there is agreement is that an Election in January is as near a certainty as anything can be.[103]

Newton's forecast was accurate. Unionists claimed over 120 seats from the Liberals in the January 1910 election, but for Midleton, writing to Theresa, the result, with Irish Nationalists still holding the balance of power in the Commons, was 'deplorable': 'This is for your private eye as I know our H[ouse] of C[ommons] friends think an addition of 100 votes is worth many risks to the H[ouse] of L[ords]. So should I, if it [did] not also mean, a majority for Asquith 9 times out of 10.'[104]

Sandars and Knollys remained to the fore in passing information to Theresa during 1910. The former urged caution, reluctant to inspire further 'wild anti-landlord talk' and another election: 'I am all for fighting - who isn't? But, on all fronts, let us see where we are going...Now please *burn this letter*...I should not like it to be found in your correspondence of 1910.'[105] Knollys was more candid, especially in relation to the king's manoeuvrability following the January election:

> I expected the Government to come back with a large majority independent of the Irish. They would then have been returned with what is called a "mandate", but they cannot say they have this now, and the King will be able therefore, if necessary, to take up a stronger line than he could have done. Therefore I do not see how they can avoid bringing in the Budget first - the House of Lords question will not come until May.

Theresa was also passing information on, in particular, regarding the mid-term implications of a Lords' reform for Ireland, forcing St. Loe Strachey, the editor of the *Spectator*, to accede:

> You have a perfect right to "rub it in" and I do not resent your exercise of the woman's privilege in the least when you say "I told you so"...your prophecies have proved correct. I can only say I did not realise the nature of the beast...there is no going back if the union is destroyed[.][106]

Towards the end of 1910, the reintroduction and passage of the budget paled to near insignificance with the introduction of the Parliament Bill. Its aim was to restrict the Lords' veto to a two-year delaying power, remove its veto regarding finance bills absolutely and, less controversially, limit the maximum life of any parliament to five, as opposed to seven, years. Knollys now sought information from Theresa:

> will they [the Lords] reject it or else alter it to such a degree as to amount to the same thing, and thus face a creation of Peers. Such action would undoubtedly damage the Government, but it would also destroy the House of Lords. I hear that some of the bolder spirits among the Conservative Leaders are in favour of such a cause.[107]

What Knollys may not have realised was that Theresa now counted amongst these 'bolder' die-hard party spirits.

As well as gathering information and exerting backroom pressure via the usual *operandi* of the political hostess, Theresa took the more unusual step, certainly for a woman of her class, of writing in protest to *The Times*. The letter, signed with the enigmatic penname of 'Not a Peer', caused the paper's editor, G. E. Buckle to muse, 'I wonder how many of our readers will recognise that "not a Peer" = "a Peeress"!'[108] Here she was conforming to a pre-set format as the Lords' reform excited many similar letters and the majority were anonymous. As in her earlier deliberations with the *Spectator*'s editor, her missive injected a longer-term perspective into the debate, emphasising that it was the Liberal conversion to home rule in the 1880s, rather than any in-built bias, that explained the composition of the upper house:

> The House of Lords is supposed to be one-sided, but the fact seems to be overlooked that it is not the fault of the Radical Party that they have not a majority there. In spite of their additions to the peerage they are in a minority, and for the following reason. Until 1886, whatever may have been the faults of the Liberal Party, they did not officially support structural alterations in the Constitution. In that year they began by advocating the separation of Ireland from Great Britain, and their numbers in the House of Lords, as elsewhere, underwent a great diminution.

She followed this with a wholesale defence of the Lords and the importance of its freedom from party dictate:

> every reform of the House of Lords should make for stability and fearlessness of action. No body of men can show such qualities unless they are independent - by which I mean independent of the suffrages of a multitude fluctuating in its opinion or oscillating violently. The day of independent members of the House of Commons is past. Subserviency to the party Whip ensures success. In the House of Lords alone can there be independence of thought; and no reform can preserve it unless its members should sit for life. Or be selected for some definite period as holders of a public position.

This view of the Lords' impartiality was, however, wholly selective: the permanent Conservative majority in the upper house and the party basis of its debate effectively denied it of any claim to independence.[109] Next came a hint of the identity, but not the gender, of 'Not a Peer':

> I have an acquaintance with many of the members who now occupy the Radical benches in the House of Lords. The attitude of the old Whigs there reminds me of Rip Van Winkle. They evidently do not realize how times have changed. They delude themselves that the Radical Party is the same as the Whig Party, advocating liberty and individualism, to which they and their forebears belonged. …There is a simplicity about this method of avoiding, mental disturbance which must command admiration; even though in some quarters such ignorance may be accounted as almost akin to high treason.
> No one reading Radical speeches and the Radical Press can fail to grasp that revolution, as Lord Rosebury said, is intended by the Radical Party. To check such revolution should be the object of the centre party in the reconstitution of our Second Chamber.[110]

That she made no inference to her sex was not surprising. To Theresa, this was an irrelevance; her belief in aristocratic right to rule meant that the power of the Lords was of huge import and she, therefore, felt duty-bound to comment.

Detailed letters written to Theresa from men like Moberly Bell who, just days before her letter was published, wrote a complex account of alternative ways for the Lords to reach a compromise, suggest that her input to this constitutional and controversial debate was valued.[111] His contention was that the upper house needed to control their destiny by preparing their own bill for reform, but whether the timing of his suggestion was coincidental with Theresa's own thoughts on reform may never be known. Thursfield was another who kept her attuned to developments although by early April 1910 he was forced to admit that 'About the political situation I'm afraid I have nothing to say that you would care to hear', suggesting that wrangles over the veto would be accompanied either by a dissolution or change in government: 'Perhaps the best thing that could happen would be that another election should make very little change. Then as neither side could do much by itself the situation would point to a settlement by compromise.'[112] Five days later, Newton advised her quick return to London from Wynyard, believing a decision was imminent, 'You had better be over here anyhow on Monday, as in the opinion of the knowing ones, that is going to be the fatal day for the Government…A. J. B.[Balfour] thinks it quite likely'. But his call for haste was premature.[113]

A constitutional conference was held to discuss the issue from June to November but procured no result. With Irish Nationalists holding the balance of power in the Commons from December 1910 and Asquith's announcement that a home rule bill would be introduced in the next parliamentary session, the idea was mooted and gained currency that new peers would be created to pass the measure. This was confirmed by George V's guarantee that sufficient Liberal peers would be made to pass the Parliament Bill should it be rejected by the Lords being made public in July 1911. This was, as is widely acknowledged, climacteric. Carson's indignation, expressed, as ever, in a letter to his confidante, was unmistakable: 'I hear no news except I am told the Government expect the Lords to give way!…I think anyone who raises a discordant note just now is a traitor. … This is a stupid letter but everything is in an unhealthy state of lull since the elections'.[114] At the same time Theresa was corresponding with the king's private secretary, Arthur Bigge who considered her 'a real friend to whom I could turn for information certain of getting it'.[115] Bigge championed the maintenance of the hereditary principle of the Lords, rejecting outright Rosebury's suggestion that an elective element should be introduced to the upper house, but urged die-hard Tories, like Theresa, to compromise:

> my informant *did* say that there was a want of activity in organisation and administration in party headquarters. …The feeling is bitter now: it will be ten times worse after the Election. Therefore I say, "compromise"! You will probably despise my suggestion…Otherwise the House of Lords is doomed - Alas! That they did not reform themselves some years ago.

And by July he reported, 'Peers will have to be made…Do *anything* rather than compel HM to make *one* Peer…will HM get away if even 50 Peers have to be created?'[116]

Knollys was moving in a similar direction, staunchly opposing the creation of peers, but Theresa could not be convinced of the merits of compromise. Instead she was key to the evolving scuffle to oppose the Parliament Bill. Indeed, contemporaries, like the Countess of Warwick, claimed that Theresa was responsible for pushing for a revolt of the peers which led to the threat that the upper house would be flooded with new blood and 'When the peers succumbed she was scornfully indignant.'[117] Like Newton in the previous year, Sir George Murray encouraged Theresa back to London in the final days preceding the Parliament Act:

> Politics and (above all) politicians are in a most effete condition here now. … Nobody seems to care a d___ about anything. …You ought *not* to stay away now for long; as you are the only person (I think) who has got any fight left in you. They are all a miserable lot…I am disgusted with them all. But the Govt. have more stuff in them than the opposition. When are you coming back?[118]

Party leader, Balfour and Lord Lansdowne, with responsibility for Unionist tactics in the upper house, as well as southern Unionist leader, Midleton all favoured an acceptance of the bill as a means to avoid peerage creation and allow their majority in the upper house to live on. Their inherent belief, not without justification, was that two years was a long time in politics and they would retain the ability to delay unpopular or controversial legislation. Theresa, however, resolutely rejected the party line and she was not alone. The shadow cabinet split on 21 July 1911 as a sizeable section of Unionist peers decided on a policy of opposition, fearing this reform would leave them defenceless against home rule, universal male suffrage and Welsh disestablishment. This rebel group included Salisbury and Selbourne (who, in protest, refused to dine at Downing Street), as well as Londonderry and Theresa's confidantes Carson, George Wyndham and F. E. Smith. But, despite the die-hards' efforts, the bill passed by a slim majority of 131 to 114 in August.

Theresa's six-page account of this period by its very existence denotes how momentous she deemed the controversy, but also makes clear her disgust at the votes of over twenty Unionist peers aiding the final removal of the veto. Carson was similarly abhorred and, worried by party unity, he called for vengeance: 'as for the Judas peers I hope they will be posted in every Unionist Club in the country until their names are a byword…so ends the House of Lords.'[119] But there was little time for contemplation. The end of Balfour's reign as party head loomed and two of Theresa's confidantes were in the running for succession.

From early 1911, as a consequence of information passed to her by Sir George Armstrong, Theresa was aware that a change in the Conservative Party leadership was imminent. Relaying details of an interview with Walter Long when the question of Balfour's successor was raised, Armstrong informed her that Long initially balked at the idea that he could lead the party. However, buoyed by a warm political reception, Armstrong was confident that Long 'will be the pivot around which the *Conservative Section* of the party will revolve…He [Long] looked like a new man when the meeting was over…[we] look forward with cheerful confidence to the future.'[120] This letter gave Theresa a head start in considering Long as a potential leader of the Conservatives but, with no agreed successor to Balfour, the possibility of a three-way contest between two of her confidantes, Long and, as an outside runner, Edward Carson, as well as Austen Chamberlain, emerged. Armstrong was, of course, not her sole party informant and Theresa's detailed account of this leadership contest also reveals Sandars passing her key information 'which you do not find in the papers' regarding the man he called the 'Chief', Arthur Balfour.

Sandars' self-proclaimed 'political gossip' letters date from 1906 and, encouraged by Theresa, he had already pushed Balfour toward an Irish agenda: in December 1907, 'I suggested he [Balfour] should talk about Ireland…and he did, and I hope you approved' and again at the start of 1909, 'I have told A.J.B. that he must advert to the condition of Ireland in his speech'.[121] Sandars was an ideal confidante for Theresa: he pushed for Charley in Commons asking if he could reject the Irish Law Bill in April 1909; from him she gleaned information on the timing of debates; forthcoming bills; registers of MPs and prospective candidates that she used to formulate her invitation lists and he also posted the parliamentary programme to her when she was away from London.[122] To Sandars, Theresa provided a 'confidential ear' and he trusted her judgement unreservedly.[123] She also proved useful in managing obtuse candidates like W. Gritten standing in Hartlepool in 1909. An invite to Wynyard, in Sandars' view, had taken Gritten 'in hand. This morning there comes a letter from him from Wynyard advising the Chief [Balfour] as to his speech, and instructing him upon the situation. This is a more friendly and favourable attitude than I should have expected.'[124] By October 1911, Sandars reinforced Armstrong's earlier inference, suggesting that Balfour, 'like Ajax', would be 'killed by his friends'. Theresa interpreted this as a prompt of Balfour's resignation but, with a third home rule bill looming, doubted whether this could be imminent. What followed, however, showed the political confidante at her most influential.

Meeting Carson in London in late October Theresa passed him the Armstrong-Sandars information. This formally opened the question of succession but Carson initially refused to take the bait. Theresa, therefore, came to the conclusion that Long, by comparison, both wanted and could probably win the leadership but would face serious opposition from Chamberlain. However, she was not ready to give up on her favourite, suggesting to Carson 'that in the event of the fight being too violent and the possibility of the Party's being split that he (Sir Edward), in view of Home Rule, would be a very suitable Leader. He did not appear to dislike the prospect, but talked much about his health and the Ulster Party.' The following day Theresa saw Long, informing him, on the one hand, that she hoped he would win the leadership but, on the other, highlighting the likelihood of bitter competition from Chamberlain. She then proposed Carson as a compromise candidate to him 'and thought W. L. [Long] seemed to consider it rather a good plan.' She next saw Sandars who confirmed her own view that Balfour would resign but not immediately. That Theresa was fully embroiled in the impending leadership fight became even more apparent on the final day of October when Balfour visited Wynyard. Here, in a private meeting, he took the opportunity to inform her that he was standing down as a result of failing health. Theresa later recorded, 'In my sittingroom, he put his hands on my shoulders and said, "my dear, you know I am going!"'. Although 'not intellectually surprised by his decision', she admitted, 'I must own that in an emotional sense I was.' She asked him to reconsider and tried to draw comment on whom he deigned as his successor but he declined on both counts: 'He gave me all his reasons which he afterwards expressed in his speech to his constituents in the Strand, and we discussed them at great length.' In the following week the king and the Balfourian faithful were informed of his resignation.

Still at Wynyard, Theresa was forced to grapple with tensions between two of her confidantes: Long and Sandars. The former told her that Sandars was working against him in the leadership tussle, backing Chamberlain's claim and, more damningly, that he 'does not fail to make use, for this purpose, of your patronage':

Of course he is not misquoting you or probably quoting you at all: he is only doing what he is thoroughly entitled to do, viz: not concealing the fact that he enjoys your friendship and confidence, and this of course helps him in his campaigns against me. But you can't help this even if you would, it is the inevitable result of your dual friendship, and I don't mention it in grievance... [only] as a fact. I am quite prepared to fight my own battle and I am happy to say I have plenty of friends.

Such strains were indicative of the deep-set party divide but Long was quick to make amends, telling Theresa later that month, 'A *real* friend such as you are is the best possession in the world.'[125] That both Sandars and Long remained loyal to Theresa was testament to her tact and skill in the 'entrancing game, that of managing men.'[126] Here she might have excelled but her timing was far from perfect.

Returning to London on 10 November, Theresa 'went straight to Mr Long's... and heard, to my utter astonishment and great regret, that Mr Long and A.C. [Austen Chamberlain] had agreed to stand down in favour of Mr Bonar Law.' She had been working towards very different ends, wanting Carson or Long at the helm and this perhaps explains why the decision was not relayed to her at Wynyard. In reaction, her die-hard principles were never more apparent:

> Everyone seems now to forget that the Tory Party existed long before we paid the Liberal Unionists so very handsomely for sticking to their principles. I was all the more annoyed, as I am sure Mr Long would have won easily...I am of the opinion that had Sir Edward Carson been properly approached at the beginning of the crisis, he undoubtedly would have led the Party; but as far as I can make out Mr Campbell went to see him...and told him Bonar Law would not stand if he...wanted to. He was ill in bed; and we know people of emotional temperament and feeling change their minds; but the idea being new, he sent a message back to say he would not stand. He did not feel at that moment that he wished to be Leader, and I must say that has said so consistently ever since.

Her sole consolation was that Chamberlain's leadership challenge had failed. She regarded him as a Liberal Unionist importation and, as a young man, one who should wait his turn for promotion, allowing those with years of party service behind them to rise to the fore. Her loyalties clearly lay with the Tory side of the Conservative and Unionist Party and she wanted this section to reassert itself. In her view, the non-appointment of Long was a lost opportunity for such a re-emergence to occur. Yet, despite Armstrong's early optimism, like Carson, Long was never keen to assume the mantle of party head, doubting if he possessed 'the health to face such a job as this would *now* be'. He subsequently beseeched Theresa on her return to London to support Law: 'you can do so much *if you like* and believe...it is right.'[127]

Theresa did not doubt the force of Law's oratory but as he was known primarily as a tariff reformer, his credentials as a Unionist leader were circumspect. Carson, by comparison, thought Law would prove an able leader and was personally relieved to be able to fight home rule without the party headship. Theresa was less convinced:

> own feeling was, very strongly, that I wished Long or Carson to lead the party; so, although I must own that personal interest in the Leadership would have been a tremendous thing to me (because I feel that Mr Bonar Law is not as interested in the various principles of the Tory Party as I should have liked - such as Church, Education and Home Rule), yet compromise seems to be the inevitable way of conducting English politics.[128]

She, thus, had to come to terms with a leader not of her choosing and Harry Chaplin, her long-term friend and father of her daughter-in-law, Edith, brought some pressure to bear on her to accept Law.

Law was not immune from hers and other society slights, feeling 'neglected and that the great political hostesses are not doing their duty by him'.[129] Although there is evidence of sporadic correspondence between Theresa and Law, as he had, for example, written to her on the difficulty he found in promoting 'personal friends' like her son, Charley without offending other prospective candidates in the 1906 election, his accession to the head of the party brought a change to their relationship.[130] In an undoubtedly politically opportunistic move, Theresa began to foster Law's trust in 1911. Carson worked along identical lines to win their new leader over to the Unionist side but found it an uphill struggle: 'I sent a note to BL [Law] and he has written to say he will dine on Sunday "but not with pleasure". However it is very important we should get in touch with all concerned. I will go to dinner "with pleasure".' Carson returned to the same subject in early March 1912 after Theresa had met with Law:

I hope your interview with B[onar Law] was satisfactory. I think there is much power of development in him and my test of his ability is that I never heard him make a bad speech...He certainly has great difficulties ahead - if we are to come in to power and to guide the evolution of events at present in the interest of the Body Politic [it] will take a really great man.[131]

Theresa was sufficiently realistic to acknowledge that Law would be 'a hard nut to crack'. Her view of him was certainly not helped by his earlier reluctance to place her son but some contemporaries alleged that she fulminated more at his lack of landed credentials.[132] Law was undoubtedly a very different party leader in terms of class, education and political experience. He was essentially a middle-class backbencher though Long tried to convince Theresa that this would be to the party's, and ultimately her own, advantage:

Everybody is pleased now...I am sure it is worth a great deal to us to get a real businessman at our head: we have wanted this badly...you can easily improve him and your influence with him will be very useful: there are others who are trying hard to get him! I hope you won't allow them to beat you!![133]

Law was gradually won over but this was due to his own pragmatism as well as the efforts of Theresa and Carson. His accession as party head increased the demands on his hospitality but he was never a keen or accomplished host or overtly *au fait* with the social niceties attached to statesmanship. This was compounded by the fact that he was widowed in 1909 and he, therefore, accepted Theresa's offer to entertain on his behalf at Londonderry House.[134] Here Law would often look visibly uncomfortable standing by her side at the top of the staircase that became a landmark of the Londonderry hostesses. Theresa also introduced Law to her son and daughter-in-law, entertained him at Wynyard and engineered political meetings at Londonderry House with the Unionist leadership. By April

1912, society acknowledged her acceptance of him and his growing trust in her and, in that month, he visited Mount Stewart with the express purpose of meeting Unionists both individually, with a house party that included Long, Hugh Cecil, Charles Beresford, Carson, Lord Hamilton and Harry Chaplin, and *en masse*, with a demonstration by the Ulster Volunteer Force at Balmoral orchestrated by Carson and Lord Londonderry. As had been their design, the spectacle of the latter, where Law witnessed the 'soul of a people', reinforced his anti-home rule stance and by 1913 he was passing information to Theresa regarding the king's anxiety over the Irish question, 'any sign of a new development...I shall in some way give you a hint of it.'[135] And Theresa returned the favour, passing on a 'rumour (from Dublin) that...the Gov[ernmen]t told Redmond he must choose between a general election and giving up Ulster - and he has given no answer yet - of course I don't vouch for this.'[136]

As in her relationship with F. E. Smith, the initial political contact developed into a friendship. As Theresa expressed after Law's October 1913 visit to Wynyard, 'I am so very pleased that you enjoyed yourself here. ...I lay great store by my friends as you know and am very grateful for political combinations which have given me what I feel to be a *real* friend'. But, just weeks later, after another meeting with Law she worried that she had overstepped the mark in this nascent relationship: 'I so enjoyed our talk yesterday...but I feel I was a little indiscreet but anyhow I trust you implicitly'.[137] Law's commitment to party unity and unionism as well as his Ulster-Scots Presbyterian heritage evidently endeared him to Theresa and she even presented his daughter, Isabel to the royal court, signalling her entry to society as a debutante, in February 1914. The result was that Theresa won an assured line of communication to the Tory command, Londonderry House remained at the kernel of Unionist politics and, as with F. E., she 'reinforced Law's natural sympathies for Ulster unionists'. She also helped ease his sense 'that he is out of his element.'[139] Law was never hostile to high society but possessed scant interest in it. He was a sombre man who seldom accepted invitations yet, in the absence of a wife, he came to rely on Theresa to organise and host the receptions expected of a party leader. He also came to regard her as a friend; writing to her for the remainder of her life. Although Theresa grew to admire, respect and even like Law, ultimately friendship could never be the foundation of effective political hostessing. Not to accept him in 1911 would have diminished her claim to be the foremost Tory hostess. So with the end of the Lords' controversy and a new leader at the party helm, especially one won over to her side, she turned her full attention to the cause that riled her from 1886: the defeat of home rule.

'The shadow behind the Throne where politics in Ulster were concerned'[140]

As Theresa and other anti-reformers predicted, the removal of the Lords' veto in 1911 injected a heightened sense of urgency into the Unionist mind. As Carson openly expressed to her: 'We cannot I think depend even on "the Lords" throwing out a bill and if anything is to be done the Ulstermen must do it for themselves.'[141] They both became fixated on the Unionist campaign. Carson declared this his last political fight and, although 'overwhelmed at all that lies before us', concerted to 'make a big effort...to stir up some life over...Home Rule':

> You cannot conceive what dissatisfaction there is everywhere at the want of life and effort in the party. I get hundreds of letters from men only begging for strong action...I want so much to have a good chat about everything with us - I feel very doubtful about the way our leaders intend to fight Home Rule but in any event I will lead for myself this time. The whole country is in a shocking state...still the country is calling out for a strong man.

It was not only Carson who was preparing himself for the final political contest of his life. Theresa was also extending the remit of the hostess further beyond the drawing room and country estate than ever before. Forewarned by Long that there was the possibility of an election in mid 1912, she saw this as the first step in maintaining the union. She subsequently threw her weight and influence behind her son's campaign in Maidstone, canvassing alongside Carson and her daughter-in-law, Edith. Her canvass did not take the form of a mute platform appearance: she addressed meetings; toured rural parts of the constituency by car and canvassed house to house on a staunchly anti-home rule manifesto:

> Not three per cent of the voters that I canvassed realised the Constitutional point. The action of the House of Lords did not seem to trouble them at all...Home Rule unless accompanied by quotations from Mr Redmond's speeches and...description of the riots, outrages and the law not running in Ireland, they did not seem to mind.[142]

Charley was also instilled with a new impetus by the advent of the third home rule crisis. He could no longer be accused of toying with politics and, once elected, was the first to acknowledge the import of his mother's influence, both in Maidstone and in pulling strings for his first post-election address: 'Thanks to the influence which I am lucky enough to obtain from yourself, arrangements had been made for me to follow Ramsay MacDonald' in the Commons' first reading of the Home Rule Bill, 'I was very lucky getting in like that on the first reading, and I need hardly say that I appreciate that to the fullest extent. ...It was very kind of W. L. [Walter Long] to sit there the whole time and he gave me every assistance by applauding my sentiments.'[143]

Changes heralded by electoral reform also brought Theresa, and many thousands of women, to more formal and public politicking. This was the first generation of wo??? able to enjoy the indirect gains of democracy as an increased, albeit still exclu???y male, electorate demanded new methods of political organisation and 'mobilising public opinion [became] a grubby, time-consuming and increasingly professional occupation'. The 1880s saw popular, but upper-class led, bodies like the Conservative Primrose League come into being, partially to harness female party workers to an electoral machine.[144] Dedicated to Disraeli and popularising the form of conservatism that he engineered into existence, Theresa's involvement with this hierarchical and imperialist organisation afforded an important opportunity for her to mount the political platform and grapple with popular, as opposed to high, politics. Although not designed as an *en masse* body, this is what the league quickly became; a multi-class hybrid with a place for men, women and children in its ranks. Yet involvement in the league in its embryonic stages could open one to derision: 'The first years of its existence were a struggle. Wearing the badge exposed one to much chaff, not to say ridicule'.[145] Theresa overcame these considerations, as well as those of social custom, when the opportunity to address a Primrose meeting arose in 1885. Though proceeding carefully as she hardly considered 'it a woman's place to address a large meeting such as this', she clearly identified a role for women within the organisation: 'surely there is no nobler work for women than endeavouring to influence all those around to preserve the empire as our forefathers handed it down to us.'

The impact of the Londonderrys' patronage of the league was especially apparent in east Durham - promoting habitations at Wynyard, Seaham, Darlington, Stockton and Hartlepool. In 1890, Lord Londonderry also led the Belfast Primrose habitation, but the north of Ireland never grew into a Primrose hotbed. Indeed, at its peak, in the 1890s, fuelled by opposition to home rule, Ireland could count only thirty-five habitations and indigenous Unionist bodies quickly took over the impetus and Primrose branches. Outside Ireland, by comparison, the league became hugely popular: mixed-sex membership numbered a million in 1891. It also appeared that this popularity transpired into votes: south-east Durham saw Conservatives retain their seats from 1895-1910, with Darlington and Stockton returning a Unionist candidate in 1895, 1892 and 1900.[146]

Theresa was appointed to the league's aristocrat-heavy executive committee in 1887 and became a key conduit between the league and the advance of popular forms of unionism. The mobilisation of women was central to this process. During the first two home rule crises of 1886 and 1893 female unionism was manifest, although much of the initiative remained localised and sporadic. There was also a clearly defined separation between male and female avenues of political activity, not only to adhere to late nineteenth-century convention but also to avoid ridiculing the rudimentary Unionist campaign. This explains women's exclusion from the Unionist Convention of 1892 but their involvement in the social niceties of the conversazione that preceded the more formal political event. In this controlled environment, Theresa emerged as a female Unionist figurehead, conveying a 350-yard anti-home rule petition with 20,000 signatures from Unionist women in Londonderry and north-west Ulster to Westminster in her carriage in 1893. And her Unionist conviction was such that she strayed close to breaching royal protocol in this year, sending Ulster newspapers covering Balfour's Belfast visit to Queen Victoria, 'thinking that although the London press have excellent accounts Her Majesty might care to see the *full* account.'[147]

Charles was also assuming a leading Unionist position, becoming one of the most vocal anti-home rulers in the Lords and president of the Ulster Unionist Council (UUC) from its formal constitution in March 1905. Theresa was similarly appointed to office on another organisation designed to popularise unionism, 'flattered and pleased' to be unanimously elected vice-president of a new and formal body of Irish-based women Unionists, the Ulster Women's Unionist

Council in 1911.[148] Although some contemporaries suggested that the initiation of this permanent organisation of women Unionists was due to Theresa, 'they all owed her a debt of gratitude for having made the suggestion', she alone cannot be credited with fashioning this association. She did, however, work hard to establish and promote this new female auxiliary, presiding over its inaugural meeting in Belfast with a rousing address where her earlier reticence to speak publicly seemed a thing of the past:

> Ulster will not consent to the tearing asunder of this country from the predominant partner - England... since Ireland has been united to England she has prospered in every way. (Applause) 'Union is strength,' and is it likely that we in Ulster would give our consent to tearing England and Ireland asunder? ('No.')...this great and important meeting will be but the beginning of real and solid work and a thorough organising of the women of Ulster. ...I feel certain that the women of Ulster will be in no way behind the men in striving for so noble a cause. (Applause).[149]

In tangent with the generic party unity she always espoused, it was her hope that this meeting would inspire the Unionist women of Ireland to band together. She also strove to personalise the appeal of the newly established body, spearheading the campaign to get women of influence on its executive committee by writing to those she deemed suitable on Londonderry House notepaper. And she made no apologies for taking such a pro-active role: 'with the political and other experience that I have, I feel it absolutely necessary that you should have my views.'[150] This was one of numerous examples where Theresa demanded a level of influence that bordered on control.

Theresa certainly believed that the UWUC was a pioneer organisation, but in directing its expansion she was undoubtedly inspired by the Primrose principles that had so effectively popularised conservatism. With leadership positions in both the league and the UWUC, she forged strong links between the two organisations and the defining Tory-Unionist principles of church, state and crown.[151] The league's neutrality on the divisive issue of women's suffrage was also mirrored in unionism's newest organisation and women's political activism was portrayed as an extension of their moral and didactic domestic role in both bodies. Also comparable was the notion that women were companionate campaigners; their role was not to rival men or push women's issues to the fore of the manifesto, but to co-operate and work toward securing a greater political good.

Theresa's influence in shaping and propagating the early UWUC was hugely significant. She was in a position to secure speakers and her close contact with the Unionist command enabled her to send Carson draft resolutions and speeches for approval. He actively encouraged her political part and made public his support of both her and the new female Unionist auxiliary. Indeed, Theresa would often begin a public address by reading a letter of support from the Unionist leader, vouchsafing her political credentials and his belief that 'No one' was 'better qualified' than she 'to express the deep sentiments of loyalty to the King and the United Kingdom which animate Ulster men and Ulster women'.[152] James

Craig, the Unionist second in command, who enjoyed a cordial, but not especially close, relationship with Theresa, also oversaw her work. Here, however, he trod carefully, commenting with some relief to Lord Londonderry that her draft Ulster Day address, 'strikes exactly the right note required at the moment...In any case, of course, none of us would have ventured to alter a word without submitting it again for her approval.'[153] One consequence of this, if at times effete, approval was that Theresa's public declarations deviated little from the divining principles of unionism. Loyalty to the crown, devotion to the empire, constitutional rights and moral sanction all featured prominently in her rhetoric. Her Ulster Day address that Craig feared changing, for instance, had imperialism and constitutionalism at its core:

> the people of England will never support that Government in attempting to carry Home Rule without the consent of the country...We in Ulster wish and intend to continue inside the Union and the protection of the British Parliament at Westminster and we *refuse* to be driven forth by legislation which Ulster rightly declares has no moral sanction whatever.[154]

Theresa grew into a confidant orator, addressing meetings in both Ireland and England, where her clarity of expression was admired to such an extent by the Duke of Portland that he admitted, 'I helped myself to your speech...for the meeting at Mansfield.' Unionist Ronald MacNeill also 'used all *your* [Theresa's] arguments and took *your* standpoint' to play devil's advocate with a radical reform group.[155] Often emphasising constitutional arguments against 'the poisonous Home Rule reptile', Theresa was fond of quoting Nationalist John Redmond at length, branding his Irish Parliamentary Party 'essentially disloyal...Redmond speaks with two voices, one in which he affects to be content with a meek and mild form of Home Rule Government...And another voice in which he breathes hatred for England'.[156] But she was equally critical of Liberal self-interest:

> You have a Radical Government in power who are always talking about 'Government for the people by the people' but yet they will not consult the people of this point - if they are sure of the verdict - why don't they do so?... a Radical Government, careless of everything but its own existence, has raked up the dry bones of the past, reopened the old sores, and brought the country to the verge of a civil war, which, if it began in Ireland, would spread through England, Scotland and Wales to the furthest confines of the Empire. For eighty odd votes a Radical Government has done this...if the Government persists in forcing Ulster under the hated domination of the Nationalists without first obtaining the sanction of the English people in a general election, the Ulstermen will be fully justified in armed resistance[.]

Female loyalty and penchant for sacrifice was another favoured theme, emotively using women's place within the family as justification for political action:

Women must suffer as women always do in times of trouble or war, in standing by the men and urging them to stand firm…of losing their fathers, husbands, sons and brothers in this terrible conflict, and yet they are firm and
unflinching and feel that they are doing their women's part in endeavouring
the save the Province they love so well from being severed from the Empire…are you prepared to allow British soldiers to fire upon loyal men
who…seek to stay with You?…I as an Ulsterwoman appeal to you [to] uphold
our principles [of] liberty, patriotism and citizenship[.][157]

To further heighten awareness of the Unionist campaign, Theresa courted
newspaper editors and wrote extensively to the press. In the latter, women, still
voteless and excluded from parliament, were arguably less constrained in the
strength of their political comment. At Craig's prompting, for example, Theresa
wrote 'a strong letter pointing out that the Radical and Nationalist Parties are
inaugurating a campaign in favour of Home Rule, despite the fact that the Bill is
not in print' and, as Craig acknowledged, 'You understand that in these matters a
man dare not interfere.'[158] Ultimately this work, coupled with Theresa's figurehead
significance, helped popularise female unionism. The very news that Lady Londonderry was 'coming to speak…put…tremendous heart into the workers' in
west Belfast in 1911 with the Londonderry name reportedly 'as popular as ever
amongst the working classes.'[159] H. G. Gwynne, editor of the *Morning Post*, was
also of the opinion that the inclusion of Theresa's name to an article 'added
weight.'[160] But the speed at which the council augmented from initiation to popularisation also suggests a pent-up female demand for organisation. Just days after
the UWUC's launch, Theresa was informed that 3,500 women had enlisted their
support in Belfast, 'arranging for their husbands to stay at home and 'mind the
weans', others want to bring their husbands with them!'[161]
    Adopting such a prominent profile in the Unionist campaign, however, also
brought negative attention. Sandars passed '*Entre nous*' information to Theresa
about the Conservative Chief Whip, Balcarres', less than favourable view of her:
'[he] yields nothing to you in the way of positive sentiments!!'[162] More concerning,
especially with regard to her personal safety, was a threatening postcard delivered
to Mount Stewart warning, '*Despite* all your subsidized Tory papers - you and your
party *know* what a great and *fatal* mistake you have made. …Your day of ascendancy is past.'[163]
    The Londonderry ascendancy, however, was far from over. Enhanced co-
operation between various Irish and English Unionist bodies was a constant in
Long's, Carson's and the Londonderrys' political agenda. Indeed, the so-called
'Londonderry House agreement' of 6 April 1911 saw representatives of the Irish
Unionist Alliance, the Ulster Unionist Council and Long's newly invigorated Union Defence League meeting at the London house. With Carson in the chair, a
decision was reached whereby a unified approach to campaign finance and propaganda were defined to prevent overlap. The Alliance and Ulster Unionist Council
subsequently continued their Irish work, but in Britain they now worked as a
collective, under the title of the Unionist Associations of Ireland Joint Committee, joining Long's league in opposing home rule.[164]

By this juncture, Carson trusted Theresa unreservedly, marking passages in his letters 'very private' and early in 1912 he confided the gravity of the situation in Ulster: 'It is nearly time.' His resolve was now for grand gestures and 'very drastic action in Ulster...There is a growing feeling we do not mean business and I certainly think this is the critical year and am prepared for any risks.'[165] He was also wholly committed:

> How I *long* to see Home Rule defeated - it is I think a passion with me and I hate the degradation of Ireland being turned into a province - and our own splendid folk being put under in the race for progress...I hope everything will be bitter this season. I cannot bear the hypocrisy of so-called political toleration. I would take it as hot as h___ on any occasion - socially or politically for the demagogues.

At the same time he privately disclosed his unease about the campaign, pondering the impact that an election would have on Unionist fortunes and admitting to Theresa that he would delight in the defeat of 'this Government of funk and feebleness'. He was, however, sufficiently realistic to conceive that unless a sizeable Unionist majority was secured their campaign could be fatally damaged. He thus predicted 'a stormy time in front of us and the weak-kneed must fall out of the ranks - that is all!...I try to get strong and well only that I may fight with all the power and resource which God has given me. Thank goodness I fear nothing and I only want to save our people'.[166] Theresa also maintained her Unionist resolve and tried to bolster a unity of purpose. In this direction she was encouraged by Arthur Bigge who determined, '*You* can do much good by preaching this policy of sticking together: you are a sincere friend and can inculcate loyalty and sincerity into those who want to be independent and stick to their own opinion. If they *do*, you would see your party back in office!'[167]

However, from Theresa's failure to persuade Carson to enter the 1911 leadership contest, there were obvious limits to her influence, but there were also very real advantages. Her close friendship with Carson, and more formal working relationship with Craig, allowed her to avoid the sense of exclusion that irked other female Unionists, who felt 'in the *cold and shade* of the men's Association...they treat us like children or troublesome suffragettes'.[168] In contrast, during the third home rule crisis Carson kept Theresa so well versed that many wrote to her in pursuit of information and some openly admired the political knowledge that she had at her command. Political wives often confided in her, anxious to glean news about their spousal prospects for promotion, suitability for office or why they had not been placed or honoured. Added to Carson's information were Commons' reports passed from her son who knew his mother would accept even 'a typewritten letter, as all you want to hear is the news' and, if Theresa was either at Wynyard or Mount Stewart, her daughter, Birdie would telegram news of voting on bills from London.[169] Even those one might presume to be politically well informed asked her for information, including Edward Saunderson, eldest son of the former Unionist leader, who was 'anxious to find out any news there might be' in exchange for what he knew 'as all incidents in the campaign are worth noting at the War Office in Ulster':

> I have very little news except that both the sittings of the Cabinet on Home Rule were entirely taken up trying to crack the Ulster nut and as far as I can gather with little success except that they have now raked up a scheme devised by Gladstone in [18]93 which never became public property and that is to place the 5 counties in Ulster that have a preponderance of Unionists under the English Home Office.
> This is a subtle scheme worthy of the serpents. I think it cannot be too much rubbed in now that nothing will cause Ulster to desert the rest of Ireland.[170]

Initially, Theresa courted friends in all political camps, including George Wyndham, Horace Plunkett, Lewis Harcourt and the Countess of Fingall. The latter mused that the Londonderrys' befriending such a self-proclaimed 'rebel and Papist' as she was an attempt 'to prove their broadmindedness', but concluded that 'their friendship was never failing and it made no difference to it that we often fought on politics'. Unionist turned home ruler, Plunkett was another rarely in agreement with Theresa's political agenda, but he corresponded with her from 1908 and enjoyed her hospitality, her company and her approach to life: 'the spirit in which you have worked for the realisation of your aims is just what the public life of the United Kingdom has lacked'.[171] Later in her own life, Theresa would claim to share the view of the late Duchess of Devonshire, another leading hostess, who 'used to say, "Never give up anything or anybody"'.[172] But the question of home rule divided society in a form reminiscent of the Foxite and Pittite biased invitations of the Regency crisis, reintroducing what Liberal, Margot Asquith termed 'old parochialisms…Our follies in Ireland have cursed not only the political but also the social life in this country.' This was apparent in Unionist, as well as more *avant garde*, circles. Ettie Desborough's 'Souls', for instance, managed a cross-party, as well as an intellectual and artistic, complexion until home rule emerged as the major political talking point.[173]

Even before this, Theresa was closing her salon doors to those whom she disagreed with: cutting Asquith and Lloyd George from her invite lists as they moved towards reform from 1906. And, always more party motivated than either her predecessor or her successor, Theresa's disdain for the Liberal Party was empathic:

> I never liked that set of people and always think they "toady" the people up but are really more autocratic, proud, and so to speak, stuck up, than anybody else. The Tories have the sense to realise that everyone has the same flesh and blood and that it is only their good luck and chance that has won them any position. The Whigs are always the first to encourage revolution and then forsake the people whom they have encouraged…They have never been sound on the established Church and many other principles.[174]

This extended, though usually in a more dilute form, to the Liberal Unionists who flocked to her party's fold after Gladstone's conversion to home rule in 1886. Yet to Theresa, the Liberal Unionists remained 'not of the blood and the faith'.[175] This was compounded by home rule, especially during the third, and most severe, crisis of 1912-14. From 1912, both parliament and high society became increasingly polarised. Lord Londonderry went as far to ask his sister, Lady Allendale, wife of a Liberal Whip, not to visit and, characteristically, Theresa made no attempt to hide the depth of her emotion, refusing a royal invite to spend Ascot week at Windsor because an Irish pro-home rule peer would be present. And, when 'feeling on Ireland was running very high':

> there were constant scenes in the House and out of it, and many former friends in opposite political parties wouldn't speak to each other. Lady Londonderry...showed her feelings very openly...on the Terrace of the House of Commons, Lady Pirrie, whose husband had ratted to the other side, rushed up to her, and after greeting her said [']What very changeable weather we are having[']; Lady L. sniffed loudly and replied, [']I dislike change of any sort['], and turned her back on her.[176]

Theresa's invitation lists became more selective and increasingly the Countess of Fingall was the lone dissenter at her receptions. Essentially this was an indirect, but effective, means of exerting influence. Indeed, during the third home rule crisis invites to Mount Stewart provided an opportunity for English politicians and journalists to witness the popular enthusiasm that opposition to home rule roused at first hand. The Down estate was, therefore, a Unionist tool to counter the mainland apathy that so worried Theresa and Carson. The value of face to face meetings such as these was inestimable. Conservative MP and founder of *The Lady* and *Vanity Fair*, Sir Thomas Gibson Bowles was one of many who admitted to Theresa, 'When we meet I will tell you things I dare not write.'[177] For convinced Unionists, like Walter Long, the visits, which included Ulster Volunteer Force (UVF) drills and Unionist demonstrations, served to reinforce a sense of camaraderie. For others, like the Duke of Portland, staying at Mount Stewart presented an occasion to meet Long as well as James and Charles Craig. Although Lady Palmerston and her successor to the title of foremost Liberal hostess, Lady Waldergrave were the first to admit newspaper editors to high society, Theresa was quick to adopt the *Observer*'s J. L. Garvin as well as H. W. Gwynne, editor of the *Morning Post* and Geoffrey Robinson of *The Times*. The latter two were invited to Mount Stewart and subsequently promised full coverage of the Unionist cause. Reginald Lucas also used his visit to gather information, 'I heard far more news and far more interesting talk at Mount Stewart than am ever like to hear amongst the amateur prophets here' and on his return to London pledged to his hostess 'if anything comes to my knowledge worth repeating, you shall hear of it.'[178]

Her efforts to popularise the UWUC were similarly constructive: by 1912 membership of the council was estimated at 80,000-90,000; twenty-seven associations were established and ninety-four meetings had been held; 5,000 letters and newspapers were being sent weekly to England and Scotland with eighteen women's Unionist associations formally linked to sister bodies in England and Scotland. She also played a pivotal role in broadening the scope of a local association beyond Ulster and into Britain: she was central in organising an Association of Unionist Ulsterwomen in London in 1912 and in the following year, in recognition of the interest that the UWUC was arousing outside the north of Ireland, successfully altered the council's constitution to allow women who were neither natives or residents of Ulster to become associate members. This was another measure of Primrose inspiration but it was nonetheless effective; paying an annual subscription fee of two guineas enabled women like the Duchess of Portland and Walter Long's wife, Doreen to be co-opted into the organisation. The monies raised were used to send literature and women workers to English and Scotch constituencies. Theresa canvassed in multiple constituencies and facilitated co-operation between the UWUC and various interested parties in England and Scotland including, unsurprisingly, the Primrose League as well as Long's Union Defence League and other women's Unionist associations who all hosted meetings for numerous female Unionist 'missionaries'.[179] Theresa also directed UWUC policy on the crucial and controversial issue of religion, advising that they 'should urge the Ulster case against Home Rule mainly on Social, Economic and Financial Grounds, by which the charge of Ulster bigotry will be avoided.'[180]

Theresa frequently called for unity when minor cavils over personality as opposed to politics caused problems within the council. One such example came soon after the UWUC's establishment when Theresa, in a letter marked specifically 'not for the press', urged, 'my earnest wish is for peace…at such a crucial moment…that should a breath of suspicion get abroad that there was any friction in the working of our Association, the enemy would rejoice and it would be a source of great weakness to our cause.'[181] Further clashes forced Theresa to intervene: in 1912 she demanded a reform of business to more clearly define the remits of the honorary and organising secretaries, warning that otherwise the council's 'usefulness as an official Unionist organization will be destroyed, and it would accordingly become necessary for me to consider whether I could with advantage to our Cause continue my connection with it.'[182]

By early 1913, Theresa was unsurprisingly being referred to as the UWUC's 'senior Vice-President'.[183] Given this position, she was widely seen as the natural successor to the Dowager Duchess of Abercorn as UWUC president in April 1913. In reality, Theresa had been leader of this organisation in all but name for some time. As president, however, she soon realised women campaigning *en masse* was a visual reminder 'that the Government were not up against a political organisation, but against a whole people.'[184] And there is no denying the success of her endeavours. Under her guidance the UWUC developed into the largest female political association that Ireland has ever seen with a membership of approximately 150,000 at the apex of the third home rule crisis.[185]

Despite the popularity and import of women's unionism, political society remained divided on gender lines. The 'man's party' held at the Commons and attended by Balfour and Craig and dinner 'being only a man's affair' at the Constitutional Club in June 1914 provide two clear examples of this separation.[186] In addition, the Ulster Unionist Council, the policy-formulating body of unionism, was still exclusively male both in its membership and organisations that it granted official representation to. But this gender-based exclusion did nothing to endear Theresa to women's rights; female suffrage had no place in her political or personal agenda. She held firm to the belief that women should to do 'a lower grade...of work' and that 'woman shriekers have handicapped women in politics.'[187] She also remained unconvinced that the female vote would 'be for the betterment of the community and the good of the wage earners' and, owing to the physiological difference of sex, declared that women were 'naturally unfitted' for parliamentary service. The idea of a female electoral majority or a women's political party was, therefore, an anathema to her and she deemed the suffrage campaign 'extravagant and artificial'.[188] Given her class, this was not an unusual stance and her anti-suffragism was in line with other prominent Primrose dames, such as Ladies Jersey and Wimborne and the Duchess and Dowager Duchess of Marlborough. Moreover, Theresa knew that she did not need a vote in order to exert political sway, leading Sir George Murray to contemplate, 'You are the only female I know who makes me doubt whether we are not wrong in refusing them [women] votes' but he added 'you have much better fun as it is.'[189]

It is, however, too simplistic to wholly discount the UWUC in the fight for women's rights. The sheer size of the council, its multi-class membership and the extent of its political work broke many boundaries for Ulster women in the early twentieth century. To Theresa this was merited only by the threat of home rule and her belief that 'Extraordinary times need extraordinary measures'.[190] She thus retained a resolute belief that women's political work should be compatible with familial and domestic responsibilities:

> I always think that as long as they do not give up their home life, women are just as good as men as far as brains and that go, but it is impossible for a young wife with a family to take much part in public life, if she does her duty to her husband and children, as I in an old fashioned way, think she ought to do.[191]

Even when the exclusively male Ulster Unionist Council pledged that women would be granted votes under their plans for a provisional government in 1913 Theresa was quick to emphasise, 'for fear of misconception', that this stance was adopted not through any support for female suffrage but 'because the Franchise...is the Local Government one and not the Parliamentary one' and 'in strict accord with the contention we have always held that any devolution of more power for the Government of local affairs in Ireland should be in the nature of extension of Local Government rather than the setting up of anything in the nature of a Parliament.'[192] Here she walked a fine line, knowing that although the issue of votes for women was politically divisive and never officially endorsed by the Unionist Party, it had some support amongst the ranks of her own UWUC. To navigate this, in a letter to her pro-suffrage daughter-in-law, Edith, she called the UWUC constitution into play whereby a member:

thinks exactly as she likes on every other subject except that of Home Rule...
The whole Ulster position is that, they are not going to have a *Parliament*, consequently no women can vote for members of it...I know that there are some
suffrage Home Rulers who are doing all they can to split up our magnificent
organisation - They know it is impossible to do it on the Home Rule question
so they are trying to drag the red herring of the Woman Suffrage across us...I
am sure you will see the point of my letter...we were banded together for one
object...it is most inopportune at this moment to bring the question of the
suffrage into a large organisation formed for a totally different object.[193]

Her view of women's involvement in unionism was, therefore, complex. Although convinced of its ancillary status, she frequently sought to avoid marginali-
sation. In 1913, for instance, she pushed for women's involvement in the Medical
Board of the Ulster Volunteer Force and issued an appeal to the 'Women of Ulster' for financial contributions to the Guarantee Fund of the Ulster Provisional
Government, 'to indemnity the members of the [Ulster Volunteer] force who
may be called upon to fight our battles. We are precluded from standing in the
ranks ourselves, though many of us are qualified for the Army Nursing Service,
so let us show our patriotism, and our deep sympathy.'[194]

But Theresa, although the best connected and informed woman in the Unionist campaign, was not privy to all decisions. The Larne gunrunning of April 1913
was kept from her as well as other prominent Unionists, like Walter Long. The
only indication she received came from Carson who, without specifying a reason,
enquired whether she wanted to leave Mount Stewart. She refused but Lord Londonderry left perhaps believing that he was more likely to come under suspicion
and possible arrest than his wife. The 1913 gunrunning was, however, an extraordinary event and under less exceptional circumstances the passing of political
information, as in the early nineteenth century, remained one of society's lynch-
pins. Lunching with Jack Mitford at Londonderry House in March 1914, for example, Theresa overheard him intimate to Lady Talbot, wife of the Common's
Chief Whip, that 'Winston [Churchill] is going to land 25,000 troops in Ulster'.
Theresa later lamented that she 'did not pay as much attention to it as I should
have done and regret now that I did not convey it to the proper quarter', but in
the same month another ominous hint came from her anonymous, but accurate,
Dublin informer who was 'always right in everything he has told me'.[195] Theresa
showed his letters to both her husband and Carson and from this source, confirmed by Ronald MacNeill, she learnt that the government planned to 'frighten'
Ulster Unionists with hundreds of arrests. This prompted Lord Londonderry and
Carson to travel overnight to Belfast, with the former of the opinion that either
widespread arrests were imminent or 'there was some idea of the Government
interfering with the volunteers [UVF].' That Carson and Londonderry acted on
Theresa's information not only emphasises her place within the Unionist command but further refutes any idea of non-communication between husband and
wife. Theresa 'naturally wished very much to accompany him, but he would not
allow this, as he did not wish to appear as Winston [Churchill] did in Belfast, with
"Clemie by his side"'. Instead she went to the Commons in search of news, but

without success. She then spoke to James Craig's wife, as well as the Portsmouth MP, Charles Beresford and her Dublin informant. But the latter warned her not to write, wire or telegraph her spouse, 'unless you want the Government to know every word you say'.[196] She also telephoned Ronald MacNeill who told her that arrest warrants would not be issued:

> I did not sleep much that night - as the Government have constantly shown themselves liars...I have heard that Sir John Simon and Mr McKenna were both privy to warrants being issued and that they were sent - 200 of them in one parcel to Dublin Castle, and sent...to Belfast...Since, we have heard that a military governor was pointed for Belfast, and appointed both a magistrate for Down and Antrim so that he would be able to sign and issue the warrants without any difficulty.

She later learnt that warrants had been sent to Dublin Castle and forwarded to Belfast but were neither unpacked nor issued and the Curragh mutiny with fifty-eight officers facing dismissal rather than take up arms against Unionists occurred on the following day. The subsequent written confirmation that the army would not be used to impose home rule on Ulster was significant, but the real import of the affair was the exposé that army loyalty could no longer be guaranteed.

News of the mutiny reached Londonderry House in the midst of a dinner with Bonar Law, F. E. Smith and co-organiser of the British covenant, Lord Milner present. The Unionist publicity machine subsequently mobilised with Theresa at its centre: 'We tried to get on to various newspapers but did not succeed until 11 o'clock...I called up the "Times" newspaper and told them about the sixteenth Lancers and my authority but I expect the paper had gone to press as the details were not in it the next morning.' To ensure accurate and full coverage Theresa dined alone with *The Times'* editor, Geoffrey Robinson the next day. Theresa's lengthy account of these heady days, working the press and central to politics, illuminates her desire to record her part in these events for posterity, but the home rule crisis darkened through 1914.[197] Many, including Bigge, continued to trade information with Theresa: 'Here we are hoping for a Conference and *some* agreement...Birrell is here and the P. Minister comes on Monday'; 'Have you any news? I am afraid nothing will come of the conversations, so after Parl[iamen]t meets the next step to be taken by both sides will have to be decided.' But with talk procuring no progress, he finally appealed to Theresa for moderation, 'Surely a mutual agreement *alone* can bring peace - and advert the shame of bloodshed... Well! The King will continue to work to that end. But there will have to be much give and take from *all* sides. There will be no secessions from the Gov[ernm-en]t!'[198]

Now in the shadow of civil war, Theresa tightened her personal control of the women's council: 'I do not wish any step to be taken, without my being consulted in the matter as it is impossible for me to the president of so great an Association unless I am kept fully informed.'[199] But tensions within the organisation aug-mented as a small grouping moved away from constitutionalism, believing contin-ued electoral work made them 'the fool of the English Conservative Party and its agents and organizations [sic], who have no regard for Ulster except as a lever for securing their own return to power'. Their closing caveat, 'force alone can decide the issue', convinced Theresa that nothing could be left to chance.[200] She countered this threatened split in the ranks of female unionism by calling on Carson. He sided with constitutional action and his old confidante, convincing the council that their political *raison d'être*, namely the defeat of home rule, should predominate.

The possibility of partition as a salve to the home rule quandary was also gaining currency. Four-county partition had been proposed as an amendment to the Home Rule Bill in June 1912 and in the same month a conference was held at Londonderry House to discuss this exclusion.[201] From this juncture, Theresa began to speak of two Irish peoples more sharply divided in race, creed and character than any other neighbouring communities in Britain: 'I always think Ireland is extremely feminine while Ulster is extremely masculine, and they are as difficult to put together (not as a married couple for that would be quite simple!) but as vinegar and oil.'[202]

In 1914 Asquith offered six-year exclusion for each Ulster county, but this was rebuffed by an increasingly entrenched Carson. The idea of six-county partition was, however, emerging, although the notion of excluding Cavan, Monaghan and Donegal from any political settlement was unpalatable to many. Carson was certainly concerned and further dissidence was apparent within UWUC ranks as its advisory committee aired its 'strong feeling' to Theresa: 'it has been much more difficult' for women in the proposed area of exclusion 'to do their duty…than it has been for us.' Theresa again sought the Unionist leader's advice, although her tone grew apologetic, 'I do feel it is a shame to trouble you about such trifles, but you know what a Women's Council is!'[203] His reply, relayed to the UWUC by Theresa, was curt: 'He begs the ladies to keep quiet as no settlement will be arrived at unless Ulster is consulted.' Theresa was now working to hold the organisation together and manage its public profile, advising that 'great care' should be exercised in 'any appeals for help made to friends in England as it was most important that the impression should not be allowed to become broadcast that the resources of Ulster were becoming exhausted.'[204]

Theresa's long-held belief that home rule would ultimately be defeated in England prompted her to hold several London drawing-room meetings and a week-long series of political rallies in south Durham during 1914. But regardless of the meeting's location, the message was clear: she spoke 'in the name of 234,000 Irish women who had signed a solemn covenant to march with their men folk in all that they did to oppose Home Rule':

> the female of the species is more dangerous than that of the male…there was nothing that the women of Ulster would not do or sacrifice in their determination to maintain the Union. The most dangerous feature of the situation was the extraordinary apathy of the people in England…[she] appealed to her hearers to "wake up England" to the peril that threatened, to spread the light among the unheeding and the indifferent and to educate the millions who had little chance to go in search of information and knowledge.[205]

However, with Carson 'feeling like a murderer in the House of Lords to hear all the same old sham and platitudes', even Theresa, one of the staunchest defenders of the union, grew dispirited.[206]

In the midst of 1914, she feared that the Unionist outlook was 'exceedingly gloomy…[there] seems to be little prospect of escaping from the necessity for the decisive action on the part of Ulster for which the preparations of the last two years have been undertaken…we must now be prepared for the worst'. As ever, this time in a prayer delivered to an UWUC Executive Committee meeting, she called for unity of purpose and action in the face of civil war: 'preserve to us and to our children that heritage of truth and liberty, of peace, and of fruitful labour'. Her address to the meeting continued the theme, 'whether the best or the worst befalls us we shall always be Ulsterwomen, and shall do all we can for the prosperity and good of our province.' But, the prospect of war was one that she, and so many others, abhorred:

> To us women the very thought of strife, accompanied by bloodshed, is an unspeakable horror. In such times it is women who suffer most. But recognising…the justice and righteousness of the cause for which Ulster has armed herself to fight, we women of Ulster are resolved not be a hindrance but a help to the men who are prepared to risk Everything for that Cause…we must give them our sympathy, our encouragement, our approval, our admiration in the noble stand they have made, and that they are ready to continue to the final issue…While there is life there is hope, I do not altogether despair of yet seeing the happy day when the poisonous Home Rule reptile shall have to be driven beyond the borders of our province, if not our island.[207]

However, as the alternatives to armed resistance diminished, those who wished for peace began to prepare for war and only the outbreak of armed conflict on an international, as opposed to a civil, stage prevented Unionists from turning to this recourse.

'No one likes stepping down from a throne'[208]
Theresa was one of the *North Mail*'s 'People of the hour' in 1914:

> the political influence of distinguished women works its way behind a curtain. Lifting the curtain that has hidden the things that have helped make the present crisis, there stands clear to vision the tall, majestic figure of Lady Londonderry. You have not seen her name in print a great deal lately?…that is the secret of her power and her success. She works by nightlight - not by limelight…Lady Londonderry has exercised an influence on the political situation of the past few months that in its scope and effect is quite incalculable…Her business has always been to know everyone worth knowing, and to be in everything. She has succeeded…[she] has the ear of the highest in the land, suggesting, hinting, advising. In the drawing room, at the small select dinner party…where much of our political history is made, Lady Londonderry has nearly always been. Beneath the shaded light she has worked, influ-

encing and helping. Her power among the leaders of the Unionist party is enormous…if she had been a man she would have made a great political wire-puller[.]

In their view, she was 'the woman who has helped to inspire no small part of the political policy of Unionism'.[209] Certainly no other woman rivalled Theresa at this time. She was at the height of her prowess: privy to advice from the highest echelons of unionism; entrusted with politically sensitive information; pumped for political news and holding the largest assemblage of political women in Ireland's history, either before or since, in check. But the First World War quickly eclipsed the Ulster crisis and, given the turmoil of the spring and summer months of 1914, one might suppose that from Theresa and the Unionist command there might have been a collective sigh of relief. Yet the war years of 1914-18 were the most trying of Theresa's life and the end of the conflict opened a new and, for many, unwelcome chapter of Unionist deliberations that would place them firmly *en route* to partition. In the early stages of the war, however, there was little to signal the tumult to come. Theresa supported the Unionist Party truce that was declared on the outbreak of war, but found inaction 'foreign' to her 'whole nature…I feel so incensed'.[210] Loyalty to the party triumphed over these private convictions as s[h]e [dive]rted the attentions of the UWUC towards war work, presiding over an Aug[ust] 1914 meeting to oversee the organisation pledge itself to care for families and de[pe]ndants of servicemen 'and that any want and suffering which may result shall be minimised as much as possible. …We will assist in the distribution…of clothing, food and other necessaries of life.'[211] The council thus turned to altruism, co-operating with the Soldiers' and Sailors' Families' Association, the Women's Legion, Queen Mary's Needlework Guild and the Ulster Volunteer Nursing Corps.

Theresa's foremost position amongst other aristocratic women also seemed assured, with Bigge relying on her to set an example to other peeresses in October 1914 when the decision was taken that the king would perform a full state opening of parliament: 'you will be there and make all the Peeresses do ditto.'[212] Theresa also used her well-established informants, many of whom, including her son, were now in army postings, to remain supremely well versed. Sir George Murray's regular updates from the front alluded to significantly higher death tolls than the press reported as well as Lloyd George's suspected political stage management; George Curzon forwarded her information and Sir Frank Sweetenham sent wartime updates from the Official Press Bureau with precise instructions as to when she could make the information public without endangering her source. Lord Selbourne kept her informed of recruiting problems and cabinet reluctance to introduce the compulsory service that she favoured while Admiral Bridgeman passed on 'secret' details of Balfour's desire to retire from the Admiralty, instructing her to 'kindly burn this letter and don't disclose your informant.' She characteristically ignored the former, but was sufficiently savvy to obey the second instruction. In return, Bridgeman acknowledged 'how much influence you have', asking her to push for larger army reverses to be sent to 'our gallant army…in great and immediate danger'. He, and many others, clearly used Theresa as a wartime channel for passing information to Carson or, in Bridgeman's case, to secure a meeting with the Unionist leader and 'break the ice with a man one has never met': within two weeks an appointment was arranged.[213] She brokered other meetings for Carson, for instance, with Sandars as well as Admiral David Beatty who asked, 'What manner of man is this Carson to be at the head of our Great Navy. Is he man enough, is he sound, do you approve will you tell me? It is a matter of utmost national importance'. Theresa obliged with 'the offer of a half way house' for a meeting and, predictably, vouched for the Unionist leader's steadfastness and ability.[214]

War, however, did not change Theresa's approach to life or politics. Although favouring 'a Moratorium in politics', she believed the government should be subject to criticism both at times of peace and war and unionism continued to preoccupy her political concerns. One of the clearest espousals of her wartime stance came in a letter to James Thursfield in December 1914:

> My party politics are stronger than ever, as I see what a disgraceful party the Radical party are. They are trying to make party capital out of every single thing…I have always thought that war was a searchlight, and in the brilliancy of the searchlight one realises true facts, and one is, that there is no more self seeking common Government than we have now…I hope the day of reckoning is not too far off, and that I shall be able to crow over it when it does come.[215]

Promotion for her son, now in a military, as opposed to a political, capacity, was another consideration. Sir John Cowans tried to assist her towards this end but, with a hint of frustration, concluded, 'I have been doing all I can and stirred up Carson to do likewise'. There were limits to what he could achieve in the face of concern amongst the general command of the Ulster Division about Charley's lack of infantry experience.[216] And, further worries, both political and private, would try Theresa in the next two years.

Theresa not only refused to cast the political past to one side for the duration of the war, but failed to comprehend those who could. The formation of a wartime coalition in May 1915 was simply unacceptable to her. Lady Talbot corresponded, sometimes daily, detailing the evolution of the cabinet and seeking information on the Unionist leader's intentions: 'Is Carson playing a deep game? has he got Ulster out and is he going to sit still, "wait and see" what happens when this wretched Govt. places Ireland in the hands of the [sic] Sinn Fein?'[217] Theresa freely admitted that her own beliefs were too deeply entrenched to support Liberals or radicals, instead backing Bonar Law, Balfour, Bob Cecil, Carson and Curzon, especially the latter three who had 'devil in them which to my mind is indispensable [in] a politician by which I mean a man to be absolutely courageous and able to take risks, and not care whether he is turned out of his place or not.'[218] When the cabinet postings were announced, she was largely satisfied to see 'all my friends' appointed, with the exception of Cecil who was made Under-Secretary for Foreign Affairs. She was also 'more than delighted that Winston Churchill has been taken away from a Executive place. …I always think he is not quite sane…he has no principles whatever.'[219] But with just eight of twenty-two cabinet places and Liberals in key postings, she was riled by what she perceived as Unionist under-representation in the coalition: 'I understand that it is to be an half in half Government, Asquith and Grey remaining in their places. A great many people think we need not have gone in. Personally, though I hate Coalitions…I think that no Party of the State could have disregarded the offer of the Government.'[220] Her belief that Unionists and Conservatives should have bargained hard for half the places remained, as did her view of the Liberals and her son offered the best précis her approach: 'I think she is the only one anxious to stir up the embers of party controversy.'[221]

Theresa was certainly a more outspoken coalition critic than many of her contemporaries. Bigge resorted to writing her a formal letter in an attempt to contain her more disparaging comments and she had clearly overstepped the mark both in terms of royal convention and her expectation that the king would share her detestation of the coalition:

> His Majesty is sorry you do not approve of the National Government: but it would have been well nigh impossible to govern the Country with an essentially Party Cabinet and had Asquith resigned the Opposition could not have carried on the Government with the present Parliament and a General Election was out of the question. The country will have to take a great pull at itself if it wishes to beat the Germans.[222]

Bonar Law similarly tried to reconcile her to the coalition with assurances that politics had not been forgotten in the name of war: 'you must not think that our old enemies are not playing the game.'[223] But she continued to refer to the coalition as two governments, deploring the sloth of wartime rule and its lack of cohesion. A quiet self-satisfaction was, therefore, evident in a letter to her grandson, Robin following Carson's resignation as Attorney General in Asquith's war cabinet in October 1915: 'I don't wonder Sir Edward Carson resigned. The two Governments seem so very slow in doing anything; I was always against their ever joining up'; 'I should resign if I had strong views one way and the Cabinet the other way…Cabinet homogeneity is what I have always been brought up to believe in'.[224]

Although the verve of the political partisan remained, Theresa was under considerable personal pressure. Through 1914 she went out with her spouse 'every day…shooting and walking, and we had many happy little days out together', but this was short-lived. Charles became seriously ill in January 1915 and was unable to write to his wife when she was in London, 'a thing he had never done in his life.'[225] Theresa nursed him at Wynyard until his death on 8 February 1915, recording that his last moments of life were 'too much for me to describe. I will only say that he held my hand for the nineteen hours and passed peacefully away at the end.'[226] Many tributes testified to Londonderry's loyalty and steadfastness, but found it impossible to write of him without mentioning the political import of his wife: 'the inestimable advantage of the co-operation of Lady Londonderry, one of the best informed and shrewdest women of her time in regard to political affairs'. Walter Long's tribute in the *Saturday Review* also highlighted Theresa's unrivalled brilliancy as a hostess and provided a classic example of the political significance of personal acquaintance, 'I remember one informal luncheon party such as probably no other hostess in London but Lady Londonderry could have brought together. Lord Lansdowne, Mr. Bonar Law, …Sir Edward Carson, Lord Curzon, the Earl of Derby and Mr. Chaplin…sat down to table at what was in no sense a political occasion.'[227] The *Northern Whig* referred to the new dowager as 'one of the most brilliant women of the present generation…her intellectual powers, wide knowledge of affairs, and passionate enthusiasm for the Union have made her a strong personality in the fight which Ulster has been waging against Home Rule'. But *Punch*'s tribute was both the most unexpected and the most exacting: 'he was encouraged and sustained by a power behind the domestic throne perhaps…more dominant than its occupant. *Cherchez la femme*. Londonderry House became the spring and centre of an influence that had considerable effect upon political events during more than a quarter of a century.'[228]

Theresa's decision to be known as the Dowager Lady Londonderry, against the growing Edwardian trend for dowagers to place their Christian names in front of their title, also attracted considerable press coverage in March 1915. Her reversion to the Victorian norm and outright, and public, rejection of the cognomen 'Theresa Lady Londonderry' did not surprise her compeers as 'few have such a horror as she of any of the attributes of advancing years.'[229] But, the changes brought by widowhood were nothing short of dramatic. Theresa lost a husband 'whose praise and approval' she was 'always so proud of' and control of her salon.[230] Londonderry House, the anti-home rule bastion, now fell under her daughter-in-law, Edith's command. This made Theresa's successor as Tory hostess and Londonderry female figurehead palatably uncomfortable. Edith, attempting to console Theresa in 1915, also felt compelled to address their changed circumstances:

> My darling Mother…I do hope you are going on all right, and not feeling too utterly lonely and desolate. I know well what splendid courage you possess, and that you will pull through, but I also know what it will cost you. I feel it myself all the more, as not only have you and beloved Pa always treated me as if I was your own daughter, but I had come to regard all the homes in the light of a daughter too, and the shock is all the greater, when through circumstances over which one has no control one is forced to step into other people's shoes.

Edith coped with her new station by striving to perform her marital dues and assist her husband, but asking for Theresa's advice on the correct way to sign her name as 'the Marchioness Londonderry' revealed her youth and desire to please:

> I have avoided signing my name as yet, w[oul]d Pa have liked me to sign it as you do with the initial only? and do you sign cheques like this too? In fact is it

the correct way to sign for me, or will it make a worse muddle for you? Let me know what you think.[231]

And Theresa's behaviour, at times, verged on the territorial. Handing over control, especially of Londonderry House, was hugely difficult for her and accusations of impropriety, although largely unwarranted, greatly affected the new Lady Londonderry. Theresa, struggling to eat and sleep in April 1915, raged to Edith:

> you never told me that my rooms would be used or that anybody would go into them...I own it gives me a *great pang* to feel *my friends* are able to run in and out of L. house before three months are over without *one* thought for me or one who has gone. ...You say I do not read your letters; you do not read mine[.][232]

Little wonder that Edith was circumspect in warning her mother-in-law that alterations might be made to the houses:

> After 70 years, there might be slight changes in taste, and a room which is intended to be for the use of one particular individual much naturally reflect that person's individuality...I should never expect future generations not to have little individual things...I have only mentioned this to you now, so that your feelings will not be hurt in the future, if some of the things in the houses are changed - but this will not be for a long time[.]

Edith was also forced to defend herself against her mother-in-law's charge that an appropriate period of mourning had not been maintained and that informal meetings held at Londonderry House with Ronald MacNeill, Walter Long and John Cowans in 1915 had political purpose:

> You know yourself that a luncheon is an invaluable means of accomplishing certain matters, especially when you don't want them to appear formal...I don't look on them in any way as entertaining - Personally, I have only dined out once since February...and I have not lunched at all - and I am quite convinced, unless you put it into their heads, that your friends have never thought or...meant to be disloyal to you...Your things here all remain *untouched*[.][233]

Charley was sympathetic to his mother's drastic change in status, instructing his wife that, 'Any servant whose demeanour to my mother alters in any way' was to be given 'one month's notice and board [and] wages and sent off.' But he was also attuned to the pressure that Edith endured and although he branded the position of dowager as 'cruel' he encouraged his wife to 'take her place and I cannot ask you to go into the background for her.'[234] Theresa's friends also rallied. For some, like Bonar Law, it was a chance to return the support that she had provided him in widowhood and he was especially sensitive to her personal loss and changed rank: 'I can fully understand how much you must feel...being out of the political current which has always been a large part of your life.'[235] Others were more forceful, persuading the woman whose appetite for life was previously insatiable that there was still much to live for. Long, for example, sympathised with her lot, but he also encouraged her not to dwell on the past:

> You have nothing to blame yourself for and you did all that any human being could do - so don't let the idea obsess you…I know *all*…you had a very difficult part to play, how difficult nobody in the outer circle of your friends could tell and few in the inner circle realise. C. was a very dear fellow…but he was in some things very, very hard to work with…he did not ever ask for obedience, much less approval or help, he demanded first to be let to his own way, unheeded, uninterrupted, and let the consequences follow. You did all you could, and this was far, far more trial than most women could have attempted - so in regard to this matter be at rest. His last words, his last movements…were his message of reconciliation…you have every reason to be pleased and comforted by the manifestations of love, respect and gratitude you always worked for…you have got your reward…you are a practical as well as a very clever woman and will face the future bravely and fearlessly.[236]

Despite these efforts, Theresa struggled to cope. Three months after her husband's death she wrote to her old friend Edmund Gosse, confiding that she could not bear to read or write and was just managing 'to wander about' Wynyard. The very thought of London and 'the loneliness of a city' appalled her. Of all her friends, Gosse refused to let her wallow: 'Are you, still so young, still so full of splendid energy and resource, going to allow life to conquer you in this wretched way? As I write, I feel as if you had taken your destiny in both hands, and determined to overcome it. Don't let me think I am too sanguine.'[237] But the Countess of Warwick's assessment was the most accurate of all. To her, Theresa was 'the most brilliant political woman of my Victorian days' who 'shone with a political sagacity and understanding that carried her to the very border of actualism', but 'actuality was the one thing she would not face.'[238] This, however, was the very thing that she could not escape.

Theresa sadly packed her possessions at Londonderry House in May 1915, savouring the chance of returning for even a few days. But her sense of isolation was very apparent: 'It seems so curious to me to be in a back-water at such a crisis, and to honestly know nothing.'[239] Though she was pleased at the dynastic continuum of Charley succeeding his father, grandfather and great grandfather by heading the Durham Conservatives from 1915 and by his appointment as Lord Lieutenant of Down in the same year, she struggled to come to terms with her new life. Overseeing the establishment of hospitals at Londonderry House and Seaham Hall, providing hundreds of beds for military causalities during the war, gave her some focus and respite, but her political drive was undiminished. Now, with just three rooms on loan from her son at Seaham Hall and permission to stay at Wynyard when she wanted, she was effectively removed from the venues she had used for political purpose for over three decades. And, many, like Walter Long, missed her greatly:

Under your long and brilliant reign all these great Houses have been really happy "Homes"…I can't bear to think of any of them without your presence: they can never be the same again…you ever able, and always willing, to help as none other could or can. Many a mountain has been removed by a luncheon or dinner at L[ondonderr]y House…I wish you were in London, I should be so thankful to be able to come and see you and talk things over. It is always such a help to talk to someone who *understands* and *knows*.[240]

Theresa was not, however, completely cut from political society as a dowager; she saw Carson, Ronald MacNeill, Lord Zetland, Balfour, Sandars and Salisbury and continued to receive information from 'GC', her shorthand for George Curzon. Indeed, for a time in late 1915 and 1916, it looked a little like business as usual. Law showed her draft recruiting legislation but, with the proposal to register men and women aged 15-65, Theresa was less than impressed, 'I think it will fail. Personally, I have no idea of recruiting anybody if the Government will not make the unmarried men go.'[241] Midleton wrote to inform her that the Pensions Bill would be delayed and agreed to her suggestion to write a letter on this subject 'to stimulate their preparation of a new Bill' and Gwynne, the editor of the *Morning Post*, asked her for a report on the meeting held to oppose this legislation.[242] She was also seeking a post for her son-in-law, Lord Ilchester and turned to Law for assistance.[243] Events of 1916 also made the Irish question impossible to ignore. Theresa retained the presidency of the UWUC, but laboured to maintain the Unionist truce in the aftermath of the 1916 Easter rising. This event hardened her political convictions. The question of Nationalist disloyalty to crown and empire previously featured in both her public and private oratory and the rising served only to further entrench this belief. Theresa depicted the event itself as 'most blood-thirsty and horrible', but spent more time expounding its political implications: 'as we always said, there is no grey: you are either a Unionist white, or a Home Ruler black; constitutional Home Rulers do not exist'. She now declared Ireland had been misgoverned over the past nine years, believing that the rising should have heralded both the introduction of martial law and the death knell for home rule otherwise 'it is exactly like giving a child what it wants after it has been naughty.'[244]

Lunching at the Treasury in June 1916, she badgered Balfour who assured her Ireland had not been discussed at cabinet level and that 'He had joined the Coalition on the understanding that no party politics were to be brought in under any pretext whatever'. For the woman to whom party loyalty was a mainstay of her life, this neared contempt. Unlike Balfour, she was 'thinking of nothing but Ireland and 'the push'. …Politics as you may suppose makes me perfectly sick':

the real trouble about Ireland was that Asquith never consulted the Unionist Members of the Cabinet when they gave Lloyd George 'carte blanche' to settle the matter. They understood…that Lloyd George was only going to throw out 'feelers' - very stupid of them! Asquith also never showed them the reports of the Sinn Feiners, and the very bad state of Ireland. Asquith minimised this for Germany forgetting that he was by so doing preventing himself

from coping with the rebellion properly. ...What it will end in I don't
know.[245]

Despite this and her struggle to come to terms with her personal loss and altered status, post-rising and with partition again mooted, she worked hard to
maintain the truce whilst Unionists gradually converted to the partitionist cause:
Carson reluctantly advised the UUC to accept six-county exclusion in 1916 and
this body accepted this in principle for the first time in June 1917. But there was
still widespread concern that, in many instances, bordered on dissent. Lady Dufferin conveyed the strength of anti-partitionist sentiment to Theresa: 'Our
women are naturally much upset by the turn things have taken, and are longing to
be up and doing. Of course we all feel heartbroken over the proposed partition of
Ulster and are still hoping some better solution may come out of the melting
pot.'[246] Indeed, proposals to omit the three counties of Cavan, Donegal and
Monaghan from an 'Ulster' settlement roused a vocal minority of UWUC members to call for the implementation of schemes to assist the movement of women
and girls out of the excluded counties. Others were coming to a different conclusion, fearing that this could be a permanent arrangement or indicative of a wider
constitutional shift in the status of the six north-eastern counties, claiming that
the truce now made political nonsense. Calling on the 'always fearless' Theresa,
this minority suggested that by making a stand on the question of three-county
exclusion, she would be taking a 'place in history'.[247] But this was a distinctly difficult place for her as she strove to uphold the party truce without shattering the
unity of the organisation that she had done so much to maintain since 1911. The
full *modus operandi* of the council was not called into play with Richard Dawson
Bates, the UUC secretary, advising Theresa to resist any pressure to hold a meeting. She also consulted Carson and the UUC on the advisability of altering the
wording of the UWUC's constitution from stating that the organisation's 'sole'
object was the resistance of home rule to now become its 'chief' purpose. She
consequently succeeded in avoiding any charge of disloyalty at a time of international crisis, but enabled Unionist women to move beyond the strict confines of
opposing a home rule bill. Even those more forthright members of the council,
like Edith Wheeler and Edith Mercier Clements, welcomed the change. As the
latter wrote:

The proposed change is most admirable, I do not think it could be improved
upon, and it will leave room for any contingency which might arise in the
future. There is not a loophole for any abuse of the liberty thus given...I believe such changes as you suggest are essential for the revivifying of our
Council which lay dormant since 1914.[248]

Notwithstanding Carson's re-entry to the coalition ranks with his December
1916 appointment as First Lord of the Admiralty, Theresa still raged against the
government. That her earlier attachment to Bonar Law was ultimately motivated
by political expediency became clearer than ever as she found his continuance at
the Conservative helm simply 'maddening'. By comparison, her belief in Carson

remained undented; watching him address the Commons from the Ladies' Gallery she could come to only one conclusion:

> Carson was splendid. He looks such a gentleman when he speaks and ought
> to be sitting as Leader. He is highly nervous, but very strong, and he has got a
> terrible sentimental strain in him. He does not push his advantage when he
> has gained it; I am afraid were I a man, and got an advantage over anybody, I
> would…push my rapier in up to the hilt.
> Each of the Ministers appears to do exactly what he likes in his own department and there is no cohesion.[249]

During 1917-18, however, at least publicly, Theresa toned down her opposition to the coalition. As F. L. Silverman wrote on behalf of Lloyd George, 'The Prime Minister is glad to know that you are speaking for the Coalition'.[250] Political propriety is the only way to explain the variance between Theresa's public façade and private utterances. This time it was not the notion of working towards a greater good that overrode her real feelings, but an ambition closer to home: securing a position for her son, now the seventh Marquess of Londonderry. This was the last political challenge of Theresa's life. And possibly she was right to intervene. This was, after all, the man who declared in 1912, 'How I hate politics and politicians.'[251] Yet, indicative of the insecurity of the dowager's lot, she was uncharacteristically sheepish when informing Charley of her efforts to secure him a position, 'I hope I did not do wrong.'[252] That old allies rallied round this cause suggests that Theresa was still influential, but this was now based on personal friendship rather than political sway. In response to Charley's 1916 lament that he did not 'have any friends to push me', she was certainly calling in old favours; telling Lords Milner and Derby that a good post would bring her son home from the front. But placing a peer was becoming increasingly difficult and Bonar Law was right to be cautious:

> I know you must have a feeling that with all the changes which have been
> made it ought to now be possible to do what you wish. If Londonderry had
> been in the House of Commons it could have been done but in the House of
> Lords it really was impossible. …Carson was really anxious to help but we
> could not do it. At most he would have got a Court appointment of the minor sort but I know for you and indeed I was certain about you telling me
> that we need not come back for that.[253]

Commons' Chief Whip, Lord Edmund Talbot also endeavoured to place Charley, but advised Theresa that an appointment to the Privy Council was simply 'out of the question' due her son's inexperience, the timing of her request and the demands for this posting. Indeed, Talbot warned that such a position would ruin Charley's political future by being interpreted as a 'way of paying him off'. Appointing him to the Irish convention seemed, to Talbot, a more realistic appointment and one that might open opportunities.[254] Theresa took this advice and pushed her son in the convention's direction, not because she believed Ireland's ills might be solved by its deliberations, but because it might further his political career. Charley was subsequently elected as an Ulster member of the hundred-strong convention which included several Londonderry allies, like UUC secretary, Dawson Bates, southern Unionist leader, Midleton and Archbishop Crozier of Armagh who all kept Theresa informed of the, supposedly, confidential proceedings. This assemblage was both ill-fated and unrepresentative and Theresa was not alone in castigating it a 'holy muddle'. She was also straining to keep hold of the UWUC, telling its members, 'I have consulted many of our friends and find that the great thing at the moment is to keep absolutely quiet, not have a meeting, write a letter or anything.'[255]

Charley's constructive input to the convention's deliberations was remarked upon, but initially, at least, he was overly optimistic of the odds for agreement and ultimately this was a wrong reading of the situation:

The Sinn Fein movement is on the wane so long as the Brit[ish] Gove-[rnmen]t do nothing foolish but you can never trust them.
The Convention is hardly nearer a solution of the problem and I doubt if it will go over Christmas but strange things always happen in Ireland.[256]

Theresa's retelling of the proceedings was more pragmatic:

I do not believe in it on the principle of oil and vinegar really mixing and the Ulster people are the good children and have always been loyal...whereas the South and West have always been disloyal, one must hope that something will come of it. ...It will only cost the country an enormous sum of money and do no good.

Regardless of her dislike, she felt isolated by her exclusion: 'It seems so curious to me not to be mixed up in the Convention when I have devoted my life to it for 32 years'.[257] Craig sympathised, but was unable to provide her with any concrete information, '[I] am quite honest in saying that there is really nothing definite to go upon as regards Ulster'.[258] Midleton, though despairing that Theresa's 'views about Irish politics are so strong', did not doubt 'the mass of Ireland will become Sinn Fein unless a strong counter movement is...made...the British Govt. have not the courage if they have the heart, to sit down and govern for 5 years.'[259] But it was the Archbishop of Armagh who sounded the death knell for negotiation: 'Here we are very near breaking point and with Lloyd George's threat that if we don't settle the [Irish] Question Parliament will do so.'[260] And, with the close of the convention Theresa remarked 'as everyone expected, it had ended in smoke. Nobody knows what the Government is going to do. Some people seem to think the Government are now going to give Home Rule on the federal principle. Ulster would then have a Parliament of her own.'[261] It spoke volumes that she made no further comment on the latter proposition.

Both Law and Carson pledged to continue to assess the political situation for Charley, but the former was becoming increasingly reticent, telling Theresa, 'if you really think it is of any value I shall gladly take it up with the Whips the next time - if there is a next time for the present govt.'[262] Curzon offered Charley a Whip in 1918. This was refused, upsetting its giver, but arousing more sympathy from men like Derby who opined to Theresa, 'it is a sinecure of the worst type and as you say simply a muzzle'.[263] Long also submitted Charley's name for the post of Irish Lord Lieutenant to Lloyd George in 1918 but to no avail.[264] That these men were working on Theresa's behalf, coupled with the requests that she received to address Conservative meetings in the north of England in the run up to the 1918 election, suggest that she was not a completely spent political force. Indeed, a letter from Bonar Law that was passed to her via Arthur Balfour in 1918 on that grounds that it was not marked private and would give her 'a halo of maternal satisfaction' showed a 'keen anxiety' to place her son: 'we are all anxious to find something for him and the first vacancy there is of any kind for which a Peer is suitable, will, I hope, be of such as kind as to make it possible to offer it to him.'[265] Charley was finally appointed to an advisory committee for the Lord Lieutenant but his mother remained dissatisfied:

> I don't quite know what is going to happen about my Charley now. For my-self, I think, it is much better for a man with any talents to be in a public of-fice than to be kicking his heels trying to look after his own affairs…Charley seems very sad about his own career and everything in general. I think he lacks confidence in himself…[he] is in a very difficult position, because he cannot take office under the Government, as long as there is any question of proceeding with the Home Rule bill. …He said the Government had alter-nately cajoled and dragooned Ireland, and ought now to let her take her place in the Empire, and undertake conscription, and everything else in the same way as Britain.

Nor was she willing to wait for the war's cessation. In an act of desperation, she seriously considered Charley returning to the Commons as a tactic to secure of-fice, travelling to Stockton in August 1918 to assess his electoral chances at first hand and even pledging to abandon party:

> I find the candidate at Stockton, is not considered a Coalition candidate, but is supposed to be an Asquithian. The great point if you have an election, is to have a "Win the War candidate". I hope we shall be able to do so and not bring in politics. The Radicals are consolidating all the time while the Union-ists as usual, are letting their opportunity slip by.[266]

Throughout the war, Theresa always maintained that the old party system would be renewed with vigour and by April 1918, she declared 'I feel terribly like Cassandra, for nearly everything I said would come to pass, has come to pass.' A few months later, Lloyd George's proclamation that he was a Liberal and a Home Ruler, therefore, came as no surprise to her. She was disillusioned, however, by both her son's and Carson's positions; the former still in pursuit of promotion and the latter overlooked for the Lord Chancellorship, 'it shows that if one ever has any political principles, as he had about Ulster, he is robbed as his right.' But this time she did not, as might have been expected, blame the coalition. Rather it was Carson's lack of ambition: 'Of course if he had done as I wanted him to when Bonar Law undertook the leadership he would now be Prime Minister I expect…He does not push his advantage when he has gained it'.[267] That another friend, the 'brilliant, and self made' F. E. Smith was appointed Chancellor offered her scant consolation. Although Long and Law continued to work in her interest, unsuccessfully venturing to place Charley as Under-Secretary for War in lieu of Lord Peel, and Curzon tried to secure him the position of Civil Lord in the Admiralty, placement instead came from the unlikely source of Winston Churchill whom Theresa was forced to admit was 'kind when it suits him':

> and was naturally very pleased to get a powerful relation as a henchman, offered him the post to answer for the House of Lords and Air Ministry. I am very pleased Charley has gone into Office for I feel quite certain that if a man is not put into harness he might degenerate. …In the political game, if one goes straight, it is possible to help the country and get influence.[268]

Although she dismissed the new government of January 1919 as nothing but a re-shuffle, her self-interest was again to the fore:

> Of course, I am very cross about Charley not having an undersecretaryship. I shall always think that Walter Long ought to have insisted upon having him for his undersecretary two years ago. As it is…he [Charley] has got nothing out of it. If he had stayed at home with a cushy job he would have done far better. …It is sickening. The Coalition Unionists number over 300, and therefore should be able to insist on getting anybody they like. I think they are like a set of sparrows, when Lloyd George comes along like a cobra. It is really very annoying.[269]

This vexation was further expressed in a letter to Law:

> I am bitterly disappointed that a place has not been found for Lord Londonderry in the new Government. All his contemporaries in the House of Commons have got places and honours…I honestly think (you know I am nothing if not honest) that with the large proportion of Coalition Unionists, it should have been *demanded* by the Prime Minister. I think, at least, he should have has an undersecretaryship in the Lords, Admiralty or Colonies or War.
>
> I will not go back to past considerations, but I think my own record, had I been a man, should have helped, but being a woman and requiring nothing, I think my work and his father's, added to his own achievements…ought to have produced something.
>
> I hope you will forgive this letter. I expect you have received many similar, as everyone thinks their own geese, swans!
>
> I view with dread the Unionist Party not exacting from the Prime Minister the price of their support. …I am coming up to London shortly and shall

hope to see you. I have seen very little of you during the war, but I have always looked upon our friendship as a very pleasant incident of my life.[270]

Her faith in the personal basis of politics was badly shaken and this was reinforced by two men she previously trusted drifting away from a strong Unionist position. For Walter Long unionism was always one of a number of interests and, despite his earlier opposition, he was moving toward federalism as Ireland's solution by 1917. In the next year he declined post of Irish Chief Secretary, but accepted the chair of the committee with responsibility for drafting of the Home Rule Bill which would, in time, become the Government of Ireland Act of 1920. Theresa was confounded:

It is an astonishing thing that it should be so. I have not had a letter from him since so I presume he knows what I think about it…I have seen Sir Edward Carson and for the life of me I cannot understand why the Unionist Party have not kicked the Government out, as we have the power to do it at any moment. I do not think we have blackmailed them sufficiently.

F. E. Smith's commitment to the Unionist cause also, as Carson earlier suspected, ebbed. Smith did not perceive the Ulster question as a block to home rule and was one of the first to support partition, but Theresa did not live long enough to witness his name, as Lord Chancellor, on the Anglo-Irish Treaty of 1921.

The last years of Theresa's life were undeniably sad. As she expressed simply yet mournfully, it gave her 'a terrible pang to see someone else in my place'. Now she was a visitor to the family homes and, even with Sandars' help, struggled to find a suitable London house: 'I tried to look at a house in London, but every house seemed to me like a pigsty. Birdie, Aline and Edith did everything that was possible to make things easy for me, but there are some things that no one can help in.'[271] She occasionally stayed at her former London home and, although this was potentially difficult for her daughter-in-law who now bore the Marchioness of Londonderry title, Theresa was always treated sensitively. On such occasions a former sense of place pervaded with the new Lady Londonderry giving up her room for Theresa and inviting Carson and Leo Amery to visit. For this Theresa was grateful: 'Edith is really too unselfish towards me, but I think you both know how deeply I appreciate it.' But the support was not only emotional. The new Marquess subsidised his mother financially and managed her monetary affairs as she acknowledged, 'hitherto I have never had any of my own to manage.' Charley also took Lumley Castle, situated ten miles from Seaham, for her in 1917. Theresa was wont to portray herself as outcast and poverty stricken, as Charley remarked, 'You are under the impression that you are a pauper. I wish I could get this idea out of your mind'.[272] But she continued to greatly exaggerate her fate; her £10,000 per year is approximate to £70,000 in today's monetary value.[273]

Theresa also berated herself for being indolent in widowhood but, in reality, she was adjusting to the dowager's dilemma. She eschewed parliament, unable to face attending the 1917 opening of parliament and often avoiding the debates. As she informed her son:

> I did not go to the Debate yesterday as really politics, without Father and you in them, and not really being able to do anything (though I still take the deepest interest) are not really congenial to listen to only...I do not care for London: being at L. House and keeping open house, with a Cabinet Minister as a husband, or in a Shadow Cabinet, is very different from living by oneself when one is a hundred with no particular object after devoting a whole life to one family and two countries.[274]

Widowhood also prompted a permanent relocation to London in 1917, a move which did not delight all. As the young Ruby Carson carped, Theresa could only talk of 'how she has nothing left to live for...we shall have no peace now she is settled in London. ...She really is a horrible old woman and everyone is fighting shy of her. She will soon lose all her friends.'[275] However, as Carson's oldest and most unfailing ally, Theresa simply had to be tolerated.

Theresa continued to see old friends and party stalwarts such as Carson, Bonar Law, Balfour, Hicks-Beach (now Lord St. Aldwyn), the Selbournes, Lords Talbot and Curzon as well as the royals, with the queen visiting her at her newly rented abode, Lady Caledon's house at 5 Carlton House Terrace in 1917 and requesting, 'Please do not ask anyone to meet us as we should rather have a quiet talk with you alone.'[276] But here too change was apparent. Attempting to advise the king on the appointment of a Lord Lieutenant for Sussex, Theresa was rebuffed, 'he said he did not know anything about it. ...He does not seem to take any part in the Gov.' She subsequently became increasingly despondent:[277]

> London is very different to me now that I am not, so to speak[,] really mixed up in Politics...Verily, being left by one's self and cut off from one's interest, if one cares for public affairs and interests is very hard, but...there is not much room for two people of the same name to act independently.

She was also lonely and isolated, in want of 'dove to send out of the ark to bring me some news'; 'With a husband you discuss everything with him but with a son, though you do so when you meet, you cannot keep telephoning to know his point of view.'[278] But the displacement, both personal and political, caused by a husband's death was not peculiar to Theresa Londonderry: Mrs. Gladstone and the Duchess of Manchester's years of widowhood were similarly testing.

Widowhood did provide Theresa with time for reflection and, encouraged by Edmund Gosse who had been pushing her toward this end from 1913, she began to write her memoirs shortly after Charles' death. But in many ways this contemplation was bitter sweet. Surveying her voluminous collection of letters proved 'more interesting than I thought it would be', but served as a reminder of how much had changed: 'It is connected with most of the great movements of the time.'[279] Even with a permanent London base she felt 'alone in a crowd...Passing the Carlton Club gave me a pang I cannot describe'; 'of course it is a great difference, but my friends all played up splendidly. I met them all, but being in London with nothing political going on - I mean party Politics - and no society except telephoning for someone to come and see one, is very lonely to me indeed.' She spent a lot of her time alone which 'when one is really terribly unhappy' she believed was 'much better...though most painful'.[280]

The London move did not signify an end to her interest in Ulster, unionism or the careers of those she favoured. Indeed, 1918 saw her backing partition, but solely to 'black-mail the Government. It would be a means of getting what we want, and I do not see why we should not have it.'[281] Theresa believed that a more consistent approach towards Ireland was needed akin to that adopted by the Unionist government of 1886-92. She oft reminded her correspondents of its merits and also urged a heightened state of organisation in the Unionist Party to capture the new female vote following the partial enfranchisement of women in 1918. Indeed, faced with the reality of women's votes, she took steps to mobilise her own organisation, the UWUC, expressing the belief that the Unionist Party was:

> very supine about looking after the women. We have had no candidates, no agents, no meetings called. A great many women know nothing of the science of politics, and has [sic] no idea of why [we] should vote, or who for. I am going to speak at a Political Meeting on Monday evening, on the subject and I hope I shall do some good.[282]

Now the avowed anti-suffragist turned her attention to the urgent need to instruct women voters on the significance and mechanics of the ballot. But there was no question of Theresa standing for election, even with her granddaughter, Maureen's lament, 'Why aren't you standing? I have no doubt that once in the "House" you would become Primeminister [sic] - before you'd finished!'[283] Instead, taking constituencies as a basis for local Unionist organisation, she advocated the establishment of parish and borough registration committees 'to rouse interest...and to make sure that when the day of election comes, every women's vote will be polled in the same way as a man's would be.'[284] Carson added his weight to these ends, writing to Theresa: 'I hope you will bear in mind how necessary it is that the women should have their full share in the organisation in Ulster. I did my best when I was over to lay the foundation of this policy.'[285] James Craig also contacted her, seeking information on the future direction of the women's council and highlighting the fact that speakers might need to be sent to England and Scotland: 'In such events the men's Associations will provide the necessary up-to-date literature; it does not take long to prepare. ...Speakers and canvassers will not be hard to find; all old arrangements have been greatly strengthened by the happenings during the war.' But Craig did not want home rule to loom large in the election campaign, 'To me it is simply unthinkable that a general election could be fought on anything but the *War!* To pledge the country into an acute Home Rule controversy would be the kind of madness the P.M. is not capable of!'[286]

Her published address of the same year also aired the possibility of fusing the male and female Unionist associations or continuing in their respective bodies but co-joined by one ruling executive 'on which women shall have proper representation.'[287] This issue was previously discussed in 1916 when Theresa successfully proposed that the council should continue as a separate organisation. But in light of the 1918 electoral changes she was now persuaded to push for formal recognition of, and representation for, the UWUC within the ranks of the UUC. Edith Wheeler, one of the most dedicated female workers, brought this to Theresa's attention in a lengthy letter of June 1918:

> I do not think you quite realise how...the whole Council have been entirely ignored...I ask for a distinct recognition of the "UWUC"...We should have a certain number of women on the "U.C." [Unionist Council] and they should be elected by our "U.W.U.C." and its associations. ...We do not ask for nor desire our full representation [of] 40 per cent - but surely we might have 10 or 12 per cent and so have some women on which to bring up the questions on which we are, in my opinion, just as well able to judge as men. I was never a suffragette![288]

Theresa passed this letter to Carson and the issue was also considered by Dawson Bates, the UUC secretary. The latter alleged that Wheeler's demands were prompted by 'mischief' on the part of a Miss Roe, a 'representative of Mrs. Pankhurst...[who] has been over in Ireland...the object...is to get control of the Ulster women, ostensibly for the purpose of the maintenance of the Union, but really for their own political ends', but whatever, or whoever, initiated this discontent, Theresa believed disregarding it would be politically dangerous.[289] So, bolstered by enfranchisement, the women's organisation took the unanimous decision to make an outright bid for formal UUC representation, like that enjoyed by the Orange Order and Unionist Clubs, in September 1918. Steered by Theresa and with Carson now on side, they were successful.

Yet, in reality, Theresa had run the UWUC long distance from 1917 and some members began to question her presidency, calling on her to attend meetings from the middle of 1918. This caused some consternation. As Hariot, Lady Dufferin and Ava expressed in a confidential letter to Carson, Theresa was 'thought to be out of touch with our affairs now...I would like to spare her the mortification of not being re-elected...resignation secures the only way to avail it'.[290] Theresa was also becoming frustrated with the council and returning from chairing a UWUC meeting in Belfast in September 1918 she noted:

> It is astonishing how very stupid women are in a body. They are told in April to get all the Unionist women on to the [electoral] register and to endeavour to work with the Mens' Associations but...they kept asking the most stupid questions. However I think we have settled them to work earnestly for the Union now.[291]

Nothing in her correspondence reveals whether the decision to relinquish the presidency in January 1919 was voluntary. Publicly she blamed widowhood for her departure and, overshadowed by 'deep regret' and 'great sorrow', her last letter to the organisation that she had led through six years of political crisis both reminisced and forebode:

> I may say with truth that there was never a prouder moment in my life than that which I was elected as President of such an influential body...we were the largest number of women to band ourselves together for political work. ...Ulster has fought her corner well, and I trust it will be long before any serious attempt will be made to separate England and Ireland. We banded ourselves together to see how we might best organise ourselves to impress our fellow-countrymen in England to the fact that Ulster will not consent to the tearing asunder of this country.

Of partition she wrongly determined, 'the North east corner will never consent to such a severance', claiming that Unionist success could be measured by the fact that the union was still intact. But her alarm at the current political situation was discernible:

> Nationalist members manoeuvred to get an English Government entirely dependent on their votes...Now what about the 73 Sinn Fein members (who boast that they are Separatists and Republicans)...returned to the House of Commons. They have...taken off the gloves the Nationalists wore from 1886 to the present time. Both Political Parties in England have lavished money upon Ireland in the hopes that she would be contented. They disestablished the Church of Ireland to please her, bought the Landlords out to please her, and gave her far more money than she returns in taxation. ...I depreciate the opening of old sores, but...We can all remember how the south and west of Ireland conducted themselves during the war, and I trust England will never forget it[.]

In reply, the UWUC acknowledged her 'constant and unflagging interest in the affairs of the Council, and by her untiring energy has largely promoted its welfare and the success of its work. Her ability and wide political experience have proved of inestimable value.'[292] Some of the most prominent female Unionists, like Edith Wheeler, privately wrote to her to record their sorrow: 'a leader is a rare thing. You certainly led us as long as you could be with us. Perhaps the fact that you led us so wonderfully during the year before the war, made everything seem so hopeless and dead when you were not there.'[293] Carson and Gosse were equally saddened by the news. Old favours were called in from Geoffrey Dawson, *The Times'* editor who 'arranged for all the space I could manage in these crowded days' to cover her resignation.[294] But the editor of the *Spectator* declined to print a copy of her farewell speech and for Theresa this more independent approach to news-gathering was another indication that times were changing: 'They do not put in what you say, and unless one goes to each separate newspaper office and states particularly what one wants putting in, the reporter chooses what he likes, and what he likes is usually the wrong thing.'[295]

Although Theresa pledged to the UWUC to 'always help forward our cause with my voice…and now also with my vote', fate intervened. Unlike previous years, Theresa attended the opening of parliament in February 1919 and delighted in seeing her son on the front bench with Lord Peel and F. E. Smith. The one regret, which she felt 'more that I can say', was Carson's absence:

> He is troubled with scruples, which I respect as I have them myself about Ulster, and he also imagines himself ill. I think marrying a woman 30 years younger than himself and not too clever a one at that, has interfered very much with what he ought to have done, which was to lead the Conservative Party.

In the same month, she began to entertain again, but only on a small, and entirely private, scale, with parties composed mainly of family and close friends, like the Desboroughs, Smith and Long.

Despite these outward signs of a return to form, from 1912 Theresa had been troubled by heart problems that caused breathlessness and she complained of 'a flabby heart' and bronchitis from early 1919.[296] She died three weeks later, on 15 March, aged sixty-two, from pleurisy following a bout of influenza and pneumonia at Carlton House Terrace, her London base since 1917.[297] That her passing was unexpected is best illustrated by her invitation of the previous week issued to her old friend, Edmund Gosse to dine at Lumley. Gosse's hand-written addendum to this invitation from the woman he regarded as 'the most precious and the most loyal of friends' reads, 'This was Lady Londonderry's last letter: she was taken ill on the same night'.[298] Her funeral was held at Wynyard on 20 March 1919 and, with a simultaneous memorial service in London, the *grande dame* of unionism was gone.

'To the last a great political leader.'[299]

Many mourned Theresa's passing. Even Ruby Carson, who always found her overbearing, recorded in her diary, 'I am sure we shall really all miss her very much.'[300] Yet in remembrance some overstated Theresa's importance, claiming she ruled 'England and statesmen used to quail before her.'[301] But she was certainly a clever and driven woman with considerable political acumen, unrivalled as a political hostess and leader of society. As the *Evening News* noted posthumously, 'to have it known that one was on terms of personal friendship with Lady Londonderry was a passport throughout Society.'[302]

The fight against home rule coincided with all of her adult life and her dedication to the Unionist cause remained undiminished: 'I have worked as hard as any woman could do, for the preservation of the Union…ever since I first took part in public life, 44 years ago.'[303] Her support bolstered the Unionist Party from the 1880s onwards, winning it both respect and influential benefactors and she was undoubtedly a party asset:

few things were hidden from her, and her extraordinary capacity for assessing character and for summing up men served her political party well on many occasions...[directing] her cool head but ardent nature into the cause of Ulster of which she became one of the chief pillars, and in the critical spring of 1914 Mount Stewart became almost the headquarters of the cause.[304]

She was no less effective as a patron. Those she supported in their youth, such as Smith and Sandars, were not reticent about paying tribute to her even whilst she lived. To the former she was 'an old friend and have always been a very kind and indulgent one to me' and the latter agreed: 'No one could have been kinder or more sympathetic or more uniform in friendship'.[305] For Long, so often entertained at Mount Stewart and Wynyard, the Londonderrys were 'the kindest and best of friends...They both left is far too soon'.[306] Her support of Carson, however, brought the most political and personal reward for both parties: 'When Sir Edward Carson raised the banner in Ulster he had no more fervent supporter than Lady Londonderry, who worked untiringly, used all her political influence, and even spoke on platforms on his behalf.' They shared a belief that apathy on the part of the British electorate posed a major threat to the Unionist cause and consequently much of her time, and his, was devoted to countering this indifference. This relationship also assured her of support and advice and this was a major succour to the unity of unionism, especially following the inauguration of the UWUC in 1911.

As 'the name of the Dowager Marchioness was...a household word', Theresa helped to popularise the UWUC during the early stages of its development and propel it into mainland Britain.[307] Paying respect to her, the council freely admitted that her influence 'amongst the Leaders of the Unionist Party in England, and her unceasing efforts' enabled them 'to obtain so many openings in Great Britain for its workers'.[308] Theresa was rarely at rest and even in the sadness of widowhood, there were 'quantities of plans seething' in her brain.[309] From 1915, however, she was effectively denied the platform from which to put these into action and she died before Unionists fully adjusted to partition and the idea of a parliament of their own.

Like the third Marchioness, Theresa's love of grandeur never left her. Some contemporaries labelled her profile the proudest they had ever seen and she liked John Singer Sargent's portrait, commissioned by her as a birthday present for her husband in 1912, again refuting the idea of a marriage lost, better than any other painting or photograph because it truly captured her hauteur. She also loved to quote her old friend, Hicks-Beach's spiky congratulations on the work, telling her she was 'very lucky to be so well done so late in the day.' Indeed, Theresa was well able to laugh at herself, once mistaken for her daughter-in-law while canvassing in Maidstone, she blamed her 'Flower Hat of the Party colours and a thickish veil I was wearing.'[310]

Birth, upbringing and personality ultimately conspired to make Theresa a great political hostess and confidante. A decade after her death, E. F. Benson included her alongside the Duchess of Devonshire and Lady Ripon, as the epitome of the Victorian great lady: 'she always wanted to manage everything for everybody...

She was always very conscious of herself…and she continually remembered who she was: you might say that she impersonated herself…with realism and gusto.'[311] Later still she inspired Vita Sackville-West's character Lady Sylvia Roehampton in her novel, *The Edwardians* that caused consternation amongst the very society it depicted when published in 1930. In its pages, fiction partially mirrored fact, as Lady Roehampton 'enjoyed all the assurance of a beautiful woman, she was always able to impose her own wishes on her audience…with a perfect grasp on life, untroubled, shrewd, mature, secret, betraying her real self to none. …She was charming, dangerous' and one of 'a very small band of the initiated.'[312]

Although an avowed opponent of radicalism and reform, Theresa was in many ways a pioneer. More party based than many of her contemporaries, she sought to win preferment for her family, her protégés and her politics. She also became a quick-witted canvasser: once when soliciting votes from a butcher's wife who claimed, 'I'm sorry mum…but we're in trade, so me husband doesn't care to mix in politics', she replied, 'But my husband is also in trade…He sells coal.'[313] She developed into a fluent and, at times, pointed platform speaker. She was a key element, therefore, in promoting popular unionism and conservatism and led the first generation of aristocratic women beyond the private realm of hostess and confidante and onto a public platform. Such duality led upper-class women to the height of their political power. But this was a position that needed to be carefully managed. As in Frances Anne's era, the indirect influence exercised by aristocratic women aroused little comment, complementary or otherwise. By comparison, adopting a more public persona could be socially compromising. And the political world was fluid. Soon patronage and endorsement from high society would be outmoded forms of preferment and, in many ways, Theresa's last years, when her position was so radically altered by her dowager status, saw her 'fighting single-handed and alone…against impossible odds, striving to maintain an empire that was already lost'.[314]

3

The last salon: Edith, seventh Marchioness of Londonderry's 'Ark'

Theresa's successor to the Lady Londonderry title remained within the fusion of public and private politics that emerged in the late nineteenth and early twentieth centuries. Edith, seventh Marchioness of Londonderry, as the daughter of Lady Florence Sutherland Levenson Gower, the eldest daughter of Britain's largest landowner, the third Duke of Sutherland, and Sir Henry Chaplin, the Tory MP commonly known as the 'Squire', possessed a considerable political pedigree. Like her predecessor, Edith's father, who held the cabinet posts of First President of the Board of Agriculture and President of the Local Government Board, inspired her political interest from an early age. His influence was especially puissant as he was widowed in 1881 shortly after his wife gave birth to their second daughter and before Edith reached the age of three.[1] He shared details of his public life with his children to such an extent that they 'grew up to think of politics as second only to hunting' but, as the eldest child, Edith benefited most.[2] Aged ten, she drove voters to the poll in her pony carriage, knew of her aunt's Primrose League habitation and was always encouraged to speak her mind. Indeed, her father demanded 'With you, having your masculine mind and... intelligence...be prepared to give me your opinion.' She was soon mature beyond her years, a trait her father commented on when she was aged fifteen, 'I feel that I can talk and write to you as if you were already a little woman.'[3] She remembered him as affectionate and entertaining and through him met numerous leading politicians, but she realised that politics was his divining light: 'The House of Commons was really his eldest child'.[4] Consequently, her aunt and uncle, the fourth Duke and Duchess of Sutherland, effectively raised her and her two siblings and their childhood was spent largely between their late mother's former home, Dunrobin Castle in Sutherland and Stafford House in London.[5]

In tangent with both Frances Anne and Theresa, Edith had a family precursor of female political activism to follow: Elizabeth, Countess of Sutherland had both command of the largest landed estates in Scotland and 'an excellent working knowledge of the political agronomy of the nation' on her majority in 1787; Harriet, second Duchess of Sutherland was an 1850s confidante to Liberal leader

Gladstone and in her lifetime Stafford House earned a reputation for reform politics.[6] And, under the tutelage of Edith's aunt, Millicent, the fourth Duchess, Stafford stood alongside Derby, Norfolk, Devonshire and Bridgewater as a great London mansion. The duchess 'had the gift of bringing all sorts of people together': the royals; visiting diplomats and society favourites, 'You met or saw at Stafford House everyone you ever heard of or hoped to meet, and her parties became the centre of a group of people in walks of life.'[7] Unlike her husband, however, the duchess was pro-Liberal and although Stafford House would also open its doors to host meetings on subjects that the duke held dear, most notably tariff reform, this was not a political salon in the mould of Londonderry House.

Edith was presented to Queen Victoria at a drawing room at the start of the 1897 season and came out at a fancy dress ball at Devonshire House in the same year. Here Theresa Londonderry was resplendent as Maria Theresa, Empress of Austria and Queen of Hungary and her son, Edith's future husband, Charley was also in attendance. Potential partners for the future Marquess of Londonderry were already being carefully screened. Indeed, 'when he contemplated wedlock he had met only six or seven possible girls. These young ladies had been purposely placed next to him at dinner because they were by birth and upbringing qualified to entertain as a great political hostess should.'[8] Theresa was a long-standing and close friend of Harry Chaplin and Edith was therefore welcomed as a choice of bride. Theresa and Harry were also related by marriage: his brother, Edward had married Theresa's sister, Guendolin. The union between Edith and Charley was, however, postponed until November 1898 due to Theresa's son, Reginald's failing health. Without a London house of their own, Edith and Charley lived at Londonderry House and the first of their five children was born in 1900.[9] Any drawbacks to such an arrangement were compensated, in Edith's view, by the 'opportunities we had for meeting everyone from London or from the continent at Londonderry House':

> My mother-in-law's friends and acquaintances ranged from crowned heads and prime ministers to poets and sculptors and men of letters. She often sent for me to have tea with her in the drawing room, but we never went there unless there was a message from her to say she wanted to see us.[10]

So, although a formality reigned at Londonderry House, Edith was essentially being groomed for futurity and familiarised with the personnel and practices of political society.

Edith, however, lacked the hauteur of both Frances Anne and Theresa and was, at times, insecure. Although she described herself in the 1930s as 'light-hearted and by nature inclined to be sceptical...fairly shrewd, and...born with a temperament that could always laugh with anyone, or at anything - which is, I think, one of the secrets of a happy life', she did not shy away from the unconventional.[11] This trait took physical form in the green snake she had tattooed winding around her leg from her ankle upwards when she was in Japan with Charley in 1903.[12] Furthermore, as a young woman she did not adopt her father's conservatism or shadow the Londonderrys' Tory and Unionist tenets. Instead it was women's suffrage an... reform that excited her. Her ardent support for suffrage certainly went against the aristocratic grain, bringing her into direct combat with her father as well as Theresa, who was an active member of the anti-suffragist movement. Edith also only managed to partially convert her husband to the righteousness of the women's cause. Her membership and public addresses on behalf of Millicent Fawcett's National Union of Women's Suffrage Societies (NUWSS) placed her firmly on the lawful side of the campaign, but even here she was an aristocratic oddity, ranking alongside Ladies Fingall and Castletown as Anglo-Irish suffragists who 'believed we should gain our ends through constitutional efforts, by speaking and writing and using such influences as we had'.[13] Edith's enthusiasm for suffrage was such that it forced her to overcome the reluctance as a public orator that was apparent in her refusal to address electoral meetings at Maidstone in support of her husband in 1905. That she raised the controversial issue of votes for women at a Conservative and Unionist Women's Association meeting in 1909 similarly reveals her determination. Some of her suffrage pamphlets, letters and articles also touched on the indirect way that disenfranchised women were forced to exert influence, comments undoubtedly inspired by her own position. As her first pamphlet of February 1909 inferred:

Is it to be wondered at, that those women naturally clever, and with woman's great adaptive quality, have had, and continually do stoop to manoeuvre, to obtain indirectly what they cannot obtain in an open manner?…How often do we hear that "so and so" owes his position politically to a great extent through the agency of a clever wife; and we know that the essential feature of her cleverness consists in disguising its existence from her husband, and only so by doing can she obtain what she is striving for, either for him or for herself.

We all admire an example such as thus, but surely we may deplore a position where abilities are employed in such an apologetic manner, and that it should be considered so derogatory, either for the man to seek political inspiration for his wife, or for the woman to acknowledge that she has any interests at all outside the hearth and home; such an attitude is neither worthy of the man, nor fair to the woman, it is a false position for either sex.[14]

In an attempt to rid women's politicking of its apologetics, Edith served with the Duchesses of Marlborough, Sutherland and Westminster and Mrs. Bernard Shaw on the council of the London-based Women's Municipal Party striving to place non-party women on local government bodies to promote female and child welfare. She also publicly refuted F. E. Smith's anti-suffrage comments, regardless of the fact that he was championed by her mother-in-law, and rallied against both Violet Markham's suggestion that women did not need the parliamentary franchise as they were in possession of a municipal vote as well as acclaimed scientist, Sir Almroth Wright's exposition that women were biologically unsuited to this responsibility:

surely it is of a minority that Sir Almoth is speaking when he refers to the grave disorders that are attendant on the sex, as if it were the rule and not the exception. Were this not the case, very few among the poorer women would be capable of being not only wives, but housekeepers, managers and holders of the purse, in addition to [attending to] the cares of the family. In actual fact, they are the householders…his remarks apply also in regard to the mental state of the other sex. How else are we to account for the frequent mention in our daily papers of terrible crimes, under lurid headings, such as…'Husband Murders Wife and Family'…Are not these persons suffering from some mental derangement, and without any of the 'physiological emergencies' which Sir Almroth thinks lie behind all similar actions relating to women?[15]

It was little wonder that Theresa decried her daughter-in-law as 'a young hound running riot'.[16] Although in the early days of her marriage unionism was certainly of secondary interest to Edith, the involvement of an unprecedented number of women in the anti-home rule campaign, spearheaded by her mother-in-law, provided a pragmatic argument against those, including Theresa, who believed that women were naturally predetermined not to vote. Indeed, in Edith's estimation, 'women can organise and become very efficient; we have seen a concrete case over in Ireland'.[17]

Theresa not only had reason to be concerned by her daughter-in-law's activities. Her son was also something of a disinclined politician. Always restless by nature, he declared himself 'hopeless and wherever I am I shall want to be somewhere else'. Charley was certainly under family pressure to abandon the army in order to forge a political name from 1899 but he initially held no ambitions in this direction and for a time his new wife agreed with him.[18] Edith spoke directly to the sixth Marquess on this subject in 1900 but with no effect: 'Lord Londonderry told my husband that he expected him to put his shoulder to the wheel and abandon soldering.'[19] And her reaction when a possible constituency was found was Charley in 1904 was unmistakable: 'Just because I hate the idea so, I feel there must be something in it…I love your being in the Regiment. At the same time nothing that is worth doing or having is ever attained without some sacrifice'.[20] Charley refused to stand for this Down seat but accepted Home Secretary, Akers Douglas' less traditional offer of Maidstone only because of its proximity to London. Nor he did cut all of his regimental ties. But in 1906, despite the Liberal majority in the rest of the country, which lost Edith's father the Lincolnshire seat that he held for over three decades, Charley was returned for Maidstone with his mother, wife and Unionist stalwarts, Walter Long and Edward Carson adding their weight to his campaign. Edith's reminiscences make plain the fact that Carson was repaying the Londonderrys for introducing him 'into English politics and society…he naturally did his utmost to secure the return of their son'.[21] But despite familial favours and Carson's oratory, 'a certain amount of "treating" by unauthorised agents' was also undertaken to secure this constituency for the Londonderry and Unionist interest.[22]

With her husband's entry to parliament, high politics demanded a larger stake in Edith's life. The Maidstone campaign provided Edith with her first taste of can-

vassing and in the two elections of 1910, she, along with her mother-in-law, encouraged party workers and brought voters to the polls to secure Charley's return
but with a diminished majority. Edith also underwent a Unionist conversion and
by 1912, with Theresa as co-conspirator, she decided the route of her husband's
future:

> This is only for you and me...I have made up my mind and I know what I
> want and that is to see Charley Chief Secretary for Ireland!!...I look upon the
> Belfast people very much as I do the Scotch I have always loathed their big-
> otry and dour non-conformist ways - but [the Unionist demonstration on]
> Tuesday completely converted me; and I should now like Charley to be an
> Irish member!! and lead the whole blessed thing. He could do it, because he is
> broadminded and moderate as well as being so closely connected by family
> ties and blood that he could never be suspected of being anything but an Ul-
> sterman first and an Irishman afterwards[.][23]

Theresa delighted in the prospect and it was no coincidence that she arranged for
Edith to be introduced to political leaders, like Bonar Law, that same year. Edith
subsequently became politically active within unionism: firstly at a provincial level
as vice-president of North Down Women's Unionist Association from 1914 and
president of the Newtownards branch of the same and then in the central body
of female unionism, as a vice-president of the Ulster Women's Unionist Council,
a position she maintained for forty years from 1919 until her death in 1959. Charley held the Maidstone seat until 1915 when, on his father's death, he entered the
Lords, but during the preceding year he pondered tendering his resignation, asking his wife, 'Will you find out from someone who knows my position now...I
don't want to disappoint Pa about getting a political job but I am not very keen as
you know. Think it over and let me know what you think.'[24] With his succession
to the Londonderry estates and titles, however, a greater sense of Unionist fidelity
and familial responsibility crept into his world view.

The death of the sixth Marquess also impacted on Edith. She was distinctly
uncomfortable succeeding Theresa as the leading Tory hostess, yet resigned herself to accept circumstance 'over w[hi]ch one has no control...one is forced to
step into other people's shoes.'[25] Edith came to share her mother-in-law's political
enthusiasm, desire to shape events, direct careers and adopt the role of political
confidante. She also gained a reputation for political empathy that led many to
seek her counsel, but with the Londonderry *grande dame* still very much alive both
women were in a testing position. And, for a time, it was the outbreak of the First
World War, rather than succession to the title of Lady Londonderry that gave
Edith the opportunity to create an organisation that embraced patriotism and her
adherence to equal rights.

During the early stages of the war, she presided over the Women's Land Army
and was Colonel-in-Chief of the Women's Volunteer Reserve established in 1914
to assist with signalling, first aid, transport, telegraphy and air raid arrangements.
In 1915, however, Edith fronted a new body, the Women's Legion. This non-
political, cross-class and non-denominational organisation was uniformed and

militaristic in both its structure and outlook. Edith's aim was for women 'to do their duties as women, and not as makeshift men…to replace working men with working women', and consequently release men for active service by training women, initially as cooks. From its culinary base, the legion augmented to include motor transport and agricultural sections, becoming the most significant of all the women's wartime voluntary associations. Edith maintained a high level of professionalism and organisational efficiency within the legion which countered some of the early ridicule and disapproval levelled at women's war work.[26] She also called social and familial networks into play. With Quartermaster General at the War Office, John Cowans as a family friend, he was able to exercise some influence over Kitchener to muster support for the legion whilst Edith's brother, Major Eric Chaplin, as Inspector of the Administrative Service, not only had access to the War Office but responsibility for monitoring the work of Cowans' department. Edith was also acquainted with Kitchener, but such personal means of exerting influence were becoming more controversial and Cowans was forced to appear before a secret Court of Inquiry to defend his position against undue 'petticoat influence' in the War Office in 1916.[27] This was not the last time that such a charge would be made against Edith, but there was no doubting either the impact or the continuance of personal influence. By Theresa's admission, Edith also 'arranged' Charley's first wartime posting with General Pulteney, commander of the Third Corps, before he resigned and returned to his old regiment, the Royal Horse Guards, serving as their second-in-command in France in 1915.[28] Edith's bearing on the legion was also marked: it was officially recognised by the Army Council in February 1916, becoming the first women's organisation to be accepted for army service; in March 1917 the Women's Army Auxiliary Corps developed from the legion and Edith was one of ten women awarded a DBE for war work in 1917. In the following year this was changed to a military award and she thus became the first woman to be recognised in this way.

War work also provided the impetus for Edith's 1915 folly, The Ark. This club of her creation aimed to continue the socio-political entertaining of the pre-war era, but this was also an attempt to re-cast Londonderry House in her mould. That she saw the establishment of The Ark as an important feature of her life is evidenced by fact that she began a book on its history in the year of her death. However, rather than having a distinct birth, The Ark evolved. Its establishment owed much to the wartime disruption of the society timetable; it began life as a Wednesday dining club for acquaintances whose war work brought them into contact with one another such as Princess Helena Victoria working with the Young Men's Christian Association, Cowans and various of the king's messengers:

we decided that once a week at any rate we would relax from serious events and be thoroughly frivolous. Any friends, too, who were on leave from the front used to turn up. Some of our friends were Cabinet Ministers or Secretaries of State…We decided to call ourselves the Ark, feeling that Londonderry House was sufficiently antiquated to merit the title.

But the name also suggested a refuge from the storms of war and its members ascribed to a fictional Order of the Rainbow, symbolising hope during wartime. The Ark was very select, with fewer than two hundred members over the decade and a half of its existence and with an elaborately named and structured Arcadian Revellers Committee to decide on the 'election or rejection of animals [members] to the Club'. This committee of nine was composed of patrons, patronesses and messengers with fictional names and bogus addresses and had Edith as chairman, Charley as treasurer, Princess Helena Victoria as grand mistress and Lord Herbert Vane-Tempest as president to attend to 'the recreation of the Revellers'. Charles Stirling was secretary and Cowans was vice-president with responsibility for the 'behaviour of the guests' and, in tangent with the animal theme, to ensure that there was 'no pouncing'.

Members received a badge depicting a dove carrying an olive branch with the motto 'Open Sesame' and a card bearing the inscription, 'The trap door of the Ark is open'.[29] Like the Revellers Committee, they were branded with the name of a bird, animal, mythical or arcane character and this further reinforced the sense of fidelity and exclusivity: 'The names either had to rhyme with that of the animal or have something to do with the work or the character of the individual, but they all had to begin with the same letter as their names, either Christian or surname.' Edith thus became 'Circe the Sorceress', daughter of the Sun God with the power to turn men into beasts:

The personality of Circe is pregnant with mysterious interest. Daughter of Helios (the Sun) out of the Ocean Nymph Perse, Circe appears to have inherited the tropical attributes of her sire in an inordinate degree. …Of pleasing exterior, with mental equipment far above the average, we have in Circe…a charming and delightful personality. Alas! that a closer acquaintance should have revealed moral delinquencies of a most serious kind. For youthful shortcomings, Circe was interned by her father in the Island of Aeoea, believed to be near where the Ark was cast ashore, and to this unpronounceable spot, under the guise of hospitality, Circe invited all and sundry. Once under her roof the unfortunate guests were plied with an inferior champagne (called… the "magic cup") of so viscous a brand that they were turned to swine.[30]

Her choice of name was not, however, universally approved. Indeed, Ramsay MacDonald frankly despaired:

Nay, nay, surely not Circe. Was she not a *wicked* witch? Witches I love, but they should be good and romantic…But Circe! Circe is uncanny. Circe's mother was met by Macbeth. Circe cannot dance, Circe cannot sing, Circe has no quaint humours…No, it must not be Circe. Circe is on the films, in the night clubs. She is a vulgar jade, a bad egg, a snare *and* a delusion. Circe is not a lassie of the hills and the heather, of our sunsets and our east winds. Only drunken men write verse to Circe. She is, in short, a hussie.[31]

For many others, however, Edith would be known as Circe for the rest of her life. Charley's Ark name of 'the Cheetah' was an interesting choice both for a treasurer and for a man not noted for his fidelity. As Edith remarked: 'The Cheetah chiefly hunts its victims when there is competition and then he runs down his prey in full view...it can, however, be caught and more or less tamed...it is always in pursuit of game of the female sex.' Significantly, the last four words of the description were later abandoned. Princess Helena Victoria was 'Victoria the Vivendiere' of 'Vive le Roi', Cowans was 'Merry John the Mandrill of Monkey House' while Theresa was 'the Tigress'. Unionist leader Carson became 'Edward the Eagle...because he sees through human beings'; Balfour was 'Arthur the Albatross...because he was over the heads of the others'; Chamberlain became 'Neville the Devil' and Churchill, although his posturing during the third home rule crisis infuriated Charley and greatly soured relations, would never be cast wholly from the Londonderry fold, became The Ark's 'Warlock' in 1919.

Society's trade in information continued during the war and therefore Henry Harris as 'Bogie the Bat' and 'an inveterate gossip' had a particular Ark function:

> Circe felt sometimes that these attributes were of use to her...[if] used judiciously, for she knew that any information given by her to the Bat which she would be unwilling to pass on herself would be quite quickly transmitted, with possible embellishment, to the right quarter.

In a similar vein, Theresa's son-in-law, the Earl of Ilchester was 'Stavie the Stoat', 'a very erudite creature, and his advice is constantly in demand at the Ark, where he is highly esteemed' while Lady Nancy Astor, the first woman to take her seat in the Commons in 1919, was 'the Gnat', who, although prone to 'bites', was still a great acquisition: 'she quipped and quizzed all around her and, wherever she was, her corner was all a 'buzz.'" Other members included Sir Samuel and Lady Maud Hoare, Lord and Lady Halifax, Lady Cunard, the Honourable Mrs. Keppel, the Desboroughs, the Baldwins, the Earls of Sefton and Lonsdale, Viscount Hailsham, Sir William Pulteney, Lord Trenchard, the Air Chief of Staff and Sir Edward Ellington of the Royal Air Force.[32] But The Ark's composition was never exclusively political. Literary and artistic members included Edmund Gosse, Sean O'Casey, John Tweed, Eleanor Glyn, Philip Sasoon and John and Lady Hazel Lavery who joined Count Grandi, the Italian Ambassador and Count Zichy, the Hungarian minister as well as Peter George Ward Price, editor of the *Daily Express*. The Ark also boasted royal patronage with the Duke and Duchess of Westminster and the Duke of York (later King George VI) as members and the Duke of Windsor, then Prince of Wales, assuming an honorary membership under the guise of 'David the Dragon'. On designated nights, members could invite a guest, but there was secrecy to the proceedings which added to the intrigue. There was also an initiation ceremony but details of this remain undisclosed and Edith made no reference to them in her unfinished volume.

Its distinctly tongue in cheek bye-laws, however, hinted to the reason for The Ark's continued popularity into the early 1930s - its originality and exclusivity:

the arctic circle is confined to certain latitudes, which must not be over-stepped. Animals whose previous habitat was nearer the Equator must on no account introduce their tropical methods of life into their new home. The Mandrill [Sir John Cowans] has set a good example by consenting (though reluctantly) to wear trousers. ...No dogs or War Babies may be deposited on the doorstep, nor may they be introduced into the club, either carried or on the lead. ...Frisking is permitted, coaxing and coquetting, and 'Gambolling' within limits. ...In order to ensure 'pleasant social intercourse' Members are asked to desist from drawing attention to some of the more pronounced peculiarities of the inmates, either in the matter of facial defects, form or colouring...Monkeys must avoid causing annoyance to other members by searching for insects, when in close proximity to the said members...Spells and witchcraft are not permitted within the confines of the Ark.[33]

The pun-riddled Ark certainly had its fair share of the trivial and this is nowhere more apparent than in the poem, 'Arkeology', which it inspired:

Much worse than the Park
In the dark is the Ark,
With its tandems of beauty and breeding
That swarm to Park Lane,
In sunshine or rain,
For Antediluvian feeding

To that classical spot
(Whether married or not)
Flock couples of fashion and passion:
Each animal toys,
By gesture and noise,
With its chosen particular ration.

You will find there a Queen,
A jockey, a Dean,
With perfect affinities sorted;
A sculptor, an actress,
A world-benefactress
By crowned Heads and clergymen courted.

By Bench and the Bar,
The latest film star,
Hobnob with the young bloods diplomatic;
Whilst foreign artistes
Play tunes to the 'beasts',
In time with their movements erratic.

Both Lib'rals and Tories
Tell Scurrilous stories
If seated beside a blue stocking;
They vie for the prize
Which is won if she cries
"That is most inexpressibly shocking!"

Their costumes do vary,
The 'beast' of the prairies
May prowl in their bare skins at random,
Or decked out in flannel,
Or trousered by Chanel,
'De gustibus non disputandum.'

Here the flow of the Soul
Is cheered on by the Bowl
Till its lost in a riot of Reason;
And epigrams shine
With the sparkles of wine
And the flavour of quail out of season.

No chapel of ease
Is as 'go-as-you-please'
As this Antient Ark, wherein Circe
(Our Arkship supreme)
With a mischievous gleam
In her eye, plays the Belle Dame sans Merci.

You see them reclining
And wining and dining
In many post-plandial poses
Then gaze at them as
They respond to the Jazz
Which the Saxophone sweetly proposes.

The hours advance;
But "On with the night"
With whoops of ecstatic delight,
Till Circe dismisses
Her herd with fond kisses
And shuts up the Ark for the night.[34]

Cynthia Asquith branded The Ark both absurd and ridiculous, while mere mention of the Londonderrys caused 'a delicate wrinkling of the nose' of the wife of historian, novelist and later Tory MP, John Buchan who believed 'the Ark business silly and vulgar, and was not pleased to see JB mixed up in it.'[35] In many ways they were right, but The Ark also served a political purpose. Indeed, as the young Lady Carson remarked, the club was 'not as silly as it sounds and outsiders are very jealous and inquisitive.'[36] Although its function echoed back to an earlier era, it was not the only grouping of its sort in the early twentieth century. F. E. Smith and Winston Churchill's 'The Other Club', established whilst the bitter wrangles of the Parliament Act were on-going in 1911, was a small cross-party grouping of approximately twelve Liberal and Conservative members who met with writers and artists in similar vein to the Asquithian 'Souls'.[37] Behind its light-hearted facade, The Ark effectively maintained personal contact between politicians and in founding it, Edith not only secured the Londonderrys' place at the centre of politics, but also her own. Here she was formalising the hostess role previously deployed by both Frances Anne and Theresa at a time when that very role and the class it represented was under increasing fire. Moreover, it enabled Edith to rise, albeit from a much smaller pool, as the 'Queen of Hostesses'; Ark invites became 'one of the most sought after in London.'[38]

Although The Ark's political purpose is clear, its treasurer, Charley remained unconvinced that his own future lay in this direction. During the war, like many other men in service, he relied on his wife to keep him informed of political manoeuvrings: 'Keep your ears and eyes open as I am powerless here and rely on you for information, in fact I really do not know how I should get on without you.' Despite his confidence in his wife, contemplating the post-war future in 1917, he was pessimistic as to the prospects for political hostessing:

> You have many difficulties, one is your name and the many 'friends' who consider themselves your equal in brain position etc etc but who have done nothing and who have consequently joined the throng of nonentities which they formerly kept out of by entertaining. Now there is no entertaining and merit is more recognised and there is no place for them. These are obstacles and handicaps which you must put at their proper valuation. You cannot ignore them but they need make no barrier in your path as they will always be there it is no use worrying about it.[39]

Eight years in the Commons had not convinced him that his future lay in politics and wartime service reinforced this belief: 'I cannot imagine resuming a normal existence after this; I shall be even lazier than before, and lead a life of pleasure… How many nice things we miss by a mistaken idea of duty…Soldiers are much nicer than politicians and the tiresome thing is that I always thought so.'[40] And, in the mid phases of the war, the often restless Charley was near content serving in France:

> I feel I have almost found the life which I have looked for and if only I could import the few people I want to see I could continue this existence indefinitely…the condition of Ireland is one more glaring instance of Government ineptitude. I must say recent events here have made me sick of party and I see myself if I survive the war [in] a position of obscure isolation and…I am not looking forward to that.[41]

This was entirely at odds with his mother's view: 'he has been in the House of Commons since 1906, and he fought for 2½ years. Surely a very good record not counting all the wonderful work that C. had done before. I always say that if one wants a thing one must work for it, and keep one's mind on it and not hesitate to take it when one gets the chance'.[42] It was Theresa's push that persuaded Charley to join the Ulster Unionist contingent of the hundred-strong Irish Convention in 1917. Here familial loyalty to the Unionist cause finally won him over as he worked toward a federal solution. But other Unionists would only nervously consider this and in a diluted form that essentially amounted to partition for Ireland: 'there is a germ of Federation, but that is all' he complained to his wife in late 1917. And Edith was more than just a sounding board during these deliberations as she facilitated co-operation between her father and husband: 'If the Convention subsides and the state of Ireland remains as it is, Father will raise the question again in the House and I suggest you make a speech. It would be a splendid opportunity and you could say what you liked then'.[43] She was also gathering information from Walter Long and Hugh Cecil and subsequently advised her spouse: 'Be very careful about your Federation scheme, won't you? and remember the chief people whose approval is necessary are the English and the North... I feel so anxious for you - you have such a difficult task and you are so fair-minded you might forget your own self in the turmoil.'[44]

Early in 1918 she wrote directly to Carson, alerting him to her husband's federal plan and seeking clarification: 'I find it very difficult to advise him (C) what to do in regard to your wishes, which he feels must always be the first consideration, but without knowing what these are, or hearing from you direct, I am inclined to tell him to go ahead, on the lines which he thinks best. Do you approve of this?'[45] She subsequently reported back to Charley:

> The Eagle [Carson] as I told you dined here last night...I asked him about your...[plan]. He said it was the only one, but that the Nationalists would not have it...I don't think he knows what to do either. He talks of going...I advise you to see Carson when he is there, or write to him and stick to your Federation plan. I think he may back you up. I should not write the letter to the papers in any case whether you stay in Belfast or return here[.]

Although Charley encouraged her political intervention, she was not given *carte blanche*. Indeed, convinced that the impetus for federalism had passed, her husband stopped her writing to Barrie in January 1918.

Serving on the convention and fresh from wartime service, prompted further reflection on Charley's part: 'A peacetime job does not appeal to me, also it is an old man's work and I do not feel old, but my ambitions in another sphere having failed, this does satisfy a desire to be someone and to be really filling a place somewhere which carries responsibility with it.' And by the end of the year despondency as to his future prospects were again apparent: 'I see my labours coming to an end soon and the disguise of the serious politician which sits ill upon me being laid aside...I am planless now. I do not know what place I drop into'.[46] That place was on the Lord Lieutenant's council of seven to advise on Irish affairs, a move that Theresa thought would mark the start of a definite political career:

> I am very glad he is such an Ulsterman and Irishman. I earnestly hope he gets a post in the new Government as I think at 40 he ought to be in harness and he has brains enough for any post. So far both in soldering and politics, in racing parlance, he had never had "the luck of the race."[47]

But increasingly political promotion owed little to fortune. As Charley intonated to Edith, merit, as opposed to birth, was the new badge of distinction and through 1918 he became more convinced that if he was appointed to a figurehead position, his political career would be effectively bedded. Indeed, he was alerted to the fact that the New York and Paris embassies were free and briefly considered the Irish viceroyalty but declared them all too much of a sinecure. Nor did he want his mother to secure an under-secretaryship on his behalf, instructing Edith, 'Tell my mother not to ask for anything…I only want to be kept before them, but I do not want to join this Government. Poor thing she is rather clumsy in putting forward claims.'[48] His wife, however, was formulating an alternative strategy to help decide his fate.

'Great traditions are always difficult to follow, and if Lord and Lady Londonderry hope to emulate the former occupants of Londonderry House their task will be a formidable one.'[49]

Despite Charley's reservations, Edith determined not only to continue The Ark's activities but also revive the entertaining of the pre-war era. Post-war The Ark's membership enlarged to embrace approximately fifty leading politicians and society notables, including every Prime Minister to serve during the 1930s. With this expansion the Wednesday dinners were abandoned in favour of more informal gatherings round small tables in the gallery of Londonderry House where 'you could eat, smoke or drink as you preferred. Later still, when the children grew up, the guest nights became small dances'.[50] Although the press now depicted it as 'a sort of social Cabinet, where important strings were pulled', to Edith it was a salon:

> where stage and star met statesmen, Liberals and Conservatives, writers and charmers, University dons, artists and Playwrights. They all scratched, pinched or bit each other jocularly or argued fiercely together but all answered to their names and replied as such to their invitations.[51]

The Ark's cross-party attendance was only to be expected whilst the coalition lived on but that this was maintained when the party *foci* of politics was fully revived attends to its inter-war popularity.

Charley sanctioned the move to continue The Ark but was more reticent about large-scale entertaining and again urged his wife to be chary: 'I do agree with you on all you say about entertaining. No one does it better than you do…I think what you do now with all that you have to do besides is enough to establish what we want...I am glad you are going out; it will help me as being Lady London-derry's husband'; 'You are an immense help to me and I value the real compan-ionship more than I can say'.[52] Despite Charley's prudence, they agreed to host a political reception for the coalition government at Londonderry House in No-vember 1919. The eve of session reception dated from the 1830s when Conserva-tive peers gathered at Apsley House for Wellington's largesse and Edith's hosting of the central event in the Tory calendar in 1919 effectively symbolised her place as the leading political hostess. For Edith, however, the event was emblematic of a post-war return to normalcy and 'Peace after wartime': in essence it was 'a vic-tory reception for supporters of the Coalition.'[53] This was also Edith's first recep-tion free from Theresa's shadow, but it was one which her always partisan mother-in-law could scarcely have envisaged. With Prime Minister, Lloyd George and his deputy, Bonar Law standing aside Edith at the top of the Londonderry House staircase, they received close to 2,000 guests and a new era of political hostessing was begun. This reception also marked the permanent move of the customary reception to meet the party leader on the eve of the opening of parlia-ment from Lansdowne to Londonderry House and here it remained for most of the next fifteen years.[54]

The press covered this revival of political entertaining on the grand scale but the reception was mixed. Some papers depicted Edith, in consequence of her war work, as the epitome of a modern woman who served the government 'even bet-ter' than her spouse. To the *Daily Chronicle*, 'The Lady Londonderry of today is herself a Parliamentary Elector and might even be a candidate for the House of Commons if she chose...she was not so much reviving the old fashioned assem-bly as adapting it to a new world' and the *Daily Express* was quick to label Edith 'the first hostess of the Coalition', uniting 'the gracious family tradition of the old regime of magnificent hospitality with a splendid record of progressive war ser-vice'. Others commended the relaxed atmosphere of the reception which they believed would prompt other events, 'while there was the old stateliness, the old dignity, there was, too...an accession of "human-ness".' By comparison, how-ever, the *Sunday Chronicle* doubted whether the event heralded a new era of politi-cal entertaining or had 'much that is permanent about it' while the *Liverpool Daily Post* questioned its whole purpose, 'what on earth was the good of it?' Even the conservative *Queen* asked, 'How far the power wielded by political hostesses in the past will have any echo in the future is something of a question. Times have changed, and the bestowal of direct power upon women may naturally detract from the indirect, great as this was.'[55] These charges opened a debate on 'The Great Hostess Question'. Would and, more crucially, should the largesse of the pre-war period be resuscitated in post-war Britain?

For several years in the early 1920s, it looked as if pragmatic, rather than ideo-logical, restraints ruled out a return to political hostessing *en masse*. High society was revived in the aftermath of the war and a return to the pre-war practices of evening courts, calling cards and late dinners to accommodate the parliamentary sitting represented a reassuring return to the norm for many aristocrats. But in many ways this was nothing more than window dressing. With the exception of Edith's large-scale receptions, a more modest approach prevailed. With Lady

Crewe, the Duchess of Devonshire and her mother, the Marchioness of Lans-downe, in retirement, only a handful of women entertained for political purpose: Lady Henry gave parties but at the Langham Hotel rather than at home; there were isolated receptions at Devonshire House and Lady Curzon entertained, but only for diplomatic purpose. Political hostessing was, therefore, responsive to a shifting climate and Edith was not immune from such change: she introduced dancing to her functions and varied the guest list from the purely political. Thus, whilst some aristocrats entered a post-war retreat, the Londonderrys dug in.

With Charley declining a Whip in the House of Lords, he took up post as fi-nance member of the Air Council in 1918. In the following year he became Lords' mouthpiece and Under-Secretary to Churchill as Secretary of State for Air, but Edith remained attuned of the real difficulty in placing a peer in the cabinet:

> you are in a position of your own making. You are looked on as an asset in Ireland. You would have been in the Government ages ago if it were not for the fact that we are living in an age of revolution though most people are blind to the fact and your class is looked upon with suspicion and a minister hardly knows how to make a peer a member of the Cabinet.[56]

Her pessimism may have been uncharacteristic but it was not unwarranted: Lon-donderry's under-secretaryship was not championed by many in the Tory Party. Rumours that he would succeed Churchill as Secretary of State heightened the opposition which was fronted by men Londonderry considered as friends: Cur-zon, Bonar Law and Churchill's eventual successor, Captain Freddie Guest. And the mean spirit of politics that so riled Charley in wartime France, coupled with a sense of familial loyalty to unionism and, more particularly, Ulster, impacted on his decision to accept the offer of becoming first Minister of Education and leader of the Senate in the newly established parliament of Northern Ireland. Though many friends thought them 'mad' for accepting this post and the Duke of Gloucester, the 'Unicorn' in Edith's Ark, urged her to 'not get shot!', she ac-tively encouraged her spouse to resign from the Air Ministry when Guest suc-ceeded Churchill on the grounds that 'there is a time after which 'staying on' merely is 'hanging on''. She believed the Northern Irish posting would fulfil the traditions of Charley's ancestry, make him more independent of party, exert influ-ence 'outside the Government' and advised, 'I should certainly take Craig's of-fer.'[57]

She also mediated in her husband's career, writing directly to Bonar Law to explain the Northern Ireland decision: 'I took the opportunity of putting my views before him'. To Charley, however, she felt compelled to explain this inter-vention: 'I hope you don't mind. I told him that you wanted Ireland first and had always said that if offered you would chuck everything else'.[58] In contrast, Charley believed that he sacrificed any hope of promotion in Westminster by accepting this position:

> This may destroy my prospects altho[ugh] if I am really good enough it can-not do that, and if I am not good enough it doesn't matter. ...I have followed

the right course. I came here to help to deal with a crisis; that crisis is not over and it amounts to running away if I follow the path of my personal ambition. ...I knew I was of a certain value here, that I filled a place which no one at the moment could fill...Nothing but conviction could have impelled me to make those sacrifices.[59]

But Edith remained convinced that, if properly managed, the move to Ulster could mark a political beginning, rather than an end. Living at Mount Stewart from 1922-26, they, like other members of the new Northern Ireland government, were guarded by B-Special forces and accompanied by detectives, 'But somehow no one seemed to treat the matter really seriously...[for] people like ourselves living in Ulster...life passed on, if not peacefully, quite pleasantly...I always had a set of day-clothes by my bed, and an Army revolver in a drawer which General Sir John Cowans had given me'. Even when Mount Stewart was raided during the night in February 1921, the alarm this caused was minimal: 'we never took it seriously - our idea being that most of the noise - shouting and shooting - came from our own defenders.'[60]

The move to Ireland could easily have tempered or negated Edith's hostessing but, with the exception of 1921 and 1922 while they relocated to Northern Ireland, the eve of parliament receptions continued. This was a deliberate manoeuvre on Edith's part; a tactic to maintain their political profile. As she explained to Charley, 'You might make Londonderry House the political centre if you chose. It is far better to do one thing a year or biennial than indiscriminate. If you did a function always for the Government it would always keep you in touch with them and at a time of year I presume you will not be wanted over here.'[61] For her there was never a sense of cutting ties with mainland conservatism or resigning her hostessing role. Indeed, her offer of assistance and Londonderry House 'as yours to command' to Bonar Law in October 1922 serves to further underline her stance.[62] As a strategy this was undeniably effective. In 1923 the Belfast press predicted Charley would be appointed to the cabinet, not as a consequence of his effectiveness in Northern Ireland, but as a result of Edith's 'continuance in the part which she fills so ideally as hostess for the Conservative Party...a sign that the Marquis [sic]...may yet appear before long in the Cabinet at Whitehall.' But Charley's reaction to this commentary was mixed, and, at times, he was privately critical of Edith's continued pursuit of prestige by association:

I never give people credit for doing things that I wouldn't do myself, and I really abhor the shoddy, and I hate running after royalties especially the lesser ones...and in this I feel I differ from E. more even than on other things; of course I can't talk to her about it. I have never made her see a big view of anything it is all the shoddy and the commonplace and I suppose it is realizing this which has destroyed my affection.[63]

Despite his misgivings, the Londonderrys' profile augmented whilst a number of the great London houses closed down and an even greater number ceased to function as political centres. Thus the reputation of Londonderry House, and that of its hostess, grew. It was, for instance, the only London house of its kind to open for an official function in 1923. This February eve of session reception was the first political entertainment of the year and, given the Prime Minister's widower status, was one of only a few likely to be held. Curzon had peers to dinner in same month but this was nowhere near the scale of the 1,000 guests assembled at Londonderry House. The next day the Londonderrys hosted a small dinner for the king and queen followed by a dance with several hundred guests present. But the reception roused the most commentary. The *New York Herald* even covered the event but closer to home the Irish press remarked of Edith, 'It is well-known in inner circles...that her say in Irish Affairs and...Ulster's...has in this indirect way been considerable during the last decade...Political hostesses are almost extinct in English society therefore Lady Londonderry's success is notable.' To the *Women's Pictorial* Edith was similarly unique and amongst the younger generation of political hostesses she was 'the one definite success...her political parties [have] a *cachet* that no other party can touch' while the *Evening Standard* was sufficiently assured of her place to confidently declare politics 'alive again. That is the conclusion one came to at the Londonderry House reception...Mr. Disraeli, who, like most of us last night...put it..."simpering in gilded saloons," might have looked into the drawing-rooms of Lady Londonderry's house and found nothing strange.'[64]

And the entertaining continued through the early 1920s, ranging from intimate gatherings and parties for members of the diplomatic corps to the huge eve of session receptions. Garden parties on a similar scale, catering for as many 5,000 members and supporters of the Unionist government, were held in Ulster as were parties to meet Northern Ireland premier, James Craig. High profile events such as Bonar Law and the Earl of Derby's visits to the Londonderrys in the newly established state in 1922 and 1923 respectively and the royal visit of the Duke and Duchess of York in July 1924 also kept the Londonderrys in the headlines. The latter was initially planned as a private visit to Mount Stewart, but a range of public functions were then worked into the week-long visit. And Edith, deemed 'the type of woman who does greatest credit to womanhood...the kind of woman who has made history...[with] a big heart, a shrewd wit, and an ability to draw the best out of everyone with whom she comes into contact that gives her what we all want, but which few of us could use to such good advantage - power', made good press copy.[65] Ultimately, this continued involvement in national politics was an effective means of preventing the Londonderry name from languishing in the provincial backwaters of Ulster.

Edith's now consuming political interest, coupled with her position of social privilege, also enabled her to effectively negotiate between leading political figures. In 1921-22 she was actively involved with Tory stalwarts, Carson, Wolmer, Gretton, Northumberland, Salisbury, Sir Henry Wilson and Ronald MacNeill in trying to build a die-hard Conservative Party under decisive leadership and independent of the coalition government. Although the plans proved abortive, Edith, in discussing the formation of a rival party and the selection of a new leader, stood as the lone woman in the midst of private negotiations amongst the party elite. With Charley incapacitated with flu late in 1921, she initially participated by proxy, but her suggestions were seriously considered and correspondence with her continued into 1922, long after her husband regained health.

As early as June 1921 Salisbury urged a Unionist withdrawal from the coalition and Carson hoped that a December dinner at Londonderry House would provide a stimulus for continued action in this direction. As he opined to Edith, 'I feel so certain that the permanence of the Coalition under any name will be a disaster and indeed prohibitive of free action and criticism'. Edith was also in contact with the right-wing backbencher, Sir John Gretton who encouraged her active participation, 'I am so glad you are interested and you can help enormously' and Northumberland echoed his remarks: 'I am so glad that you are taking the lead in getting all those who think like us to meet. It is not at all pushing and there is nobody else who could do it as well.' Edith identified Salisbury as the best potential leader for this breakaway group and though Northumberland agreed, he advocated caution:

> don't you think that what we ought to do is just to keep our small "die-hard" party together for the next few months in view of the probability (and I should regard it almost as a certainty) that the whole Conservative party will eventually come round to us?...there must be some rallying point for Conservatives which we must provide. We must try and meet when you come North...This is a tiresome tale and you must forgive me pouring it out to you. I wish I could have talked to you.[66]

By the start of 1922 Salisbury and Carson could rally fifty to sixty MPs to the die-hard cause. Edith's considerations were for unity of purpose and action, anxious to avoid any split between Gretton's call for immediate action and Northumberland's more measured and strategic approach. In this Carson was in complete agreement, 'I quite agree that no pronouncement is to be made until we see what the Gov[ernmen]t are going to do but I think no time sh[oul]d be lost in organising and being ready.'[67] As in the third home rule crisis, Londonderry House provided a meeting ground for interested, though not unanimously agreed, parties. Wilson, for instance, lunched at the house alone in the company of his hosts in January 1922 to discuss the 'possibility, necessity and probability of forming a real Conservative party. Lady Londonderry is working hard to this end...and I am sure this is the right thing to do and I believe if they could get a fine leader it is a real possibility.'[68] Later in the month, Londonderry House was again the venue for a die-hard meeting, this time with Carson in attendance. However, the façade of the Londonderrys' support for the coalition was maintained with 'all the devils' attending a March party in Londonderry House. Ruby Carson was disconcerted by this, 'I can't think why they asked them' and condemned Charley for being 'so half hearted one can see it all the time.'[69] But maintaining an illusionary support for the coalition was an effective means to avoid alienation whilst the deliberations continued. The die-hards went public on 8 March 1922 sending a collective letter from sixteen MPs and peers, counting Lord Londonderry amongst their number, to *The Times*, setting forth their manifesto of loyalty to the throne, the established church, the restoration of the Lords' veto, strict economy in national

finance to end excessive taxation as well as liberty, stability and peace. But the
gender divide in parliamentary politics still pervaded in the post-suffrage era:
Edith's name was not included.

More evidence of this exclusion came later in the same year when Edith was
asked by the Northern Ireland government to organise an Ulster Women's Volunteer Association to enlist and train a body of 'loyal' women who would be prepared to assist 'in case of extreme emergency, and to replace men called out for
active service'.[70] Edith was an obvious choice for this position: a dedicated and
influential Unionist with key experience in female organisation. The Ulster
scheme was avowedly non-political in nature but, as the enlistment of women
was undertaken through the organisational machinery of the UWUC, the government's identification of 'loyalty' with unionism was clear. Edith appointed salaried
country organisers to administer the scheme and formulated detailed plans to
prepare for an emergency situation 'arising either of a serious military nature due
to Sinn Féin or an internal nature due to strikes on a large scale'.[71] Should such a
situation arise it was envisaged that this association would ensure that 'the essen-
tials of life to the community...that is, the supply of food, water, fuel and light'
were maintained and women, as in wartime under the auspices of the legion,
would substitute government personnel, the police, St. John's Ambulance and the
Red Cross.[72] By late 1922 Edith had mustered some 230 recruits, carefully managing the scheme as government service could not be officially conducted under the
auspices of any political association, but her work for the Unionist cause in the
early years of the Northern Irish state was soon overshadowed.

The rumour that Edith could be the 'Lady L' romantically written to by Nationalist Michael Collins in 1922 lingered until the 1990s. This, however, was a long-
lived case of mistaken identity: it was not Lady Londonderry but Lady Hazel Lavery who was being addressed. It seems Hazel Lavery, in an act befitting her noto-
rious reputation for indiscretion, passed Charley Londonderry Collins' letter
which he then transcribed as well as keeping the original, but whether this was by
accident or design remains unknown. Collins included messages to the cabinet in
his letters to Hazel which she then showed to Churchill and Londonderry and so
it is plausible that the latter would be given a dispatch to read and copy. Having
previously refused to meet Collins during complicated wrangles over the Anglo-
Irish Treaty in 1921, Charley was wrong footed after his first meeting with him
in Churchill's room at the Colonial Office on 30 March 1922. Discussing the rise
in sectarian outrages in Northern Ireland, Charley recorded: 'I spent three of the
most delightful hours of my life...and I formed a conclusion which was quite
different from the one which I would have formed if I had only known him as I
had read of him before'.[73] Collins' letter written after this meeting suggests a similar appreciation, but also reveals his insecurity, believing Londonderry was a rival
for Lady Lavery's affections:

> Forgive me. I bitterly regret my outburst about L[ondonderry]. You were very
> kind to arrange the meeting...It is all very well to tell me as you do that he has
> no 'interest' in you. But how can you expect me to believe that, feeling as you
> know well how I feel? So you must forgive my bitterness, and try to imagine

what it means to a man like myself, entirely self-made, self-educated, without background and trying to cope with a man like Lord L., a man who has every advantage I lack. This is not self-disparagement, a mean quality that I think I do not possess; but I cannot help recognizing the fact that you and he speak the same language, an alien one to me, and he understands to perfection all the little superficial things that matter in your particular world - unimportant things maybe - but oh! my God, not to be underestimated with a woman like you. I know that instinctively. I feel savage and unhappy, and so I blame you for a situation for I alone am to blame, but I contrast myself with him, my uncouthness with his distinction, my rough speech with his unconscious breeding and the worst of it is I *like* him and admire him, and feel that he is brave and honest[.][74]

But such qualities would be insufficient to guarantee Charley a place at Westminster other than in the House of Lords. In consequence, strenuous efforts continued to be made to maintain the Londonderry political profile on the mainland. In August 1924 a Conservative rally for 5,000 was held in the Wynyard grounds, making it the largest political assemblage ever held at the Durham estate. The eve of session reception at Londonderry House of the same year was attended by some 1,100 people, 'who had to get up the staircase...some gave up the attempt and got up the back stairs instead!'[75] Those assemblages included many from Northern Ireland, thus bridging the gap between the Londonderrys' two political worlds and, despite the crush, Stanley Baldwin commended Edith's efforts and took no umbrage at her recommending a name for that year's honour's list:

Your party was a great success and you made many people very happy. I am not one who takes these things as a matter of course: I know (in a small way) the amount of trouble and work involved and I want to thank you and your husband most warmly for what you have done...I thought you played your part marvellously.[76]

No other event of 1924 rivalled this reception. The Marchioness of Salisbury's dinner held on the same day, for instance, was much more intimate and was timed to allow guests to go on to Londonderry House. Nor was there any doubt as to who was in command at Londonderry House: the order of merit at the top of the now infamous staircase saw Edith greet guests with the Prime Minster while Lord Londonderry stood behind.

A more cordial relationship with the Churchills was also being built with Charley encouraging Winston back to the Conservative fold from 1922 and canvassing for him during the 1924 Westminster election. But this backing was not without price. As Charley wrote to Churchill, 'how delighted I am that we shall have the full value of your powerful support. ...As you know it is what I have always hoped, and yet the bridge seemed impossible to build.'[77] Edith was also active, addressing a series of women's meetings in support of various Conservative candidates in north-east England in October 1924. Standing on an avowedly anti-

Socialist and anti-Communist platform, she also championed the women who had been elected to parliament and, in a letter to the *Morning Post* on the third of the following month, denied the charge that they had failed to defend their seats effectively.[78] This early feminist, therefore, maintained her belief in equal rights.

Her view of the Northern Irish post as a stopgap was similarly static. And, from Charley's correspondence with Churchill, it seems that he was coming round to her way of thinking. Unsettled by the uncertainty of partition, he confided to Churchill:

> it is merely a question of whether at some stage of the descent of Ireland to anarchy and chaos the British Government will step in, and tan Ireland like a large nanny which has mutinied against a long suffering nurse. If Ireland is to be left to its own devices, it is an ugly sore and in the end may poison the whole body of the Empire. ...There is really no inbetwixts and betweens... You must be independent or dependent...I feel very depressed from a source of impotence and inability to do anything to save the disaster.[79]

In 1925 he mused over the possibility of becoming Governor of India, a post he coveted from 1916, but Edith curtailed his ambition with pragmatic considerations of not only his own, but also their children's, future: 'at the end of five years we should return quite old, having lost every younger friend we ever had and out of touch with everything - children strangers and altogether finished.'[80]

The sense of obligation that brought Charley to Northern Ireland ultimately held him in post until the question of territorial boundaries was settled in the newly established state. But in November 1925, with the Boundary Commission report imminent, he believed 'the situation becomes much easier for me, as the process of loosening roots here should reach its maximum point when I am free.'[81] In January 1926 he informed Craig that he wanted to resign from Northern Irish politics, blaming a pre-occupation with the general strike and a pressing need for closer management of his mining interests in Durham. This resignation ended his Irish political career, at least in any official capacity, but he remained ambitious. Within months of his resignation there were rumours, especially prevalent in Dublin, that he would become Irish Lord Lieutenant. The press also speculated that Edith, especially after her public defence of the revised Church of England prayer book, would stand for parliament. The possibility of the Paris embassy also emerged but Charley questioned why the Prime Minister would want to send him:

> I don't think it is my job at all. I am rather liking the free lance complex and expect to continue in that state altogether...I regret India very much. It would have been just the climax and after it I could have come home and adopted the sort of life I am leading now. I apologise for egotism[.][82]

Edith, now ranked as a figure of national importance by *Woman* magazine, also felt a sense of freedom on leaving Northern Ireland. As she wrote to her husband's secretary whilst devising the eve of session guest list in 1926: 'The situation is different now…it is unnecessary for Lord Londonderry to ask more than a certain number of the more prominent officials and his own friends.'[83] With Prime Minister Baldwin in attendance, northern Nationalist Joseph Devlin was now amongst the 2,000 invited. To the pro-Socialist press, however, this was 'an orgy of wasteful spending' and the *Daily Herald*'s message was clear in both visual and narrative form: the cartoon of a poor woman clasping a child ignored by peers in robes and coronets published the day after the Londonderry reception was coupled by their questioning the sincerity of Baldwin's calls for economy when he was involved in 'the pantomime tinsel of yesterday's procession and ceremony'.[84] Though the *Evening Standard, Daily News, Northern Whig* and *Belfast News-letter* all rallied against this charge, the days of glorifying the splendour of aristocratic display were nearing their end. Given this, it is perhaps understandable that Edith was still subject to bouts of insecurity, unnerved by making daily electioneering speeches in 1927, especially with the heightened interest in what she had to say. As she expressed to Charley: 'I discover that being your wife adds great importance to what I say [and] I have to be careful…How I hate it and it frightens me very much.'[85]

Although disappointed that Charley was not in office, she was unwilling to reconsider the Indian viceroyalty, writing to her spouse: 'your real good work lies at home in my opinion…this Government will be dead and buried before long… and your trip forgotten or else the decision thrown into the waste paper basket'.[86] Instead Churchill was faithful to kin and directed Baldwin toward Charley who was subsequently appointed first Commissioner of Works and Public Buildings in October 1928, an office that on this occasion, as it did more often than not, came with cabinet rank. Some doubted whether Londonderry deserved the honour and were barbed in their congratulation, viewing the appointment as a reward for Edith's hostessing. As prominent Durham Conservative, Sir Cuthbert Headlam contemplated in his diary, 'One can't use a man's hospitality and not give him a job if he wants it.'[87] And, although Edith labelled the following letter 'Too amusing to destroy', the charge was clear:

> naturally we are very glad to think that all of his work, and the marvellous entertaining you have given the Conservative party, being recognised in this way by the Conservatives…your gorgeous parties will now have an added splendour, when you ask Conservatives to the house of a minister, as well as being the great political hostess you have always been. I do think a party like ours enjoys, and needs, your entertainments very much. The Liberal and Labour Party hope to destroy and rebuild everything, but you show the Conservatives what we have got to preserve.[88]

Londonderry was in this particular harness for just eight months. In June 1929 with Baldwin's defeat at the polls and the Londonderrys' only son, Robin failing to secure a seat at Darlington in spite of the efforts of Edith and two of her daughters in 'a new feature at which quiet talks are had with the women voters', they now looked to another, this time from outside the party fold, for preferment.[89]

'Shine and sing in the realm of feeling.'[90]

Edith's relationship with the premier of the first Labour government, Ramsay MacDonald, brought her new found notoriety with politicians, the public and the press. Widowed at the age of forty-five in 1911, MacDonald came to rely on Edith as his closest friend and confidante from the mid 1920s. They first met at a Buckingham Palace dinner in 1924 when he was already Prime Minister and she was surprised to learn that he was to walk her into dinner: 'I had always detested his views on Russia, and disliked what I heard of him.'[91] Despite these unlikely beginnings, a close friendship with serious political implications ensued, lasting until MacDonald's death in 1937. They discovered a shared love of the Scottish highlands, Gaelic myths and a dislike of the mediocrity of the wartime coalition, but they were politically poles apart. Edith often stood on anti-Socialist platforms while MacDonald had criticised conservatism for attracting 'a certain type of blatant background and is therefore worst and its press is also the worst.' In regard to Ireland, whose fate occupied the Londonderrys for decades, his ill-concealed distaste for unionism made him an unlikely confidante to one of conservatism's and unionism's leading promoters in the early twentieth century: 'What have the Unionists been doing all these 20-40 years but wasting time and disgracing their country…a party that is a class…It is hard not to hate them deeply'.[92]

But MacDonald was also, in many ways, an unlikely Labour leader. In 1924 Beatrice Webb believed him a poseur, 'an aristocratic charmer and courtly society man' and she uncannily predicted the future course of politics:

> his present pose as a political charmer of no particular party and as a capable citizen anxious to carry on in the business of the country with the consent of all parties - with special compliments, by the way. To the Conservative Party and their leader. …We are inclined to think that he consciously and subconsciously desires continuance in office - from what his friends say, he is enjoying himself vastly[.][93]

Two years later it was 'so plain' to Tom Jones that MacDonald's 'distinguished head, his address, his ring' meant that he was 'not a T.U. leader, but an aristocrat.'[94] MacDonald was, therefore, a brooding and often reluctant Labour leader, focussing on work to detract from the personal tragedy of burying both a wife and a son, losses that coloured the rest of his life:

> I am bodily and spiritually tired of all this notoriety and would welcome gratefully a summons to the silences. But the end is not yet and I am doomed to my burdens…Reflections nothing but sad. The dead came to be with me and I look downward along the road of uncertain length and events into shadows.[95]

Baldwin's resignation in 1924 paved the way for the first Labour ministry, although one lacking a Commons' majority, with MacDonald at the helm. This was a huge turnaround in fortune both personally for MacDonald and for the party he led. But any sense of achievement quickly gave way to melancholic reflection:

The people of my heart are Dead; their faces on my walls; they do not share with me. ...How vain in honour now...I returned to the world of politics and premiership, and a press that wonders why I take so little delight in publicity.[96]

Indeed, MacDonald's loneliness holds the key to understanding his friendship with Edith Londonderry.

MacDonald wrote to Edith the day after their first meeting and though she claimed to have been labelled 'a dangerous woman' by an undisclosed female Socialist, most probably Beatrice Webb, in an attempt to warn him off her, he was either undeterred or intrigued, inviting both she and Charley to Chequers.[97] This quickly prompted complaints that he interacted more with Conservatives than with members of his own party and certainly offended his Home Secretary, Arthur Henderson who was excluded from the inaugural Chequers invite. The Londonderrys subsequently became the first to sign MacDonald's Chequers visitors' book in May 1924.[98] Scathing comments about this association continued and Beatrice Webb entrusted hers to her diary, noting in early March 1924:

The longer I watch the newspaper paragraphs about the Labour Ministers and their wives going to great houses to meet Royalties - the Londonderrys' for instance! - the greater seems to me the mistake that is being made from the standpoint of the morale of the Party...I cut the knot by refusing...to take the first step into the charmed circle, and I shall not be troubled again![99]

This early critic's opinion only hardened as MacDonald's association with Edith grew closer.

In return for the Chequers' hospitality, Edith invited MacDonald to call at Londonderry House on his way back from the Commons and to visit Mount Stewart. He deemed the 'Ulster proposition...not at all a bad one...I really should like very much to go. The only trouble is the Irish sea and the time. If the one could be kept calm and the other made a little more generous than it now is, I should dearly like to go and see our troublesome folks'. In March 1924 she invited him to dine at Londonderry House with the king and queen and although she met with him later that month, their early correspondence remained formal, if jovial. At the end of April he wrote:

What a burden you all are upon my poor back. Never in all my life did I wish the country to Jericho until I came here. Do tell your friends to turn me out or I shall become a blasphemous and an otherwise sinful man. You really are as bad as Poincare [the French Prime Minister] with your bargaining...I should really like very much to go to Ireland once more...But if I could get my storms here calmed and so be able to breath freely and with some certainty I should gladly accept your invitation to see your folks and your land. Ishbel [his daughter] would come too...she belongs to the *old* aristocracy and does not love the new. So I think you will like her[.][100]

Pressure of work, with every day bringing 'its difficulties' for MacDonald, pro-hibited a visit to Mount Stewart and he admitted, 'there is not much chance of my being able to get away to Ireland', but he also alluded to the personal criticism he was being subjected to: 'You may have noticed that the papers have been at-tacking my "social engagements" and accusing me of neglecting my Parliamentary Duties.'[101] His acceptance of the traditions of the prime ministerial role, such as court dress, caused a crisis of conscience amongst his own party. This was the first of several but MacDonald believed the success of this, the first Labour min-istry, would be measured in the amount of respect and confidence it could muster and in maximising policy debate as opposed to party pettiness: 'It is a great ex-perience and an enlightening one. Perhaps we must fail. We are the first. Can we be more than a hope mingled with a warning. I shall be content with that.'[102] Al-though MacDonald believed his would be a short ministry, perhaps of only one session's duration, it coincided with the Boundary Commission, established in 1924 in accordance with article 12 of the Anglo-Irish Treaty to consider the terri-torial definition of Ulster. The commission unnerved Unionists, but Edith's new association with MacDonald enabled her to exert some influence on him, work-ing to ensure that Unionist interests were represented in the report. The signifi-cance of this influence was undoubtedly heightened by the Northern Ireland gov-ernment's refusal to appoint a delegate to the commission.

Through 1924 Ulster's boundary became a common topic for discussion in both their letters and conversations as Edith outlined Unionist fears and the need for compromise and trust between the London and Belfast administrations. In early August MacDonald and Henderson met Lord Londonderry and Hugh Pol-lock as formal representatives of the Northern Ireland government in order to ratify an agreement to appoint commissioners to review the boundary: if North-ern Ireland refused to appoint a commissioner, Britain would do so on their be-half. And in a private letter written the day after this meeting, MacDonald con-fided to Edith:

I was sorry that the Irish project could not be carried out. You knew how I was placed. The burden of Atlas was nothing to mine. His was the world; mine is the follies of the real world. Between the weight of the two there is no comparison. This new Irish trouble is most worrying. I am rigidly opposed to hasty legislation but I must make it plain that the Government means to keep faith. I know you will do your best to get your friends to meet us reasonably within the period between now and the end of September. Do not let us re-vive those evil passions of hate and strife. We were not meant to be torn by such things and I shall not countenance in any way the too evident intention of Mr. Lloyd George and his miserable minded following to make party capi-tal out of a grave tragedy. This is a thing to settle between friends who wish to be happy rather than to squabble over by dishonest politicians or hard mouthed bigots.

This was a remarkable outpouring from one of just a few months acquaintance and it is clear that MacDonald wanted Edith to comprehend the limitations of his own position:

> The difficulty about our expressing a view that Clause 12 was meant to be a rectification of [the] boundary is that apparently the South people had a different pledge from Mr. Lloyd George…If the Govt. here began to contemplate this, it could only be jumping out of the frying pan into the fire. You are all on the other side of the world of people and ideas from me and when I go from this I hope it will be never to emerge again from my own fireside; but…I am doomed to bear these burdens and because I really did enjoy our talks, I beg you to help like a good dear woman to give us peace.[103]

Edith, by return, did not discuss her husband's views or the earlier meetings. Instead her focus was on the thorny issues of security and loyalty:

> I never expected you to write in the midst of all your work and worry…Will you forgive me if I ask you a few questions and say a few things to you on paper as, unfortunately, I cannot say them in person…I wish more than ever now that I had had the luck to get you over here, as in my view, it is absolutely impossible to gauge the situation here from the other side of the water.
>
> When reading your letter, I could not fail to be reminded of the parable of the lost sheep. Are you quite sure that the sheep you have found is not a goat? And if a sheep has it really repented? Did you know that this same sheep fired six shots over the Fermanagh Border at one of our Specials last week?…The Southern Irish can be very charming but they certainly are an inconsequent race - in fact, very like children and when given too much latitude, they get out of hand. It does not really signify what Government they have, they must always "be agin it". Hence the present attitude of the self styled Republicans who really represent the anti Government Party. The mere fact of two British Cabinet Ministers going over to negotiate with the Free State will give them an entirely wrong idea of their power for doing either good or evil. Too much attention is bad for the young and causes them to show off.

Her allegory was clumsy but the idea of two nations and the strength of her own conviction was unmistakable: 'You ask me to do my poor best to help towards peace and get my friends to help you reasonably - but to enable us to do this, you must be reasonable too and keep the faith with Ulster.' She felt MacDonald needed to remain by the 1920 Government of Ireland Act and inferred that the boundary question had been discussed during their Chequers visit:

> I do not call it a debt of honour and I am too cynical to apply this word to the Treaty!! But if those who signed the Treaty regard it as a debt of honour which Great Britain owes the South, she owes an equal debt of honour by the 1920 Act to the North of Ireland.

Ulster never asked for this form of self government and when it was reluctantly accepted, it was accepted for a certain clearly defined territory. It is most important to my mind that the British Government should say what Ulster's territory is under the 1920 Act, seeing that it is an accomplished fact and was forced on her by Great Britain on the understanding that it was absolutely final. ...Won't you...extend to us...the right hand of fellowship and maintenance and throw us the olive branch. This is my request to you. I am on the other side of the water, but not the world, as you suggest, nor do I think that though we are certainly in opposite camps, that our ideas are necessarily so wide apart or that we may not have the same goal in view. I certainly did not receive this impression at Chequers and I shall be surprised if the future makes me feels otherwise. ...You may rely on my helping you all I can to keep the peace only you must help us too[.]

MacDonald replied the next day, confirming that Northern Ireland would not appoint a boundary representative and thus 'It is no use pursuing the subject further...though I wait events with some disquiet of mind. ...You gave me a terrible dressing down. Ah, that red hand of Ulster. Why will you always think we are your enemies? Especially when we are giving you such good advice.'[104] When the commission finally reported in 1925, the territorial boundaries were unaltered. It is difficult to ascertain the exact impact of Edith's influence in securing these ends, but her persuasive arguments with MacDonald seem, at least, to have helped to maintain a Unionist perspective in the commission's deliberations. That she wasted no time airing her opinions to MacDonald in the early months of their association perhaps suggest political expediency. More certainly, however, there was an augmenting rapport and empathy in their epistolary and the settlement of Northern Ireland's boundaries did not mark an end to their relationship. Their friendship continued, especially after the Londonderrys' return from Northern Ireland in 1926, when the tone of their often weekly letters grew more familiar. But they were far from political allies and this was nowhere more apparent than in Lord Londonderry's public challenge to MacDonald to visit the Seaham constituency in the midst of the 1926 general strike to adjudge the condition of his miners after making claims that they were starving. The press mused on the 'interesting spectacle' that the triumvirate of Londonderry, MacDonald and Sidney Webb, MP for Seaham and husband of the already critical Beatrice, might make, but although the invite was refused, the Londonderry and MacDonald names would soon be inextricably linked.[105]

MacDonald's continued friendship with Edith and his interaction with London society continued to worry Beatrice Webb: 'As I write these words [in 1926] I see him purring in the home of a high-placed woman friend...enjoying his social prestige as an ex-Premier'.[106] But strictures remained. MacDonald occasionally addressed Edith by her first name in 1926 but more commonly, at least until 1928, she remained Lady Londonderry. A brief period of coyness and uncertainty followed when he addressed her as 'Me' and signed himself as 'Me too' before adopting Christian names in 1929. After 1930 he addressed her interchangeably as 'My dear Lady', 'My dearest friend', 'best friend' and 'Dearest one' and began to sign himself with his Ark nomenclature. But there was no drastic change in his outlook or approach to life: 'no rest, no gaiety, no lilt in life...I am like a man wading a river with the water up to his neck and not knowing but that the next step will take him out of his depth.'[107]

Edith's early letters to MacDonald adopted the same casual and familiar style that she used for the rest of her correspondents and he evidently found some solace in writing to her, joking in the midst of a 'perfectly rotten time' in 1927 that if her son turned his into a Conservative:

> I shall never look with any favour on the name Londonderry and when I come in I shall forfeit all your heirlooms without a halfpenny compensation and if my Left is too strong I shall allow you to be guillotined, though, as I could not bear to see it, I shall turn my back upon the scene. On the other hand if yours becomes a decent Labour Man, I expect to receive from you and your husband your warmest congratulations!

In a similar vein, her tease that that he was a Tory provoked a reaction of, 'If you say that I shall put a Chinese cracker under you the next time you sit in state in the House of Lords'. Edith became convinced that she lifted his spirits, 'I am sure that I do you good!! Now don't laugh - you have often told me you felt better after you have been here [at Londonderry House]'[108] and believed that writing to her provided him with some respite, 'I hope and feel that it is restful for you to write to me - as you can be just yourself - really and truly'.[109] More seriously, he sought her company: 'I sometimes do hate politics...I should be glad to have a talk on the far off things and the battles long ago which become more and more one's life. After 60, the dead, and the past.'[110] However, she had little impact on his political demeanour and his distaste for the class basis of the Conservative Party remained: 'The present government represents Society and papers and people support it as they do the Church and whatever is the expected thing amongst those who are consciously respectable...With their resources, their screens, their devotees, the Tories should rule for the next generation were they not stupid.'[111] Even though he was not in line for a Conservative conversion, central Labour Party figures still advised him against becoming too closely associated with the Londonderrys. However, with MacDonald's 1929 return for the constituency of Seaham, a town literally hewn by the Londonderrys, there was a further moulding of interests. This prompted Sidney Webb to caution him not to accept Edith's invite to a Seaham Harbour centenary function in late 1928, believing 'they must not shadow each other'.[112]

With the fall of Baldwin's short-lived ministry, MacDonald became Prime Minister for the second time in June 1929. The problems of his first government quickly returned: cabinet creation and governing without a Commons' majority remained problematic and his insecurity as party leader was clear: 'We have more who would like to see empty shoes above them and be ready to knife away any leader who slips.' He also faced mounting press criticism and an aggressive Conservative opposition whose tactics verged on obstruction: 'We are not accepted. We are ugly ducklings in authority.'[113] Edith did little either to ease her party's approach to the Labour premier or his sense of solitude but her relationship with him was bearing results: her husband retained his position as Commissioner of Works:

> Ramsay asked me to join the Gov[ernment], and I became First Commissioner of Works once again…[with] this gesture from the Prime Minister, I was marked down as "Ramsay's man" by several of my colleagues in the Conservative Party, just as in the days of the L.G. [Lloyd George] Coalition, Bonar Law and Curzon had always looked on me as "Winston's man". It would have made the world of difference had I simply been a "party man".[114]

Londonderry's retention of office caused some consternation and Headlam was not alone in remarking, 'Circe has played her cards well.'[115] Tensions were further raised by the failing performance of Conservatives in Durham and Edith, in a move that was reminiscent of Frances Anne in 1861, rallied against what she perceived as undue interference on the part of Conservative Central Office. Their oversight to consult her before the district agent of the Northern Area Office was moved provoked a swift and severe reaction. As president of this body, her letter to J. C. C. Davidson, the National Chair of the party, revealed a continued sense of proprietorship over the north-east of the country:

> If you do not realize yourself how rude the whole thing is…[and] only confirms to my mind how hopeless the management of our central office is. If you treat *me* in this very off-hand fashion, I hardly like to contemplate what occurs elsewhere…it is I who organized the Ball which produced all the money for the anti-Socialist campaign in the North, and it is to my husband that you owe everything in these quarters, the only time there has been a failure was in the last election when the Central Office ran the campaign and they lost *nearly every* seat. I do not accuse the Central Office naturally of any discourtesy, but of gross ignorance in the management of affairs of this sort.[116]

She was similarly infuriated by the press coverage of her large-scale receptions, controversial from 1919, but now attracting even more negative commentary. The reception to meet Baldwin in July 1929 had fewer attendees than the previous year due to the party's recent electoral defeat, but the *Daily Sketch* believed that on the eve of a Socialist government, the event symbolised 'the end of the *ancien régime*.'[117] Although in this year Lady Beauchamp entertained the Liberals at Halkyn House in Belgrave Square, hostessing on this scale was rare and, in the midst of an economic depression, questions were being asked of propriety. Edith was also coming under provincial fire with Headlam, whose relationship with the Londonderrys was soured by their continued paternalistic belief that they controlled Durham conservatism, confiding to his diary: 'that wretched woman…she really is about the silliest and most conceited donkey that ever lived. She is a perfectly valueless person politically in this part of the world - or anywhere else - except that she is only too willing to entertain the Party in London.'[118] But within two years the extent of Edith's political influence was being talked of far beyond Durham.

To many of his party's dismay, MacDonald delighted in his invitation to join The Ark's ranks in 1929:

What ponderings it awakens! Am I to escape the flood which is sure to come upon this ungodly nation? What am I to be? A bear? A serpent? A wolf (in sheep's clothing or not -?) A lamb? What?...I am in the midst of a dispatch to a friendly power so I cannot pursue the speculation. ...Life is really hard and I am trying to stave off the day when you and yours will enter the prison house where I am and you will put your thumbs down and stiletto in and Chequers and Downing St. will see me no more.

In The Ark he was known as 'Hamish the Hart', a name he believed represented the different traits of his personality, 'a bit of everything wild and tame, good, bad and indifferent. But that is to be the name of my Olympian friend who stands in glory at the top of the Londonderry House staircase.'[119] Some claim that this was Edith's conquest of MacDonald, but a real change in their relationship came in the following year.

Tom Jones' diary entry for 16 January 1930 accentuated the increasing social and political fusion between the Londonderrys and MacDonald as well as the sense of unease that this caused. Jones refused his invitation to "At Homes' at Londonderry House' although the 'P.M. would issue invitations to delegates and Londonderry's friends', he deemed the disadvantages 'overwhelming.'[120] In the next month MacDonald made his first sparse mention of the Londonderrys in his diary, noting an 'Evening of feasts. Londonderry Opera by Broughton; Admiralty reception for [US] delegates' with the Churchills, Baldwins and Chamberlains present. Coverage in the *Daily Express* of this event was similar in brevity, but was cutting in tone, 'A Socialist Prime Minister sat amicably with the greatest Tory hostess of her generation. And the music which they applauded was composed by a Communist. The lion had indeed, lain down with the lamb.' Later that month MacDonald attended another Londonderry House reception, this time for naval conference delegates, accompanied by his daughter and his secretary and prompting the *Northern Whig* to comment that 'strange faces were seen' at the former Unionist bastion.[121] Soon MacDonald and Edith were the fodder of gossip columnists whose clamour for social tattle was a salient feature of post-war Britain. Indeed, in mid April 1930 under the headline of 'Premier and Lady Londonderry', the *Daily Sketch* noted:

It is not often that Mr. Ramsay MacDonald is seen dining in a public restaurant. But on Budget night he had evidently decided to forget politics...He and Lady Londonderry were dining together...Both were in good spirits - the one because and the other in spite of the Budget - and neither finance nor politics appeared to be occupying their conversation.[122]

By July, MacDonald recorded a 'Happy lunch' at Londonderry House with 'herself' in attendance and in October he was received again with the 'Hostess charming as ever'. He was clearly comfortable in their company but the enigmatic entry of the following day saw him noting his closest friend in the Labour Party, J. H. Thomas' words, '"Didn't she look like a Queen last night", said J.H.T. rolling his eyes and his mouth. "You and she together were the only two in the room".'[123] MacDonald's lack of comment was significant as were the three sonnets he penned and sent her, though 'I really should not let you see'. One, with second and third stanzas entitled 'The joy of it' and 'The sadness of it', referred to Edith 'amongst other things and shows how you bring me back to stern realities':

And if God's heart is moved by sympathy
And is not only just, but also kind,
Amongst the whims an angel I shall with azure scarf blowing in the wind
Her harp and crown she will have left behind,
But she will smile a greeting as on earth;
Music will steal from her approaching feet;
From shy glad eyes will rosy love have birth;
My hungering lips her joy crowned brow will greet
From Time and Heaven I then shall find release
And midst the golden broom know perfect peace.
Alas! Alas! 'Tis only a vain dream
Born of the beauties of a Lossie day –
The magic of the whin and broom in gleam –
And like a dream, 'tis doomed to fade away.
The sunlight earth will shiver into grey.
The moment's peace die into lasting care;
Soon will the Tory archers bend their bows
The Tory hordes wind up their Park Lane stairs
And smirk at Circe - how she does't God knows –
The world will bow to Mrs Baldwin's plume
A lonely outcast, I will dream of broom.

The following day he penned another. Under the title 'Political love rejected', this was to be sung at Tory gatherings and with Edith, Baldwin and MacDonald as its subjects, although less obvious than the above, there can be little doubt who was his 'jo', the Scots colloquialism for a loved one:

But oh she bothers me gie sair [sic],
For Stanley Baldwin is her jo
An' jauntily she's said me "No".[124]

Herein lies the clearest indication that MacDonald's feelings for Edith were changing. Their correspondence developed a wistful romanticism from 1930 and both agreed that political divergences in opinion should not hinder their friendship. As he wrote on the day preceding the king's speech in 1930: 'it is the moment when we feel enemies. Let us shorten it'. He continued to often write in jest. Indeed, knowing that he would soon be out of the premier's job, he applied for an imaginary manager's post at one of the Londonderry pits in September 1930. But Edith began to worry about the political damage that their association could cause, reacting so badly to the gossip column in the *Evening News* that she wrote directly to the paper's proprietor, Rothermere in complaint. She also aired her concerns to MacDonald but he was unrepentant: 'Promise to let me judge whether accepting invitations from you damage me or not. My fear is that you may be injured amongst your folk for asking me to sit at your table. And for harbouring hesitations as to what people may say are we not fools?'[125]

It was to Edith that MacDonald turned when Thomas, Secretary of State for Air in both his cabinets, was killed on the maiden flight of airship R101: 'I am lonely and broken and just want to go away and be alone and try to forget what has happened.' But soon he was attending another Londonderry reception, this time to meet dominion representatives at the Imperial Conference and the public association between Edith and MacDonald continued to grow: he introduced her as a speaker at the Sutherland Association in Glasgow and the press also carried photos of them sitting beside one another at a banquet in the Connaught Rooms for the Maharaja of Alwar.

Edith held her now customary eve of session reception for Baldwin and the Conservatives in October 1930 and with an estimated 1,000 present there seemed to be no sign of the event's popularity diminishing. The *Sunday Graphic* subsequently entered into a lengthy, and ultimately complimentary, examination of the alternatives open to a hostess of Edith's ilk:

> In the first case the hostess might say to herself:- "It is up to me to represent the pre-war idea of Conservatism. Times may change, but I shall not..."... This is a very reasonable point of view and much safer...than trying to move with the times.
> A Middle Course. - It sounds easy enough - but how much easier to be a little too free, a little too Bohemian, and a little too democratic. By sticking to what has always been done the hostess knows that she is safe, but by launching out into unknown spheres she has to rely on her own judgement to progress, and yet keep intact the grandeur and dignity with which she has been entrusted... Lady Londonderry was the first hostess to realise that it was possible to organise a political reception in such a way that people could *enjoy* it.[127]

Although other aristocratic women, such as the Duchesses of Norfolk, Roxburghe and Devonshire as well as the Countess of Derby entertained royalty, the Duchess of Sutherland and the Countess of Ellesmere gave a couple of political receptions in the 1926-28 period at Bridgewater House and there was some diplomatic entertaining at London embassies, society guide, *The Queen*, placed Edith in a category of her own: she was the one 'who can give any kind of entertainment.'[128]

The increased press attention of early 1930 was, however, nothing in comparison to what would follow. Edith's cousin, the Duke of Sutherland, accompanied her to Chequers in November where, by MacDonald's admission, she raised 'in a more virulent form the project of a national government'[129]:

> The proposal is that the Government somehow (events will show) should resign, that there should be no election (no one except a group of Tory partisans want it and it would not be good for the country) but a cabinet formed from all parties. From one quarter I am urged to remain Prime Minister, but others think that none of the leaders should take that office. Lady L. says she thinks I should go to the F.O. [Foreign Office], 'departyise' it and remain after the next change. My own feeling is to go out altogether, give a pledge that I shall not hamper the govt., but be free to express views of my own which party responsibility renders impossible (difficult role but possible) and offer to do anything for the Govt. which it wishes but out of office. This I fear would break the [Labour] Party but it has broken itself.[130]

Perhaps this was no more than a discussion of current political cabal but late 1930 also provides the first firm evidence of Edith exerting influence on Mac-Donald. Charley's name, along with that of Lords Zetland and Lothian, was aired for the Indian viceroyalty, a posting Londonderry coveted each time it became vacant since 1916. Edith, however, remained opposed and thus canvassed Mac-Donald to take the Indian position for himself: 'Lady L. urges strongly, claims support of Princes, mentions [it] to several important persons.' The following day he noted in his diary: 'Lady L. returned last night to subject of India and Duke of York present. Have mentioned subject to Ishbel; neither of us likely to bite, though I confess to feeling a grim humour.' By mid December Lord Londonderry was pushing MacDonald in the same direction and, in tangent with his wife, aired the possibility of a national government.[131] MacDonald was yet to be convinced of the merits either: unsure that he could end his political career in India and finding the Tories 'offensive and cocky' in the lower house. The latter, however, did not prevent him visiting Edith's childhood home and Sutherland's seat, Dunrobin Castle and staying with the Londonderrys at Loch Choir. Beatrice Webb vented her spleen to her diary:

> Alas! Alas! Balmoral is inevitable; but why the castles of the wealthiest, most aristocratic, most reactionary and by no means the most intellectual of the Conservative Party? "Because," J. R. M. [MacDonald] would answer if he laid bare his heart, "I am more at home with them than I should be with you or with any other leader of the Labour Party." Considering that he represents Seaham his friendship with the Londonderrys almost amounts to a public scandal. This silly little episode will do the P.M. untold damage…He *ought* not to be more at home in the castles of the great than in the homes of his followers. It argues a perverted taste and a vanishing faith.[132]

Webb's pique was not unique and Edith, alone amongst her aristocratic compeers, would soon be referred to as 'the siren'.[133] Even former detractors, like

Headlam, were forced to acknowledge, 'Circe is full of life and as you get to know her better you appreciate her charm - apparently Ramsay MacDonald is more than ever at her feet and writes to her every day. How ridiculous it is for a Socialist P.M. to make such an ass of himself with a Society Queen'.[134] But this 'Society Queen' was becoming more politically influential, pushing her own party and MacDonald towards non-party government. Lloyd George 'went so far to claim that Lady Londonderry's influence lay behind the very formation of the National Government'.[135] And he was not alone. Sean O'Casey advised her, though with his tongue firmly in his cheek, 'God help you all to use your victory wisely, for it is far easier to be wise in a defeat than it is to be wise in a victory…You have played Judith in this fight, though Holofernes hasn't yet lost his head. Who is Holofernes? Ah, guess.'[136] Other correspondents, like Professor Lindeman, also accredited her with the move towards a more collective form of government but as The Ark's 'Philosopher' he was not the most objective commentator: 'I am sure we must thank you more than any one person in England…That the appeal was a national one, that the most unexpected yet vigorous assistance was enrolled on the side of the angels, is to be put down almost entirely to you. You are not called Circe for nothing.'[137]

In considering these claims MacDonald's opening speech to parliament in 1929 is significant as he hinted at a desire to move toward a less partisan state: 'I wonder how far it is possible, without in any way abandoning any of our Party positions, without in any way surrendering any item of our Party principles, to consider ourselves more a Council of State and less as arrayed regiments facing each other in battle.'[138] But he was soon tried by more pressing concerns. No solution to the crux problem of unemployment could be found, indeed, perhaps there was none, but the government struggled to offer any alternative in the face of Conservative and Liberal demands to cut unemployment benefit. By early February, Hugh Dalton, Henderson's parliamentary secretary in the Foreign Office, wished Labour's term in office was over: 'High hopes are falling like last autumn's leaves…one wishes we had never come in. We have forgotten our programme or been bamboozled out of it by officials. One almost longs for an early and crushing defeat.'[139]

Plagued by the budget, unemployment, international affairs and industrial disputes in the cotton and coal industries, Lloyd George and Conservative MP, John Buchan appear to have been the first to suggest the idea of a national government to MacDonald in September 1930 and in the following month Buchan was certainly the first to raise the idea in parliament. Whilst Edith talked privately to MacDonald at Chequers, Buchan, with fellow Conservatives Stanley, Elliot and Horne, called for an end to party government in The Times. Edith made her support for a national government public on the following day. Her letter to The Times was essentially a rallying call for action, 'for deeds and less words…fiddling with facts instead of fighting them':

There is no confidence left in those who only talk. Criticism without construction, platitudes without a policy, are worse than useless at this moment. The man in the street is waiting for a lead. It is not so much a question of which party, but of good government…What is the use of asking for sacrifice and talking of discipline if they do not define the path of duty? We know by past experience of the War that the nation is always more truly responsive to an appeal to duty than to self-interest, and that they are ready to respond to a call for a great effort. But for a great effort the issues must be clear-cut, and there must be loyalty to their leader, otherwise the effort must fail.[140]

Edith certainly helped to persuade MacDonald that this was the best and, indeed, the only, course of action to 'save the country'. Such influence provided inspiration for Michael J. O'Prune's 1931 poem, 'Circe Old and New', where he compared her to her mythical namesake:[141]

Another Circe on another Isle
So works her wonders to our admiration
We pass the older Circe with a smile
As nothing but a wash-out imitation.

She's brought the other's system up to date
And makes it serve a crying public need
We know its Circe, though the TIMES says FATE
Has turned its solemn preachments into deed.

She took the direst creatures she could find,
With horns and tails and fangs and fearsome yells,
And to our joy she's changed them and their kind
To nation-leading statesmen by her spells.

She saw the job to do and none to do it,
So put a leader where none grew before,
Showed him the chance to serve and led him to it,
To save the day and thrill us to the core.

WHAT DOES THE OLD ENCHANTRESS LOOK LIKE NOW?
An aimless joker and a shrewdish Tartar.
While modern Circe steals our hearts AND how!
And richly earns the Order of the Garter.[142]

But Conservative acceptance of MacDonald as a potential leader of any national administration was far from absolute by the start of 1931. Within Londonderry ranks, by comparison, empathy, familiarity and, most crucially, trust already existed. Privately MacDonald pondered whether this relationship would compromise his opposition to the Conservatives but convinced himself that it would not: 'Dined à trois Park Lane. Ought I? Can I attack his institutions as it ought to be attacked? I can, and at any rate I shall.'[143] Despite the pricks at his conscience, he continued to socialise with them and spar with Edith on their different political outlooks: 'How wrong you are about Socialism…Shall I throw one of my poor books at your head? I shall not because I don't want to convert you. You would be a Left Winger and do nothing but give me trouble.'[144] Essentially he believed they could 'be friends without besmudging our principles' and, in terms of the response that the 1931 political situation demanded, party diminished in import.[145] By late August MacDonald was convinced of the need to 'commit political suicide to save the crisis...decided only Nat[ional]: Gov[ernmen]t: wd. do to meet the crisis, and on urgent request of all, I consented to continue as P.M. ... this is a lonely job...We are like marooned sailors on a dreary island'.[146]

In the approach to the election Edith was tireless in her promotion of the National Government, addressing some twenty meetings in the north of England in the space of eight days and speaking on seven platforms on the eve of the poll. And she was frequently encouraged by the reception. In Newcastle and Jarrow, for example, where 'we were all howled down at the pervious elections...they listened quite attentively and in the end I was embraced by two of the filthiest old hags I have ever seen, waving Labour flags.'[147] Edith was, however, uncompromising in differentiating between the outgoing Labour administration and a new national basis of government, emphasising MacDonald's loyalty and self-sacrifice in the face of his former 'inefficient spendthrift' colleagues who 'ran away from the crisis which they themselves created'. Nor was she adverse to scaremongering, suggesting that 'The National Government is the one safeguard today against a Socialist dictatorship [and] the forces of anarchy.'[148]

MacDonald wrote to her on the day of the formation of the National Government, 24 August 1931, addressing her as his 'best friend':

> Your letter with its patent specific for burden lightening has just come...my clouds have darkened. ...The general opinion amongst my friends here is that I have committed suicide. ...I shall welcome a sight of you again and put on a collar and a shirt which will hide the hangman's rope around my neck. As you know you are mine.[149]

This ministry, with MacDonald at its head, was sworn in two days later and his worst fears of a Labour desertion were soon realised: only a few, including Snowden and Sankey, remained loyal and MacDonald was expelled from the Labour Party in September.

However, this was no ordinary coalition. Rather it was an emergency suspension of party politics to meet the twin crises of finance and unemployment. But Edith became one of its most vocal defenders. She corresponded with Baldwin in November who, although on side, believed he was 'up against the job of my life to keep our huge majority happy and make Ramsay's curiously composite government function' and he was, therefore, 'really grateful' for her letter and 'the friendship and support I have always had from you and Charlie.'[150] Through the early 1930s, when opening church fêtes, charity fundraisers and delivering more formal political addresses to Conservative and Unionist associations Edith's message never wavered in calling for unity and support for continuing the non-party basis of politics. Although pragmatic in her assertion that 'nobody loves a government which represents all Parties as much as...a government that represents...

Party alone; for a Party government commands a loyalty which a coalition can never expect to enjoy', she often faced virulent criticism.[151] Catcalls of jobbery in the midst of her widespread electioneering in the north-east of the country in October 1931 forced her to defend her husband's re-appointment as Commissioner for Works in MacDonald's new government even though he no longer had a cabinet place.[152] And at a Barnard Castle meeting on 23 October 1931 Edith responded directly to Beatrice Webb's accusatory questioning of Londonderry's place in the new government by asserting her spouse's patriotism and her defence was not only verbal. Three days later in a letter to the *Evening World* she tackled the 'falsehoods' that were circulating about her husband at more length. Under the headline of 'Election lies exposed by Lady Londonderry' and 'Husband's name defended', she not only cited Beatrice Webb as the source of the rumours behind her husband's re-appointment, but also scorned the Webbs' record of public service. In Edith's view, Charley, silenced and excluded from the electoral contest in Durham by his Lord Lieutenancy, had been subject to much abuse:

> His name is either mentioned as an object of derision, or held up to obloquy as a blood-sucking landlord - with the additional crime of being a peer...I dislike very much to have to mention these things, but I intend to do so in order that once and for all the people shall judge for themselves between those who do nothing but stir up class prejudice...I regret very much to have had to write at such length about my husband; nothing could be more distasteful to both of us, but I felt after having spoken at a great many meetings in the country where these ridiculous rumours are being bandied about I would tell the electors the plain and untarnished truth...For the sake of this old country, do let us sink our party differences and prejudices, and work together for the common cause.[153]

On the same day she published an election message to women in the north of England, again deriding Webb as well as Lansbury's simplified statements on the economic crisis, 'written with the specific object of deluding well-meaning working men and working women...If it was "such a simple matter" why did the last Socialist Government resign?...We are standing on the edge of a precipice...The choice now is - *National Co-operation and Reconstruction or National Bankruptcy and Disaster.*'[154]

Politically isolated as the pariah of his party, the loneliness that long plagued MacDonald intensified and his need for Edith's sympathy cemented the change in his sentiments that emerged during the previous year.[155] Now he often he addressed her as 'dearest Friend':

> "I am just off" you say "When I might see you and be a help". I unsay nothing in that message. You do cheer me up and when you are not about I imagine you...The political situation is full of current and counter currents[,] reasonable and unreasonable, so how long we [the National Government] shall last I know not yet... My love has not yet been dried up by my worries, so you can come in exchange.[156]

A few weeks later the tone was the same, but he also expressed his gratitude to Charley, 'your better half - or is that quarter?':

> I have always stood for the equality of women and their identity in all things with husbands, pray observe that we now enter upon new relations and you too must obey my orders...I lay the laurels aside and think of those who are gone and feel very lonely. I hope that what I have done may help the country and perhaps stir the hearts of people outside...I shall take the liberty of kissing your hand when I see you for have I not defied all your pet horrors from the T.U.C. downwards.
>
> But they have hoisted the "Jolly Roger" and shots will soon be whizzing about our ears. With you in the boat I shall keep away from port as long as I can, and what would you say if I ran you in the end on a desert island? I am a rash Captain and the crew could easily be persuaded to become mutineers. Gretton, Churchill and a few like are on board without oars in their hands and with pistols at their belts. So with such a skipper and such a crew you must keep a vigilant eye upon your own safety, but I can still subscribe myself with affection to be always yours[.][157]

And Edith's letter to Charley written on the following day hinted that she might be able to secure him a cabinet place: 'Not that I flatter myself that it has made the change but it won't have done any harm...I should stick to your decision about a seat in the Cabinet unless there is a very obvious reason for not being in'.[158]

With Conservatives holding eleven of the twenty cabinet seats, MacDonald was considering an autumn increase in their number to reflect their Commons' majority. This prompted a competitive clamour for office, but the appointment of Charley as Secretary of State for Air with a cabinet seat took even him by surprise. Edith had been at Chequers a few days earlier and went for a long walk with MacDonald as her 'attendant gillie'. Their surviving letters fail to detail what passed between them but even family biographer and former private secretary to Lord Londonderry, Montgomery Hyde admitted that Edith's 'strong friendship' with the Prime Minister was influential, tipping 'the balance in Londonderry's favour in the face of rival claimants such as Hoare...Edith Londonderry's day at Chequers had not been in vain...The choice of this ministry was certainly not Baldwin's.'[159] Nor was it Churchill's: he disapproved of the appointment, doubting both Londonderry's credentials for the post and that an effective air department could be run from anywhere but the Commons. But Londonderry was not a wholly spent political force, advising MacDonald that Ponsonby 'should be appointed leader of the Lords' and being offered, for the third time, the post of Governor of Canada in 1931. His rough rebuke to the king with regard to the latter possibly alludes to the fact that he knew, or at least hoped, that he had an alternative: 'The positions in which we are invited to represent your majesty are rapidly becoming sinecures, and apart from entertaining and visiting different parts of the area...there was almost nothing to do.'[160] He believed acceptance would essentially result in 'being completely extinguished and by making what would be a real sacrifice I could not see that I could do very much good...So I have definitely chosen the arduous path of politics here'.[161] But that path was considerably less testing with his wife and MacDonald on side.

Despite MacDonald's close relationship with Edith and the worst suspicions of Labour, he never converted to conservatism. Indeed, one constant in his leadership of the National Government was his determination to prevent the re-emergence of party, but this was an increasingly difficult stance to maintain. On a personal basis he found many of the Conservatives convivial company, but noted towards the end of 1931:

the political company in which I find myself gets increasingly distasteful. I cannot live in it...I am worn out and feel more and more isolated. I must not let this go too far. Better retire and gain some vigour for work in the country to rally Labour round a policy of Socialism. Close acquaintance with the Tories does not improve one's respect for nor interest in them.[162]

As 1931 drew to a close, Edith again offered him some words of comfort, insinuating that she, at least, would remain loyal:

Whatever this year may bring to us all - it has cemented our friendship so I hear it, no ill will - for better for worse - for richer for poorer, in sickness or in health - and I shall hold you to it, no matter how far you wander - I'll not let you escape. As for growing older - what matter...remember what I said to you that day - you can't be General, and all the other ranks besides...now it is yourself I am thinking about - time will show - I'm not sure where any of us stand - so let us keep a port hole open - but come what may - feasts or no feasts - you are not going to escape from my Ark ever - you are not the Raven so I shall not let you out - and you will end in being quite a nice Minotaur[.][163]

And MacDonald seemed more than happy to oblige the woman he now addressed as 'Dearest Friend o'Mine'; 'You do not know how helpful you are' with her letters 'a refuge in memory...My dear, my love.'[164]

Edith's importance in MacDonald's ministry was further increased by its cross-party strata: not all its members were well acquainted with one another and, with no processes of familiarisation with colleagues as was the norm in a party government or shadow cabinet, most were unused to working with one another. Her Londonderry House receptions on behalf of the new government, therefore, now provided another important political function. Yet Edith regarded making the arrangements for her first National Government reception in February 1932 as simply 'business' and informed MacDonald:

the tea party - so called - is to meet "first yourself"...which means all the supporters of the National Party - The one difference from other parties of all sorts, will be the hour. It was a bitter day for me to stand on those stairs with L.G. in the coalition days - but no one will be more happy than I shall when *you* are there - and both of us[,] C[harley] and I[,] are pleased to think you will be receiving your supporters - You are the first National Prime Minister.[165]

But this 'business' provoked widespread rumours about her influence as 'the Mother of the National Government' and *The Star* was one of several papers to comment on the political capital that MacDonald gained from her[166]:

Londonderry House is being used for those entertaining duties which are so necessary to a Prime Minister with a mixed team to drive…Londonderry House proved a useful card recently to take a 'Churchill' trick. Certain inexperienced, but enthusiastic back benchers were being carefully played by the Churchill fisherman.
    A dinner at Londonderry House, a little stiff instruction to political wisdom by the Marquis [sic], much talk and sweetness by the Marchioness and the erring ones were coaxed back into the MacDonald Street.[167]

By comparison, the *Evening Standard* sniped that the time change of this reception from its customary evening slot to the afternoon on the grounds of economy turned the event into a 'glorified tea party…[in] the place of the stately reception of former days.'[168] Others were more explicit, musing that the cause of the time change was political, 'for a Prime Minister of Socialist views to stand at the head of a great double staircase in one of London's most aristocratic mansions receiving the fine flower of the Conservative party at a glittering evening assembly might worry some of his own special and ancient following.'[169] MacDonald's brief mention of the event also alludes to the fact that he felt there was 'something lacking. Big afternoon receptions too much like herds to be satisfactory.'[170] He was also uncomfortable: 'If I stick to this job and be your supporter at the top of the stairs, I shall be a more solitary figure than ever - a mule, in short, with a hybrid ancestry and no possible posterity.'[171] But neither the timing of the event nor the negative press commentary impacted on its popularity or consequence. The press estimated 1,500 to 3,000 guests were present and the reception was a visible expression of the national composition of the new government.
    But Edith was sufficiently incensed by some of the coverage, especially in the *Daily Express*, to write at length to Lord Beaverbrook:

I regret very much that you will not even trust yourself to telephone this house. I know you are too nervous to come here and this I appreciate.
    The question I wished to ask you is this. Do you really wish to quarrel with me personally? and, if so, for what reason?…Do you think it better to try and pick a quarrel with this house - or to be friendly? Which will be of most use to you. There are many ways in which your paper has been of the greatest help to me in the past…There are many ways, I expect in which I might also be of help to yourself. But since you have, through your paper, chosen to single me out as a butt…I cannot but feel that your attitude is most unfriendly…and you have never sent me any apology, in spite of having directed your attention to it myself.

I do not consider the matter is of sufficient importance to have a real feud and I would prefer to be on friendly terms with you, but if your people persist in writing about this house - I shall have to take other steps, which will mean a vendetta and will be unseemly for both of us. The choice lies with you...I wish to know whether it is friend or foe - peace or war.[172]

Beaverbrook, in tangent with much of the press, chose the latter course. On Edith's arrival at Mount Stewart in November 1931, for example, 'there were camera men and reporters everywhere - so we fled into the men's room - It really is too bad - one climbed over the wall last night'.[173] Press interest in the Prime Minister's social activities increased, covering the weekends he spent with the Londonderrys in December 1931 and January 1932. By March photographers were banned from the Spanish Infantas' visit to Mount Stewart for fear that it would be misconstrued: 'such photographs in the newspapers do a great deal of harm as they always appear to be a display of extravagance and self-advertisement and are likely to give an entirely wrong impression.'[174] Edith, a shareholder in the *Morning Post*, mistakenly believed that this entitled her to 'a certain amount of consideration from the Editor'.[175] But innuendo and Labour, as well as some Conservative, disapproval of their friendship, such as F. E. Smith's censure that Charley was 'catering his way to the cabinet', brought MacDonald and Edith even closer: 'I...according to many of your friends, was a traitor and a spy during the war, but you know I was not; whilst you, according to many of my friends, are a horrid and bad women, and I know you are a dear good creature.'[176] By 1932, however, with the joke that MacDonald no longer sang 'The Red Flag' but 'The Londonderry Air' doing the rounds, Charley admitted to his wife:

I am really rather frightened at the gossip and believe there has been some talk in the papers about 'petticoat influence': the P.M. said something about this at lunch. ...You will find out if he is thinking anything about it when you see him before he leaves for Geneva; but you must remember that everyone is ready to gossip and say unkind things.

Edith's reaction was more stoic, 'any good either of us do - or myself in particular - outweighs the bad of any gossip.'[177]

The increasing controversy surrounding this friendship caused unease and this is evident in both MacDonald's and Edith's collection of papers. He wrote her some 400 letters and postcards, but her name is almost wholly absent from his diaries.[178] His first mention of her only comes in 1930, six years after their first meeting. Moreover, in their correspondence some of their opening addresses of 'dearest' have been scored out or the '–est' blacked out. Her use of the abbreviated forms of his Ark pseudonym, 'dearest H', banal though they may appear, have received a similar treatment while closures such as, 'fondest love' have also been concealed although it is impossible to tell at what stage, or by whose hand, this was done. Even Montgomery Hyde's innocuously titled manuscript, 'Mount Stewart and its owners' is censored with the sentence reading this 'controversial friendship which undoubtedly helped her husband's career' defaced.[179]

Despite the gossip and disquiet, Londonderry House was also being put to dip-
lomatic use to improve Anglo-French relations. This was proclaimed by the *Daily
Telegraph* to be 'the outcome of a conversation which [the French Prime Minister]
M. Tardieu had with Lady Londonderry when she was recently in Paris' attending
the British ambassador, Lord Tyrell's dinner for over sixty people in her honour.
There Edith took Tardieu into dinner, relaying a message to him from Mac-
Donald: 'your love message to him, through me!!! and Heaven knows what I did-
n't say to him about you - all lies of course! but you will guess that!'[180] She also, in
a clear indication that her faith in personal contact for political purpose was undiminished, encouraged him to meet MacDonald. This led *Le Cri de Paris* to declare
her MacDonald's muse, a 'political woman…who knows about all the most arduous, internal and external political questions' of the type that no longer existed in
France and without whom 'MacDonald does nothing'.[181] On her return, Edith
initiated a correspondence with the French premier which resulted in him pledging that he would be 'happy to see' MacDonald again:

> in the great hope that we will be able to do some useful work.…I shall be
> delighted to dine informally at your house…with our mutual friend…We shall
> meet on Monday morning at 11 am for the official conversation but I think
> that it would be good if, before that, the Prime Minister and I were to have a
> one-to-one conversation for about half an hour.
> Do you agree? If so, could you set that up?[182]

To the press, there was no doubt that this was 'a diplomatic move in both ori-
gin and intent' with Edith using Londonderry House to provide 'a mellow atmosphere in which the acid rivalries of Europe can be discussed and neutralised'.[183]
She was obviously delighted with the outcome of her diplomatic manoeuvres,
telling MacDonald that she deserved 'a good mark…Tardieu's earnest wishes to
see you - only you - and nothing but you!! are partly the outcome of that luncheon in Paris'.[184] The British Ambassador to Paris was working toward the same
end, impressing upon Tardieu the importance of cultivating a personal relationship with MacDonald and writing to Edith, 'It is going to be a vital meeting and
again it is with the same Circe that brought Ramsay and S.B. [Stanley Baldwin]
who is bringing these two Prime Ministers together.'[185] Tardieu and MacDonald
subsequently had a private meeting at Londonderry House on the night of 4 April
and for her part in this, Edith was widely commended. As one correspondent
observed, 'I am a great believer in personal interviews as the best way of achiev-
ing satisfactory results for if I may presume to say so, I think you are a very good
hand at 'willing a bird off a bush".[186] And A. L. Kennedy of *The Times* mused,
with an illusion to her predecessor Frances Anne, 'How much more open these
friendships can be now than in the days of Dizzy!'[187] But by May 1932 this
'friendship' was over and Tardieu's last letter to Edith feared difficult days lay
ahead, hinting at the growing drift between Anglo-French reactions to German
renewal: 'I'm afraid that in Britain people are not inclined to watch too closely
what is developing in Germany. In Berlin, they seem to be *completely* mad!'[188]

Within three years, Edith would again use identical personal tactics of persuasion, only this time in an attempt to salve Anglo-German relations.

By the middle of 1932 MacDonald was tired, increasingly worried that his memory was failing and disillusioned by Conservative commitment to the government. But there was no doubting Edith's allegiance to the national cause: she espoused the pro-national message to a politically mixed meeting of women at Seaham on 26 October and in the next month the eve of session reception at Londonderry House caused the *Yorkshire Evening Press* to echo sentiments previously expressed in 1930, 'Have we come to a new Liberal understanding or is it due to Lady Londonderry's genius as a hostess in making the lions lie down with the lambs?'[189] MacDonald was evidently grateful for her continued support:

> I have to tell my hostess how she mothered me, and try and tell her how I loved it. One evening she rubbed a startled nerve and soothed it by the magic of her hand and I could hardly bear her going away, I felt so miserable and deserted…for three days I seemed to be living an old existence, and my hostess and I had known each other from the beginning when there was only the Word and nothing but the Word, and would know each other until the Word resumed its empire, and that with her I wandered in rich autumn pastures where gentle winds blew and the air was benign?[190]

As MacDonald became increasingly worn down by the pressures of office, his attachment to Edith deepened: 'We are silly, aren't we? - and yet I confess I love to be silly - with *you*. I wish I could write what I feel, but in the first place I am tired and dull and in the next it would be indiscreet' and, in a phrase that was reminiscent of Frances Anne's association with Alexander I, he concluded, 'we are both clad in the armour of discretion.' Soon there could be no mistaking his feelings: 'the silly fact is that I love you. Isn't it a nuisance?'[192] In a letter written in May 1932, after Edith called to see him in court dress, he addressed her as 'My Dearest of Dear Persons' and though he hesitated to 'embarrass her' with his emotional confession, he enclosed an additional note with an, obviously ignored, instruction to turn it 'to ashes':

> You were very beautiful, and I loved you. The dress, dazzling in brilliance and glorious in colour and line, was you, and my dear, you were the dress. I just touch its hem, and pray for your eternal happiness wondering at the same time what generous hearted archangel ever patted me on the back and arranged that amongst the many great rewards that this poor unwelcome stranger to this world was to receive that he would be permitted before he returned to his dust to feel devotion to *you*.[193]

His tone was similarly expressive a few days later, 'My trouble with you is that you make me so happy that I *will* be dainty with you, will pull your leg, will approach you as a *devoué*. And you will say: "Tiresome creature, why this inferiority complex?" Why because I am a devotee…So don't be silly and delightful and don't apply democracy to love.' He ventured further in a postscript:

Of course those who are bearing heavy burdens, or who work amidst gloom or discouragement, or who have to draw heavily upon nervous and spiritual energy, or who work by faith or by visions, should have the frankest friendship with the right kind of the other half. The tragedy of the misfit is heartbreaking and irreparable but the bliss and power of the heaven-chosen mating cannot be told. Perhaps I have made a mistake in taking memory as the constant companion, but who can say with assurance? The (what I might call) mechanism of mating is so delicate and so apt to get out of order that no one can assume the ideal...Bless you always.

Edith was never as dramatic as MacDonald, but she showed genuine concern and affection for him: 'I do hope you are not doing too much and worrying - I wish I was with you to have a good laugh - which is all that matters. My v[er]y fond love to you - you dear and great soul - I love you v[er]y much and admire you more'.[195] She was also not adverse to ask for help: canvassing his support, for example, to move the British Ambassador at Prague to Vienna and secure the Prince of Wales for the opening of the Northern Ireland parliament in 1932: 'If anyone can get him - it can only be you. ...You are such a dear to me - and I love you so much and no wonder.' A week later the royal opening was arranged, 'You have been an angel about H.R.H. - it is all settled now - and I as distinct from an official thing - have settled that you are to come here - *Please* do - I have let it be known all over Ulster - the Prince's visit is due to you - so you must come - Anyhow begin thinking of it'.[196] During the Spanish Civil War, she passed him letters from the exiled King Alfonso and the former Foreign Minister, the Duke of Alba, marking envelopes with the command, 'You must look at these - For P.M.'[197] She again sought his assistance in seeking royal patronage for the Personal Services League and attaining cabinet sanction for training women in the inter-war period on the same lines as wartime Voluntary Aid Detachments. In return, she freely offered him her advice: advising him, worried by his memory in 1931, to write his speeches out; encouraging him, unsuccessfully, to accept an honour for his services in 1933 and making her own recommendations for the 1935 honours list.[198] She was also politically uninhibited. In response to his qualms about German militarism, for instance, she opined: 'Personally I should *go* for the Germans - t[he]y can't fly - and you and France between you can coerce them - I *hate* seeing you worried'.[199] Another letter, most likely written in 1932, saw her recommending axing disruptive elements, like Johnnie Baird, from the government as well as trying to convince MacDonald that the Tories were his allies:

it is quite the height of absurdity that S.B. [Baldwin] should obstruct you...a heart to heart between you and me - would help everybody - I am not good at seeing both sides of the question - and in your case I may be too partisan - but I am supposed to be quite logical - and level headed - and I feel sure I can help...it matters very much - that the best and highest motives that caused you to save the country at the last Election are not to be lost.

I am going to talk to you now quite openly…I know you resent the conservative Party v[er]y deeply - but t[he]y have helped you in a great crisis too -
you must not forget that there is more than a possibility of points of view
coming quite close to-gether…therefore it is all the more necessary for the
sake of all - for Johnnie [Baird] to be removed - If I might s[a]y so - you have
played your lot - and those who are left are those you can depend on - We
have still to do this - it will happen but don't condemn all - Please let me see
you and talk this all over - Might I suggest it would be far better and far more
efficacious - if a few of our representatives were called to-gether and JB's letter read to them - This is what I should do - you must always attack the enemy - The other way will make real mischief - and it would be cruel to undo in
such a way all that you have sacrificed…You are too wise to do anything as
you suggest[.][200]

Edith's dual interest in the National Government and the Conservative Party
led her to write on the same topic to Baldwin. Declaring herself the 'official
watch dog for you, in your party', she again pilloried Baird 'the most tactless man
I know':

he has now driven a wide breach between the Prime Minister, himself and
what really does matter, the conservative Party - for some time I have known
there was going to be trouble…as a rule - I never - nor does the P.M. ever
touch on Conservative Policy - What's the good?

And, ignoring MacDonald's plea for privacy, she quoted him verbatim to Baldwin, adding her own view that Baird's want of tact 'causes the P.M. to be unreasonable':

Should J.B. drive the P.M. out it would be a blow our Party could not stand
up to at present…the P.M. should have no party - and he should never be
within sight of a party machine…I have written to the P.M. saying he much
better hand the letter over to his Tory supporters and let them deal with it
through you…I hope you will approve of what I have done.[201]

Baldwin's feelings on Edith's level of influence were mixed, but others happily
came on board to use her as a means to sway the premier. From Paris, Tyrell
encouraged her to keep MacDonald at the government's helm whilst Sankey saw
a central place for her and her political salon in the deliberations of the 1932 Ot-
tawa conference to negotiate free trade within the empire: 'The 'Ark' will be
more useful than ever in the deluge'.[202] And, as interest in this relationship intensified, even the king was tempted to comment:

Obviously he wanted to say something about you to me - Stopped with great
difficulty - and said it was a dirty story he could not remember!! Isn't it a pity
for all of you - I can guess what is going to be said before the words are spo-

ken!!...When you write - just tell me this - as it is what I want to know most...that matters are a little less perplexing[.][203]

Some sections of the press, however, especially in Northern Ireland, rallied to Edith's defence. The *Belfast New-Letter* chose not to announce MacDonald's 1932 visit to Mount Stewart on the grounds that this 'would give rise...to inferences which are unwarranted', making clear that he was simply 'an old friend of his host and hostess'. But much of the national press, like the *Daily Independent*, was less politic, suggesting with on-going wrangles with de Valera, 'it was slightly less than prudent for him [MacDonald] to go anywhere in Ireland at the present time. For the rumours and expectation which were inevitable do less than good'.[204] The gossip continued and Edith, exasperated by 'talk' in the *Morning Post*, shared her frustration with MacDonald:

of my poor self insinuating myself with people and getting round them - I am not "in" it with you. ...*How* I want to see you - I would love a gossip - and you here...I shall re-read your letters both again tonight I love them so much - almost as much as the owner whom Circe is v[er]y v[er]y fond of[.][205]

Edith was also becoming increasingly territorial and her sense of proprietorship, previously displayed in wrangles over Durham conservatism, re-emerged in November 1932. Infuriated by her husband's cousin, Lady Wimborne holding a party with the express purpose of meeting Foreign Secretary and, more importantly, Liberal, Sir John Simon on the evening of Edith's afternoon eve of session reception, she complained to both MacDonald and Simon about the party basis of such entertaining. To the former she recorded that Liberals 'absolutely crowded out of hearth and home' at her own reception:

As this Party is held in your honour, we have all agreed to refrain from Party politics, I cannot understand Sir John Simon lending his name for this purely party manoeuvre. ...It has placed Charley and myself in a most awkward position as I now feel my party should have been for Mr. Baldwin. Had I asked him to do such a thing, he would have refused straight away. I have seen him about the matter and he was, like myself, very surprised...Unless there is some substantial reason forthcoming, I feel that I can never give another National Government reception. I absolutely refuse to be made a fool of by anyone.[206]

She was even more forthright to Simon:

Why did not the Wimbornes give the National Government reception? We should have been delighted if they had. ...We agreed to drop party politics for the time being...This sort of thing is not playing the game. I have not put Mr. Baldwin's name on my card, out of deference to Liberal feelings. He has far more right and reason to have a party given for him, in view of the immense preponderance of his party in the "House". ...I want you to be perfectly frank with me and tell me if this sort of thing is going to happen regularly. If so, I shall most naturally refuse to invite any Liberals here at all. This at least is logical - you cannot eat your cake and have it.

Simon responded to the letter, which made him 'sad all day', from the Geneva disarmament conference in late November, with a firm denial of party competition, government opposition and game playing.[207] Edith, however, remained unconvinced that the Wimborne party was anything other than a Liberal manoeuvre and, in a less official letter to MacDonald written on the same day as her former dispatch, she noted:

I could not be more flabbergasted by such behaviour - moreover you are playing with fire - the Austrian Minister rang me up this morning and asked if the Wimborne party was not very peculiar - I am so sorry about it all - I only wish now we had not given a party at all - owing to the Liberal influence there are just under 3,000 acceptances - You don't do these things, nor do I - I hate underhand tactics I don't do them myself and certainly don't expect our colleagues to do them.[208]

MacDonald was similarly tried by the non-party basis of politics and Edith increasingly had to bolster his spirits:

You must not be depressed about the future but take as much rest as you can…however dark the horizon may appear - there is an end to ev[er]y storm…You are such a magician and although I know all that you have to contend with, with you at the helm - you will weather the storm. …I do hope you will be successful with the European powers - If you can only get them into your web - you will be able to handle them, as you always do[.][209]

In another letter she urged him to care for himself:

Please take my advice and do not try to write until you feel less exhausted - First of all if you play a tired brain - the result is never good - and it requires twice as much energy to write…I should be so interested to hear your memorandum - I feel quite sure nothing in it would anger me - How could it - If friends must always think the same on every minute details how dull the friendship would be - nothing to discuss or talk about - What signifies is the ultimate object to be achieved - what each has in mind as the goal - this is all that really matters - and you and I think - practically the same in the end - only that you are far more autocratic - I can see you smile - but fundamentally you are and you are right - because you have that in you to lead and compel - if I wasn't myself I might do both - but in the days in which we live - to be born an aristocrat - means that it must be something v[er]y exceptional to be allowed to lead at all - and to compel - hardly ever - In the great aristocracy of brain - a leader will be accepted when found - with enthusiasm but leaders are rare - rarer still like yourself - to refuse to play when you can - it is not your *rôle* - but you are so right to survey your position from all angles[.][210]

His letters to her became increasingly reflective and sad, questioning the transitory nature of their friendship and highlighting his sense of isolation: 'The day is sure to come when I shall again be of the sea and the mist, and you will continue to reign at your fireside and amongst your own people. "Once I knew him", you will say and maybe sigh. And that will be all.'[211] But, ultimately, to MacDonald, 'What a difference it makes having a friend who knows and sympathises and helps'.[212] Many, however, worried about just how susceptible MacDonald was to her influence. As Conservative MP and opponent of the National Government, Robert Bernays recorded with 'great indignation…the PM that afternoon had spent his time at a charity matinee with Lady Londonderry…at least he could have been reading his papers'.[213]

Charley was no longer being described in reference to his cabinet position or political dogma but, in a reversal of the normal descriptors applied to political wives, in relation to Edith: 'the husband of the most important political hostess the Government has'. By 1933 the press had also decided Edith's fate. She had 'already won her place in history as the *Grande Dame* of the twentieth-century thirties…having greater personal power than any other women in Britain', but, like MacDonald, she paid the price of such notoriety: she resigned from the presidency of the Personal Services League as her name was 'objectionable to them' in 1933.[214] To the *Evening Standard*'s cartoonist, David Low, the Londonderrys were akin to the Borgias[215] while to others MacDonald was Edith's 'protégé' and she was 'the *via media* of the Cabinet.'[216]

Despite the criticism, Edith's remained the National Government's official hostess. In June she invited the World Economic Conference to meet the Prince of Wales and MacDonald at Londonderry House, but the latter was increasingly worried by the Tory dominance of his administration and, in a probable reference to his hostess, hinted at tension: 'My good companion is helpful but headstrong and like her kind goes like a Bull at a gate and has strong dynamitish dislikes.'[217] He continued in this vein through the next month when, in Edith's opinion, he was 'Too tired to care much for anything…Not knowing if you want to see me or not - Irritated at me and everyone - Terrified I might say anything to you - All on the edge and a bit sour face - There! I know so well… as it so happens - nothing will be said to you at all'. His reply of the following day again showed his irritability, 'I want a word or only just a look before you go…What an ass I am to want petting. Burn this and I shall confess that I do, for the world is horrid.'[218]

Even with his petulant state of mind, the correspondence continued and Ireland returned as a topic for discussion in mid 1933. Indeed, her dispatches of August reveal how unconstrained she was in letting him know her view of the Irish Free State reworking its constitutional position, informing him she that had no doubt that an Irish Republic would come, 'and the sooner the better - as it is absolutely one now':

then - and then only - will [we] be able to make terms with them for a future occasion …In the meantime the office of Governor [General] is being made fun of daily and hourly - I should withdraw it - It is most insulting…As I can not [sic] talk to you - I have sent you a screed - just what I would have said to you - It reads as rather cheek[y] - My presuming to write this - but anyhow it is partly your fault and what I would urge you to do - you see - you are such a much greater man than you allow yourself to think - and you have a position in Europe like no one else - and only you can handle America - what do party squabbles matter - where all genuine people want you and a Nat[ional] Gvt - this is what I feel so strongly - All the best elements in all three parties want you…for a Nat Gvt, there must be sacrifices - and the Conservatives being the largest homogenous whole - have to sacrifice more…but this is private between you and me[.][218]

With these concerns and MacDonald's continued harrying by some Conservative members, she urged him to visit Mount Stewart, but her letter of invitation also showed a degree of political calculation:

I note your remarks...A lot of this - *must be squashed* and it can be - by us in concert - but please keep this private - between you - C[harley] - and I. It does not represent the party as a whole…you - in yourself are so much more than anything conservative I have ever seen - a *great* gentleman - an autocrat - equal opportunities for all - and where you lead us - you give us a clear lead, no nonsense about democracy - you accept the best, reject the impossible - either ours or socialists. You really are a Heaven made dictator - It is imperative you come here to have a nice long free talk…We see so much in common - what I feel is - that our people can be controlled - the others can not, but you know best - S. B. [Baldwin] will never move again, unless you force him to, and though I know you hate Disraeli…[he] v[er]y surely remarked - "there is no reason why you should not use anyone, although you may not trust him" I commend this to you heartily.[220]

He acceded to the invite, flying to Mount Stewart in September 1933 where the Hailshams and Castlereaghs were also present, but nothing lessened his disillusion with party secessions. Although Edith did her best to counter his reservations, this was in vain:

I don't mind what you say about mere politicians…but you are a Statesman, a proper one - and about the only one…I want to have a long long talk with you about things - not a vague one - but a direct one - I am certain of two things - the first and most important one is that it is absolute nonsense your even thinking of leaving for a long long time the post you are in - the 2nd is that, as we shall have to be a National Party for a long time too - a lot can be done to ease matters for you - you must make more use of S.B. [Baldwin]…and you must learn to like and trust the nice Conservatives. You really must - as we are your real friends. Neither of the parties will absorb each other but we can be real friends…nothing will ever arise that permits you to leave…you are the only human being who can do anything - you have all my love and prayers for your success.[221]

MacDonald also felt increasingly hounded by the press, recording in his diary, 'no one is safe. Soon no wise person will write a letter except of the most guarded and formal kind, certainly none sent from heart to heart, free, gay, casual and confidential.'[222]

However, the seventeen-page invitation list for the 1933 Londonderry House eve of session reception and the 1,500 guests who attended the event suggests that negative press commentary did not impact on its popularity. Foreign ambassadors, leading political figures, including the Baldwins, mayors, cabinet members, representatives from the Admiralty, Air Ministry and War Office, European nobles like Prince Pierre of Monaco and peers like the Grevilles, Hardinges, Westminsters and the Earls of Dudley and Halsbury, were all invited.[223] The timing of this reception also reverted to the evening, a move which some of the more optimistic sections of the press deemed indicative of a return to national prosperity. MacDonald, however, was far from sanguine. Grave and pre-occupied, he found the 'crush' trying: 'Did not enjoy it a bit. The more one knows the Tory Party as a crowd the less one likes it, but of many of its individuals the opposite is true.'[224]

He was similarly worried about Charley as Secretary of State for Air, personally amending his white paper and erasing references to armament competition in October 1934. This previously marginal ministry with a decreasing budget in the early 1930s was now being scrutinised both from within government and without, its actions seen as a predictor of rearmament and the resumption of international conflict. Although Edith was a leveller, providing a sense of perspective 'on the things that matter in life',[225] MacDonald, 'the most human and understanding of men', wondered how much longer he could continue to play the lead and others were asking the very same question.[226]

Edith's notoriety also continued to grow. The *New York World Telegram* included her in its series on the great women of Europe, declaring her a 'Power in Britain' due to her 'close friendship with Prime Ministers and the royal family':

If some few years ago anybody had predicted that Ramsay MacDonald and the swank Londonderry family would become intimate friends, that the Marquess of Londonderry would become one of his stoutest supporters and that the Marchioness would have him at her famous parties as their favourite guest, English people would have doubted the sanity of the speaker…Today she is one of the most powerful people in Great Britain. If anybody holds a salon in the ancient term of the word, it is she.[227]

But, just as doubts multiplied on MacDonald's ability to lead, public opinion turned further against Edith. By early 1935 Lloyd George called her 'the Mother of the National Government' with MacDonald 'as her tame lion' in comparison to 'the old Lady Londonderry [who] had a regular zoo'.[228] An anonymous letter sent to Edith, futuristically dated AD2035, described the visit of a mother and daughter to Londonderry House, 'The child, pointing to a portrait of 'the Duchess of Ulster' (i.e. Circe Londonderry) asks 'Who is that pretty lady?' 'Don't look at it - she was an evil woman who tempted the Labour Prime Minister, Ramsay MacDonald, and turned him into a Tory. She ruined England and was very wicked." Although Edith's reaction to the letter was one of delight, 'enchanted with the ingenuity of the malice', MacDonald, by comparison, was an intensely private man and was 'very annoyed'.[229]

Feeling his age, burdened by trying to retain the national focus of the government under Conservative encroachment and anxious about the domestic and international consequences of his retirement, MacDonald was 'gloomy and worrying, and I cannot escape the conclusion…that Germany is preparing for war in the sense that it is going to do what it likes and is willing to accept war as an issue.' Edith was also thinking to the future and not just on MacDonald's behalf: 'if and when you ever leave your present job - you must give me a fair warning - We don't want to go on without you - The only thing Charley would like, supposing you do not intend to stay - is to go to India - to finish off, out there…I should be quite willing - but not if it entailed deserting you.'[230] And time was drawing to a close for both MacDonald and Lord Londonderry. An early warning sign for the latter came in February 1935 when Chamberlain and Churchill aired their hostility to him retaining the Air Ministry. Indeed, Churchill warned Charley of political intrigues in April, although he skirted over his own involvement in the same. Charley was already aware of his vulnerability and acknowledged to his wife, 'I have several enemies and…there are one or two who would like to have my place. If I survive I think it will be on your merits. I am sure the P.M. would never sponsor me again and SB [Baldwin] has always resented (I think) our support of the P.M. …I see myself being squeezed out.'[231] By May rumours were rife concerning the reconstruction of the government and Churchill was encouraging Londonderry to resign before he was axed.

Even MacDonald believed Charley had been complacent at the ministry:

He has not been very well used but he is much to blame: when he disagrees he is cantankerous and when he acquiesces he surrenders his rights. He has not developed the Cabinet mind or art of persuasion in getting on with others; he has been as I first met him as an M.P. I am sorry as he is a good hearted friend and not without ability.

But MacDonald's 'Talk at L.H. on the political situation' in late May suggests that relations were not wholly soured by the growing crisis as would be expected if this was purely a relationship of convenience. And, in the same month, he forewarned Edith of his resignation:

Frequently I have told you about party developments, but never could get a private word so matters have drifted, as I really could not write of them. Now, my health compels me to ease myself of the weight of my burdens. That is inevitable, and when it comes I shall be pretty well out of it and decisions will be more in Conservative hands than ever. For weeks I have been struggling to keep going against heavy odds and great depression and the limit is passed.[232]

Her reply also saw tensions coming to the fore as his ministry drew to a close:

Far from anger - I have been feeling deeply for you - It hurts me to think of you - after all you have done being treated like this - You keep saying you have tried to talk with me - but dearest H - you have avoided me - I have tried all I can to see you - I have been at home a lot - but nothing seemed to suit you…another thing - you say you warned me about all this - I can not call it to mind - only the vaguest references to intrigues which I thought referred to yourself - and I have had a few encounters on this score - I longed to know more - so as to lend any weight I had to counter attack - as soon as we meet - we can compare notes - Your decision is perhaps best - but it disquiets me - but the F.O. [Foreign Office] is the most frightening without you - as Anthony [Eden] is not man enough for the job now…So dearest - let us try and meet soon - I so want to see your dear self - and hold your hand and thank you for all too!![233]

Baldwin was confirmed as MacDonald's successor in that month and the latter was realistic about the consequences. Writing to Edith four days prior to his formal resignation on 6 June, he informed her that a 'National Govt. controlled by a Conservative maj. - is what is being worked out'.[234] MacDonald took over as Lord President of the Council, the post Baldwin occupied since 1931, but this change made Londonderry's position far from safe: underlining the insecurity of patronage in an increasingly meritocratic world. MacDonald warned Londonderry to be careful in July, but this only provoked an embittered response:

I wish you had more of the Dictator spirit. I have got it, but neither the capacity nor the power. You have both and seem not to realize it…I do not accept your ideas about the Conservatives. I do not believe it at all. I feel I know that if you summoned them and discussed things with them and by that I mean "us", we should all feel we knew better what you wanted.
I am not complaining because I know your tremendous preoccupations, but a ten minutes talk would have explained to me what was in your mind…Forgive my outspokenness but I will not accept the situation as you put it to me very privately and very confidentially, and I hope you will stick to it.[235]

However, Charley's sense of loyalty to the Conservative Party was misplaced. To Baldwin he was MacDonald's man and, in consequence, had been promoted beyond his abilities. There was also growing personal hostility. Although Baldwin was party to many a Londonderry House reception and was an Ark member, he disliked the continued fusion of politics and society a decade after what he deemed 'the golden age of corruption'. That the Londonderrys 'proceeded to entertain politically on a vast scale with, of course, the set purpose of political advancement...It was very magnificent and beautifully done', but to Baldwin it was out of date and at times 'in dubious taste':

> It did not fit in with my idea of the Tory democracy. Central Office, of course, loved it. These methods were not calculated to make him popular with colleagues...He appeared to be donning the mantle of Castlereagh a little too often. Frankly I do not think he had a flair in that direction; he was not a success at Geneva. I have always thought that his knowledge of history was too scanty to support the role to which he aspired...the worst thing of all was the alliance with Ramsay MacDonald. I have Highland blood in me and I understand the bond which unites all Highlanders, but 90% of people do not. To them her [Edith's] friendship with Ramsay is purely an act of political expediency to help his political career. All his life Ramsay has fought against everything he [Londonderry] stands for. The abrupt change is too good to be true in their eyes[.][236]

Baldwin was ruthless in his determination to be free of Londonderry. He sacked Charley from the Air Ministry, appointing him, under Lord Hailsham's persuasive reasoning, Lord Privy Seal and leader of the Lords. Londonderry alleged that the latter was his for as long as he wished but Baldwin always maintained this was a misunderstanding. Some were surprised that Londonderry was retained at all, especially with cabinet rank. Indeed, in theory his appointment as Privy Seal was a promotion but, in reality, it was little more than a sop and he accepted it reluctantly and against Edith's counsel: 'I was glad to continue my connection with the National Government because I felt that my knowledge of the air might be of some service.'[237]

Although Hailsham played a part in Charley's political survival, Edith was again believed to have been instrumental: 'Circe Londonderry, the only political hostess left, bullied Ramsay MacDonald into stipulating that Londonderry should not be dropped altogether.'[238] On this occasion, however, the pundits were mistaken. As Londonderry freely admitted, 'My wife was against me taking this offer from the very first, feeling instinctively that it was merely another stage in the plot of squeezing me out altogether. She said I ought to refuse office under the new P. M. and begged me to retire.'[239] Hailsham even apologised to Edith for his part in keeping Charley in office: 'I feel very responsible if I have influenced Charley against your judgement which is almost always right. I was so anxious that he should seem at least to fair promotion, and I couldn't bear the idea either that he should appear to be discarded, or to be throwing in his hand.'[240]

Whether due to inside information or intuition, Edith was proved right. Londonderry only held these appointments for a matter of months. With Baldwin's reconstruction of the government in November 1935, he was the only minister to be dropped in an act that, in Charley's own words, effectively wiped him 'off the face of the political map'.[241] His son's description of him learning that he was dismissed recorded 'a pathetic figure...He was sitting sideways on a chair with his legs dangling over the arm. Holding a letter in his hand with tears running down his cheeks he kept muttering, 'I've been sacked - kicked out'.'[242] Baldwin justified the decision with Churchill's earlier adage that an Air Minister could not be in the Lords. This, however, was solely a pretence: five months later Baldwin elevated Londonderry's air successor, Sir Philip Cunliffe-Lister, to Viscount Swinton and, more importantly, the upper house.

That Edith was acknowledged as the political force behind her husband was nowhere more apparent than in Baldwin's letter to her, stating his regret at Londonderry's loss of position. More sincere was the recently appointed Foreign Secretary, Samuel Hoare's letter of sympathy to her that despaired of 'troubles of politics…if we took them too seriously we should all become embittered cynics. As it is, we must take the new world as we find it. It is an unpleasant place and it is no good thinking that it is anything else…one's real friends come forward when things are going badly'.[243] But things continued to go 'badly'.

A November 1935 press statement, approved by Baldwin, was issued from Londonderry House in response to press claims that Edith had decided not to entertain, 'This is incorrect, as Lord and Lady Londonderry offered the house as usual to the Prime Minister, but Mr Baldwin considered that the present moment was not opportune.'[244] Thus, the *Evening Standard* could only satirise the eve of session reception with a cartoon showing the empty splendour of Londonderry House and kinsman Winston Churchill the lone attendee in 1935.

The idea of a long-standing rift between the Londonderrys and the Baldwins should not, however, be overdrawn. The Baldwins were invited to Mount Stewart in the summer of 1936 and socialised with the Londonderrys during the next year. It was also Londonderry who, with Derby, was responsible for the customary introduction of new peer, Earl Baldwin of Bewdley to the House of Lords in 1937. Edith certainly showed great fortitude and a grim determination to continue the familial political tradition with her husband sidelined. For a time she harboured a hope that he would be re-instated once Baldwin fell from grace and in a May 1935 letter to Ark 'Devil', Neville Chamberlain she asked him to back her husband:

I am so worried over Charley - I do not discuss Cabinet secrets with him - but I have other means of knowing what is going on - What I was going to ask you to do, is to support him - He has had a most uphill job all these years… He has had no support at all…Charley has succeeded in making the Air Force and the Air Ministry really efficient…now that at last it is realised what an important post the Air Ministry is - other people are anxious to fill the position…The only reason that my informant vouchsafed to me - was that the post was so important - it was considered necessary that it should be held by someone other than a Peer in the House of Commons!! This was what made me write to you - as I look on you - as the one person who has authority in the Cabinet - I was so upset by the statement…It is far better for the 'Air' in any way that it can not be made a party question in the House of Commons… Now please say nothing about what I have written - as my source of information is unknown to Charley - nor does he know that I have heard anything in particular…I do ask you to help him to see this sudden 'Air Mindedness' of the Cabinet[.][245]

This approach, however, produced nothing to salvage her spouse's political career. Indeed, Chamberlain took some reproach at her dispatch, telling Charley, in person and in writing, that it inferred 'intrigue' on his part. With this reprimand, Edith was at pains to explain her motivation:

> I had in my mind to place on record exactly what had been told to me - and the answers to the accusations that were being bandied about - I wrote direct to you - because these things were being connected with your name - I thought you ought to know…Had you not been a real friend - I should have done otherwise…Forgive me if I have wounded you - but I only meant to act quite straight and openly about what I actually knew - My letter was not meant to be angry with you - but I am incensed at the attitude of our people and v[er]y fearful of the results[.]

Despite her apologetics, Chamberlain still smarted. In a sparse note, marked private and personal and written after tearing up one reply, he made his position clear: 'I am very glad to know that your previous letter was not intended to bear the construction which I put upon it, and which, in fact, it was difficult to avoid. Charley is, I know, satisfied that I have not acted otherwise than as a friend to him, and I hope you now feel the same.'[246] But when he succeeded Baldwin as premier in 1937, Edith was again disappointed with the result. Chamberlain did, however, request a Londonderry reception in October 1937, underlining the value of the event, especially for provincial members of the party faithful:

> I know how greatly our people always look forward to Londonderry House parties, and how much they have missed them on the occasions when they have not been given.
> "De Mortuis Nil Nisi Bonum"…I can only repeat that your readiness to help us on this occasion, in spite of anything that happened in the past, is deeply appreciated by me and I am grateful to you both.

Chamberlain's decision to revive the reception was also carefully calculated, aware that he was 'running some risks', but he 'considered that they were well worth taking':

> and I have no regrets. It is difficult to realise what a party at Londonderry House means to the provincial Conservative…a Birmingham man who has given a great deal of money and time to the cause there…wrote me a letter of thanks that was quite touching …so once again I want to thank you and Charley…for your great service to the party.[247]

Although attended by 2,000 guests and received in some sections of the press as continuing the tradition of political entertaining, this was the last event of its kind. In the following year no reception was held, a decision applauded by 'other political hostess in London. They feel as she [Edith] does that the burden resting on the shoulders of the Prime Minister and his colleagues scarcely permits them to undertake what may be regarded as a purely social engagement.'[248] Underlying this explanation, however, was Lord Londonderry's growing political discontent, 'We get the smug-faced citizens of London with their wives and daughters who vote Conservative anyway...I always wish that we could touch the other strata where the bulk of the votes lie.'[249]

Edith supported MacDonald throughout and beyond his years at the head of the National Government. Solitary, lonely and cast aside by a party whose Socialist faith in a classless society was incompatible with his own acceptance into the Tory elite, he needed her compassion. By nature, he shied away from large assemblies, 'My social habits do not make me run to crowds but to a few where there is companionship and not entertainment'[250] and as a hostess, Edith was, therefore, invaluable. She also became his 'dearest of all friends and most desired of all companions', someone he loved to 'to gossip with...over a cigar and prattle...like an old fool'.[251] Yet even in the 1930s when his diary mentions of Edith became more frequent, if still cloaked, he continued to complain of loneliness and depression. He remained devoted to his wife, finding the 'desolation of loneliness... terrible' and believing 'One good personal friend would make all the difference in the world'.[252] But he was closer to Edith than anyone else in that decade and she frequently countered his not insignificant insecurities as head of the National Government:

> Who would ever say now that you let anyone down...nor will you allow to yourself the conviction that you have won admiration from all ranks - a real deep admiration...Please - Hamish dear - get quite still - and take stock of your assets - What you have saved - What you have won - What you have discarded and what still can be discarded!! You can sift the chaff from the corn quite well - We want no battles...Democracy is changing every day...of the old - the new will be fashioned - After your day and mine something quite different will arise - We must have started a new epoch - I think[.][253]

If political expediency lay at the core of this relationship, we have to consider whether Edith would have remained in contact when MacDonald was on the backbenches of the Commons, with failing health and feeling all of his years, where he could be of no political capital either to her standing, her family or her party. Although claims have been made that it 'was indeed a capture to have the leader of the Socialists dining at the Mansion of a Tory hostess. It was a very different thing when MacDonald was merely one of themselves. No longer either a Socialist or a Premier he was absolutely *de trop*', Edith remained in contact with him until his death.[254] After his resignation they continued to correspond and meet, although less regularly than before. They lunched and dined together approximately every six months in 1936 and 1937 and, although in September 1937 Edith complained that she had not seen him, she noted, 'I often think of you and miss you'.[255] He considered dedicating his new study of Burns to her, but feared, like their relationship, it would be misconstrued: 'If I dedicated it to you, would be too much mixed up and would have to blush for the rest of days, as there are so many nasty minded people about'.[256] In the last year of his life, 1937, they exchanged more than twenty letters and his affection for her was still apparent in his last dispatch, written before he left for South America and 'sorry to leave without a real goodbye':

> I shall have to take your memory away with me. The result of the journey will remain uncertain, though I shall face it whatever it may be and make the best of it. So let us 'greet the unseen with a cheer', whatever it may be. I shall think much of you as I go along from pagan to saint and pray do not altogether forget me.[257]

MacDonald died after two days at sea.

Much of their affectionate tone could, if taken out of context, be misunderstood as romance. But MacDonald's relations with Charley remained cordial with no identifiable sense of resentment or jealousy. Moreover, nothing was hidden from him and he delivered his wife's letters to MacDonald, sometimes carrying them from Mount Stewart to London and sanctioned her passing information to him. The April 1934 ceremony to inaugurate air travel between London, Liverpool and Belfast on a plane named the Marchioness of Londonderry with MacDonald and the Londonderrys on board also raises the question of whether there would have been such openness if this was an affair?

Although this relationship provided literary inspiration for Howard Spring's 1940 novel, *Fame is the Spur*, its basis lay in friendship.[258] It was, however, still of consequence. Edith did not promote MacDonald in the early stages of his career as was common for both Frances Anne and Theresa's confidantes. She did, however, have some bearing on his difficult and career-defining decision to front a National Government in 1931. This, illuminated by the fact that he wrote to her more times in 1932 than he did in any other year, was when he needed her most. She was, in essence, the lynchpin between MacDonald and the Conservatives and continued to bolster him to remain firm at the national helm from 1931-35.

MacDonald's three terms as Prime Minister were all riled with difficulty. He never served with a Commons' majority composed of his own party. He also paid a heavy and personal price for heading the National Government. In 1933 the word 'Ramsay' came into American dialogue as an expression for political treachery of the highest order and in the 1935 election the only defeated ministers were MacDonald and his son. He took much of the criticism levelled at him personally. Indeed, much of it had this as its intent. His relationship with Edith, as Marquand has remarked, certainly damaged 'his reputation at the time and, in some quarters at least, it has dogged his memory ever since.'[259] Without Edith he would not have been perceived as so Tory biased and as 'the defender of Londonderry House', but her fate, for many, was not a consideration.[260]

Baldwin was of the opinion that Edith's befriending of MacDonald ultimately led to her husband's downfall and somewhat surprisingly informed their son and heir, 'I do not think your Mother has been a very happy influence on your Father in politics', though he conceded, 'She is a very remarkable person. She was a creative genius in the war…She has great charm, vitality and courage…Your mother certainly provided a refuge for Ramsay for which your Father paid a high price.'

The little comment that has been made of Edith is similarly negative: 'It was sup-posed, on all sides, that Lady Londonderry had meddled too much in the coun-try's affairs.'[261] Further still, her association with MacDonald 'effectively discred-ited lavish, cross-party political entertaining for ever.'[262] But Edith remained val-ued as a confidante and astute commentator. Samuel Hoare, in a remark that was reminiscent of many made of her mother-in law, still wanted to discuss politics with her in 1936: 'You must let me talk over these...political questions with you...Your mind is so fresh and vigorous that it does me a great deal of good to discuss politics with you.'[263] Nor was Londonderry House wholly redundant as a political salon without MacDonald's patronage. Large-scale entertaining contin-ued here until the late 1930s with ambassadors, visiting royalty and cabinet mem-bers present. During the coronation season of 1937 the focus became, however, more imperial than party, entertaining dominion and foreign power representa-tives with the express desire that 'nothing could promote a feeling of good will in the Empire and amongst other nations better than this kind of entertaining...to carry on in the traditions that were established by the late Marquess and Mar-chioness, and to revert in a manner to the grand traditions of Edwardian times.'[264] Edith also entertained formally for Queen Mary in this year, submitting guest lists and seating plans for her approval and she remained one of the few whom the queen dined with privately. But the distribution of a pamphlet at a Londonderry House reception for 1,000 members of the diplomatic corps in May 1937 remind-ing them that the venue 'has been the scene of many distinguished gatherings in the past, and played a significant part in the social and political life of the nation', left an unmistakable aftertaste of decline.[265] Hyde's publication of *Londonderry House and its pictures* as well as a photographic spread on the house in *Country Life* in the same year fall into this same category of reminiscence: it was the end of an era.

A 'better understanding of our two countries'.[266]

After his unceremonious sacking, Lord Londonderry retained his seat in the Lords and the only other political activities that he undertook were the now noto-rious visits to Nazi Germany in the 1930s. This was a well meaning, though po-litically myopic, attempt to promote better understanding between the two coun-tries, but the visits prompted yet more criticism to be directed at the Londonder-rys: they were widely branded as Nazi sympathisers. A consideration of context and an abandon of hindsight are, however, essential to understand this involve-ment. As early as the November 1933 eve of session reception at Londonderry House, MacDonald recorded meeting an unnamed Nazi 'here on business, but mainly to see some of us and explain Hitler's position. Interesting talk from which I expect some important results.'[267] This was most likely to have been Joachim von Ribbentrop and suggests that the Londonderrys' Anglo-German embrace was not solely a time-filler after Londonderry lost his government place.[268] Charley clearly felt that he had disappointed his wife by 1936: 'I feel I have let you down...and it is for these feelings really that I feel irritated with Baldwin and those who brought about my downfall' and this impacted on his desire to continue to contribute to the diplomatic dialogue.[269] He certainly later interpreted his overtures to Nazi Germany in this light:

> I went to Germany as one deeply interested in foreign affairs. My social contacts were the usual contacts which in peace-time are utilised for establishing an understanding and gaining a knowledge of those individuals involved in governing…I came away from Berlin with an uneasy feeling…It was obvious that the country was becoming an armed coup.[270]

The visits undoubtedly gave Londonderry a chance to operate on the European stage, if only in an informal capacity, but numerous other men of his class did likewise and Ribbentrop's attendance at the 1933 event was indicative of high society's interaction with the Nazi command. The Marquess of Lothian, the Dukes of Bedford, Westminster and Buccleuch, Viscount Rothermere, Barons Mount Temple, Brocket, Allen, Semphill, McGowan, Mottistone and Redesdale as well as the Earl of Glasgow all counted as pro-appeasement aristocrats.[271] In addition, MacDonald and Sir John Simon met Ribbentrop privately at the Baldwins in late November 1933; Ribbentrop weekended with the Astors at Cliveden and was hosted by Mrs. Greville and Lady Cunard who also courted the Fascist, Count Grandi. Indeed, of the 1930s hostess set only Sibyl Colefax was consistently anti-Nazi and she still invited Ribbentrop to her receptions, assembling those, including Conservative MPs, who shared her concerns and allowing him 'to talk as much as he liked so that others present would see him as he was. Gradually Ribbentrop's nature revealed itself without provocation.'[272]

Londonderry was encouraged to interact with the German command as early as February 1933 after compeer, Lord Lothian paid a visit to Hitler, conveying details of the meeting to him and calling for more of the same: 'It is going to be a difficult job but I think it is possible to get a basis of agreement of assured peace in Europe for ten years if we go about it in the right way.'[273] Further contact between the Londonderrys and Nazi regime came, with Charley still in office, in the somewhat unlikely form of two of their daughters, Maureen and Margaret, visiting Germany in October 1934 when they met Göring. The visit, possibly arranged by the German Embassy, perhaps saw 'his daughters acting as intermediaries, Londonderry had forged an unofficial link with Göring, one of the most powerful men in the Nazi hierarchy.'[274] It is more probable, however, that they simply met their father's counterpart as Commander-in-Chief of the German air force. By this juncture Londonderry was of the view that the third Reich should be admitted to the League of Nations to hasten accommodation and believed that the alternative was bleak: to 'find ourselves up against ultimatums from Germany and a power behind those ultimatums which will plunge the world once more into the catastrophe of war.'[275] The visits that he and Edith made to Germany from 1936 were, therefore, never about a blanket acceptance of Nazi creed. Indeed, the full intent of that ideology was still to be realised and if they were duped by Hitler, so too was much of Europe. As Harold Macmillan later remarked, the Nazi propaganda machine of the 1930s was devilishly ingenious, but the private audiences 'were equally dangerous. It is no mean feat to have charmed such varied and distinguished men as Lansbury, Lothian, Rothermere, Arnold Toynbee, Londonderry, Allen, Tom Jones, and Lloyd George.'[276]

As ever, Edith was not a passive bystander in her husband's affairs. Her part in the campaign to ease relations between Britain and Germany by courting Göring, Ribbentrop *et al* bears a striking similarity to that of the French Prime Minister, André Tardieu just three years previously. Like other foreign dignitaries in 1930s London, the German ambassador, Hoesch had been invited to Londonderry receptions and as he addressed Edith as Circe, it is also likely that he attended Ark functions. This certainly laid the basis for discussion but, unlike the Tardieu encounter, Edith was working more closely with her spouse. She, along with their youngest daughter, Mairi accompanied Charley to Germany in January 1936, taking in the Winter Olympics in southern Bavaria *en route*. From the Reich Chancellery, they witnessed tens of thousands of stormtroopers processing to mark the third anniversary of Hitler's accession to power, but Edith's reaction to the enormity of the militarization was stark: 'This means war, Charley.'[277] Their resolve to avoid such a conclusion was certainly strengthened by this visit. They were also entertained by Göring and met Himmler, the Ribbentrops, the German Foreign Minister, Baron von Neurath as well as Rudolf Hess and were privy to a two-hour meeting with Hitler, Hess and Ribbentrop. They met Hitler and Göring again at the Olympics and Londonderry also saw Göring, von Neurath and Hess alone. Although he issued a statement to the Press Association on his return, addressed a meeting in Durham recounting his experiences in Germany and spoke to several members of the cabinet, including Austen Chamberlain, few were responsive.

Edith also publicised the visit by writing an article in the *Sunday Sun*, under the title of 'Hitler - man of simplicity and action'. Here she recorded her 'prejudice, imbued with the antipathy, towards a dictator, of a woman who has always upheld the right of women to equal status with men - and one who has fought strenuously to that end'. Though she had qualms about the possible illusionary nature of his command, Edith was mesmerised by Hitler. Seeing him at first hand, sitting beside him at a Berlin dinner given in their honour, she 'beheld a man of arresting personality':

a man with wonderful, farseeing eyes. I felt I was in the presence of one truly great. He is simple, dignified, humble. He is leader of men...The last thing Germany wants is another war in the first place they are not ready: in the second place they have suffered too greatly...But even if Hitler is not all that he wishes us to believe he is, might we not, ourselves, take advantage of his step to try to bring about a change of heart and policy so that we come to know that peace we all so greatly desire?[278]

She subsequently forwarded a copy of the article to Ribbentrop and thanked Hitler effusively for his hospitality:

It was a very great pleasure to meet you and to have seen all that you have done in Germany in the last three years. To say that I was deeply impressed is

not adequate. You and Germany remind me of the book of Genesis in the
Bible. Nothing else describes the position accurately...to the best of your
abilities, in our different ways, we will do our best to help towards a better
understanding of our two countries.[279]

She also began to correspond with Ambassador Hoesch, the Görings as well as
Magda Goebbels who offered to translate both her husband's and Hitler's
speeches into English. The letters were also often translated by the Foreign Office so nothing that passed between the Londonderrys and the German command was unknown to the authorities.

One of Edith's letters, dated February 1936, to German General der Fliegar
also highlighted the continued importance of personal means to exert political
sway: Edith informed him that she was using her own contacts to bring her, and
by association, the German, influence to bear:

you may rest assured we shall do all that is possible to help forward the cause
of peace between our two countries, coupled with France. The difficulties are
very great...fear and an ingrained dislike of certain things in your country on
the part of many very nice people here, who have been led by the Government in the past, to pin their entire faith on the Geneva [disarmament] policy,
in order, so they imagine, to create a more humane world - The Press too - as
you know is largely hostile and controlled to a great extent by Jews. Besides
this...is another smaller section - though vociferous and strong, whose sympathies are secretly with Russia to some extent, and all the Trades Unionists
quite openly - Together all these parties combine to make a situation which
will be difficult for the present Prime Minister, to steer another course. No
one in this country wants War - On the contrary, they are almost hostile in the
cause of peace!!...Your help will be a great assistance to us. You are a pillar of
strength in your country. If you will make your people realise that our difficulties are not that "we will not", but that "we can not" without a good deal of
preparation. Public opinion has not only to be led but swayed...My husband
has already seen several people - and I have seen many M.P.s[.][280]

In the next month she invited Ambassador Hoesch to spend Easter at Mount
Stewart and though he declined, his reply intimated the depth of her involvement
in diplomatic manoeuvrings:

I was very glad to talk through the telephone with you the other day...but it
was not easy to discuss the matter openly...It is very difficult to foresee how
things will develop...We will not accept the proposals of the Locarno-powers
in so far as they are not in conformity with the principle of equal rights, but
we do not reject them as a whole...Our desire to come to practical negotiations remains as strong as it was[.][281]

The Londonderrys' German visit was, however, controversial and some sections of the press were quick to scorn their efforts. The fact that Londonderry had so recently served in an official position, more particularly one dealing directly with the question of disarmament and air policy, aroused suspicion and, compounded by his ill-disguised bitterness at being dismissed, many wondered if he could be trusted to keep his counsel. As Harold Nicolson expressed to Vita Sackville West, 'I admire Londonderry in a way, since it is fine to remain 1760 in 1936; besides he is a real gent. But I do deeply disapprove of ex-Cabinet Ministers trotting across to Germany at this moment. It gives the impression of secret negotiations and upsets the French. But we are incorrigibly irresponsible in such things.'[282] MacDonald was similarly perplexed, already convinced that there was a considerable discrepancy between Hitler's pacifist rhetoric and the preparations that were being made for war. He noted Charley's cousin, Lady Wimborne's 'rather spiteful talk' on the Londonderrys' German visit but believed 'they have certainly laid themselves out for it…I get more and more inclined to believe that Germany is staging a war.' But as his doubts about German intentions intensified, he, like the Londonderrys, continued to work towards peace: he met Ribbentrop twice in 1935 and again in April 1936. And, more accurately than most, he summarised high society's approach to European affairs: it was, as a whole, 'pro-German eg like the rest of the country anti-French and anti-war.'[283] And it is in this context that the Londonderrys' interaction with Nazi Germany must be adjudged.

Edith's correspondence with the Nazi command continued and Göring, in particular, replied at length. In a letter of April 1936 he expressed his belief that 'The German people…brave, decent and honest…can no longer be expected to live as a second-class nation':

I know that you have familiarised yourself with the new Germany and understand better than many others, and I am convinced that you know how much the Leader and all of us desire and love Peace. We are also very happy to see that England shows full understanding of the recovery of German independence. I am following the English press with great interest on this point. I only fail to understand how the Government can put the letter of an agreement before the spirit, and the French have broken the spirit of agreement by their Soviet Treaty. The Irreconcilable attitude of the French shows that they do not desire any understanding with Germany, and that they consider it is more important to win Great Britain for their policy…for an ally…for an attack on Germany. They know quite well that Germany has no intention whatever of ever attacking France. This is quite out of the question.

Edith sent a copy of this letter to Chamberlain. Indeed, the Nazis that she corresponded with were aware that she passed their letters onto government officials and this may explain why they wrote at such length using her, not the first time for a Marchioness of Londonderry, as a conduit. But a new sense of urgency was apparent in Göring's next dispatch which he wanted her to show to her spouse:

Politically, things look somewhat unpromising...especially for England. The quick Italian victory and the complete annexation of Abyssinia may mean a great danger for England in the long run. Mussolini will make the brave Abyssinians within a few years into an army of millions...Abyssinia will also become a very strong naval and aviation base...he will threaten the Sudanese frontier from Libya. Moreover, I happen to know that Italy is now beginning to develop her fleet and submarines. All this is extremely serious for England's position in the Mediterranean and particularly for navigation through the Suez canal. I must confess that I have seldom seen in history a combination of circumstances which so directly affects England's vital nerve as the present situation in Abyssinia...Italy makes extraordinary efforts to secure German friendship. You know however that the Fuhrer has provided for cooperation with England in his political programme...I trust that England will at last make English politics and not be dependent of French politics. A great deal now depends on England's attitude in the Locarno and Rhine question. This will be the test question for our people in our relations with England... these are very uncertain times...God grant that the two great Germanic nations, England and Germany may come together in future to guarantee world peace, or a least peace in our own countries...you are also looking towards this end...I...hope that we can discuss it frequently and fully.[284]

This letter, making clear Germany's conditional approach to Britain, might have been expected to provoke a government response, but the opposite was true, although it certainly roused a reaction from Edith.

She subsequently wrote to der Fliegar blatantly asking for information and counting the French out of the diplomatic loop, highlighting the anti-French attitude that MacDonald had referred to:

what is going to happen now?...As France is at present, there is no use trying to negotiate with her. She is just drifting about helplessly...I think a great deal of the violent anti-German feeling has been engineered in France for electioneering purposes...I think France is in a very dangerous state. It only shows how necessary it is that our two countries should remain firm friends.[285]

Another dispatch to de Fliegar pointed in the same direction, but simultaneously sought reassurance as to Nazi intent:

I am going to speak to you with the frankness permitted to a woman who wants to help...it is necessary to give an assurance that you really will stick to your word...it is vital to future arrangements to remove this mistrust concerning Germany's foreign policy in relation to ours...we are both doing all we can to foster friendship and I am sure you will[.][286]

In pursuit of these ends, Ribbentrop and his wife spent Whitsuntide at Mount Stewart in late May 1936. Also present was Prince Viktor zu Wied, later the German envoy to Stockholm, his wife and two daughters whom the Londonderrys had met on their earlier visit to Germany, Ribbentrops' two adjutants, Werner von Fries, the legation secretary at the German Embassy in London, Air Marshall and RAF Chief of Staff, Sir Edward Ellington, Edith's brother, Viscount Eric Chaplin, American heiress and socialite, Laura Corrigan, Durham landowner Sir Hedworth Williamson and the pro-German foreign correspondent of the *Daily Mail*, George Ward Price. And, just as during their German visit, Londonderry was privy to private meetings with Ribbentrop. Here then was another classic example of the personal mingling with the political. But, despite the hospitality, like the bulk of the Nazi regime, neither of the Londonderrys was fond of Ribbentrop and, with the benefit of hindsight, Charley later declared that he 'never had any illusions about him [Ribbentrop]. He was shallow, loquacious and self-opinionated...well aware of what was in Hitler's mind all along.'[287] However, the Ribbentrops had been hospitable during the Londonderrys' recent German visit, engineering the meeting with Hitler, so there was an element of reciprocality in the Mount Stewart weekend. This was certainly the public façade, but Charley was both sensitive and defensive about local headlines such as 'swastika over Ulster' and the punning of 'The Londonderry Air' to 'The Londonderry Herr'.[288]

The Mount Stewart visit reinforced Edith's view of Ribbentrop and, in early July 1936, she confided her misgivings to Göring. In a long reply, which Edith passed to Samuel Hoare, he defended his colleague, reiterating the German desire for peace and his 'unshakeable conviction that the day will yet come when England...will recognise that there so no firmer bulwark against the disintegrating efforts of Communism and against total anarchy and disorganisation in Europe than German and the German Government':

> That will also be the day when English statesmen will have to recognise that no constellation will be better fitted to ensure prosperity and peace that the co-operation of England and Germany...Germany has no interest in English embarrassment within the concert of the British Empire, nor indeed of its collapse...we too have our vital interests...such a powerful nation as ours cannot be permanently excluded from all the world's goods...Germany cannot for ever go on making offers to England, but that she is forced, in case England rejects the proffered hand, to seek her friends were she can find them.[289]

The conditional nature of German rapprochement towards Britain was becoming ever clearer, but there was no escaping Ribbentrop who was appointed German Ambassador to London in October 1936. In the same month the Londonderrys travelled to Germany for a second time, staying with Göring and seeing Hitler and in mid November Ribbentrop was again their guest, joining a shooting party at their Durham seat with photographs of his sojourn being reproduced in the Berlin press. As the Wynyard visit coincided with Londonderry's inauguration as mayor of Durham, family members as well as local magnates, like the Earl and Countess of Durham and Sir Hedworth Williamson, were present along with the Spanish Duke of Alba and Sir Ronald Graham, the former British Ambassador to Rome.[290] And, regardless of the misgivings about Ribbentrop, his interaction with the Londonderrys and London society continued. In May 1937, for instance, he and his wife attended a Londonderry House dinner, with an eclectic mix of guests from King Farouk of Egypt, King Gustav Adolf of Sweden, the Maharajah of Jaipur, Prince Bernhard of the Netherlands to the Brazilian, French, Italian, Belgian, Japanese and German ambassadors in attendance.[291]

The Londonderrys accepted a second invitation from Göring in September 1937 and spent three days with Von Papen but Charley denoted 'a marked falling off in the friendliness of the Germans toward ourselves...I found General Göring far less conciliatory and rather impatient of the attitude which we seemed to adopt towards his country.'[292] As Göring's earlier letter to Edith made clear, Germany was forging allies of Italy and Japan. Londonderry, 'very gloomy as to the future', shared his misgivings about German rearmament and international intent to Ribbentrop and, closer to home, to Chamberlain, Halifax and Sir Neville Henderson, the British Ambassador in Berlin.[293] He continued, however, to hope that personal appeasement would procure diplomatic results. In return for the Görings' hospitality, Londonderry invited them to London in 1937, mooting the idea of them attending the coronation of George IV. This caused a furore in the press: questions were accusingly asked in the Commons and a mass protest in London numbering some 3,000 people provided a clear indication of how out of step Londonderry was becoming with public opinion. But Göring's refusal also epitomised the growing distance between the two countries.

Edith was becoming equally disenchanted. Her autobiography, *Retrospect*, written in 1937 and published in the following year, declared, 'The more positive "isms" are taboo, like Nazi-ism or Fascism, because they imply doing something', but she was never an active advocate of Nazi policy.[294] The publication of *Locarno: eine Dokumenten - Sammlun*, with a preface by Ribbentrop, greatly alarmed her as she believed twenty to thirty documents were missing from the German edition and that declaring the British *Blue Book* as prejudiced was greatly damaging. Although Edith, Mairi and Charley left for Germany in late January 1938 and again saw Hitler, Göring, Ribbentrop and Hess, Charley now found the plans for German expansion 'somewhat disturbing'.[295] Edith's disillusionment with Nazi aspirations was compounded by the arrest of two Austrian skiing guides she was personally acquainted with in 1938 and she aired her indignation in letters to both Göring and Ribbentrop. To the latter she noted:

> German mentality and ours must be poles apart - With what object must you antagonise all your erstwhile friends over here - What good do you do by imprisoning honest men...I feel so v[er]y strongly about it all that I might even go to Vienna myself to find out what is going on...I cannot express in sufficiently strong words the chagrin I felt, at what is happening and the utter impossibility of finding any common ground to work on between English and Germans when these sort of outrages are permitted.[296]

This letter further suggests that it was never a policy of rapprochement at any cost that Edith pursued. Göring responded within days, telling her he had instructed the police to inquire as to the nature and legality of the arrests but Ribbentrop was less hasty and less accommodating in reply: 'You will understand that it is not possible for me to indulge any details, especially as the details you mention were, in most instances, not according to the actual facts'. But, like Göring, although somewhat less convincing, he hoped their acquaintance and work for improved Anglo-German relations would continue.[297] In Germany, this time at Göring's invitation, in June 1938 Edith again raised the issue of the Austrian guides with Ribbentrop and also with Himmler and, according to her husband, used 'far more outspoken language that I would have had the audacity to make use of in relation to the imprisonment and maltreatment of Austrians'.[298] Göring agreed, somewhat grudgingly, to look into the matter and the guides were later released. But for Edith there was no going back: her resolve to abandon her part in personal appeasement was made public in a letter to *The Times* in October 1938: 'On the...issue of resisting world domination by a Great Power I have always believed...that we should be prepared to fight.'[299]

Charley's belief in appeasement unravelled at a slower pace.[300] However, with the Nazi invasion of Prague and the intent of their racial ambitions becoming clearer, he was an appeasement promoter no more. The last letter he penned to Göring was written in August 1939 and with a charge that the policy of the German government 'opposed all those doctrines of Government, which, I am quite convinced, in the end make for the progress and well being of the nations', it was not surprising that he received no reply.[301]

Appeasement's reputation as a salve for European strife was ruined once it transpired nothing could quell Nazi ambitions. But the Londonderrys were far from alone in putting their faith in this policy in the 1930s. Their endeavours were never about befriending either Hitler or the Nazi party, nor were they privy to the true extent of Nazi intent which could never be curtailed by personal means or one country's stand. The time for talk had passed, but the pro-Nazi tag attached to the Londonderrys remained.

So much criticism was directed at Lord Londonderry, in particular, and at Edith, by association, because of the position he had held in the National Government. What, it was asked, was he telling Hitler about the pace and magnitude of British armaments and air power? In consequence, from the late 1930s, the Londonderrys were on the defensive. Edith's anti-Nazi pronouncements that began in October 1938 continued throughout the next year as she urged the women of the UWUC, 'If every mother who knows the awful result of the Nazi doctrine on young children, the teaching they have been given when of tender years which is almost impossible to eradicate, would insist on her child being given the religious education that she believes in'.[302] But her declarations had little impact. And, although Charley had proclaimed himself 'an interested dilettante' but 'no pro-German' in a letter to Lady Milner in March 1937, few shared his vista: 'We beat the Germans and I am very glad we did and it is just because I don't want to have to do it again that I have gone all out to capture the Germans another way...I am looking gloomily at the future now, because we are just sliding into the 1914 alignment...I believe all generations do exactly the same thing'.[303] He was later forced to admit that 'the general public...simply regard me as one who has entertained von Ribbentrop here, and who received lavish entertainment from the Germans when I went to Germany and therefore I became a violent pro-Nazi', but his claim 'that my efforts have been completely ineffective has tickled my sense of humour rather than stimulated any feeling of irritation and annoyance' was less credible.[304] He increasingly distanced himself from the Anglo-German crusade, refusing the presidency of The Link, a newly formed pro-German organisation and was sufficiently riled to write *Ourselves and Germany*. Published in 1938, the book expounded his views on Anglo-German co-operation and the fact that he was certainly alive to the possibility of warfare:

> I have been careful, in my efforts to bring about a better understanding be-tween this country and Germany, to avoid, so far as I have been able to do so, adopting what might be interpreted as a critical and censorious attitude to-wards the internal administration of Germany...Much of the anti-Semite propaganda carried on in Germany to-day is of an exceedingly crude and vio-lent nature...it would be wrong to give the impression that I viewed them with indifference. On the contrary, as one who has been brought up in an atmosphere of Christian idealism, I deplore what appears to me to be a perse-cution of a considerable section of the community for its religious beliefs.[305]

The book was hugely popular, running to a fourth impression and a second edi-tion within six months of publication, illuminating the huge public interest not only in Nazi Germany but also in Londonderry at this time.

It is clear that the Londonderrys formed part of an aristocratic grouping striving to improve Anglo-German relations in the 1930s. Their pro-German stance con-sequently caused no social ostracisation. Edith, for instance, played a small part in the abdication crisis, alerting Wallis Simpson at one of Emerald Cunard's parties to the extent of popular opposition to her relationship with Edward. Wallis wrote to Edith on the following day:

> I have been thinking over all you told me last night. I have come to the con-clusion that perhaps no one has been really frank with a certain person in telling him how the country feels about his friendship with me...I feel that he should know...I am going to tell him the things you told me...I am afraid I am the innocent victim put "on the spot" by my own country.

Edith, now seasoned to press criticism, advised her to 'remain calm' and ignore the personal attacks that were being made, 'I am quite sure that if his real friends all help - much can be done to silence this wicked conspiracy...I am so sorry for you and only write now to tell you that any indirect help I can give to help "him" - I will, and do all I can quietly'.[306] Queen Elizabeth dined at Londonderry House in the aftermath of 1937 crisis and was grateful to Edith for her tact in forward-ing a list of possible guests for her scrutiny: she suggested Emerald Cunard and Laura Corrigan be cut. The royals dined with the Londonderrys again in the fol-lowing year and Charley and Edith were also amongst an exclusive party of twenty-four invited to Chamberlain's dinner for the king and queen at Downing Street in March 1939, only the third time that a monarch dined at this address.

Despite their continued part in society, the Londonderry name, especially that of Charley, was popularly tainted. In September 1939 press rumours that he had been interned as a spy were speedily dismissed as nonsense but illuminate his, albeit unfounded, reputation as a chief Nazi promoter. He tried to defend himself in several news articles in 1939 and early 1940, attacking those he blamed for his downfall. As relations with former allies, such as Neville Chamberlain, became increasingly strained, Edith also felt compelled to champion her husband. In a dispatch to the latter she was openly critical:

> It would have been so easy for you and would have appealed to him, had you ever asked him to go and see you…but he has always been studiously ignored and he could have given you v[er]y useful help. This is at least what we both feel C[harley] is the only independent link in those days - [19]36 - to [19]38 between this Country and Germany, you never once mentioned the matter to him.[307]

By 1940, instead of vilification, there was, at least, some vindication for Londonderry's term as Secretary of State for Air, when he urged investment and expansion. As the *Daily Mail* noted: 'In 1940, the nation knows that Londonderry was right'.[308] But many remained unconvinced. During the war, with Wynyard used for evacuee children and the London house closed with furniture removed to save rates, Edith and Charley resided mostly at Mount Stewart. In September 1940 Londonderry House was hit by a bomb but, unlike Charley's reputation, the damage was only superficial.

'That is the whole story really.'[309]

The Nazi branding left a bitter aftertaste and helps explain the Londonderrys comparatively low political profile during the 1940s. This was compounded in November 1945 when Ribbentrop's defence counsel requested that Lord Londonderry, the Duke of Windsor, Winston Churchill and other notables, be called as witnesses to his Nuremberg trial. Ultimately Londonderry, and others like him not in possession of public office, were permitted to submit written depositions. News of the request, however, reached the press and for a short time there were calls of treason, but these were soon silenced.[310]

Churchill's accession to the premiership briefly raised Charley's hopes for placement both in the coalition and the 1945 Conservative ministry but lobbying for a cabinet seat proved unsuccessful and by 1947 he was forced to acknowledge that his political life was over. He resented both Baldwin and Churchill, writing of the latter, 'I shall never know why he went out of his way to destroy me which he certainly did.'[311] Weakened by failing health, he was exhausted 'trying to do every little job because I have had to realise that I do not come into the bigger ones'. He confided his sense of failure to the woman he always wrote most openly to, Ettie Desborough:

> Well, I have been ill but am all right now in the sense that I have had a light warning and that I have got to go slow…I have only just realized that I have

never stood still, that I have never stayed in the same place for 10 days and in these forties 1940-1947, the war years and after I have had endless worries and sorrows with you and Edie as my only real friends and supports.

He was even more expressive in another letter to her, this one of eleven pages in length:

When Baldwin removed me I instinctively knew that I had finished...I have touched almost the lowest depths of despair...I tried loyally to carry on out-side, then I dabbled in diplomacy with an idea which I know was correct but I somehow could not work it with anyone who counted...I made speeches which people seemed to want to hear, we went on entertaining and everyone seemed to want to come. Then I had some bitter exchanges with Baldwin and Chamberlain...then I fell out with Winston because I wanted to achieve by what I thought was statesmanship what he wanted to achieve by war...So I really planned a bad crash and was not strong enough or clever enough to strike out on my own. So the war, the crisis of our lives finds me completely isolated and under a sort of shadow which I cannot get away from...I have no illusions about it and that I am bitterly disappointed. I had great chances and I missed them by not being good enough and that really sums up the whole thing...It all has worked out badly and I know it is some inherent fault in myself.

But his greatest regret was for the woman who stood by him through all his per-sonal and political trials, 'I have been a miserable failure. I think poor Edie real-izes this and I know Robin does too but E. is constant in her support and care for me and I never would know from anything she says or does that I have failed to give her the position she should have had.'[312]

The best gauge of Edith's reaction to her husband's displacement, MacDonald's death and the personal criticism of her role both as hostess and diplomatic com-panion to Nazi Germany can be found in her 1938 autobiography. With a chronological span from childhood to the present day, her decision to write it raises interesting questions. Did she see her public life as at an end and believe, therefore, that the time was opportune for reflection? Alternatively, does the memoir mirror her husband's self-defensive publications of the late 1930s and early 1940s? The latter supposition is the most likely. Indeed, given the level of controversy and negative commentary that her relationship with MacDonald raised, Edith unsurprisingly wanted *Retrospect* to tell her story. Relating their first meeting and their common Celtic bond in a chapter entitled 'Personalities and people, 1915-31', she depicted him as an 'old fashioned Socialist' who 'fought against privilege and inequality of opportunity' and 'Contrary to the opinion of the day - and anyone who did not know him in these days would have been bound to misjudge him and his actions - Ramsay was really a very brave man, and certainly had the courage of his convictions and opinions'.[313] She also made the nature of their association clear: he was nothing more than a friend. Edith was, however, displeased by the book and its reception and, writing to Hyde after its publication, hinted at a near compulsion to write it: 'I don't like "Retrospect", as you know, but perhaps for this reason - it will sell better - it certainly has had a most frightening press - I was v[er]y angry.'[314]

Londonderry House had been closed since in the winter of 1939 but within months of the cessation of the war, Edith returned. However, her reign here was effectively over. The death of her daughter, Maureen from tuberculosis in 1942 and her son, Robin's refusal to seek re-election to the Down seat he had held since 1931 in 1945 both took their toll. Charley attempted to find his son and heir a Durham seat, writing to Headlam, chair of the Northern Area Conservatives. But Headlam's response to the 'rather pathetic letter' expressed disquiet about the Londonderrys' fulfilment of their duties, doubting 'whether Robin would want [a Durham seat]...nowadays, and I doubt very much whether any Association (except a very derelict one) would want him. He and his father have been too long absentees from the county.' To Headlam, Lord Londonderry was now 'no more use...than a sick headache in the north...he was probably lucky ever to get into the Cabinet. However, he was badly treated...He has nothing to do now and, like me, feels that the world is crumbling before his eyes.'[315]

Edith also had to come to terms with change. That political entertaining and personal endorsement were no longer guarantors of position was most apparent when she sought a place for her son-in-law, Derek, husband of her youngest child in the 1940s. Edith was warned, 'Any suspicion of stringpulling is very badly regarded nowadays and does more harm than good', but an approach was still made to the War Office although 'in such a way that no umbrage can be taken... this particular door is not banged shut yet.'[316] Now there was no escaping the fact that Londonderry House was defunct and in 1946 the Royal Aeronautical Club negotiated a take over of the house using it as a national aviation centre with the family retaining a twenty-two room flat.

Charley died a disappointed man in 1949. Injuries sustained in a gliding accident in 1945 were followed by a series of strokes, the most debilitating of which in April 1948 deprived him of the ability to speak and move freely. Edith tried to remain positive but resignedly admitted, 'It has been such a long and trying time.'[317] His will and codicil made provision for her 'to live according to the same standard to which she has been used during his lifetime', granting her up to £15,000 per annum and the use of an apartment in Londonderry House for life. But more personal trials were to come. Robin, now the eighth Marquess, was widowed in 1951 and died of heart problems at the age of fifty-two, just six years after succeeding to the marquessate, in 1955.

Edith was also upset by her nineteen-year-old grandson's (now the youngest ever Marquess of Londonderry) written outburst against the royal family in 1957. In a letter to the *New Statesman* he attacked their 'toothpaste smiles...[and] deplorable taste in clothes'. Edith, now aged seventy-seven, still assumed the mantle of family head and issued a statement from Mount Stewart criticising the letter as 'not only vulgar but also silly and childish' and the new marquess was subsequently forced to publicly apologise.[318] Unsurprisingly the press had a field day with the *Irish Times*' tagline epitomising many others: 'He's just at the awkward age - one doesn't know which end to slap...'[319]

In widowhood, Edith resided mainly at Mount Stewart where the history of The Ark was quite literally set in stone. The Dodo terrace at Mount Stewart, created by Edith in the early 1920s, is still studded with animals, an ark and loggia inspired by the club of her making. She maintained contact with the royals and occasionally entertained at Londonderry House: hosting an 'At home' in 1955; a coming-out dance and dinner in 1958 and celebrating her eightieth, and last, birthday with a swansong reception in 1959. With Prime Minister, Harold Macmillan in attendance, he was the seventh premier of her acquaintance and the event was reminiscent of an earlier era. Many of the tributes paid to her on this occasion were also reflective and some still referred to her by fictional persona, Circe but four months later, on 23 April 1959, Edith died at Mount Stewart.

After a private funeral in the house chapel, she was buried alongside Charley at Tir-N'an Oge (the Land of the Ever Young), a walled burial enclosure watched over by statues of Irish saints at Mount Stewart and a visible reminder of their Anglo-Irish pedigree.[320] Edith's death sealed the end of an era: she was the last great political hostess. Her determination not to surrender to the aristocratic anti-suffragist norm in the early years of the twentieth century show that she possessed an independence of thought and strength of character. She was also a woman of great vitality and humour once, rushing home to change her clothes after attending the opening of parliament to go and vote in 1933, telling the waiting pressmen, 'I can't go to the poll in a tiara.'[321] Some of her *joie de vive* was, however, a façade: a manufactured construct to cope with the realisation that hers was a companionate marriage by 1918. This turned Edith, by her own admission, from being:

> rather stodgy but adoring and for *me* v[er]y unselfish...into a rather hard, cynical woman, but only outwardly...I only ever had an inferiority complex when I was frightened of being the dull and pitied wife!! As soon as I found the way to be really nasty and make people laugh I prospered!...I am not really like this at all[.][322]

This also made Theresa's bolstering of her confidence all the more significant: 'she always told me I looked nice - that I was clever - and could do lots of things if I wished...I owe her so much.'[323] And Edith remained loyal: to her spouse; to the Londonderry interest and to conservatism. It was this trait that close friend, Harold Macmillan, believed was her greatest flaw, 'Her friendship and confidence, once given, were lasting and immutable'.[234]

Like her predecessors, Edith was remembered as an outstanding woman of her time. The French, American and Australian press all carried articles on her in the 1930s and she was awarded an honorary Doctorate in Law from Queen's University, Belfast in 1949. But the *Sunday Graphic*'s depiction of her as the 'most famous political hostess of the century, friend, adviser and confidante of the greatest figures of the three reigns' exaggerated her role.[325] As a confidante and hostess, however, Edith befitted the Londonderry mould cast by the third Marchioness in the 1820s. The scale, longevity and calibre of Edith's receptions were remarkable but in this role she attracted more controversy than any of her forebears and wide criticism came to be directed toward Londonderry House and its hostess as the world changed round them. Even the 1928 eve of session reception at London-derry House was seen as 'a lingering oasis in Thackeryan London' and Chips Channon's affirmation of her as the 'only political hostess left' by the mid 1930s cannot be denied.[326] Her influence on MacDonald may have been, as is alleged, 'damaging', but this was inadvertent.[327] Without her bridging the Conservative-MacDonald divide his acceptance as leader of the National Government would perhaps have been even more troubled. And without her sympathy and support MacDonald may have abandoned this administration earlier in the 1930s or may have been even more reticent about accepting it in the first place. As he openly acknowledged to her, 'I sustain myself with your regard and with all my affec-tions.'[328] Moreover, Charley freely admitted that he owed his last political posting to her influence: 'I got the Air Ministry through Ramsay and I am eternally grate-ful…That was part of the assistance that you gave Ramsay at a very critical time when your help and support and mine too in a much smaller way was vital to him.'[329] In later life Charley clearly felt that he failed her, but she reciprocated the sentiment, 'You always try and say that you have failed me - I am thinking often that it is the other way - Had I thought more of you and been more of a help it would have been much better.'[330]

This raises an interesting question of self-definition. Although an equal rights feminist, Edith defined herself very much in relation to her husband: 'I am like a sideboard…I am only of use and feel happy with the wall to support me and then I display all your trophies on myself and do very well.'[331] Perhaps this came from an awareness that she owed her position to her marriage. She claimed her sole purpose in adopting the mantle of political hostess was to serve her husband and, at times, seemed to have felt this was not a question of choice, but of duty: 'I only have to do them because I am your wife'. Accepting Charley's thanks when his political career was effectively over in 1936 she remained unassuming: 'I don't know what to say - except my v[er]y v[er]y greatest pleasure in life is to do you credit - in return for all you do for me.'[332] Others, however, rarely saw her in such a self-effacing light. The press, especially in the 1930s, often defined Charley in relation to his wife and he often did the same.

Edith's life also epitomised how much had changed for women since the 1800s. For her, women's war work proved the fallacy of the anti-suffragists' physical force argument more eloquently than any protester or pamphleteer ever could. But the Restoration of Pre-War Practices Act and the popular clamour for women to return to domesticity in both its paid and unpaid forms reaffirmed her feminist thinking. She subsequently issued a stark warning to the younger genera-tion of women:

Women must resolve now that they will not allow themselves to be ruthlessly flung aside as they were after the Armistice in 1918…The younger generation must plan now how best to safeguard woman's future. They must resolve to unite and work as hard as did the Suffragettes to win their aims and gain real equality for the sexes. Women may very well have to brave unpopularity and dare once more to become a nuisance in order to bring home to the public at large that at the end of this war the sex bar must be banished for ever and efficiency become the only test…There should be no distinction between the sexes, either in pay or rations. When we are all doing equal work it is absurd. …In the political arena, why are women content to allow the illogical and archaic position of Peeresses in their own right being debarred from sitting in the House of Lords? Women should insist on this absurdity being removed… When you encounter prejudice and opposition and are beset by opponents…'You must fight until you overcome.'[333]

Reflecting on her life she still believed women's twentieth-century progress had been rapid, especially in terms of their public representation. Her own work played a part in this process of female transition. As the founder and director general of the Women's Legion from 1915-18 and its president from 1939-45, the subsequent acceptance of uniformed women into military ranks was groundbreaking. In 1918, she accepted Lord Birkenhead's invite to form a central committee in London to advise on the selection of the first female JPs. This committee, chaired by Lady Crewe, included Mrs. Lloyd George, Elizabeth Haldane, Gertrude Tuckwell, Mrs. Humphrey Ward and Edith's future arch-critic, Beatrice Webb amongst its number. Edith subsequently became the first woman, both in Northern Ireland and Co. Durham, to serve as a JP. Her vice-presidency of the UWUC and presidency of both North Down Women's Unionist Association and the Women's Advisory Committee of the National Union of Conservative and Unionist Association of Northern England as well as her membership, along with seven other women, including Ladies Carson and Craig and the Duchess of Abercorn, of the Standing Committee of the Ulster Unionist Council from 1919 was also significant: exemplifying the rapid absorption of women into the formal political process in the aftermath of their enfranchisement.[334]

However, the most striking change of all was not in relation to her sex, but her class. Edith believed that her father's death in 1923 completed a chapter without a sequel, one which told of an irrevocable aristocratic decline and 'men and women and modes of life that will not come again' and she was forced to conclude[335]:

Now you very rarely see anyone who looks like a lady…It would be wrong, however, to imagine that none of the pre-war types exist. They do - but not in the glaring light of the Press. There is still…an Upper Class, its ranks diminished and impoverished by the war. These people, in pre-war days, never encouraged the limelight on their doings…They still wield a certain influence behind the scenes, and, in times of crisis, their presence will still be felt, something solid and very British and, above all, they are the people who were born and bred to the old tradition - that possessions carry duties with them, before pleasure.[336]

By her time of writing, however, politics, the most public arena where this duty had been lived out over the preceding centuries, was so radically transformed that an aristocratic retreat was all but complete.

x.   *Above left*, photograph of Edith, seventh Marchioness of Londonderry in court dress, *Country Life*, Nov. 1932.

xi.   *Above right*, chalk drawing of Charles, seventh Marquess of Londonderry by Ivan Opffer, 1934, © National Portrait Gallery, London.

xii.   *Above left*, photograph of Edith, seventh Marchioness and Ramsay MacDonald at the Maharaja of Alwar's anniversary banquet, London, *The Graphic*, 27 Dec. 1930.

xiii.   *Above right*, photograph of Edith, seventh Marchioness addressing electors at Newcastle, *Newcastle Evening Chronicle*, 26 Oct. 1931.

xiv.   David Low cartoon of the eve of session reception at Londonderry
        House, *Evening Standard*, 22 Nov. 1932.

xv.   David Low cartoon of the eve of session reception at Londonderry
        House, *Evening Standard*, 26 Nov. 1935.

Conclusion

Living with the revolution: women and aristocratic decline

The anonymous, futuristic letter dated AD2035 and sent to Edith in remonstration at her continued association with MacDonald in March 1935 predicted a defunct aristocracy where Londonderry House would function only as a museum.[1] The reality was even more crushing and took far less than a century to arrive. The gradual dismantling of the Londonderry properties from the 1920s was a visual reminder that theirs was a class in decline: Seaham Hall was turned into a municipal tubercular sanatorium in 1928; 9,000 acres of land were sold in Merioneth in the 1930s; Plâs Machynlleth was donated to Wales in 1945; the Mount Stewart gardens, so much of Edith's creation, were given to the National Trust in 1957; the estate's neo-classical Temple of the Winds passed to the trust in the year of Edith's death and the house and its contents were handed over in 1976.[2]

During the 1930s, the seventh Marquess could not 'help feeling that the so-called big houses are becoming in a sense, anachronisms...I find myself quite unable to foresee the future of Londonderry House.'[3] By this time, the house was one of only five surviving great London mansions. Others, like Stafford House, succumbed to financial pressure and were sold even before the outbreak of World War One, while Devonshire House and Grosvenor House could only endure until the 1920s. Even in that decade Londonderry House was being singled out as unique, the only mansion 'which links up the pomp of yesterday with the ceremony and festivities of today.'[4] Despite Charley's pessimism, the house, although partially leased from the 1940s with the result that in 'most of the rooms only the ghost of the old glories remains...The magnificent ballroom is drab and discoloured', only met its physical demise two decades later.[5] A wake for the house was held in July 1962 with a party for three hundred hosted by the twenty-four year old ninth Marquess. A week later it was sold at auction to a property developer and quickly demolished with the Londonderry Hotel on the site serving as the only monument to the venue for so many political receptions and entertainments. Wynyard was then the sole Londonderry survivor but, from the mid 1940s, it was used primarily as a teacher training college with one wing kept for private use. Its seventy rooms and 5,400 acres were finally sold in 1987.[6] So, although a decline in the Londonderrys' position, power and prestige undoubtedly occurred, this process was neither swift nor in line with the majority of their compeers.

Any sweeping approach to the question of aristocratic decline ill explains the Londonderrys' comparative longevity. A gendered approach to the same question further complicates any notion of a seamless downfall of a once powerful class. The 1880s certainly saw high society augment: the aristocracy began, often grudgingly, to share power with the middle classes and by the end of the nineteenth century some 4,000 families swelled its number, but this remained a 'face to face community' fused together by hearsay and information exchange.[7] The formerly strict process of screening admittance to its ranks waned, but its demise was not caused by it increasing to such a size that it became unsustainable. Rather, it was the dual and interconnected processes of economic and cultural change that led to its ruination.

Death duties, introduced in 1889 and augmented in 1894, hit landed incomes hard. The 1914 increase in income tax raised four per cent of gross rental on any one estate and by the start of the First World War 800,000 acres of land had already passed from aristocratic hands. In 1919 income tax on estate rentals rose to thirty per cent and the levy of death duties of up to forty per cent on estates worth over £2 million heralded extinction for many. By the middle of 1919 the Londonderrys had paid £361,753 in death duties, but their combined landed and industrial pursuits temporarily buffered this loss.[8] While their coal, and sometime political, rivals the Earls of Durham had opted out by the 1890s, the Londonderrys continued to mine the land inherited by Frances Anne until the mid 1940s. For much of the early twentieth century, therefore, the seventh Marquess was one of the richest mine owners in Britain and one of just six millionaire peers in the half century from 1900-49: he sank a new pit in 1928; employed 7,000 colliery and dock workers with an annual coal production tonnage of over one million. Seaham colliery remained under Londonderry control until nationalisation in 1947 and British Coal closed the Seaham and Vane collieries two years later.[9]

Casting aside the political dominance of the aristocracy was a similarly slow and uneven process. MPs were unsalaried until 1912 and electoral contests remained expensive. In 1939 it was estimated that to be adopted as a Conservative candidate entailed an annual subscription of between £250-£1,000 to the local association and personal payment of at least half the election expenses of £400-£1,200.[10] Fewer seats could be categorised as safe in the 1920s and 1930s with the result that the number of electoral contests increased and ministerial office was subject to considerable flux. Cabinet aristocrats, however, still outweighed their Commons' representation: sons of peers and baronets made up thirteen per cent of the inter-war House of Commons but held a quarter of cabinet positions. The familial tradition was especially marked amongst Conservative cabinets: from 1886 to 1935 only nine of forty-one Conservative cabinet members had neither a politically active father nor grandfather.[11] The Londonderrys' longevity of parliamentary service, therefore, ranked amongst a handful of aristocratic families who were still politically active in the 1930s including their kin, the Churchills, as well as the Salisburys, Stanleys and Cavendishes.

Down and Durham still dominated the Londonderrys' electoral vista in the 1930s, just as they had a century earlier. Robin, later the eighth Marquess of Londonderry, held the Down seat from 1931 but commentators not only remarked on his 'being decidedly gifted' but also on his lack of 'a little ambition'; he was 'not so keen on Irish affairs as his father.'[12] The sacrosanct obligation that kept Robin in this seat was not everlasting: he resigned in 1945, severing the familial tradition of entering parliament. Financial pressures also came to bear. On the death of seventh Marquess in 1949, though leaving £1,021,754, he denoted by will that the 'heavy burden' of death duties would amount to over £110,000 and this was a conservative estimate that excluded the Irish estates.[13] Robin's early death in 1955 meant the payment of a second set of duties within six years and this took a heavy financial toll. The final death knell came when the ninth Marquess did not take his seat in the Lords' reform of 1998.[14]

The idea of an aristocratic decline certainly gained currency in the early twentieth century. Some pre-war publications, such as Lady Dorothy Nevill's reminiscences, doubted whether high society continued to function at all so flexible were its rules of admittance and so materialistic were its new adherents. At the same time, Lady Randolph Churchill decried the decline of the season: 'The London season of thirty years ago was far more prolonged and its glories more apparent than they are now. It was looked upon as a very serious matter.'[15] In a similar vein, Arthur Ponsonby's 1912 volume, *The decline of the aristocracy*, made clear by its very title what he believed would be the final outcome, with 'their actual political power a mere ghost of what they formerly enjoyed'. It was, however, a transitional aristocracy that he identified, one in the throes of an inevitable, but gradual and intermittent, decline from the time of the great Reform Act of 1832: 'the rise of democracy entails the decline of the aristocracy…the aristocracy is now in an entirely false position.' Ponsonby also inferred that the aristocracy was out of sympathy 'with progressive thought', concluding that their 'growing unpopularity is a consequence of the defensive attitude'.[16] But did the traditional ruling class need to side with progressive thought?

Previously the aristocracy made no apology for their rank: 'they found themselves born into a position of comfort and command and did not see any necessity for explaining…that they were not such bad people after all.'[17] But, as Ponsonby implied, heightened criticism prompted a defensive aristocratic response. It also forged an alliance: the sense of there being an old aristocracy and a new elite more rooted in monetary gain than in landed wealth waned in the immediate post-war period. The sale of honours, commonplace up to the 1840s, diminished under Liverpool and Peel only to be revived in 1891 with Gladstone's sale of two peerages in return for donations to Liberal Party funds. Of more import was that great manufacturer of title, Lloyd George whose creation of the rank of OBE widened entitlement to honours beyond those who were traditionally ennobled or, as had become common in the more recent past, to those who could afford to pay for the privilege. Of the two hundred and forty-six new titles granted in the period 1886-1914, for instance, over eighty per cent entered the nobility for the first time. Placed in context, with the English peerage in its entirety numbering approximately three hundred in 1820, this was a dramatic augmentation.[18] Although titles became more available, for many who fell under the 'old aristocracy' banner, including the Londonderrys, a sense of duty to serve remained. This was more than a Victorian construct and for the Londonderrys it remained a divining principle that was alive and well, if not loved by all, into the 1940s. As one newspaper observed in 1933, 'Park Lane changes: not so Londonderry House'.[19] The Londonderrys were also distinct from other Anglo-Irish aristocrats. This bloc came together for the last time with any sense of cohesion and common identity in the deliberations of the Irish Convention of 1917 and in the years of political turbulence and the more than occasional attack on their properties that followed, they erred on the side of caution, reluctant to draw attention to themselves as a class apart.

By comparison, there was a continuum in the Londonderrys' aspirations and actions from the 1800s to the 1900s. This is not to claim that this was the aristocratic norm, rather that such exception, coupled with the fact that much of the driving force behind the family came from a feminine source, heightened the import of the Ladies Londonderry. From their perspective, in the 1920s, just as in the century before, there was work to be done, alliances to be made and promotions to be pursued. Moreover, these women were able to cling onto the remnants of influence for longer than their male counterparts as a consequence of the very way they exercised power. The customary socio-political mix, with its merger of private and public, was certainly less criticised than open patronage or a continued sense of aristocratic propriety over electoral candidature.

From the 1820s the women of the Londonderry family impacted significantly on its financial and political status without attracting much negative commentary and this continued for the best part of a century. Therefore, the decades that some posit for the decline of female aristocratic influence, the 1880s and 1890s, cannot be applied to this particular case.[20] The changes which occurred in the political system as a result of an increasingly democratic electorate were undoubtedly momentous. Victoria's long reign from 1837 and the increasingly centralised and party basis of politics dented the generic importance of the political hostess, but fewer women were needed to carry out the remaining political functions of society rather than none at all. Nor did these changes extinguish the ambition of women like Theresa and Edith Londonderry. Politics as a familial enterprise continued and thus so did the female endeavour to promote, profile raise and influence. In consequence, the informal work of the Londonderry political hostess proved to be her saviour until the mid 1930s.

Class and gender provide the common denominators between the three Marchionesses of Londonderry who were otherwise united only by ties of marriage. Although not constrained by poverty, domestic responsibility or working conditions, they were limited by definitions of female aristocratic acceptability that impacted on their education, their marriage partners and all of their adult lives. In consequence, their world view was not identical to that of the men of their class. Yet, although they shared a marital name and warrant the title of political hostess and confidante, there were subtle gradations of activity and experience within their lives. Frances Anne, though a high Tory, was primarily focussed on familial gain: her life revolved around political and economic investment for futurity. Her determination and wealth built on Castlereagh's substantial achievements and established a metropolitan platform for the family that moved them from provincial to national standing. This was best visually referenced by Sir Thomas Lawrence's time of engagement portrait of Frances Anne where he depicted her as literally holding the key to familial advancement, the land and wealth that could win political position, in her grasp. Due to social constraints, however, Frances Anne knew that it was impossible to work alone: she needed alliances, most famously with Disraeli, to exert influence. She subsequently stage-managed her position; issuing joint statements to voters, tenants and workers as a way to have her voice heard but, as her husband admitted and society, sometimes bemusedly, acknowledged, she was the dynamic force in this union. Widowhood, although emotionally devastating for her, ironically, was also akin to a personal emancipation; she was freer as a dowager than she ever was as a wife.

Theresa, by comparison, was always more party and principle focussed. In consequence, she gave patronage to men like Carson and Bonar Law who could assist her in these ends. She had a discernible impact on unionism and the careers of those she patronised both from within her family circle and without. By the 1880s she was also able to embrace the opportunities for public action that were opening up for women, but this had nothing to do with feminism. Instead it was a strategy to maintain the status quo, the union and her family's position. In the closing stages of the First World War and its immediate aftermath, Theresa was much attuned to the rapid transformation of society but her reaction was a steadfast refusal to change.

Absolute aristocratic survival may have no longer been an option but Edith proved more adaptable than her predecessor in her attempts to maintain the family's political profile. Moreover, feminism was ever-present in her ideological composition and, uniformed and in a leadership position, during the First World War she, in many ways, symbolised how much had changed for women from the turn of the century.[21] However, she never sought to break free from the familial bond of duty and ultimately this fuelled her continuance as a political hostess and confidante throughout the 1920s and 1930s. Just as Theresa had been 'the moving spirit in private discussions which had a placating effect on the course of public events', something of that tradition survived in Edith's reign at Londonderry House.[22] But Edith was increasingly alone in these endeavours and, as the *London Mail* remarked in 1924, 'So few big houses are open now for entertainments of this kind that Lady Londonderry's parties will become historical.'[23]

Edith's relationship with Ramsay MacDonald was, however, more readily remembered than her hostessing. This association not only helped to secure cabinet rank for her spouse in the 1930s, but also revealed the potency of the political influence which aristocratic women could still exert through personal means of friendship and entertaining. This, coupled with women's heightened public profile, meant that an undercurrent of aristocratic female influence endured and this is crucial in gaining a fuller understanding of the working of politics in the nineteenth and twentieth centuries. But times were changing and Edith was unquestionably the last great political hostess. By the middle of the 1930s critics were describing her political receptions as too ostentatious for a time of economic depression. The role of familial patronage was also diminishing as Lord Londonderry tried in vain to persuade Winston Churchill to secure a cabinet appointment for him in the 1940s. Four years after Edith's death, Sean O'Casey reflected that she 'had to live through a decline and fall; a shock, for she, and all of her class, refused to believe that social evolution was bound to write Ichabod on the lintel of every grandee house in the land.'[24] The seventh Marquess never reconciled himself to his own or his family's fate, but Edith's autobiography reveals she was more pragmatic than O'Casey believed. She resignedly acknowledged the change that had occurred:

Society, as such, now means nothing except wealth and advertisement. The Peerage, to a great extent, has replenished its waning fortunes from the ranks of those who, before the War, would not have formed part of...'Society'. Therefore, it...does not represent what it formerly did.[25]

With this transformation nothing would ever be quite the same for the aristocracy in general and the Londonderrys in particular and it is difficult to disagree with Edith's final assertion that she had witnessed nothing short of a 'revolution'.

Notes

Epigraphs

1. Durham Record Office [hereafter DRO], Londonderry Archives, D/Lo/Acc:451 (D)/11/32.
2. Public Record Office of Northern Ireland [hereafter PRONI], D/2846/2/26/40.
3. PRONI, D/3099/3/2/927.

Introduction

1. Lady Castlereagh was the youngest daughter and co-heir of the second Earl of Buckinghamshire. Although christened Amelia Anne, she was always known as Emily. She married Castlereagh in 1794 and was widowed in 1822. She died in 1829 without issue. Little of her correspondence has survived.
2. Holdernesse was re-named Londonderry House by Henry, fifth Marquess of Londonderry and eldest son of Frances Anne, in 1872. See H. Montgomery Hyde, *Londonderry House and its pictures* (London, 1937) and Christopher Simon Sykes, *Private palaces. Life in the great London houses* (London, 1985).
3. Edmund Burke, *Reflections of the Revolution in France* (London, 1986 reprint of 1790 ed.), pp 194-95.
4. See, for example, Stella Tillyard, *Aristocrats. Caroline, Emily, Louisa and Sarah Lennox, 1740-1832* (London, 1995); Amanda Foreman, *Georgiana. Duchess of Devonshire* (London, 1998); Judith S. Lewis, *Sacred to female patriotism* (New York and London, 2003); Patricia Jalland, *Women, marriage and politics, 1860-1914* (Oxford, 1986); P. J. Jupp, 'The roles of royal and aristocratic women in British politics, c. 1782-1832' in Mary O'Dowd and Sabine Wichert (eds), *Chattel, servant or citizen. Women's status in church, state and society* (Belfast, 1995); K. D. Reynolds, *Aristocratic women and political society in Victorian Britain* (Oxford, 1998); Esther Simon Shkolnik, *Leading ladies* (New York and London, 1987) and Susan A. Williams, *Ladies of influence. Women of the elite in interwar Britain* (London, 2001). See also Peter Mandler, 'From Almack's to Willis's: aristocratic women and politics, 1815-67' in Amanda Vickery (ed.), *Women, privilege, and power. British politics, 1750 to the present* (Stanford, 2001), pp 152-67.
5. H. Montgomery Hyde, *The Londonderrys. A family portrait* (London, 1979) and Anne de Courcy, *Circe. The life of Edith, Marchioness of Londonderry* (London, 1992 reprinted as *Society's Queen. The life of Edith Marchioness of Londonderry* (London, 2004)). For Powell's review see *Books and Bookmen*, Sept. 1979.
6. See Ian Kershaw, *Making friends with Hitler. Lord Londonderry and Britain's road to war* (London, 2004); N. C. Fleming, *The Marquess of Londonderry: aristocracy, power and politics*

in Britain and Ireland (London, 2005) and Annabel Goldsmith, *Annabel, an unconventional life* (London, 2004).

7. For details of Frances Anne's [hereafter FA] travels see W. A. L. Seaman and J. R. Sewell, *Russian journal of Lady Londonderry, 1836-37* (London, 1973); Frances Anne, Marchioness of Londonderry, *A journal of three months' tour of Portugal, Spain and Africa* (London, 1843) and *Narrative of a visit to the courts of Vienna, Constantinople, Athens, Naples and c.* (London, 1844). For her handwritten account of the Vane-Tempests see PRONI, D/3030/RR/1 and for the Peninsular War correspondence see PRONI, D/3030/GG/1-5 and D/3030/P.

8. Theresa, sixth Marchioness of Londonderry [hereafter T], *Robert Stewart. Viscount Castlereagh* (London, 1904). In Nov. 1904 the *Times Literary Supplement* applauded this seventy-eight page volume as 'a very laudable endeavour and it is very skilfully and gracefully pursued...even though family piety may have tempted her to soften the harsher features of the portrait'.

9. Raymond Mortimer to Edith, seventh Marchioness of Londonderry [hereafter E], 17 July 1958 (PRONI, D/3099/3/49/1). Edith was the author of *Henry Chaplin. A memoir. Prepared by his daughter* (London, 1926); *Character and Tradition* (London, 1934); *Retrospect* (London, 1938); *The Land of the Living Heart* (privately printed, undated [c. 1940s]) and *The life and times of Frances Anne Marchioness of Londonderry and her husband Charles third Marquess of Londonderry* (London and New York, 1958). With H. Montgomery Hyde she co-edited the following: *Letters from Benjamin Disraeli to France Anne Marchioness of Londonderry, 1837-61* (London, 1938); *The Russian journals of Martha and Catherine Wilmot, 1803-08* (London, 1934) and *More letters from Martha Wilmot: Impressions of Vienna, 1819-29* (London, 1935). She also authored a children's book, *The Magic Inkpot* (London, 1928). Her memoir of Chaplin was extracted in the *Yorkshire Post*, the *Morning Post* and the *Glasgow Herald* in 1926.

10. The comparable Scottish figure was twenty-one per cent (Lewis, *Sacred to female patriotism*, p. 40).

11. See John Bateman, *The great landowners of Great Britain and Ireland* (Leicester, 1971 reprint of 1876 ed.) and W. D. Rubinstein, *Men of property. The very wealthy in Britain since the industrial revolution* (London, 1981). The country residences were Wynyard and Seaham Hall in Co. Durham, Mount Stewart in Co. Down, Garron Tower in Co. Antrim, Oakham near Rutland and Plâs Machynlleth in Merioneth, Wales.

12. On Mount Stewart see Edith, Marchioness of Londonderry's pamphlet, *Mount Stewart* (Belfast, 1965) and H. Montgomery Hyde and G. Jackson Stops, *Mount Stewart* (London, 1978).

13. Stewart was widowed in 1770 after his wife, Lady Susan experienced complications during her third pregnancy. Their first born, a son, died aged one but their second child, Robert became Lord Castlereagh. Stewart remarried in 1775 and Lady Frances, the first Marchioness of Londonderry from 1816, bore three sons and eight daughters. Three of the children died young but the eldest son, Charles later became the third Marquess of Londonderry.

14. Hyde, *Londonderrys*, p. 47. Widowed in 1822, Lady Frances left Mount Stewart and retired to Hastings where she died in 1833.

15. J. C. Beckett, *The Anglo-Irish tradition* (London, 1976), p. 10.

16. Anita Leslie, *Edwardians in love* (London, 1972), cited p. 127.

17. Frances, Countess of Warwick, *Afterthoughts* (London, 1931), p. 45.

18. Leonore Davidoff, *The best circles* (London, 1973), p. 63.

19. For a contemporary description of the ideal characteristics of a political hostess see Mrs. R. Niall, 'The political salon of today' in *The Lady's Realm*, vol. 26 (Oct. 1909), pp 150-57.

20. Vita Sackville-West, *The Edwardians* (London, 1930), p. 16.
21. Ralph Nevill (ed.), *The reminiscences of Lady Dorothy Nevill* (London, 1906), p. 216.
22. T. A. Escott, *Society in London* (London, 1886), p. 19 and pp 53-54 and J. S. Sandars to T, 4 June 1909 (DRO, D/Lo/C671 (31)).
23. See Elaine Chalus, "To serve my friends': women and political patronage in eighteenth-century England' in Vickery, *Women, privilege, and power*, pp 57-88.
24. J. M. Bourne, *Patronage and society in nineteenth-century England* (London, 1986), p. 5.
25. In the unemployment-ridden 1930s, for example, Edith was overwhelmed by the number of requests for assistance that she received.
26. Ralph Nevill (ed.), *Lady Dorothy Nevill. My own times* (London, 1912), p. 129.

Chapter 1
1. Disraeli to FA, 26 Dec. 1846 (DRO, D/Lo/C530 (30)).
2. Jonathan Powis, *Aristocracy* (Oxford, 1984), p. 5.
3. See Dena Goodman, 'Public space and private life: toward a synthesis of current historiographical approaches to the Old Regime' in *History and Theory*, vol. 31, no. 1 (Feb. 1992), pp 1-20. Goodman's comments on eighteenth-century France have a wider geographical and chronological resonance. As she notes, 'We need to get away from the rigidly oppositional thinking that assumes two spheres or two discourses, one public and the other private', p. 14.
4. Lewis, *Sacred to female patriotism*, p. 3.
5. See Joan Perkin, *Women and marriage in nineteenth-century England* (London, 1989), p. 53.
6. The Wynyard estate consisted of 1,350 acres. The house was re-built in 1826 on a design based on Wellington's Waterloo Palace. An 1841 fire caused devastation and damage estimated at £200,000-300,000 (see the *Morning Post*, 23-24 and 26 Feb. 1841 and *The Satirist*, 21 Mar. 1841). Although uninsured the house was rebuilt on a larger scale and completed in 1849. The estate was also enlarged by some 50,000 acres. See Brian Masters, *Wynyard Hall and the Londonderry family* (Teeside, 1973); Adrian Liddell, *An illustrated history of the Wynyard estate* (Wolviston, 1989); John Martin Robinson, *The Wyatts: An architectural dynasty* (Oxford, 1979) and N. Pevsner, *The buildings of England: Co. Durham* (London, 1953).
7. On the death of Frances Anne's mother, Anne Catherine in 1834 the majority of the Antrim estate and the title of Countess of Antrim and Viscountess Dunluce passed to her sister, Charlotte, wife of Vice Admiral Lord Mark Robert Kerr and aunt to Frances Anne. Frances Anne inherited only a sixth of the estate, amounting to 9,800 acres with an annual rent roll of £2,630:0:0 in 1844 (see PRONI, D/2977/6/3). See also the Earl of Antrim's memorial to the Duke of Rutland, Lord Lieutenant of Ireland to have his titles continue, undated (PRONI, D/2977/5/1/6/10).
8. Frances Anne, for instance, hoped in vain that her mother would re-settle the Antrim estate to allow it to pass either to her or her progeny. See solicitor Richard Groom's letter to Charles, third Marquess of Londonderry, 2 Jan. 1846 (DRO, D/Lo/C505 (4)).
9. Alan Heesom, *Durham city and its MPs, 1678-1992* (Durham, 1992), p. 63.
10. Typed copy of FA's handwritten memoir of 27 Dec. 1848 [hereafter 'Memoir'], undated (PRONI, D/3048/C/A/7/1), pp 3-4.
11. FA to her mother, 27 Oct. 1807 (PRONI, D/3030/RR/1). Her father assured her that she could write to her aunt whenever she liked, 'but be sure you always begin the first word of every Sentence with a large letter' (H. Vane-Tempest to FA, 26 Oct. 1807, transcribed in 'Memoir').
12. 'Memoir', pp 5-6. In 1819 the gross rental of Frances Anne's Durham estate was £11,136:16:8 and in the first six months of 1822 her collieries at Rainton and Penshaw earned £61,364:2:11 (DRO, D/Lo/E/489 and D/Lo/B/249). In the 1820s her aver-

age annual income was £60,000 which is equivalent to approximately £3.6 million in today's values.

13. FA to her aunt, Frances Taylor, 13 Sept. [1816] (DRO, D/Lo/C544 (1)) and FA to her mother, 21 Feb. 1817, transcribed in 'Memoir'. Frances Anne wanted her copy letters dealing with the Duke of Leinster's proposal to 'be burnt unopened' on her death (see DRO, D/Lo/C535 (3)). The practice of making substantial heiresses wards of court continued into the twentieth century. Trustees demanded, for example, that the daughters of George Curzon be made wards of court following the death of their mother in 1906 (see Anne de Courcy, *The Viceroy's daughters. The lives of the Curzon sisters* (London, 2000)).

14. 'Memoir', p. 13. Phelps, the son of an auctioneer, was also private secretary to Lord Burghersh. He changed his name to McDonnell after his marriage and was a trustee of the Londonderry estates until 1853.

15. FA to her mother, 24 Mar. 1818, transcribed in 'Memoir'.

16. Archibald Alison, *The Lives of Lord Castlereagh and Sir Charles Stewart, the second and third Marquesses of Londonderry* (Edinburgh and London, 1861), vol. III, p. 213.

17. 'Memoir', pp 14-15.

18. Alison, *Lives*, vol. II, p. 213.

19. Charles Stewart to Castlereagh, *ante* Apr. 1818 (PRONI, D/3030/P/155/1). The 1819 marriage settlement of Frances Anne was revised in 1822 (see DRO, D/Lo/E (1)).

20. In 1804 Stewart married Lady Catherine Bligh, daughter of the third Earl of Darnley. They had one son, Frederick (1804-72). Catherine died after a minor head operation in 1812. Frederick, Viscount Castlereagh and fourth Marquess of Londonderry from 1854, inherited the family's Irish estates and was MP for Co. Down from 1822-52. He held junior ministerial office under Wellington and Peel respectively in 1828 and 1834 whilst his father was politically isolated. He married Elizabeth, daughter of the third Earl of Roden and widow of the sixth Viscount of Powerscourt, in 1846 but they were without issue.

21. Tempest v. Ord, Chancery Papers, brief *affidavit* of Mrs. Michael Angelo Taylor, 11 Apr. 1818 (PRONI, D/654/G1/3).

22. Ibid., letter from Dr. McDonnell, Belfast, 14 May 1813. Sir Walter Farquhar and Dr. Thomas Duncan echoed his remarks in letters dated 25 May 1813 and 2 June 1813 respectively.

23. Ibid., brief *affidavit* of Mrs. Taylor.

24. A. W. P. Malcolmson, *The pursuit of the heiress: aristocratic marriage in Ireland, 1750-1820* (Belfast, 1982), p. 30. Marriage settlements dated from early eighteenth century and after 1750 the average Irish jointure ranged from £500-£3,000 per year. See also David Large, 'The wealth of the great Irish landowners, 1750-1815' in *Irish Historical Studies*, vol. XV, no. 57 (Mar. 1966), pp 21-45.

25. Tempest v. Ord, Chancery Papers, brief *affidavit* of Lord Charles Stewart, 17 Apr. 1818 (PRONI, D/654/G1/3).

26. Castlereagh to Charles Stewart, c. Apr. 1818 and Lord Liverpool to Castlereagh, 4 Sept. 1818 (PRONI, D/3030/P/156/1 and 161). Liverpool was Prime Minister from 1812-27.

27. Cited in the *Irish Times*, 25 Dec. 1937.

28. Tempest v. Ord, Chancery Papers, brief *affidavit* of the Countess of Antrim, 20 Apr. 1818 (PRONI, D/654/G1/3).

29. Malcolmson, *Pursuit of the heiress*, cited p. 39.

30. 'Memoir', pp 15-16.

31. FA to Mrs. Taylor, 13 July c. 1818 and to Lord Eldon, 9 July 1818 (Centre for Kentish Studies, Maidstone, Kent [hereafter CKS], U840/C63-4).

32. R. W. Surtees, 'The Londonderry trust, 1819-54' in *Archaeologia Aeliana*, 5th series, vol. 10 (1982), p. 180.

33. Londonderry, *Frances Anne*, p. 42.

34. Lewis, *Sacred to female patriotism*, p. 12.

35. On the exceptions to and the variations of coverture see ibid., pp 12-13.

36. 'Memoir', p. 18.

37. Castlereagh to Lord Londonderry, 11 Apr. 1818 (PRONI, D/3030/P/157/1).

38. FA to her mother, 16 Dec. 1819, transcribed in 'Memoir'.

39. Martha Wilmot to Viscountess Ennismore, 8 Dec. 1819 and to Lady Bloomfield, 12 Dec. 1819 (PRONI, D/3084/C/E/1/6-7).

40. 'Memoir', p. 19 and pp 21-22. The 1820 Congress at Troppau aimed to quell the revolutionary spirit in Italy. In December the congress moved to Laybach where discussions ended on 6 May 1821.

41. Londonderry and Hyde, *More letters from Martha Wilmot*, pp 80-81 and p. 86.

42. FA to her mother, 16 Dec. 1819, transcribed in 'Memoir'.

43. Francis Bamford and the Duke of Wellington (eds), *The journal of Mrs. Arbuthnot, 1820-32* (London, 1950), vol. I, p. 68.

44. Londonderry and Hyde, *More letters from Martha Wilmot*, pp 108-09.

45. Peter Quennell (ed.), *The private letters of Princess Lieven to Prince Metternich, 1820-26* (London, 1937), p. 164. The Londonderry jewels are now in the Victoria and Albert Museum.

46. 'Memoir', p. 24. For a discussion of Frances Anne's childbearing experiences, along with forty-nine of her upper-class contemporaries, see Judith S. Lewis, *In the family way. Childbearing in the British aristocracy, 1760-1860* (New Jersey, 1986). The child was known as Henry (1821–84) and married Mary Cornelia, only daughter of Lord John Edwards, in August 1846. He was known as Viscount Seaham until his father's death in 1854 and then as second Earl Vane until his half-brother, Frederick's death in 1872 when he succeeded to the marquessate. Although MP for Durham 1847-54 and Lord Lieutenant of the County Palatine, he maintained a lower profile than his predecessors and mainly resided on his wife's Welsh estate, Plâs Machynlleth in Merioneth. They had six children, including Charles, later the sixth Marquess of Londonderry.

47. Londonderry and Hyde, *More letters from Martha Wilmot*, p. 110 and p. 115.

48. Quennell, *Private letters of Princess Lieven*, p. 171.

49. Lady Frances Anne Emily (1822-99) married the Duke of Marlborough in July 1843. Known as Duchess Fanny she was mother to Randolph Churchill as well as ten other children and was grandmother to Winston Churchill.

50. FA to her mother, 27 May and 11 June 1822, transcribed in 'Memoir'. Holdernesse was rebuilt under Frances Anne's supervision.

51. Sykes, *Private palaces*, p. 243. For a history of Holland House see Leslie Mitchell, *Holland House* (London, 1980).

52. 'Memoir', p. 31. As Castlereagh and his wife, Lady Emily had no issue the Irish estates and titles passed to Charles. Castlereagh succeeded to the marquessate in 1821.

53. Charles (now the third Marquess of Londonderry) to Lord Liverpool, 28 Oct. 1822 (PRONI, D/3030/DD/6). Castlereagh fought and injured Canning in a duel in 1812 with the event leading both to temporarily resign from the government.

54. FA to her mother, 3 Sept. 1822, transcribed in 'Memoir'.

55. Tsar Alexander I of Russia to FA, Dec. 1822 (PRONI, D/3030/NN/1). My sincere thanks are due to Dr. Ian McKeane for his skilful translations of this correspondence from the original French and for his insightful comments on the nature of this relationship.

56. Transcribed and translated letter from FA to Alexander I, Sept. 1822 in 'Memoir', p. 34.

57. Transcribed letter from Alexander I to FA and her reply, Sept. 1822, ibid., pp 33-35.

58. 'Memoir', pp 35-36.

59. Two transcribed letters from FA to Alexander I and his replies, Sept. 1822 in 'Memoir', pp 36-38.

60. Alexander I to FA, undated [1822] (PRONI, D/3030/NN/1).

61. 'Memoir', p. 45 and FA to her mother, 26 Oct. 1822, transcribed in the same.

62. 'Memoir', pp 38-39. Charles was a patron to Sir Thomas Lawrence and brought him 'into touch with all the most celebrated personages in Europe' (George Soames Layard (ed.), *Sir Thomas Lawrence's letter-bag* (London, 1906), p. 100).

63. Transcribed letter from FA to Alexander I, Nov. 1822 in 'Memoir', p. 40.

64. Madame La Comtesse de Choiseul-Gouffier (trans. by M. B. Patterson), *Historical memoirs of the Emperor Alexander I and the Court of Russia* (London, 1904), p. 70. Janet M. Hartley in *Alexander I* (Essex, 1994) concurs with this view. It is widely acknowledged that Alexander had numerous dalliances, including one of sixteen years duration with Countess Maria Naryshkin.

65. 'Memoir', p. 41.

66. H. Montgomery Hyde, *Princess Lieven* (London, 1938), pp 144-45.

67. Sir Herbert Maxwell (ed.), *The Creevey papers. A selection from the correspondence and diaries of the late Thomas Creevey, MP* (London, 1904), vol. II, p. 58.

68. Londonderry, *Frances Anne*, cited p. 103.

69. 'Memoir', p. 42.

70. Alexander I to FA, Dec. 1822 (PRONI, D/3030/NN/1).

71. 'Memoir', pp 43-48 and transcribed letter from FA to Alexander I, 11 Dec. 1822 in the same.

72. FA to her mother, 26 Dec. 1822, transcribed in 'Memoir'.

73. Londonderry and Hyde, *More letters from Martha Wilmot*, p. 206.

74. 'Memoir', p. 52. Alexandrina Octavia Maria was born following a twenty-six hour labour on 31 July 1823. She married the third Earl of Portarlington in 1847 and died in 1874.

75. Alexander I to FA, 14 June 1823 and 29 Feb. 1824 (PRONI, D/3030/NN/1). FA's written memoirs come to a close with her arrival at Glenarm in late 1823.

76. Londonderry, *Frances Anne*, p. 138 and Reynolds, *Aristocratic women*, p. 63.

77. Henri Troyat, *Alexander of Russia: Napoleon's Conqueror* (Kent, 1982), cited p. 216. Troyat makes no mention of Frances Anne.

78. Alan Palmer, *Alexander I. Tsar of war and peace* (London, 1974), pp 382-83. Palmer notes the tsar's congressional melancholy was caused by venereal disease. Alexander died of typhoid in 1825.

79. Charles to Castlereagh, referring to his plans to seek peerage promotion, 6 Dec. 1821 (PRONI, D/3030/P/194).

80. Wellington to Charles Arbuthnot, 4 Oct. 1822 cited in Londonderry, *Frances Anne*, p. 102. Sir George Hill was appointed to the Derry militia command in 1823.

81. Peel's reply to FA stated his regret at being unable to comply 'with the wish with you have conveyed to me on the part of Lord Londonderry', 22 Dec. 1822 (DRO, D/Lo/F/1055 (vii)). Frances Anne championed her husband in another letter to Peel of 13 Dec. 1842, noting her spouse's 'deep anxiety and just expectation' that he should succeed Lord Hill as Colonel of the Blues. Peel, however, informed her on 22 Dec. that Lord Anglesey had been appointed to this position (British Library, 40520).

82. W. D. Rubinstein, 'The end of "Old Corruption" in Britain 1780-1860', *Past and Present*, no. 101 (Nov. 1983), p. 58.

83. FA to her mother, 28 Nov. and 26 Dec. 1822, transcribed in 'Memoir'.
84. Quennell, *Private letters of Princess Lieven*, pp 170-71. Londonderry's financial position was seen as a barrier to the £2,000 pension he claimed. Mrs. Arbuthnot was not alone in declaring, 'He has above 2000£ a year of his own and married a woman with 60,000 £ a year!!!' (Bamford and Wellington, *Journal of Mrs. Arbuthnot*, vol. I, p. 238).
85. Ibid., Bamford and Wellington, p. 246.
86. Londonderry, *Frances Anne*, cited p. 127.
87. Hardinge, later Viscount Hardinge, MP who married Charles' sister, Emily Jane in 1821.
88. Frances Anne's fourth child, her second and favourite son, Adolphus, was born on 2 July 1825. He was MP for Durham city from 1852 to June 1853 but was unseated by petition. He succeeded his older brother, Henry as MP for the N. Division of Durham, 1854-64 and served as Lieutenant Colonel in the Scots Fusilier Guards. He fought in the Crimea from 1854-59 and died in 1864. August 1826 saw the birth of Frances Anne's fifth child, a daughter named Sophia Henrietta Charlotte. She died from inflammation and suspected pneumonia aged eight months on 11 April 1827. Her sixth child was Adelaide Melina Caroline who was born on 31 Jan. 1830 with the Duke and Duchess of Clarence, later William IV and Queen Adelaide, as godparents. She eloped and married Rev. Francis Henry Law, vicar of Wellington in Derbyshire and her brother's tutor, in Feb. 1852. She was ostracised by her family but as she comforted her mother in widowhood in 1854 some entente was obviously reached. She died in 1882. Frances Anne's seventh and last child, Ernest was born on 29 Feb. 1836 and with the king as godfather the family were evidently in royal favour. Ernest served in the Life Guards but was dismissed. He married Mary, daughter of Thomas Hutchinson of Howden Hall, Co. Durham in 1869. He died, leaving one son, in 1885.
89. Charles to Camden, 3 Dec. 1822 (CKS, U840/C61/20). On the peerage see M. W. McCahill, 'Peerage creations and the changing character of the British nobility, 1750-1850' in *English Historical Review*, vol. XCVI (96) (1981).
90. Charles to Camden and 26 Oct. 1822 (CKS, U840/C504/5).
91. Ibid., 22 Nov. 1822 (CKS, U840/C61/17).
92. Ibid., 10 Oct. and 20 Nov. 1822 (CKS, U840/C504/6-7).
93. FA to Camden, 10 Dec. 1822 (CKS, U840/C510/1).
94. FA to her mother, 26 Dec. 1822, transcribed in 'Memoir'.
95. 'Memoir', p. 50.
96. Unidentified newspaper cutting from 1815 (PRONI, D/2846/3/24/1).
97. J. M. Turner to FA, 7 June 1822 (CKS, U840/C168).
98. Lord Colchester (ed.), *Lord Ellenborough. A political diary, 1828-30* (London, 1881), vol. I, p. 131.
99. Duke of Wellington (ed.), *Wellington and his friends* (London, 1965), p. 74.
100. Londonderry, *Frances Anne*, cited pp 150-51.
101. Bamford and Wellington, *Journal of Mrs. Arbuthnot*, vol. I, p. 254. Lord Maryborough was appointed to this post.
102. Alison, *Lives*, vol. III, p. 253.
103. Cumberland was the fifth son of George III, a staunch Tory, Grand Master of the Orange Order and, from 1837, King of Hanover.
104. The predicted cost of purchasing and developing Seaham was £70,000 but by 1845 £180,000 had been expended. Repaying monies for the purchase and refurbishment of Holdernesse, plus the remodelling of Wynyard, cost over £10,000 per annum from 1821-29. In 1829 Charles' personal expenses, although it is possible that this covered political expenses and the £3,000 annual upkeep of Wynyard, amounted to £43,000.

105.There are certainly similarities between the hostesses and the formalities that   reigned at both Holdernesse and Holland House. At the latter, for example, it has been remarked that, 'For beginners, the experience of dining at Holland House could be terrifying' (Mitchell, *Holland House*, p. 32).

106.Perkin, *Women and marriage*, p. 79.

107.Ione Leigh, *Castlereagh* (London, 1951), cited p. 223.

108.C. J. Bartlett, *Castlereagh* (London, 1966), cited p. 261.

109.Leigh, *Castlereagh*, p. 310 and p. 326.

110.Londonderry, *Letters*, p. xii.

111.Alison in Londonderry, *Letters*, cited p. xii.

112.Ralph Nevill, *The life and letters of Lady Dorothy Nevill* (London, 1919), p. 177.

113.Maxwell, *Creevey papers*, vol. II, p. 80.

114.Guy Le Strange (ed. and trans.), *Correspondence of Princess Lieven and Earl Grey* (London, 1890), vol. I, p. 10.

115.Bamford and Wellington, *Journal of Mrs. Arbuthnot*, vol. I, p. 313 and unidentified newspaper cutting of 1824 (PRONI, D/2846/3/24/1).

116.Louis J. Jennings, *The correspondence and diaries of the late Right Hon. John Wilson Croker* (London, 1884), vol. I, p. 426. At the time of her marriage in 1819, Frances Anne's debts, accumulated by neglect of her mining interests whilst she was in minority, amounted to £123,400. From 1825 Charles was unable to place an annual £10,000 aside for Adolphus, his second son by Frances Anne, and was thus in breach of their marriage settlement. By 1830 their debts stood at £233,990 and in the following year bankers demanded the lease of a Londonderry colliery as security for loans. Frances Anne's trustees retook command of the Vane-Tempest financial concerns in 1834 and retained it for the next eight years. See Surtees, 'The Londonderry trust'.

117.Bamford and Wellington, *Journal of Mrs. Arbuthnot*, vol. II, p. 280. From Arbuthnot's journal it appears that Lord Londonderry's brother-in-law, Col. Wood tried similar reasoning tactics in June 1830, again, without success, see pp 363-64.

118.Londonderry, *Frances Anne*, pp 164-65.

119.Aspinall, *Correspondence of Charles Arbuthnot*, vol. LXV, p. 128.

120.Wellington to the Duke of Buckingham, 12 Oct. 1830 in Duke of Wellington (ed.), *Dispatches, correspondence and memoranda of Field Marshall Arthur Duke of Wellington* (London, 1868), vol. VII, p. 248.

121.Bamford and Wellington, *Journal of Mrs. Arbuthnot*, vol. II, p. 410.

122.Abraham D. Kriegal (ed.), *The Holland House diaries. The diary of Henry Richard Vassall Fox, third Lord Holland* (London, 1977), p. 32 and p. 122. See also the anonymous printed account of Lord Londonderry's career to 1838, c. 1840 (PRONI, D/3030/HH/1).

123.Bamford and Wellington, *Journal of Mrs. Arbuthnot*, vol. I, pp 119-20 and Colchester, *Lord Ellenborough*, vol. II, p. 40. Ellenborough also deployed language such as 'insane' and 'painful' in relation to Londonderry's Lords' contribution. Le Marchant used similar terminology for Londonderry in his diary.

124.Unidentified newspaper cutting, 1832 (PRONI, D/3030).

125.Unidentified newspaper cutting and anonymous epigram to Lord Londonderry, 1832 (PRONI, D/2846/3/24/1). In 1824 news of Charles' duel with Cornet Battier, a member of his own regiment, the tenth Hussars was, according to Wellington, 'in every body's mouth, in all the newspapers, and on the theatres' (Wellington to Charles, 9 Apr. 1824 in Wellington, *Dispatche*s, vol. II, p. 248). The Duke of York wanted Charles tried by a court martial, but Wellington intervened. Charles was, however, censured by the king for fighting an inferior officer. In 1839 another duel, this time with Irish MP, Henry Grattan again caused furore.

126.Londonderry, *Frances Anne*, p. 171.

127.Bamford and Wellington, *Journal of Mrs. Arbuthnot*, vol. II, p. 410.

128.Wellington, *Wellington*, pp 106-07.

129.Heesom, *Durham*, p. 22.

130.Alan Heesom, "'Legitimate' *versus* 'Illegitimate' influences in aristocratic electioneering in mid-Victorian Britain' in *Parliamentary History*, vol. 7, part 2 (1988), p. 290.

131.Hardinge to FA, 4 Feb. 1820 (CKS, U840/C530/1). Hardinge was re-elected to Durham in 1828.

132.N. J. Nossiter, *Influence, opinion and political idioms in reformed England. Case studies from the North-East, 1832-74* (Brighton, 1975), cited p. 118.

133.Heesom, "'Legitimate' *versus* 'Illegitimate'", p. 290. Heesom also effectively highlights the conditional nature of Durham workers' allegiance to their employer. See also Nossiter, *Influence*, p. 30.

134.Heesom, "'Legitimate' *versus* 'Illegitimate'", p. 289.

135.*The Times*, 21 Mar. 1835. The Commons also voted Manners Sutton out of the chair of the house at this juncture.

136.Le Strange, *Correspondence of Princess Lieven*, p. 94 and p. 98.

137.Disraeli to FA, 7 Jan. 1858 (DRO, D/Lo/C530 (179)).

138.J. A. Gunn, John Matthews, Donald M. Schurman and M. G. Wiebe (eds), *Benjamin Disraeli letters: 1815-34* (Buffalo and London, 1982), vol. I, pp xiv-xv. The first sale of Disraeli's missives occurred during his own lifetime in 1866. Much of the Disraeli/ Frances Anne correspondence is now missing, especially an uninterrupted run of her letters. Indeed, Edith, seventh Marchioness of Londonderry, the editor of their letters, claimed that Coningsby 'destroyed the whole lot' in 1955 (E to Hugh Alexander Boyd, 23 May 1956 (PRONI, D/3084/C/D/3/7)).

139.Ian Machin, *Disraeli* (Essex, 1995), p. 2.

140.As Disraeli noted, 'in England personal distinction is the only passport to the society of the great. Whether the distinction arises from fortune, family or talent is immaterial; but certain it is, to enter high society, a man must either have blood, a million or be a genius' (Christopher Hibbert, *Disraeli. A personal history* (London, 2004), cited p. 19).

141.Ralph Disraeli, *Lord Beaconsfield's correspondence with his sister, 1832-52* (London, 1886), p. 26. Disraeli unsuccessfully contested three seats at Wycombe between 1832-35.

142.Robert Blake, 'The rise of Disraeli' in H. R. Trevor-Roper (ed.), *Essays in British history. Presented to Sir Keith Fielding* (London, 1964), p. 229 and p. 232.

143.Philip Magnus, 'Disraeli' in Duff Cooper (ed.), *British Prime Ministers* (London, 1953), p. 113.

144.Londonderry, *Letters*, cited p. 3. Frances Anne's first wore her Cleopatra costume at Prince Borghese's ball in Florence shortly after the congress.

145.Disraeli to FA, 6 Aug. [1837] (DRO, D/Lo/C530 (5)) and FA to Disraeli, 13 Dec. 1837 (PRONI, D/2846/2/37)).

146.Edgar Feuchtwanger, *Disraeli* (London, 2000), p. 24.

147.J. A. Gunn, John Matthews, Donald M. Schurman and M. G. Wiebe (eds), *Benjamin Disraeli letters: 1835-37* (Buffalo and London, 1982), vol. II, p. 70. The Londonderrys purchased Rosebank near Fulham in 1831 as a summer retreat from London. Disraeli used Rosebank as the fictional home of Lady Everingham in his 1844 novel, *Coningsby* (Hibbert, *Disraeli*, p. 163). The property was sold in 1854.

148.On Disraeli's earlier unsuccessful attempts to join White's, the Travellers' Club and the Athenaeum see Hibbert, *Disraeli*, pp 63-64.

149.See for example, FA to Disraeli, undated (DRO, D/Lo/C530 (3)). In this dispatch, she asked him to look over an article she was submitting to Lady Wortley as she felt 'one of my boy's exercises would be as suitable'.

150.Disraeli to FA, Aug. 1837 in Londonderry, *Letters*, p. 8 and 26 Dec. 1846 (DRO, D/ Lo/C530 (30)). Disraeli admitted to Matthew Arnold that he was a flatterer: 'You have heard me called a flatterer and it is true. Everyone likes flattery; and when it comes to royalty you should lay it on with a trowel' (Hibbert, *Disraeli*, cited, p. 271).

151.Ibid., undated (DRO, D/Lo/C530 (67)). Bradford and Feuchtwanger both note that servility remained a constant in their relationship.

152.M. G. Wiebe, J. B. Conacher, John Matthews, Mary S. Millar (eds), *Benjamin Disraeli letters: 1838-42* (Buffalo and London, 1987), vol. III, pp 25-26.

153.Letter from FA and Charles, 18 July 1837 (PRONI, D/3084/C/C/6/88). Other aristocratic women who participated in electioneering included Ladies Palmerston, Guest and Jersey and the Duchess of Sutherland.

154.FA to Disraeli, 6 Aug. [1837] (DRO, D/Lo/C530 (5)).

155.Ibid., undated and 8 and 11 Aug. 1837 (DRO, D/Lo/C530 (6, 7 and 17)). Electoral contests were costly and it was, therefore, in local grandees' interest to have candidates returned unopposed. This was evident in the N. Durham division in 1841 when Liddell and the Earl of Durham's brother, Hedworth Lambton, were returned unopposed. That this was purely a financial consideration on Londonderry's part is evidenced by that fact that Liddell's re-election was not initially supported. This seat was perceived as belonging to Frances Anne's eldest son, Seaham and as he was not yet of age the Londonderrys threatened to bring in a temporary caretaker. The financial implications of a fire at Wynyard, however, prompted a re-think and Liddell was consequently supported.

156.Disraeli, *Lord Beaconsfield's correspondence*, p. 26. Disraeli's success owed much not only to his growing social acceptance facilitated by women like Frances Anne but also to Lord Lyndhurst's patronage from 1834. At this juncture Lyndhurst had no seat to offer Disraeli but drew him into the Tory Party and, in time, he was named as a parliamentary candidate.

157.Wiebe *et al*, *Disraeli letters*, vol. III, p. 25.

158.W. F. Monypenny, *The life of Benjamin Disraeli, Earl of Beaconsfield* (London, 1912), vol. II, p. 35.

159.Disraeli to FA, 20 Apr. 1850 (DRO, D/Lo/C530 (87)).

160.Leonore Davidoff, *The best circles* (London, 1973), p. 73.

161.Disraeli to FA, 19 Dec. 1861 (DRO, D/Lo/Acc: 451 (D)/11 (45)).

162.Ibid., 8 May 1839 in Londonderry, *Letters*, pp 8-9. At this juncture, their correspondence, although frequently rushed on Disraeli's part, was usually at least weekly and he also sent her copies of newspapers.

163.Wiebe *et al*, *Disraeli letters*, vol. III, p. 146.

164.Disraeli, *Lord Beaconsfield's correspondence*, p. 132. In 1839 FA also hosted a banquet at Holdernesse for Czarewich Alexander II, grandson of Alexander I and a ball at Wynyard that was attended by 300, including the Dukes of Cleveland, Devonshire and Rutland.

165.Wiebe *et al*, *Disraeli letters*, vol. III, p. 202.

166.Robert Blake, *Disraeli* (London, 1966), cited p. 152 and p. 155.

167.Wiebe *et al*, *Disraeli letters*, vol. III, pp 131-32.

168.Ibid., p. 187. Disraeli wrote to his sister of his regret at not being able to attend these Londonderry fêtes.

169.FA to Disraeli, 14 Aug. 1839 (DRO, D/Lo/C530 (22)). Her next letter, dated 20 Aug. 1839, suggests that he replied to her earlier dispatch as she thanked him 'for remembering me at such a moment and I beg you will accept my sincere congratulations and very best wishes for your happiness. ...Adieu, you shall hear again before I leave England' (DRO, D/Lo/C530 (23)).

170.Blake claims Disraeli was 'unperturbed' by the split: 'He probably guessed that they [Ladies Londonderry and Jersey] would change their attitude sooner or later - and of course they did' (*Disraeli*, p. 158). Feuchtwanger and Sarah Bradford in *Disraeli* (London, 1982) concur with this view.

171.Benjamin Disraeli, *Sybil or the two nations* (London, 1927 reprint of 1845 ed.), p. 312.

172.Disraeli to FA, 13 Sept. 1853 (PRONI, D/3030/JJ/24B).

173.Heesom, "Legitimate' *versus* 'Illegitimate", p. 292 and Nossiter, *Influence*, p. 121. The Corn Laws were designed to prevent the price of wheat falling from inflated wartime levels when normal trading resumed.

174.M.G. Wiebe, J. B. Conacher, John Matthews and Mary S. Millar (eds), *Disraeli's letters: 1842-47* (Buffalo and London, 1989), vol. IV, p. 103.

175.Disraeli, *Lord Beaconsfield's correspondence*, pp 199-200.

176.Lord Sudley (ed. and trans.), *The Lieven-Palmerston correspondence, 1828-56* (London, 1943), p. 253 and pp 295-96.

177.Earl of Ilchester (ed.), *Elizabeth, Lady Holland to her son, 1821-45* (London, 1946), p. 208.

178.Wellington, *Wellington*, pp 188-89.

179.Quote from *Sybil* in W. F. Monypenny, *The life of Benjamin Disraeli, Earl of Beaconsfield* (vol. II, London, 1912), p. 262.

180.Disraeli to FA, c. 29 June 1845 (DRO, D/Lo/C530 (24)).

181.Ibid., 26 Dec. 1846 (DRO, D/Lo/C530 (30)).

182.FA to Disraeli, 30 July 1845 (DRO, D/Lo/C530 (26)).

183.Disraeli to FA, June 1845 in Londonderry, *Letters*, pp 13, 18-19.

184.Wiebe *et al*, *Disraeli's letters*, vol. IV, p. 178. In the same letter he notes Lady Jersey was 'in a stupor of malice and astonishment' at his wife, Mary Anne partaking in society.

185.Disraeli to FA, 1 Sept. 1846 (DRO, D/Lo/C530 (28)). In 1851 he also sent her the first copy of his *Life of Lord George Bentinck*.

186.Disraeli to FA, 30 Apr. 1849 (DRO, D/Lo/Acc: 451 (D)/9 (24)) and Wiebe *et al*, *Disraeli's letters*, vol. IV, p. xliii.

187.Disraeli to FA, 1 Sept. 1846 (DRO, D/Lo/C530 (29)).

188.FA to Disraeli, undated [c. 1845-46] in W. F. Monypenny and G. E. Buckle, *The life of Benjamin Disraeli, Earl of Beaconsfield* (London, 1914), vol. III, p. 18.

189.John Lanktree, Antrim estate agent to FA, 25 Jan. 1845 (PRONI, D/2977/6/4A-C).

190.See printed poster, undated (PRONI, D/2977/5/1/8/20/1).

191.1847 report on Antrim estate to FA (PRONI, D/2977/6/4B).

192.Note by Hugh Alexander Boyd on Garron Tower, undated (PRONI, D/3084/C/D/3/6). In 1850 FA sent her Durham agent to report on the Antrim estate, suggesting a concern for future profitability. He reported favourably on 'a sober, respectful[,] well disposed people…warmly attached to the noble landlord and Landlady. They acknowledge with gratitude the favours they have from time to time received', but the tenantry was still wedded to the Rundale system and potato cultivation on badly drained land (David Cowan to FA, 29 July 1850 (PRONI, D/2977/6/6)). Little changed over the next decade: in 1850 rent arrears amounted to £2,000; blight re-emerged in 1858 and 1861 and the Clothing Society, established in 1845, was still in existence in the early 1860s.

193.Disraeli to FA, 26 Dec. 1846 (DRO, D/Lo/C530 (30)). Anne, Duchesse de Longueville was the mistress of the Duc de la Rochefoucauld and possessed considerable political sway in the seventeenth century.

194.Ibid., 7 Nov. 1847 (DRO, D/Lo/C530 (34)).

195.Ibid., 1 May 1848 and 12 Mar. 1849 (DRO, D/Lo/Acc: 451 (D)/9 (3) and (22)). Again, this time on 3 Aug. 1848, Disraeli noted, 'I can scarcely guide my pen from sheer fatigue and hurry, but I hope you will pardon this letter and accept it, at least, as a proof of devotion, tho' it will cost an extra stamp to gain the ½ past 6 o'ck post' (DRO, D/Lo/Acc: 451 (D)/9 (14)).

196.Bentinck patronised Disraeli from 1842 and was leader of the protectionists in the Commons from 1846. Guizot succeeded Soult as French premier but resigned in 1848. He spent approximately a year in London from 1848-49.

197.Disraeli to FA, 1 May 1848 (DRO, D/Lo/C530 (44)).

198.Ibid., 5 Sept. 1848 (DRO, D/Lo/C530 (63)). In 1859 the French monarch's son, the Comte de Paris and the Duc and Duchess d'Aumale visited Garron Tower in Antrim where the Londonderrys regularly spent the summer and early autumn months. The tower, designed by Lewis Vullimany and modelled on Burg Rheinstein, a thirteenth-century castle on the left bank of the Rhine, was built in 1848 at a cost of £4,000.

199.*London Illustrated News*, 22 July 1848 and 8 June 1850.

200.Disraeli to FA, 9 Aug. 1848 in Londonderry, *Letters*, pp 40-41. The Prussian-Danish conflict over Schleswig-Holstein was settled in Denmark's favour in 1850.

201.Disraeli to FA, 12-14 Aug. 1848 in Londonderry, *Letters*, pp 43-44.

202.Feuchtwanger, *Disraeli*, p. 83. Frances Anne thanked Disraeli for 'sending such interesting accounts' of parliament to her at Wynyard in a letter of mid 1848, especially as 'it is so purely disinterested on your part for I can send you nothing in return but lamentations about the wet and the hay' (DRO, D/Lo/C530 (46)).

203.Disraeli to FA, 7 Aug. 1848 (DRO, D/Lo/C530 (48)).

204.Ibid., 29 Aug. 1848 (DRO, D/Lo/Acc: 451 (D)/9 (15)).

205.Ibid., 12 Apr. 1849 (DRO, D/Lo/C530 (71)).

206.Ibid., 19 and 21 Aug. and 30 Dec. 1849 (DRO, D/Lo/C530 (53 and 75-6)). From 1848, Frances Anne maintained her father's practice of keeping a bear garden, along with some monkeys, at Wynyard although Disraeli playfully chastised her, 'when the [bear]…ceases to kiss your fair hand, and begins to lick his own paws, he is getting dangerous.' The Young Ireland rising probably served to reinforce Frances Anne's earlier views that Ireland and England's relationship was akin to that of Poland and Russia, noting in 1836: 'a conquered country, a subdued kingdom that can never forget it was once independent, but is always internally agitating and bringing down misery and forging for itself fresh claims' (Angela Antrim, *The Antrim McDonnells* (Belfast, 1977), cited p. 54).

207.FA to Disraeli, 30 Aug. 1853 (PRONI, D/3030/JJ/22B). The Disraelis declined her invite.

208.Disraeli to FA, 20 and 27 Mar. 1850 in Londonderry, *Letters*, pp 78-82.

209.Ibid., 20 Apr. 1850 (DRO, D/Lo/C530 (87)). Blandford succeeded to the dukedom of Marlborough in 1857.

210.Disraeli to Charles, 26 May 1850 (DRO, D/Lo/Acc: 451 (D)/2 (4)).

211.Sidney Webb, *The story of the Durham miners, 1662-1921* (London, 1921), p. 50.

212.Disraeli to Charles, 27 Aug. 1850 (DRO, D/Lo/Acc: 451 (D)/2 (6)).

213.Disraeli to FA, 2 Aug. 1850 (DRO, D/Lo/C530 (89)). Frances Anne thanked Disraeli for his intervention in the passage of this legislation on 6 Aug. 1850, noting 'It is hard to add to your Labours' (DRO, D/Lo/C530 (90)).

214.Disraeli to Charles, 29 Dec. 1850 (DRO, D/Lo/Acc: 451 (D)/3 (1)).

215.Disraeli to Lord Stanley, 21 Jan. 1851 in Monypenny and Buckle, *The life of Benjamin Disraeli*, vol. III, p. 277.

216.Disraeli to FA, 27 Mar. 1851 (DRO, D/Lo/Acc: 451 (D)/10 (2)).

217.Ibid., 20 Apr. 1851 (DRO, D/Lo/Acc: 451 (D)/10 (3)).

218.Ibid., 28 Dec. 1851 (DRO, D/Lo/Acc: 451 (D)/10 (5)). He also enclosed a copy of a letter sent to him concerning Palmerston's resignation.

219.FA to Disraeli, 7 Jan. 1852 (PRONI, D/3030/JJ/2B).

220.Disraeli to Charles, 29 Feb. 1852 (DRO, D/Lo/Acc: 451 (D)/4 (2)).

221.A. C. Benson and Viscount Esher, *The letters of Queen Victoria. A selection from her Majesty's correspondence between the years 1837-61* (London, 1908), vol. II, p. 392.

222.The sixth and seventh Marquesess were awarded the Garter in 1888 and 1919 respectively.

223.Disraeli to Charles, 29 Dec. 1850 (DRO, D/Lo/Acc: 451 (D)/3 (1)) and Heesom, "Legitimate' *versus* 'Illegitimate'", p. 283.

224.FA to Disraeli, 12 June 1852 (PRONI, D/3030/JJ/6B).

225.Ibid., 20 June 1852 and his reply of 26 June 1852 (PRONI, D/3030/JJ/8B and 9B).

226.Ibid., 2 July 1852 (PRONI, D/3030/JJ/11B).

227.Disraeli to FA, 30 Sept. 1852 and 21 June 1853 (PRONI, D/3030/JJ/13A and 18B).

228.Ibid., 13 Sept. 1853 (PRONI, D/3030/JJ/24B).

229.Disraeli to Charles, 31 Dec. 1853 (DRO, D/Lo/Acc: 451 (D)/4 (8)).

230.Disraeli to FA, 4 Aug. 1853 (PRONI, D/3030/JJ/20B).

231.Ibid., undated in Londonderry, *Letters*, p. 118.

232.Ibid., 11 Feb. 1854 (DRO, D/Lo/C530 (107)).

233.Ibid., in Londonderry, *Letters*, p. 259.

234.FA to Mary Anne Disraeli, 29 Mar. 1854 (DRO, D/Lo/C530 (110)).

235.Disraeli to FA, Apr. 1854 (DRO, D/Lo/C530 (111)).

236.FA to Disraeli, 6 Apr. 1854 (DRO, D/Lo/C530 (112)).

237.Charles to Castlereagh, 6 Dec. 1821 (PRONI, D/3030/P/194).

238.FA to Disraeli, 24 July [1854] (DRO, D/Lo/C530 (118)).

239.Disraeli to FA, 4 Mar. 1856 (DRO, D/Lo/C530 (162)).

240.Reynolds, *Aristocratic women*, cited p. 69. Other aristocratic women involved in mid nineteenth-century estate management and business included Georgiana, Duchess of Somerset who ran the family estate whilst her husband held political office.

241.*The Times*, 3 Mar. 1856. The speech reflected her philanthropic interests: visiting the poor; temperance and the education of workers' and tenants' children in Durham, Antrim and Down.

242.Geoffrey Best, *Mid-Victorian Britain, 1851-75* (London, 1971), p. 265 and unidentified newspaper cutting, 1857 (PRONI, D/2864/3/24/1).

243.Hugh Alexander Boyd's address to the Glens of Antrim Historical Society on Frances Anne Londonderry, 20 Oct. 1972 (PRONI, D/3084/C/F/6/286), cited pp 14-15.

244.Surtees, *Aristocrat in business*, p. 183 and p. 190. The revision of marriage settlements and aristocratic insolvency were not unusual. In the 1840s it was estimated that the Londonderrys owed £600,000. By comparison, the Duke of Devonshire and Earl Fitzwilliam owed £1 million and £800,000 respectively. See C. W. Chalklin and J. R. Wordie (eds), *Town and countryside. The English landowner in the national economy* (London, 1989), p. 94.

245.Disraeli to Mrs. Brydges Willyams, 8 Dec. 1861 in Buckle, *The life of Benjamin Disraeli*, vol. IV, cited p. 304.

246.Frederick, fourth Marquess of Londonderry to FA, 30 Nov. 1854 (PRONI, D/3084/C/A/5/13). The fifth Duke of Rutland also commended her commercial pursuits: 'when I think of the works the completion of which you have energetically accomplished (...to pay the costs and not to leave them to your stepson!) I am in amazement' (Rutland to FA, 3 Feb. 1856 (DRO, D/Lo/Acc: 451 (D)/18 (5)).

247.Disraeli to FA, 7 Aug. 1854 (DRO, D/Lo/C530 (120)). He and his wife again invited Frances Anne to Hughenden: 'Here you, at least, will find sympathy, and we can talk for ever of all that interests you' (Disraeli to FA, 28 Oct. 1854 (DRO, D/Lo/C530 (128)).

248.Ibid., 21 Oct. 1854 (DRO, D/Lo/Acc: 451 (D)/11 (9)).

249.FA to Disraeli in Londonderry, *Frances Anne*, cited p. 262.

250.Disraeli to FA, 22 Nov. 1854 (DRO, D/Lo/Acc: 451 (D)/11 (12)).

251.FA to Disraeli, 20 Dec. 1854 (DRO, D/Lo/C530 (135)).

252.Ibid., 1 Jan. 1855 (DRO, D/Lo/C530 (136)).

253.FA to Mary Anne Disraeli, 30 Jan. 1855 (PRONI, D/3084/C/A/5/4).

254.FA to Disraeli, 10 Oct. 1854 (DRO, D/Lo/C530 (125)).

255.Disraeli to FA, 1 Jan. and 2 Feb. 1855 (DRO, D/Lo/C530 (136 and 143)).

256.Ibid., 9 Aug. 1854 (DRO, D/Lo/C530 (121)).

257.FA to Disraeli, 9 Feb. 1855 (PRONI, D/2846/2/37).

258.Disraeli to FA, 29 Apr. and 31 July 1857 (DRO, D/Lo/Acc: 451 (D)/11 (29-30)).

259.Ibid., 9 Nov. 1861 (DRO, D/Lo/C530 (198)).

260.One of the few recorded instances of open patronage between Frances Anne and Disraeli also occurred during her widowhood. In Sept. 1858 she personally recommended a Mr. Coleman to him and he agreed 'if I see the opportunity of engaging… [him] in a public service it shall not be lost. There is no one whose opinion on men, and especially men of business, I esteem as highly as your own' (Disraeli to FA, 24 July 1858 (DRO, D/Lo/Acc: 451 (D)/11 (37)).

261.Londonderry, *Frances Anne*, cited p. 292.

262.In 1861, for example, Adolphus was charged with disorderly conduct at Marlborough Street Police Court 'evidently suffering from a disordered mind' having 'brought together a crowd of 500 persons' in Coventry Street (unidentified newspaper cutting of 1861 (PRONI, D/2846/3/24/1)).

263.FA to Disraeli, 11 Nov. 1861 (DRO, D/Lo/C530 (199)).

264.Ibid., 20 Dec. 1861 (DRO, D/Lo/C530 (206)). The telegraph from the clerk at Sunderland to Seaham expressed sheer disbelief that another fire could have occurred: 'Have you heard that Wynyard is on fire. Do you think it can refer to the name of a ship?' (telegram from Holmes to Arnold, 19 Dec. 1861 (PRONI, D/3084/C/A/6/1)).

265.Stanley Weintraub, *Disraeli. A biography* (London, 1993), pp 385-86.

266.Disraeli to FA, 14 Dec. 1861 (DRO, D/Lo/C530 (202)).

267.FA to Disraeli, 17 Dec. 1861 (DRO, D/Lo/C530 (204)).

268.W. Lindsay to FA, 18 Apr. undated (DRO, D/Lo/C182 (4)) and Lord Loughborough to the same, 24 Jan. 1864 (DRO, D/Lo/C 182 (23)). See also D/Lo/C182 (6) and (21) and D/Lo/C183 (1-2) and (4) and Reynolds, *Aristocratic women*, p. 141.

269.FA to Disraeli, 3, 12, 16 Aug. 1863 (DRO, D/Lo/C530 (212-14)).

270.Disraeli to FA, undated in Londonderry, *Letters*, p. 194.

271.FA to Disraeli, 11 Nov. 1853 (PRONI, D/3030/JJ/27B).

272.Ibid., 22 Oct. 1862 (DRO, D/Lo/C530 (209)).

273.Some have claimed that Disraeli's last letter to FA was written in 1861. FA to Mary Anne Disraeli, 4 July 1864 (PRONI, D/3084/C/A/5/11). This despondency also clouds Frances Anne's personal writings, as she noted, 'I am of those whose sense of being is in the past' (Observation and quotation book of FA, undated (DRO, D/Lo/F/1052)).

274.Earl Vane to Disraeli, 17 Oct. 1864 (DRO, D/Lo/C530 (218)).

275.Winston Churchill on his grandmother, Frances Anne, cited in Boyd's address to the Glens of Antrim Historical Society on FA, p. 16.

276.'Memoir', p. 1.

277.Benson and Esher, *Letters of Queen Victoria,* vol. II, p. 362.

278.Perkin, *Women and marriage*, cited p. 82.

279.Earl of Malmesbury, *Memoirs of an ex-Minister. An autobiography* (2nd edition, London,1884), vol. I, p. 284.

280.Disraeli to FA, 2 Sept. 1855 (DRO, D/Lo/C530 (53)).

281.Disraeli to Montagu Corry, 14 Sept. 1873 in Buckle, *The life of Benjamin Disraeli*, vol. V, p. 260.

282.Zetland, *Letters of Disraeli*, vol. I, pp 74-75.

283.Disraeli to Henry, fifth Marquess of Londonderry, 12 Dec. 1879 (PRONI, D/2846/3/1/1).

284.Zetland, *Letters of Disraeli*, vol. II, p. 175.

285.Perkin, *Women and marriage*, citing Lady Dorothy Nevill, p. 82 and *Ulster Tatler*, Sept. 1979.

286.*Belfast News-Letter*, 27 Jan. 1865.

287.For the 'Wynyard Post' see PRONI, D/3030/QQ/1.

288.Observation and quotation book of FA, undated (DRO, D/Lo/F/1052).

289.Frederick's mental illness was apparent from 1862. He spent the last eleven years of his life in White Rock Hospital in St. Leonards. Elizabeth was thirty-six when she married Frederick. She was devoted to her three offspring from her first marriage but was unable to bear any more children. She died in 1884.

290.Hyde, *Londonderrys*, p. xv.

Chapter 2

1. Edith Wheeler to T, 8 July 1916 (PRONI, D2846/1/8/39).

2. Arthur Balfour was Conservative leader from 1891. He was Prime Minister from 1902-05 but was overthrown as leader in 1912. Austen Chamberlain was a Liberal Unionist in political persuasion and replaced Bonar Law as Conservative leader in 1921.

3. T's resolution to the Ulster Women's Unionist Council [hereafter UWUC], 18 Jan. 1912 (DRO, D/Lo/F580 (22)).

4. Charley, later the seventh Marquess [hereafter Charley] to Lady Desborough, 12 Jan. c. 1915 (Hertfordshire Archives and Local Studies [hereafter HALS], DIERV C2482/5). Walter Long also frequently despaired of Theresa's handwriting, noting in a letter to her on 19 Nov. 1909, 'I find it awfully hard to read some of your sentences!' and on 4 Feb. 1910, 'I tried the magnifying glass but to no avail' (DRO, D/Lo/C666 (98) and (108)).

5. John Sandars, political secretary to Arthur Balfour and go-between between Balfour and senior members of the Conservative and Liberal sections of the Unionist Party. Sandars occasionally passed letters to Theresa as on 27 Nov. 1911 when he enclosed a letter from T. Gibson Bowles written to encourage Balfour to partake in a debate on foreign affairs (see PRONI, D/2846/2/28/12). The Hon. Sir William Gervase Beckett was MP for Whitby and N. Leeds. There was some press speculation that Theresa's diaries would be published in 1919.

6. The Londonderrys first met Hicks-Beach when he served as Irish Chief Secretary during the first part of their viceroyalty, 1886-89. Although Hicks-Beach 'seldom visited any but his nearest relatives', he was 'always glad' to visit Londonderry House 'to enjoy its congenial atmosphere and the stimulating sympathy of his hostess [Theresa], upon whose very true friendship he set a high value' (Lady Victoria Hicks-Beach, *Life of Sir Michael Hicks-Beach* (vol. II, London, 1932), p. 73).

7. T, 'The life of the Dowager Marchioness of Londonderry', 19 Apr. 1915 [hereafter 'Life'] (PRONI, D/3084/C/B/3/1). Her father was a Conservative MP for South Staffordshire and then Stamford before entering the House of Lords in 1868. Disraeli celebrated Alton Towers in his novel *Lothair* under the name of Muriel Towers at the suggestion of Theresa's younger sister, Muriel.

8. 'Life', 21 July 1915.

9. T to Guendolin and Muriel Chetwynd Talbot, 1873 (PRONI, D/3084/C/E/1). Guen-

dolin married Col. Chaplin and then Major Cosmo Little. Muriel married Viscount
Helmsley and then Hugh Owen. Her brother, Charlie became twentieth Earl of
Shrewsbury but his life, in Theresa's view, was unhappy.

10. Political notes of T, 10 Aug. 1915 (PRONI, D/3084/C/B/1/3) and 'Life', 17 Aug.
1918.

11. T to Guendolin and Muriel Chetwynd Talbot, 1873 (PRONI, D/3084/C/E/1).

12. In 1885 Charles, later sixth Marquess of Londonderry (1852-1915), was granted permission by royal license for he and his issue to resume the original family surname of
Vane-Tempest-Stewart. The former two surnames have since fallen out of use. The
marriage took place on 2 Oct. 1875 at Alton Towers with 1,000 guests in attendance.
In their early years of marriage they resided at Kirby Hall in Bedale, Yorkshire but
moved to Wynyard on Charles' succession to the Londonderry titles and estates in
1884.

13. T to her uncle, Reginald Talbot, undated (PRONI, D/2846/2/15/89).

14. Volume of newspaper cuttings relating to the 1878 Co. Down election (PRONI,
D/2846/3/8/1).

15. 'Life', 17 Aug. 1918.

16. Warwick, *Afterthoughts*, p. 105. Theresa and the Countess of Jersey have been identified
as women who exercised considerable authority over their husbands. See Martin Pugh,
The Tories and the people, 1800-1935 (Oxford, 1985), p. 47.

17. E. F. Benson, *As we were. A Victorian peep-show* (London, 1971 reprint of 1930 ed.), pp
177-78.

18. Sir Alfred Fripp to T, 14 Jan. 1917 (PRONI, D/2846/2/23/44) and Henry Stracey to
the same, undated (PRONI, D/2846/2/8/39).

19. Benson, *As we were*, pp 177-78.

20. Sir Edmund Gosse was a writer and famed conversationalist. He became acquainted
with Theresa after revising an essay for her in 1899 and remained a close friend until
the end of her life. He had visited Mount Stewart eleven times by 1912 and it
'remained his favourite of all the great country houses' (Ann Thwaite, *Edmund Gosse: a
literary landscape, 1849-1928* (London, 1984), p. 406).

21. Fingall, *Seventy years*, p. 163. Wyndham was MP for Dover and Irish Chief Secretary
from 1900-05.

22. John Vincent (ed.), *The Crawford papers. The journals of David Lindsay twenty-seventh Earl of
Crawford and tenth Earl of Balcarres, 1871-1940 during the years 1892 to 1940* (Manchester,
1984), cited p. 330. Special galleries were provided for women at Westminster after the
fire of 1834.

23. Margot Asquith, *Autobiography of Margot Asquith* (London, 1920), p. 191 and T to Charley, 22 Dec. 1916 (PRONI, D/2846/1/13/1).

24. Diary of Lady Ruby Carson, 23 May 1916, 8 Feb. and 1 Mar. 1917 (PRONI,
D/1507C/2-3).

25. Warwick, *Afterthoughts*, p. 105.

26. Fingall, *Seventy years*, p. 163. Similar comments have been made of other hostesses such
as Mrs. Arbuthnot and the Duchess of Rutland. See Jupp, 'The roles of royal and aristocratic women', p. 105.

27. *The Times*, 17 Mar. 1919.

28. Sir Almeric Fitzroy, *Memoirs* (London, 1938), vol. I, pp 356-57.

29. Birdie married Lord Staverdale, later the sixth Earl of Ilchester in 1902; Charley married Edith, the subject of chapter 3 and Reginald, who was widely acknowledged to
have been fathered by Theresa's brother-in-law, Lord William Reginald Hemsley, suffered from hip problems and tuberculosis. He died, aged twenty, in 1899. There is no
evidence that Reginald's paternity caused long-term family estrangement. Theresa

continued to see her sister, Muriel and Charles was affectionate towards Reginald. Although Theresa requested to be alone with Reginald at the time of his death, Charles recorded in a 1899 letter to his mother-in-law, the Countess of Shrewsbury, that he then 'went with her [Theresa] to her rooms…Poor little chap' (PRONI, D/2846/3/21/17). On the sexual mores of aristocratic society, see Perkin, *Women and marriage* who notes, 'Aristocratic wives were as likely as their husbands to have extra-marital affairs', p. 90. This was especially true once an heir had been produced and if a public scandal could be averted.

30. Charley, 'In the days of my youth' in *TPs and Cassell's Weekly*, 21 Mar. 1925.
31. Thomas Hardy to T, 2 Dec. 1895 (PRONI, D/2846/2/26/72).
32. Life', 17 Aug. 1918.
33. Pugh, *Tories*, p. 45.
34. Lady Eglinton was the only daughter of the sixth Earl of Essex and wife of Archibald Montgomerie, the thirteenth Earl of Eglinton. I am grateful to Dr. Martin McElroy for providing me with information on Earl Talbot.
35. Mrs. George Cornwallis-West, *The reminiscences of Lady Randolph Churchill* (London, 1908), p. 85.
36. Charles Cameron, *Anecdotes and memories of a Freeman of Dublin* (Dublin, 1913), p. 3. Cameron suggests that the Londonderrys refused a second term in this post as they did not want a repetition of the large expenditure required. Hicks-Beach championed Charles' cause after he refused the post of Privy Seal and let Theresa help him choose a name when he was created earl in 1917. He subsequently became, at her suggestion, Lord St. Aldwyn.
37. Thomas Wodehouse Legh (Lord Newton), *Lord Lansdowne. A biography* (London, 1929), p. 18.
38. Andrew Adonis, *Making aristocracy work. The peerage and the political system in Britain, 1884-1914* (Oxford, 1993), p. 233.
39. Salisbury to Charles, 27 June 1895 (PRONI, D/2846/3/10/6). 1900 also saw Charles appointed Lord Lieutenant of Bedford and from 1902 of Co. Down.
40. Earl Grey to T, 8 Nov. 1902 (PRONI, D/2846/2/20/23).
41. Masters, *Wynyard*, cited p. 56.
42. Fitzroy, *Memoirs*, vol. I, pp 169-70. Theresa had a lifelong interest in education. She was a member of Durham Education Committee and was appointed to the Senate of Queen's University of Belfast in 1909, one of only three women on this body at the time. She also promoted Irish industries and was president of the London Committee of the Royal Irish Industries Association. Throughout her life she supported various philanthropic causes such as the Red Cross and discharged prisoners. During the First World War she became involved in the Women of the Land Committee and Voluntary Aid Detachments as well as the military convalescent homes established in Mount Stewart, Londonderry House and Seaham Hall. She was active in the Primrose League, the anti-suffrage society, the Girls' Friendly Society and the Victoria League as well as being a keen sailor and, along with her son, Reginald, a gifted photographer.
43. Sir Robert Morant to T, 20 Sept. 1904 (PRONI, D/2846/2/32/54).
44. *Church of Ireland Gazette*, 10 Dec. 1904.
45. Fitzroy, *Memoirs*, vol. I, p. 161 and p. 273.
46. Arthur Bigge to T, 4 Feb. 1911 (PRONI, D/2846/2/18/37).
47. Pugh, *Tories*, p. 44. See also Reynolds, *Aristocratic women*; Lewis, *Sacred to female patriotism*; Jalland, *Women, marriage and politics*; Shkolnik, *Leading ladies* and Julia Bush, *Edwardian ladies and imperial power* (London and New York, 2000).
48. Shkolnik, *Leading ladies*, p. 153.
49. See, for example, Leslie, *Edwardians*; Perkin, *Women and marriage*; Robert Rhodes James

(ed.), *Chips. The diaries of Sir Edward Channon* (London, 1967). In Channon's version, Theresa's dalliance was with not with Cust but with the father of her youngest son, Lord Helmsley. By comparison, de Courcy in *Circe* more accurately claims that Charles and Theresa were reconciled by 1899.

50. Harry Cust to T, undated (PRONI, D/2846/2/25/52).

51. Charles to T, undated and 15 Jan. 1908 (PRONI, D/2846/2/2/27, 32, 39 and 119).

52. Letter from T to the UWUC, 2 Jan. 1911 (DRO, D/Lo/F/580 (15)).

53. Christopher Sykes, *Nancy: the life of Nancy Astor* (London, 1972), p. 117.

54. Cited in PRONI, D/2846/2/19/49. Politician and writer, Lord Morley was a Liberal and pro-home ruler and, as a consequence, would not remain on Londonderry invite lists in the early twentieth century.

55. Cornwallis-West, *Reminiscences*, p. 86 and Warwick, *Afterthoughts*, pp 45-46.

56. Fitzroy, *Memoirs*, vol. I, p. 140.

57. Fingall, *Seventy years*, p. 121.

58. Rosebury to T, 2 July 1894 (PRONI, D/2846/2/19/67).

59. George Wyndham to T, 14 Feb. 1896, 26 Dec. 1911 and 29 Apr. 1905 (PRONI, D/2846/2/19/114, 122 and 116).

60. Lord Esher to T, 20 Dec. 1906 (PRONI, D/2846/2/25/78) and Gosse to T, 12 May 1909 (PRONI, D/2846/2/26/36). From 1895 Esher was permanent secretary at the Office of Works which included the maintenance and decoration of royal palaces in its remit. Of the monarchs he served, Esher was particularly close to Edward VII.

61. Robert C. Self (ed.), *The Austen Chamberlain diary letters* (Cambridge, 1995), p. 156.

62. Sir George Murray to T, 7 Jan. 1915 (PRONI, D/2846/2/10/65). Murray was Secretary of the Post Office from 1899; joint permanent secretary of the Treasury from 1903 and sole secretary from 1907. From 1909 he also audited the civil list. He retired in 1911.

63. Diary extract of T, 20 Dec. 1915 (PRONI, D/3084/C/B/1/10) and Reginald Lucas to T, 5 Apr. 1910 and 7 Nov. 1913 (PRONI, D/2846/2/14/3 and 20).

64. Hon. Schomberg McDonnell to T, 3 Aug. 1910 (PRONI, D/2846/2/28/33A). McDonnell was the fifth son of the Earl of Antrim, private secretary to the third Marquess of Salisbury and secretary to the Office of Works, 1902-12.

65. For example, in a letter from Charley to T dated 25 Oct. 1906 he noted his doubts on the existence of 'real sympathy between father and a son' (DRO, D/Lo/C682 (53)).

66. Charley to T, 28 Dec. 1905 and 25 Oct. 1906 (PRONI, D/3084/C/E/3). Carson addressed the Maidstone electors twice during Charley's 1906 election campaign. In the 1910 Maidstone election Theresa and Lady Boyne toured polling stations in a car bedecked with party colours.

67. Harcourt to T, 21 Feb. 1906 (PRONI, D/2846/2/19/43). This was the ninth such petition to be brought in Maidstone since 1900. Although Charley was returned, the 1906 election was a disaster for Conservatives and Unionists. They won just 157 seats whilst Liberals, Labour and Irish Nationalists won a total of 513 seats.

68. Midleton to T, 19 Sept. 1907 (PRONI, D/2846/2/28/50). St. John Broderick, first Earl of Midleton was a Conservative MP from 1880; Secretary of State for War from 1900-03 and Secretary of State for India from 1903-05. Lansdowne remained Unionist leader of the Lords until Dec. 1916.

69. Political notes of T, 20 Dec. 1915 (PRONI, D/3084/C/B/1/10). F. E. Smith, Conservative MP, barrister, Solicitor-General from 1915 and Attorney-General and Lord Chancellor from 1919-22.

70. Smith to T, 20 Oct. 1909 (PRONI, D/2846/2/20/70).

71. John Campbell acknowledges the significance of Theresa's patronage in *F. E. Smith. first Earl of Birkenhead* (London, 1983), p. 163.

72. See John Kendle, *Walter Long, Ireland, and the Union, 1905-20* (Montreal and London, 1992).

73. Walter Long to T, 29 Oct. and 18 Dec. 1907 (DRO, D/Lo/C666 (20) and (29)).

74. Ibid., 24 Nov. 1907 (DRO,D/Lo/C666 (23)).

75. Ibid., 1 Feb. 1910 (DRO, D/Lo/C666 (107)).

76. T to Charley, 19 Mar. 1916 (PRONI, D/2846/1/13/1).

77. Edward Carson to T, 23 Dec. 1913, 30 May and 15 Aug. 1918 (PRONI, D/2846/1/1/112 and 151-2). Again on 23 Dec. 1913 Carson proclaimed to Theresa, 'What a dear friend you have been to me I never for a moment forget' (PRONI, D/2846/1/1/112).

78. Fingall, *Seventy years*, pp 206-07. Carson was appointed Solicitor General for Ireland in 1892 and for England in 1900. Fingall does not specify which appointment the Londonderrys were meant to have influenced but the Irish post seems most likely.

79. Carson's first wife, Annette died in 1913. He married Ruby Frewen in 1914. Notes of conversation between Mrs. St. George Robinson with H. Montgomery Hyde, 22 July 1950 (PRONI, D/3084/H/3/9).

80. Carson to T, undated [c. 1913] (PRONI, D/2846/1/1/157).

81. Ibid., undated [c. 1909] and 22 Sept. 1907 (PRONI, D/2846/1/1/40 and 6). See also, for example, Carson to T, 8 Sept. 1908 where he noted, 'as you know I never go anywhere but to Wynyard or Mount Stewart' (PRONI, D/2846/1/1/16).

82. Ibid., undated [c. 1908] (PRONI, D/2846/1/1/25). See also his letter of 1 Nov. 1909 where he noted, 'I have been more than usual dining about and going to the play and trying to imagine that such trivialities are satisfying!' (PRONI, D/2846/1/1/37).

83. Ibid., c. 27-28 Oct. 1910 (PRONI, D/2846/1/1/55).

84. Ibid., Sept. 1908 and 12 Mar. 1912 (PRONI, D/2846/1/1/18 and 85).

85. Ibid., undated [c. 1908] (PRONI, D/2846/1/1/25).

86. Ibid., 16 Sept. 1913 (PRONI, D/2846/1/1/104).

87. Ibid., 16 Sept. 1911 (PRONI, D/2846/1/1/69).

88. Political notes of T, 15 Oct. 1916 (PRONI, D/3084/C/B/2/76).

89. Ian Colvin, *The life of Lord Carson*, vol. III (London, 1936), p. 443. Carson often complained of rheumatism and neuralgia.

90. Carson to T, undated [1914] (PRONI, D/2846/1/1/123).

91. T to Bonar Law, 17 Sept. [1913] (Parliamentary Archives, House of Lords [hereafter HL]/BL/12/4/5).

92. Carson to T, 23 Dec. 1907, 6 June 1909 and c. early Mar. 1912 (PRONI, D/2846/1/1/9, 38 and 82).

93. Ibid., 24 Jan. 1910 (PRONI, D/2846/1/1/44).

94. Long to T, 25 Aug. 1910 (DRO, D/Lo/C666 (124)) and 12 June 1911 (DRO, D/Lo/C666 (145)).

95. Carson to T, 23 Dec. 1910 (PRONI, D/2846/1/1/59). See Ronan Fanning, 'Rats versus ditchers: the die-hard revolt and the parliament bill of 1911' in A. Cosgrove and J. I. McGuire (eds), *Parliament and community: historical studies, 14* (Belfast, 1983), pp 191-210; David Brooks, *The age of upheaval. Edwardian politics, 1899-1914* (Manchester, 1995) and P. Kelvin and C. C. Weston, 'The 'Judas group' and the parliament bill of 1911' in C. and D. Jones (eds), *Peers, politics and power: the House of Lords, 1603-1911* (London, 1986), pp 527-39.

96. Carson to T, 29 Oct. 1908 (PRONI, D/2846/1/1/20). The bill was defeated in the Lords.

97. Sandars to T, 9 Dec. 1908 (DRO, D/Lo/C671(21)).

98. Lord Burham to T, 20 Feb. 1909 (PRONI, D/2846/2/7/7). Burham visited Wynyard and Mount Stewart in 1912 and 1913 respectively and provided Theresa with further

information. For example, at her request he told her which Unionist was passing information to the press in 1913.

99. Address by T, 6 May 1909 (DRO, D/Lo/F1126 (9)).

100.Typed notes by T, undated [c. 1909] (DRO, D/Lo/F1126 (49)).

101.James Thursfield to T, 23 Sept. 1909 (PRONI, D/2846/2/23/83). Thursfield was a leader writer in *The Times* and a self-professed radical who enjoyed a political joust with Theresa whom he regarded as a close friend. He was entertained at Wynyard in 1909 and continued to correspond with Theresa thereafter.

102.*Daily Chronicle*, 11 Dec. 1909.

103.Lord Newton to T, 6 Oct. 1909 (PRONI, D/2846/2/25/96). Newton visited Wynyard again in 1912.

104.Midleton to T, 28 Jan. 1910 (PRONI, D/2846/2/28/51).

105.Sandars to T, 18 Oct. 1910 (DRO, D/Lo/C671 (51)).

106.J. St. Loe Strachey to T, 26 Jan. 1910 (PRONI, D/2846/2/26/104).

107.Knollys to T, 7 Feb., 11 Nov. and 28 Dec. 1910 (PRONI, D/2846/2/18/21-2 and 24).

108.Buckle to T, 8 Feb. 1910 (PRONI, D/2846/2/26/11).

109.As Adonis remarks in *Making aristocracy work*, the Lords was 'a party assembly: almost all peers took a party whip, party constituted its organizing principle', p. 48.

110.*The Times*, 9 Feb. 1910.

111.C. Moberly Bell to T, 2 Feb. 1910 (PRONI, D/2846/2/26/6).

112.Thursfield to T, 8 Apr. 1910 (PRONI, D/2846/2/23/88).

113.Lord Newton to T, 13 Apr. 1910 (PRONI, D/2846/2/25/99).

114.Carson to T, June 1911 (PRONI, D/2846/1/1/64).

115.Bigge to T, 8 Apr. 1910 and 30 Sept. 1911 (PRONI, D/2846/2/18/30 and 44).

116.Ibid., 25 July 1911 (PRONI, D/2846/2/18/40). Bigge visited Theresa at Wynyard in 1911.

117.Warwick, *Afterthoughts*, p. 104.

118.Sir George Murray to T, undated (PRONI, D/2846/2/10/36).

119.Carson to T, 11 Aug. 1911 (PRONI, D/2846/1/1/67). Balcarres, Austen Chamberlain and James Craig also sided with the die-hard group.

120.Sir George Armstrong to T, 13 Jan. 1911 (PRONI, D/2846/2/28/1).

121.J. S. Sandars to T, 19 Nov. 1907 and 10 Feb. 1909 and Harriet Sandars to the same, c. 1905 (DRO, D/Lo/C671 (i), (5) and (26)). Sandars corresponded with Theresa until her death in 1919.

122.Sandars' request for Charley was, however, rebuffed as it was believed that this duty should fall to front bench members.

123.J. S. Sandars to T, 4 Nov. 1908 and 26 Dec. 1916 (DRO, D/Lo/C671 (15) and (113)).

124.Sandars to T, 22 Sept. 1909 (DRO, D/Lo/C671 (37)).

125.Long to T, 3, 5 and 29 Oct. 1911 (DRO, D/Lo/C666 (165-7)).

126.*Sunday Herald*, 13 Feb. 1927.

127.Long to T, 11 and 12 Nov. 1911 (DRO, D/Lo/C666 (172-3)).

128.Untitled typescript by T, undated (PRONI, D/2846/2/20/16).

129.Vincent, *Crawford papers*, cited p. 273. On the difficulties facing Law on his accession to the Conservative Party leadership see Jeremy Smith, *The Tories and Ireland, 1910-14. Conservative party politics and the home rule crisis* (Dublin, 2000), pp 38-51.

130.Bonar Law to T, 9 Jan. 1906 (PRONI, D/2846/2/20/9).

131.Carson to T, 15 Oct. 1911 and 12 Mar. 1912 (PRONI, D/2846/1/1/74 and 85).

132.Lord Redesdale to T, 20 Dec. 1911 (PRONI, D/2846/2/22/72) and Vincent, *Crawford papers*, Sandars cited p. 247.

133.Long to T, 19 Nov. 1911 and 10 Oct. 1912 (DRO, D/Lo/C666 (175 and 218)).

134.For instance, Law asked Theresa to entertain Canadian premier, Sir Robert Laird Borden at Londonderry House in 1912 (see Bonar Law to T, 1 June 1912 and T's reply, 4 June 1912 (Parliamentary Archives, HL/BL/33/4/41 and HL/BL/26/4/8)).

135.T to Bonar Law, 19 Apr. [1912] (Parliamentary Archives, HL/BL/12/4/5 and Bonar Law to T, 15 Sept. 1913 (PRONI, D/2846/2/20/49)). Theresa also asked Law to keep her informed 'of any steps' as she left England to spend new year at Mount Stewart in 1913 (T to Bonar Law, 29 Dec. [1913] (Parliamentary Archives, HL/BL/12/4/5)).

136.T to Bonar Law, 11 Dec. 1913 (Parliamentary Archives, HL/BL/12/4/5).

137.Ibid., 6 and 25 Nov. [1913].

138.Patrick Buckland, *Irish unionism: Two. Ulster unionism and the origins of Northern Ireland, 1886-1922* (Dublin, 1973), p. 51.

139.Reginald Lucas to T, 7 Nov. 1913 (PRONI, D/2846/2/14/20).

140.*Glasgow Herald* making reference to T, 6 Feb. 1923.

141.Carson to T, 30 June 1911 (PRONI, D/2846/1/1/66).

142.T's typescript, 'Electioneering 1911 and 1912 Maidstone', undated (DRO, D/Lo/F580 (17)).

143.Charley to T, 12 Apr. 1912 (PRONI, D/2846/1/12/4).

144.Domonic Lieven, *The aristocracy in Europe, 1815-1914* (London, 1992), p. 5.

145.Cornwallis-West, *Reminiscences*, p. 99. See also Pugh, *Tories*, p. 215 and J. H. Robb, *The Primrose League, 1883-1906* (New York, 1968).

146.Pugh, *Tories*, p. 58 and p. 127. The league declined in popularity in the 1920s but Conservative associations formed separate female sections after women's partial enfranchisement in 1918 (Vickery, *Women, privilege, and power*, p. 46). See also R. F. Foster, "Tory democracy and political elitism': provincial conservatism and parliamentary Tories in the early 1880s' in Cosgrove and McGuire, *Parliament and Community*, pp 159-60. Other Anglo-Irish women involved in the league included the Marchioness and Dowager Marchioness of Waterford and the Countess of Bandon. Fanny, Duchess of Marlborough, a daughter of Frances Anne, third Marchioness of Londonderry, was president of the Ladies' Guild Council of the Primrose League and her daughter-in-law, Jennie Churchill, wife of Randolph, was Dame President of several habitations.

147.T to Sir Henry Ponsonby, 5 Apr. 1893 (PRONI, D/2846/3/20/19).

148.For a history of the UWUC see Diane Urquhart, *Women in Ulster politics, 1890-1940: a history not yet told* (Dublin, 2000) and "The female of the species is more deadlier than the male'? The Ulster Women's Unionist Council, 1911-40' in Janice Holmes and Diane Urquhart (eds), *Coming into the light. The work, politics and religion of women in Ulster, 1840-1940* (Belfast, 1994). For an official history of the UWUC see Nancy Kinghan, *United we stood. The story of the Ulster Women's Unionist Council, 1911-75* (Belfast, 1975). The records of the council are reproduced in Diane Urquhart (ed.), *The Minutes of the Ulster Women's Unionist Council and Executive Committee, 1911-40* (Dublin, 2001).

149.R. H. Reade's address to the inaugural meeting of Dunmurray and District Branch of Lisburn Women's Unionist Association, cited in the minute book of the same, 31 Jan. 1912 (PRONI, D/1460/11). Edith Mercier Clements is credited in UWUC records as having the initiated the establishment of a formal association of female Unionists. For Theresa's address see the *Belfast News-Letter*, 24 Jan. 1911.

150.T to unknown recipient, 23 Feb. 1911 (DRO, D/Lo/C686 (26)).

151.For example, in 1913 the Primrose League's 'Help the Ulster Women Committee' organised evacuation schemes for women and children in the event of civil war, securing promises of accommodation for 8,000 and raising some £17,000 in funds. This type of work particularly appealed to the league whereas only 300 habitations signed a Primrose memorial to Carson in the following year (Pugh, *Tories*, p. 165). For Theresa the latter provided another example of English political apathy.

152.*Glasgow Herald*, 20 Nov. 1913.

153.James Craig to Charles, 12 Sept. 1912 (DRO, D/Lo/C686 (164)). Craig was a Unionist MP from 1903 and the first Prime Minister of Northern Ireland, 1921-40.

154.Address by T, 17 Sept. 1912 (DRO, D/Lo/C686 (170)).

155.Duke of Portland to T, 8 Feb. 1912 (PRONI, D/2846/2/29/63) and Ronald MacNeill to the same, 29 Mar. 1913 (PRONI, D/2846/2/14/24). MacNeill visited Theresa at Mount Stewart and Wynyard in the same year and was described by Lady Fingall as 'a political follower of Lady Londonderry's' (Fingall, *Seventy years*, p. 209).

156.*Northern Whig*, 15 July 1914 and *Belfast News-Letter*, 24 Jan. 1911.

157.Speech delivered by T at a Stockton anti-home rule meeting, 17 Nov. 1913 (DRO, D/Lo/F580 (1)).

158.James Craig to T, 30 Aug. 1911 (DRO, D/Lo/C686 (54)).

159.S. A. Finlay, UWUC honorary secretary, to T, 19 Nov. 1911 (DRO, D/Lo/C686 (75)) and Ronald MacNeill to the same, 17 July 1918 (PRONI, D/2846/1/8/71).

160.H. G. Gwynne to T, 20 Nov. 1918 (PRONI, D/2846/2/26/67).

161.S. A. Finlay to T, 3 Jan. 1911 (DRO, D/Lo/C686 (1)).

162.Sandars to T, 10 Feb. and 17 Apr. 1912 (PRONI, D/2846/1/6/16-17).

163.Anonymous postcard to T, 9 Feb. 1912 (PRONI, D/2846/1/2/4).

164.The Londonderry House agreement is reproduced in Patrick Buckland, *Irish unionism 1885-1923. A documentary history* (Belfast, 1973), pp 318-21.

165.Carson to T, 20 Jan. and 27 Mar. 1912 (PRONI, D/2846/1/1/70 and 86).

166.Ibid., undated [c. early Mar. 1912] and 16 Aug. 1912 (PRONI, D/2846/1/1/82-3 and 89).

167.Bigge to T, 4 Oct. 1912 (PRONI, D/2846/2/18/49).

168.Marchioness of Dufferin and Ava to T, 10 Aug. 1912 (DRO, D/Lo/C686C (151)) and 21 Sept. 1912 (DRO, D/Lo/C686C (175)).

169.Charley and Birdie Londonderry to T, 12 Apr. and 11 Nov. 1912 (PRONI, D/2846/1/12/4 and 10).

170.Edward Saunderson to T, 1 and 7 Feb. 1912 (PRONI, D/2846/1/7/46-47).

171.Fingall, *Seventy years*, p. 163 and Horace Plunkett to T, 14 Oct. 1914 (PRONI, D/2846/2/7/78). Plunkett chaired the Irish Convention of 1917 which counted Theresa's son, Charley, amongst its members.

172.'Life', 17 Aug. 1918.

173.Asquith, *Autobiography*, p. 139. See also Max Egremont 'Lady Desborough. The Souls of London' in Peter Quennell (ed.), *Genius in the drawing room. The literary salon in the nineteenth and twentieth centuries* (London, 1980), pp 117-28. Lady St. Helier also highlighted the divisive nature of home rule, noting 'Nothing divided society like the Home Rule question' (Lady St. Helier, *Memories of fifty years* (London, 1909), p. 210).

174.Diary extract of T, 1 Dec. 1917 (PRONI, D/3084/C/B/1/103).

175.Warwick, *Afterthoughts*, p. 104.

176.Diary of Lady Cecil Craig, 17 Jan. 1913 (PRONI, D/1415/B/38). Pirrie was head of Harland and Wolff shipyard in Belfast. In 1911 Theresa persuaded Bigge to complain about Pirrie's appointment as Lord Lieutenant of Belfast. Pirrie returned to the Unionist fold in 1921.

177.T. Gibson Bowles to T, 11 Nov. 1913 (PRONI, D/2846/2/28/14).

178.Harry Lawson to T, 30 Jan. 1914 (PRONI, D/2846/1/6/8) and Reginald Lucas to the same, 17 Apr. 1914 (PRONI, D/2846/2/14/22). Ian Malcolm, MP for Suffolk; Harry Lawson, MP for Tower Hamlets; Samuel Robert, MP for Sheffield and John Crozier, Archbishop of Armagh, were amongst the many politicians and clerics who visited Mount Stewart during the third home rule crisis.

179.Missionary was a contemporary term used for those who spent between three and nine months in mainland Britain during the third home rule crisis to espouse the Unionist message. For example, in 1912 forty UWUC 'missionaries' visited over sixty-six Scottish and English constituencies. During 1913 the number of women working in this capacity increased to ninety-three. See UWUC annual reports for 1912 and 1913 (PRONI, D/2688/1/9).

180.Minute book of UWUC Executive Committee, 30 Jan. 1911 (PRONI, D/1098/1/1).

181.Letter from T read at meeting of UWUC Executive Committee, Belfast, 6 Feb. 1911 (DRO, D/Lo/C686C (115)). The chair of the UWUC had resigned.

182.Statement by T to the UWUC Executive Committee, 19 Mar. 1912 (PRONI, D/2846/1/8/10).

183.Minute book of UWUC, 1 Apr. 1913 (PRONI, D/1098/1/3).

184.*Darlington and Stockton Times*, 22 Nov. 1913.

185.This formed part of 'the first "modern" mobilization of Ulster Unionism. It was also the first truly popular mobilization of Unionism' (T. A. Jackson, 'Unionist myths, 1912-85' in *Past and Present*, no. 136 (Aug. 1992), p. 184).

186.Diary of Lady Cecil Craig, 14 Jan. 1910 and 25 June 1914 (PRONI, D/1415/B/38).

187.Mrs. Sinclair to T, undated [c. 1911] (DRO, D/Lo/C686 (33i)).

188.Handwritten notes by T, undated (DRO, D/Lo/F 1126 (36)).

189.Sir George Murray to T, 9 Jan. 1906 (PRONI, D/2846/2/10/5).

190.T's resolution to the UWUC, 18 Jan. 1912 (DRO, D/Lo/F580 (22)).

191.Diary extract of T, 5 Dec. 1918 (PRONI, D/3084/C/B/1/14).

192.T to John Hamill, UWUC secretary, 13 Sept. 1913 (DRO, D/Lo/C686C (239)).

193.T to E, 30 Sept. 1913 (DRO, D/Lo/C686 (248)).

194.T typescript, 'Women of Ulster', 1913 (DRO, D/Lo/C686 (211)).

195.It is possible that Edward Saunderson, eldest son of the former Unionist leader, was Theresa's informer. From 1912, he was certainly feeding her information as, for example, on 10 Dec. 1912 when he wrote, 'I wish you would stir up the Ulster people as I have heard on authority which I have always found absolutely reliable that the government are changing their view as to Ulster's opposition being really serious. No one can stir them up as well as you and I am sure if you will move in the matter a really efficient organisation in Ulster will be [the] outcome' (DRO, D/Lo/C672 (4)).

196.T typescript, 'The Ulster crisis and the plot that failed', undated (PRONI, D/2846/1/2/18).

197.Ibid.

198.Bigge to T, 2 Oct. 1913, 14 and 22 Jan. 1914 (PRONI, D/2846/2/5/3 and 6-7).

199.T to unknown recipient, undated (DRO, D/Lo/C686 (219)).

200.UWUC memorandum, 9 June 1914 (PRONI, D/1507/A/6/6).

201.Fleming, *The Marquess of Londonderry*, p. 30.

202.Political notes of T, 3 Aug. 1918 (PRONI, D/3084/C/B/2/145).

203.T to Carson, 10 June 1914 (PRONI, D/1507/A/6/5).

204.UWUC Advisory Committee minutes, 12 and 14 May 1914 (PRONI, D/2688/1/6) and Executive Committee minutes, 21 Apr. 1914 (PRONI, D/1098/1/2).

205.*The Standard*'s coverage of T's speech delivered at Mrs. D. Reid's Unionist drawing room meeting in London, 24 Feb. 1914.

206.Carson to T, 24 June 1914 (PRONI, D/2846/1/1/116).

207.*Northern Whig*, 15 July 1914.

208.Political notes of T, 22 Feb. 1919 (PRONI, D/3084/C/B/2/163).

209.*North Mail*, 26 Mar. 1914.

210.T to Gosse, 29 Apr. 1915 (Brotherton Collection, Leeds University Library).

211.Minute book of UWUC, 18 Aug. 1914 (PRONI, D/1098/1/3).

212.Bigge to T, 20 Oct.1914 (PRONI, D/2846/2/18/63).

213.Admiral Sir F. Bridgeman to T, undated and 12 and 30 Dec. 1916 (PRONI, D/2846/2/8/1-5).

214.Admiral David Beatty to T, 11 and 22 Dec. 1916 (PRONI, D/2846/2/25/11-12). Others asked Theresa for assistance in securing honours such as OBEs and sought her advice on the suitability for men for colonial postings.

215.T to Thursfield, 14 Dec. 1914 (PRONI, D/2846/2/23/97B).

216.Sir John Cowans to T, 5 Oct. 1915 (PRONI, D/2846/2/24/11).

217.Lady Talbot to T, 27 June 1915 (PRONI, D/2846/2/21/111).

218.Diary extract of T, 20 May 1915 (PRONI, D/3084/C/B/1/2).

219.Notes of T, 26 May 1915 (PRONI, D/3084/C/B/2/19). Theresa claimed to have disliked Winston Churchill since he was fourteen. He defected to the Liberals in 1904 and in 1906 Theresa contributed to the Tory indignation at his Common's speech against Milner, writing in protest to the king who replied, 'I quite share you views concerning certain proceedings in the House of Commons, and the conduct of a certain relation of yours is simply scandalous...Alas! nowadays Party comes before country.' The king then wrote to Churchill's colleague, Crewe (Randolph S. Churchill. *Winston S. Churchill*, vol. II (London, 1966), p. 185)). Theresa remained scathingly critical of Churchill: 'I am always delighted to think that I was one of those who prevented him from speaking in the Ulster Hall, and eating up his father's words "Ulster will fight and Ulster will be right." When I love at all, I love passionately, but I like most people and it is very few I hate. He is one of the few and the reasons I can give are very inadequate. I think he does not love his country at all but only cares for his own skin' (Diary extract of T, 23 Dec. 1918 (PRONI, D/3084/C/B/1/15)). Churchill returned to the Conservative Party in 1924.

220.Account by T, 25 May 1915 (PRONI, D/3084/C/B/112).

221.Charley to Lady Desborough, 5 Feb. 1915 (HALS, DIERV C2482/7).

222.Bigge to T, 25 June 1915 (PRONI, D/2846/2/18/69).

223.Bonar Law to T, 6 Aug. 1915 (PRONI, D/2846/2/20/56).

224.T to Robin, 3 Nov. 1915 (PRONI, D/2846/1/13/1) and political notes of T, 2 Nov. 1915 (PRONI, D/3084/C/B/2/44).

225.Political notes of T, 26 Aug. 1914 and 12 Jan. 1915 (PRONI, D/3084/C/B/2/7 and 12).

226.Notes on T by H. Montgomery Hyde, undated (PRONI, D/3084/C/B/2/15).

227.*Saturday Review*, 15 Feb. 1915.

228.*Northern Whig*, 9 Feb. 1919 and *Punch*, 17 Feb. 1915.

229.*Liverpool Daily Post and Mercury*, 6 Mar. 1915.

230.Lady Julia Wombwell to T, 25 Dec. 1915 (PRONI, D/2846/2/31/109).

231.E to T, 16 Feb. 1915 (PRONI, D/3084/C/E/2/13).

232.T to E, 29 Apr. 1915 (PRONI, D/3099/3/11/2).

233.E to T, 4 Aug. [1915] (PRONI, D/3099/3/11/6).

234.Charley to E, 7 Mar. 1915 and 21 Mar. 1917 cited in Jennifer Anne Pauley, 'The social and political roles of Edith, Lady Londonderry, 1878-1959' (unpub. D.Phil. thesis, University of Ulster, 1994), p. 409.

235.Bonar Law to T, 1 May 1915 (PRONI, D/2846/2/20/55).

236.Long to T, 14 Feb. 1915 (DRO, D/Lo/C666 (262)).

237.T to Gosse, 27 Apr. 1915 (Brotherton Collection, Leeds University Library) and Gosse to T, 3 Sept. 1916 (PRONI, D/2846/2/26/46).

238.Warwick, *Afterthoughts*, p. 105.

239.T to Charley, 20 May 1915 (PRONI, D/2846/1/13/1).

240.Long to T, 12 Apr., 14 July and 12 Sept. 1915 (DRO, D/Lo/C666 (265, 273 and

275)). Irish Unionist, George Holmes of Booterstown, Co. Dublin concurred in a letter to T, 7 Apr. 1915, 'You were so completely the moving spirit, the centre of force in your surroundings that it is impossible for me to imagin[e]…them without you, or you without them…I find myself quite dazed as to what you will do in the future' (DRO, D/Lo/C657 (4)).

241.T to Bonar Law, 1915 (PRONI, D/3084/C/B/2/33).

242.Midleton to T, 10 Nov. 1915 (PRONI, D/2846/2/28/53).

243.In 1916 Law was initially optimistic about securing the post of Lord Lieutenant of Dorset for Ilchester but found that Lansdowne had already spoken to Asquith and Shaftsbury was subsequently appointed.

244.Political notes of T, 28 Aug. 1916 (PRONI, D/3084/C/B/2/63-4) and T to her granddaughter, Lady Maureen Stanley, 13 June 1916 (PRONI, D/2846/1/13/1).

245.T to Charley, 17, 27 and 30 June 1916 (PRONI, D/2846/1/13/1).

246.Lady Dufferin to T, 6 July 1916 (PRONI, D/2846/1/8/38).

247.Edith Wheeler to T, 8 July 1916 (PRONI, D/2846/1/8/39). John O'Stubbs highlights the illusionary nature of the truce in 'The Unionists and Ireland, 1914-16' in *Historical Journal*, vol. 33, no. 4 (1990), pp 876-93.

248.Edith Mercier Clements to T, 13 Oct. 1916 (PRONI, D/2846/1/8/54). As a consequence of this constitutional change the UWUC updated electoral registers and held a series of imperial lectures in late 1916. Theresa was also fielding personal appeals for help from women in the three potentially excluded counties: 'Do do everything you can for us poor devils in the border counties and don't let them leave us out', Olive Guthrie to T, undated (PRONI, D/2846/1/9/18). There was further discontent as press claims that Ulster Unionists were willing to compromise on a home rule settlement led to calls for a public meeting of women Unionists to be held. Such a public display would obviously violate the truce and therefore holding the UWUC in check was crucial. Unsurprisingly Carson advised against any meeting.

249.Diary extract of T, 1 Dec. 1917 and 26 June 1918 (PRONI, D/3084/C/B/1/101 and 109).

250.F. L. Silverman to T, 14 Dec. 1918 (PRONI, D/2846/2/19/47). For example, addressing a West Pelton Mothers' Union meeting for women voters on 18 Nov. 1918 Theresa supported the coalition and her letter to the *Morning Post* less than ten days later on 27 Nov. 1918 noted that this form of government was essentially a 'compromise', urging women that it was their responsibility to vote and 'join the old political associations, and…never form a Women's Party, as the interests of men and women are one and the same in the long run'.

251.Charley to T, 27 Sept. 1912 (PRONI, D/2846/1/12/5).

252.T to Charley, 29 Mar. 1917 (PRONI, D/2846/1/13/1).

253.Charley to T, 20 May 1916 (DRO, D/Lo/C682 (194)) and Bonar Law to the same, 15 Dec. 1916 (PRONI, D/2846/2/20/63).

254.Edmund Talbot to T, 30 May 1917 (PRONI, D/2846/2/21/93).

255.Political notes of T, 28 Aug. 1916 (PRONI, D/3084/C/B/2/64) and minute book of UWUC Advisory Committee, 18 Apr. 1917 (PRONI, D/2688/1/7).

256.Charley to T, 23 Nov. 1917 (PRONI, D/3084/C/E/2/8).

257.Diary extract of T, 24 May and 10 Sept. 1917 (PRONI, D/3084/C/B/2/84 and 89).

258.James Craig to T, 24 Jan. 1918 (PRONI, D/2846/1/3/9).

259.Midleton to T, 29 Sept. 1917 (PRONI, D/2846/2/28/55).

260.Archbishop Crozier of Armagh to T, 27 July 1918 (PRONI, D/2846/2/27/28).

261.Political notes of T, 3 Apr. 1918 (PRONI, D/3084/C/B/2/122).

262.Bonar Law to T, 30 May 1917 (PRONI, D/2846/2/20/65).

263.Peter Martin, 'Irish peers, 1909-24: the decline of an aristocratic class' (unpub. MA thesis, University College Dublin, 1998), p. 172.

264.Kendle, *Long*, p. 145. Long's other suggestion to Lloyd George, than Ian Macpherson be appointed Irish Chief Secretary, was acted upon.

265.See Wilfrid Short to T, 5 Mar. 1918 (PRONI, D/2846/2/20/20).

266.Diary extracts of T, 16 Apr., 15 May, 22 June and 7 Aug. 1918 (PRONI, D/3084/C/B/1/123, 126, 133 and 150).

267.Political notes of T, 13 Dec. 1916 and 26 June 1918 (PRONI, D/3084/C/B/2/56 and D/3084/C/B/2/109). Milner, who stayed with Theresa at Wynyard for a short time in 1916, believed Carson was the one man who had grown in political stature during the war but, like Theresa, worried about the Unionist leader's approach to life, 'If only he does not get ill or think himself ill, he will be able to do what he likes with them in the near future...though he always complains of his health I don't think there can be much the matter with him' (Milner to T, 13 Aug. 1916 (PRONI, D/2846/2/14/81)).

268.Diary extracts of T, 16 Apr. 1918 and 16 Jan. 1919 (PRONI, D/3084/C/B/1/122 and 160). Gwynne, Lord Talbot and Law remained at the forefront of trying to match Theresa's ambitions for her son to the reality of the political score but, as late as 1919, Law still struggled to find a definite appointment for him, 'I am sorry that I do not find this feasible' (Bonar Law to T, 23 Jan. 1919 (PRONI, D/2846/2/20/66)).

269.Diary extract of T, 1 Feb. 1919 (PRONI, D/3084/C/B/1/161).

270.T to Bonar Law, 13 Jan. 1919 (Parliamentary Archives, HL/BL/102/1/22). Law's response of 23 Jan. 1919 noted, 'I should have liked if it had been possible to get a definite appointment for Lord Londonderry, but I am glad to think however that the work which he has undertaken in connection with the Air Ministry will be interesting to him' (ibid.). Charley was appointed Under-Secretary of State for Air in Apr. 1920.

271.Political notes of T, 25 May, 2 Nov. 1915 and 15 May 1918 (PRONI, D/3084/C/B/1/52, 112 and 126).

272.Charley to T, 23 Apr. 1915 (DRO, D/Lo/C682 (147)). In the same letter he tried to reassure her that she was 'rich...I never had more than £7000 a year'.

273.Lumley Castle was licensed in 1389 and modified by Vanbrugh in 1721. Charles' will, where any deep-rooted sense of resentment or estrangement might be discernible, gives little hint of a lifelong rift; in 1905 he bequeathed £20,000 to his 'dear wife' with additional monies coming from family settlements. This amount was increased in three codicils so that by 1913 Theresa stood to inherit £100,000, a carriage, a car and horses (see PRONI, D/2846/3/11/1 and the *Irish Times*, 3 Mar. 1915).

274.T to Charley, 8 Mar. 1917 (PRONI, D/2846/1/13/1).

275.Diary extract of T, 29 Nov. 1915 (PRONI, D/3084/C/B/1/7).

276.Queen Mary to T, 28 Feb. 1917 (PRONI, D/2846/2/5/55).

277.T to Charley, 19 Mar. and 13 Apr. 1916 and 5 Mar. 1917 (PRONI, D/2846/1/13/1).

278.Political notes of T, 4 Oct. 1916, 10 Sept. 1917 and 22 Feb. 1919 (PRONI, D/3084/C/B/2/86, 91 and 163) and T to Charley, 23 Feb. 1917 (PRONI, D/2846/1/13/1).

279.T to Charley, 25 Apr. 1917 (PRONI, D/2846/1/13/1). See, for example, the calendar of her letters compiled under family sponsorship (PRONI, D/2846/2/37).

280.Ibid., 7 Feb. 1917 (PRONI, D/2846/1/13/1) and diary extract of T, 10 Aug. 1916 (PRONI, D/3084/C/B/1/11).

281.Political notes of T, 30 Jan. 1918 (PRONI, D/3084/C/B/2/114).

282.Ibid., 17 Nov. 1918 (PRONI, D/3084/C/B/2/158).

283.Maureen to T, 7 Dec. [1918] (PRONI, D/2846/2/11/131).

284.Speech by T to UWUC, 28 Apr. 1918 (PRONI, D/1507/3/11/15).

285.Carson to T, 4 Sept. 1918 (PRONI, D/2846/1/1/153).

286.James Craig to T, 20 Sept. 1918 (PRONI, D/2846/1/3/12).

287.Published address by T as UWUC president, 18 Apr. 1918 (PRONI, D/1507/A/27/3-4).

288.Edith Wheeler to T, 20 June 1918 (PRONI, D/1507/A/28/9).

289.Richard Dawson Bates to T, 18 June 1918 (PRONI, D/1507/A/28/5). The UWUC had twelve representatives on the UUC per annum from 1918-29.

290.Hariot, Lady Dufferin and Ava to Carson, 25 Sept. 1918 (PRONI, D/1507/A/28/32).

291.Diary extract of T, 28 Sept. 1918 (PRONI, D/3084/C/B/1/153).

292.Minute book of UWUC, 29 Jan. 1919 (PRONI, D/1098/1/3). Although there was some speculation that Edith would replace her mother-in-law as UWUC president, the Duchess of Abercorn was elected to this position.

293.Edith Wheeler to T, 19 Jan. 1919 (PRONI, D/2846/1/8/73).

294.Geoffrey Dawson to T, 31 Jan. 1919 (PRONI, D/2846/1/10/7).

295.T to Charley, 24 Apr. 1916 (PRONI, D/2846/1/13/1).

296.Diary extract of T, 22 and 27 Feb. 1919 (PRONI, D/3084/C/B/1/16 and 164). The latter is the last diary extract included in the H. Montgomery Hyde papers.

297.Minute book of UWUC, 29 Jan. 1919 (PRONI, D/1098/1/3). Theresa is buried in the family vault at Long Newton.

298.Gosse to T, 5 June 1910 (PRONI, D/2846/2/26/38) and T to Gosse, 11 Mar. 1919 (Brotherton Collection, Leeds University Library). Theresa left £141,088 in her will (see *The Times*, 24 June 1919). Her political favourites, Carson, Long, as well as the sixth Duke of Portland and first Marquess of Zetland, were bequeathed pins and rings. Sandars and Beckett did not publish any of her letters. Indeed, that her wholesale collection of letters and papers was deposited by the Londonderry family to repositories in Belfast and Durham suggests that they never collected this material.

299.*Morning Post*, 16 Mar. 1919.

300.Diary of Lady Ruby Carson, 16 Mar. 1919 (PRONI, D/1507/C/5).

301.Fingall, *Seventy years*, p. 163.

302.*Evening News*, 25 June 1919.

303.Minute book of UWUC, 29 Jan. 1919 (PRONI, D/1098/1/3).

304.*Morning Post*, 16 Mar. 1919.

305.Sandars to T, 29 Dec. 1911 (DRO, D/Lo/C671 (72)) and Smith to T, 29 Jan. 1919 (PRONI, D/2846/2/20/75).

306.Walter Long, *Memories* (London, 1923), p. 363.

307.*The Times*, 17 Mar. 1919 and *Belfast Telegraph*, 17 Mar. 1919.

308.UWUC annual report, 1919 (PRONI, D/1098/1/3).

309.T to Charley, undated (PRONI, D/3099/2/2/6).

310.T, 'Electioneering 1911 and 1912 in Maidstone' (DRO, D/Lo/F580 (17)).

311.Benson, *As we were*, p. 178.

312.Sackville-West, *Edwardians*, p. 30, p. 48 and p. 111.

313.*Answers*, 13 July 1918.

314.Warwick, *Afterthoughts*, p. 49 and p. 105.

Chapter 3

1. Londonderry, *Retrospect*, p. 72. Edith was born in 1878.

2. E in Margot, Countess of Oxford and Asquith, *Myself when young by famous women of today* (London, 1938), p. 191. Lord Chaplin died in 1923.

3. Henry Chaplin to E, undated [c. 1890s] (PRONI, D/3099/3/1/42 and 52). He wanted her to comment on plans to modify the family home. As a correspondent Edith was no less prolific than her predecessor and thousands of her letters survive, but she was more selective, certainly than Theresa, in what she preserved for posterity. Many lett-

ers are labelled 'Keep' and she separated her political correspondence from that she
deemed of a more social nature.

4. Asquith, *Myself when young*, p. 189.

5. Stafford House was later renamed Lancaster House and later still was home to the
   London Museum.

6. Lewis, *Sacred to female patriotism*, p. 36.

7. Londonderry, *Retrospect*, p. 40. See also Denis Stuart, *Dear Duchess. Millicent Duchess of
   Sutherland, 1867-1955* (London, 1992).

8. Leslie, *Edwardians*, p. 33.

9. Their first born was Maureen and their second child, Edward (always known as Robin)
   was born in 1902. Margaret was born in 1910, Helen in 1911 and Mairi in 1921. Robin
   had a difficult relationship with his parents in the 1930s and 1940s. He succeeded to
   the marquessate in 1949. He married Romaine Combe in 1931 and they had three
   children, Jane, Annabel and Alexander, known Alistair. Alistair succeeded to the title in
   1955 becoming, aged eighteen, the youngest ever Marquess of Londonderry. He married Nicolette Harrison in 1957 but divorced in 1970. They had two children, Sophia
   and Cosima. In 1972 he remarried Doreen Mills and they had one son, Frederick.

10. Londonderry, *Retrospect*, p. 46.

11. Asquith, *Myself when young*, p. 213

12. Charley got the insignia of his regiment, the Royal Horse Guards, tattooed on his arm
    at the same time. Tattoos were not uncommon amongst the upper classes of both
    sexes from the 1860s and were distinctly fashionable from the 1890s onwards. The
    snake motif was also popular as Jennie Churchill, for example, had a tattoo of a snake
    coiled around her wrist. See Elizabeth Kehoe, *Fortune's daughters. The extravagant lives of
    The Jerome sisters. Jennie Churchill, Clara Frewen and Leonie Leslie* (London, 2004), p. 181.

13. E, typescript, 'Armistice Day, 1932' (PRONI, D/3099/3/25). Edith also believed that
    women should ride astride.

14. E, 'Woman's indirect influence, and its effect on character; her position improved by
    the franchise, morally and materially', Feb. 1909, pp 6-7. See also her 'The origin of the
    vote and other historical facts' which was a reply to the Countess Dowager of An-
    caster's pamphlet, 'The vote, not a right, but a trust', Apr. 1913 (PRONI,
    D/3099/3/6/2 and 7).

15. *The Times*, 1 Apr. 1912.

16. Londonderry, *Retrospect*, p. 104.

17. E, 'Women and war', *Daily Sketch*, 5 Apr. 1919.

18. Charley to Lady Desborough, 27 May/June 1917 (Hertfordshire Archives and Local
    Studies [hereafter HALS], DIERV C2482/51).

19. E, *Sunday Graphic*, 20 Oct. 1935.

20. E to Charley, 8 June 1904, cited Pauley, 'Edith', pp 227-28.

21. Londonderry, *Retrospect*, p. 75.

22. Martin, 'Irish peers', p. 9. A petition with ninety-seven allegations of electoral bribery
    was lodged by Charley's Liberal opponent, Sir Frances Evans and a week-long trial
    ensured. The judgement ruled in Charley's favour but heavy costs were incurred.

23. E to T, 12 Apr. 1912 (PRONI, D/2846/1/12/7). Walter Long had entertained the
    same idea in 1907.

24. Charley to E, 7 Aug. 1914, cited Pauley, 'Edith', p. 233.

25. E to T, 16 Feb. 1915 (PRONI, D/3084/C/E/2/13).

26. E, 'Armistice Day'. For correspondence relating to the Women's Legion, see PRONI,
    D/3099/14. During the coal strike of 1926, Edith re-assembled the legion and placed

it at the disposal of the authorities. It was revived in 1934 and in World War Two women were paid for their legion services.

27. Pauley, 'Edith', p. 88.
28. Diary extract of T, 26 July 1914 (PRONI, D/3084/C/B/2/3).
29. For a collective list of Ark members and their fictional nomenclatures in the period 1921-31 see DRO, D/Lo/Acc: 1251 (D) (28).
30. E, typescript chapter on 'The Ark', c. 1959 (PRONI, D/3099/3/12/5). Members of the Order of the Rainbow were decorated with a small bronze ark on a rainbow ribbon.
31. Brian Masters, *Great hostesses* (London, 1982), cited p. 46. It has also been claimed that Edith's choice was influenced by a desire to have a name beginning with 'C' to represent her former courtesy title of Castlereagh as well the torpedo boat of the same name (see Pauley, 'Edith', p. 100).
32. Edith lodged a £200 guarantee for Sean O'Casey when he went to America for the opening of *Within the gates* in 1934. He referred to Londonderry House as 'Richer England's tapestried tavern of the Rose and Crown' and its hostess as charming, 'I was content with her friendship without ever seeming to agree with political affinities' (Sean O'Casey, *Rose and Crown* (London, 1952), p. 94 and Eileen O'Casey, *Sean* (London, 1971), p. 73 and p. 76). In 1933 Edith invited George (AE) Russell to supper and in 1935 extended hospitality at Londonderry House to W. B. Yeats. She was also patron to composer Rutland Boughton whose support for communism lost him both work and admirers. He was, therefore, grateful for her support: 'thanks to you, I have a new chance in the world' (cited Pauley, 'Edith', p. 191).
33. E, 'Ark', c. 1959 (PRONI, D/3099/3/12/6-116).
34. 'Arkeology', author unknown, 1932 (PRONI, D/3099/3/12/1-39).
35. William Buchan, *John Buchan. A memoir* (London, 1982), p. 192. Buchan was known in The Ark as 'the Buck' and assisted Edith with her biography of her father in the early 1920s. He was a regular visitor at Londonderry House into the 1930s.
36. Diary of Lady Ruby Carson, 31 May 1916 (PRONI, D/1507/C/2).
37. The Other Club was still in existence in the 1980s. See Pugh, *Tories*.
38. Sykes, *Private Palaces*, p. 335 and p. 339.
39. Charley to E, 18 Nov. 1917, cited Pauley, 'Edith', p. 246.
40. Charley to Lady Desborough, 2 Jan. 1915 (HALS, DIERV C2482/3). Ettie Desborough was also close to George Wyndham, Arthur Balfour, Evan Charteris and Lord Revelstoke.
41. Charley to Lady Desborough, 24 Apr. 1916 (HALS, DIERV C2482/29).
42. Diary extract of T, 28 Dec. 1916 (PRONI, D/3084/C/B/2/59).
43. E to Charley, 27 Feb. 1918, cited Pauley, 'Edith', p. 245. When the Irish Convention met in Belfast, Charley, in tangent with the hospitality extended by other landed members, invited them to Mount Stewart. On Charley's contribution to the convention, see Fleming, *The Marquess of Londonderry*, pp 50-66.
44. E to Charley 18 Nov. 1917 and his reply, 20 Nov. 1917, cited Pauley, 'Edith', pp 242-43.
45. E to Carson, 17 Jan. 1918 (PRONI, D/3099/13/2/524).
46. Charley to Lady Desborough, 1 Sept. and 22 Dec. 1917 and 16 Mar. 1918 (HALS, DIERV C2482/52, 54 and 56).
47. Diary extract of T, 8 Dec. 1918 (PRONI, D/3084/C/B/1/14).
48. Charley to E, 27 Feb. 1918, cited Pauley, 'Edith', p. 247.
49. *Sunday Times*, 16 Feb. 1919.
50. E, 'Ark'. The Ark met, at least, until 1932.
51. *Cambridge Daily News*, 7 Feb. 1930 and E, 'Ark'.

52. Charley to E, 29 Jan. and 26 Feb. 1918, cited Pauley, 'Edith', p. 32 and p. 246.
53. Londonderry, *Retrospect*, p. 173.
54. Lord Lansdowne resigned office in 1916.
55. *The Globe*, 10 Dec. 1919; *Daily Express*, 19 Nov. 1919; *Daily Chronicle*, 19 Nov. 1919; *The Queen*, 29 Nov. 1919 and 2 Dec. 1922; *Sunday Chronicle*, 23 Nov. 1919 and *Liverpool Daily Post*, 20 Nov. 1919.
56. E to Charley, 14 Sept. 1919, cited Pauley, 'Edith', p. 251.
57. Duke of Gloucester to E, 10 Jan. 1921 (PRONI, D/3099/3/13/69B) and E to Charley, 20 Jan, 2 and 4 Apr. 1921, cited Pauley, 'Edith', p. 256 and p. 282. On Charley's record of service in this posting see Fleming, *The Marquess of Londonderry*, pp 88-113.
58. E to Charley, Apr. 1921, cited Pauley, 'Edith', p. 267. See also E to Bonar Law, 29 Jan. [1921] (Parliamentary Archives, HL/BL/100/1/47).
59. Charley to Lady Desborough, 25 Oct. 1922 (HALS, DIERV C2482/61).
60. Londonderry, *Retrospect*, pp 215-18.
61. E to Charley, 12 July 1922, cited Pauley, 'Edith', p. 283.
62. E to Bonar Law, 26 Oct. [1922] (Parliamentary Archives, HL/BL/109/2/13a).
63. Charley to Lady Desborough, 10 July 1923 (HALS, DIERV C2482/82).
64. *New York Herald*, 18 Feb. 1923; *Belfast Telegraph*, 2 Feb. 1923; *Women's Pictorial*, 10 Mar. 1923 and *Evening Standard*, 13 Feb. 1923. In addition, at the behest of the *Saturday Review*, Edith fed them information about the Irish situation, especially in relation to the north of the country in the early 1920s.
65. *Women's Pictorial*, 18 Apr. 1925.
66. Carson to E, 22 Dec. 1921; Gretton to the same, 23 Dec. 1921 and Northumberland to the same, 23 and 25 Dec. 1921 (PRONI, D/3099/3/17/1-3 and 8).
67. Carson to E, 1 Jan. 1922 (PRONI, D/3099/3/17/13).
68. C. E. Callwell, *Field-Marshall Sir Henry Wilson. His life and diaries*, vol. II (London, 1927), p. 320.
69. Diary of Lady Ruby Carson, 21 Mar. 1922 (PRONI, D/1507/C/7).
70. UWUC annual report, 1922 (PRONI, D/2688/1/9). Women appointed under this scheme were trained as telephonists, nurses, telegraphists, cooks, policewomen and searchers to deal with women suspected of carrying arms or documents.
71. Notes on the Ulster Women's Volunteer Association, 20 July 1922 (PRONI, FIN/18/2/56). The association had offices at King's Chambers in Belfast.
72. Ibid., 1 July 1922 (PRONI, FIN/18/2/78).
73. See Sinead McCoole, *Hazel* (Dublin, 1996), p. 86 and Tim Pat Coogan, *Michael Collins. A biography* (London, 1990), p. 291. For the suggestion that 'Lady L' was Edith Londonderry see Masters, *Great hostesses* and de Courcy, *Circe*.
74. Michael Collins to Lady L, Apr. 1922 (PRONI, D/3099/3/15/52A).
75. Lucy Baldwin writing to her mother-in-law, 1924, Williams, *Ladies,* cited p. 15.
76. Baldwin to E, 18 Nov. 1924 (PRONI, D/3099/3/15/13). Baldwin was the Conservative Party leader from 1923-37 and held the position of Prime Minster three times: 1923-24; 1928-29 and 1935-37.
77. Martin Gilbert (ed.), *Winston S. Churchill*, vol. V (London, 1966), p. 53.
78. In 1928 Edith hosted several anti-Socialist fundraisers. For an example of her anti-Socialist pronouncements see her 17 Nov. 1926 speech to the Central Women's Unionist Association bazaar (DRO, D/Lo/F615 (8)).
79. Charley to Winston Churchill, 19 Jan. 1923 (PRONI, D/3084/C/E/7/4).
80. E to Charley, undated [1925], cited Pauley, 'Edith', p. 255.
81. Charley to Winston Churchill, 2 Nov. 1925 (PRONI, D/3084/C/E/7/7).
82. Charley to Lady Desborough, 21 Nov. 1926 (HALS, DIERV C2482/68).
83. E to Hendricks, Jan. 1926 (PRONI, D/3099/15/3).

84. *Daily Herald*, 3 Feb. 1926.
85. E to Charley, 1927, cited Pauley, 'Edith', p. 300.
86. Ibid., 6 July 1927, p. 296.
87. Stuart Ball (ed.), *Parliament and politics in the age of Baldwin and MacDonald. The Headlam diaries, 1923-35* (London, 1992), p. 155.
88. Monica Winterton to E, 19 Oct. [c. 1928] (PRONI, D/3099/3/2/413).
89. *Darlington Times*, 29 June 1929.
90. MacDonald to E, 28 May 1932 (David Marquand, *Ramsay MacDonald* (London, 1977), cited p. 691).
91. Londonderry, *Retrospect*, p. 223. She notes that they became 'firm friends'.
92. MacDonald diary, 2 Jan. 1917 and 6 Dec. 1921 (Public Record Office, London [hereafter PRO] PRO/30/69/1753/1).
93. Margaret Cole (ed.), *Beatrice Webb's diaries, 1912-32*, vol. II (London, 1956), p. 18 and p. 25.
94. Keith Middlemas (ed.), *Thomas Jones Whitehall diaries*, vol. II (Oxford, 1969), p. 56.
95. MacDonald diary, 1 Oct. 1914 and 30 Dec. 1917 (PRO/30/69/1753/1).
96. Ibid., 10, 13 1924 (PRO/30/69/1753/1).
97. Londonderry, *Retrospect*, p. 224. MacDonald's adoption of John and Hazel Lavery in 1930 bears a striking similarity to his relationship with the Londonderrys. They too were invited to Chequers within weeks of their first meeting and MacDonald also wrote much more extensively to Hazel than to her husband. The flirtatious tone of their often weekly letters and notes is, at times, reminiscent of those he wrote to Edith. He also wrote poems for her but there was a reversal in affections as Hazel, jealous that he wrote prose for others, had her ardour cooled by his disparaging wit. Mac-Donald, for example, chastised her in 1931, 'Now! now! now! My dear Hazel, if you are in love don't show signs of it'; 'Hazel, behave yourself or I shall pull your leg and make you feel uncomfortable. I shall dip you in buckets of cold water and hang you out to dry.' He was also concerned about gossip which he referred to as 'a forked tongue jake who spares no-one and who is most devoted in her attentions to figures on pedestals' and feared their letters would stray into the wrong hands: 'You need not burn when the letters are only chaff, but I have a horror of letters lying about and perhaps published when I am dead'. Fewer letters passed between them from 1931 but they remained friends until at least 1933 (McCoole, *Hazel*, cited p. 166, p. 168 and p. 172).
98. Marquand, *Ramsay*, p. 405.
99. Cole, *Beatrice Webb*, pp 11-12.
100. MacDonald to E, 9 and 30 Apr. 1924 (PRONI, D/3084/C/D/4/9-10).
101. Ibid., 17 June 1924 (PRONI, D/3084/C/D/4/11).
102. MacDonald diary, 2 Mar. 1924 (PRO/30/69/1753/1).
103. MacDonald to E, 5 Aug. 1924 (PRONI, D/3084/C/D/4/16-7).
104. E to MacDonald, 12 Aug. 1924 and his reply, 13 Aug. 1924 (PRONI, D/3084/C/D/4/18-24).
105. *Birmingham Evening Dispatch*, 19 Aug. 1926.
106. Cole, *Beatrice Webb*, vol. II, p. 120.
107. MacDonald diary, 3 Apr. 1927 (PRO/30/69/1753/1).
108. E to MacDonald, 20 May 1930 (PRO/30/69/752/79). Another letter jests, 'Don't you want a female Minister or Mistress of Education!!! I should make such a good "Maitresse du Cabinet." I think it an excellent idea' (E to MacDonald, undated (PRO/30/69/760/59)).
109. Ibid., 22 Dec. [c. 1931] (John Rylands University Library, University of Manchester [hereafter Rylands], RMD/1/13/27).

110.MacDonald to E, 11 June 1927 (PRONI, D/3084/C/D/4/28). Their sons were part of an official contingent to Honolulu.

111.MacDonald diary, 20 Jan. 1928 (PRO/30/69/1753/1).

112.Norman Mackenzie (ed.), *The letters of Sidney and Beatrice Webb*, vol. III (Cambridge, 1982), p. 309.

113.MacDonald diary, 17 Nov. 1929 and 14 Jan. 1930 (PRO/30/69/1753/1).

114.Marquess of Londonderry, *Wings of destiny* (London, 1943), p. 44.

115.Ball, *Parliament and politics*, p. 214.

116.Robert Rhodes James, *Memoirs of a Conservative. J. C. C. Davidson's memoirs and papers, 1910-37* (London, 1969), pp 311-12. Davidson was chair of the Conservative Party from 1926-30.

117.*Daily Sketch*, 5 June 1929.

118.Ball, *Parliament and politics*, p. 183.

119.MacDonald to E, 8 July 1929 (PRONI, D/3084/C/D/4/41).

120.Middlemas, *Thomas Jones*, vol. II, p. 236.

121.MacDonald diary, 5 Feb. 1930 (PRO/30/69/1753/1); *Daily Express*, 7 Feb. 1930 and *Northern Whig*, 20 Feb. 1930.

122.*Daily Sketch*, 16 Apr. 1930. Patrick Balfour also remarked in *Society racket. A critical survey of modern social life* (London, 1933), 'you can see Mr. Ramsay MacDonald...dining *tête-tête* at *Boulestin's* with Lady Londonderry, the official Conservative hostess, on the night of the Budget!', p. 125.

123.MacDonald diary, 1 July and 20-21 Oct. 1930 (PRO/30/69/1753/1).

124.Ibid., 13-14 June 1930 (PRO/30/69/1753/4) and MacDonald to E, 12 June 1930 (PRONI, D/3084/C/D/4/47). He dedicated this song to the dames of the Primrose League.

125.MacDonald to E, 12 Sept. and 27 Oct. 1930 (PRONI, D/3084/C/D/4/53 and 57).

126.Ibid., 7 Oct. 1930 (PRONI, D/3084/C/D/4/55).

127.*Sunday Graphic*, 26 Oct. 1930.

128.*The Queen*, 15 Apr. 1931.

129.MacDonald diary, 9 Nov. 1930 (PRO/30/69/1753/4). This point is reinforced by Philip Williamson who infers in *National crisis and national government: British politics, the economy and empire, 1926-32* (Cambridge, 1992) that Edith was in favour of a coalition from 1930, pp 150-51.

130.Marquand, *Ramsay*, cited p. 577.

131.MacDonald diary, 2-3 and 16 Dec. 1930 (PRO/30/69/1753/1).

132.Cole, *Beatrice Webb*, p. 249. MacDonald was not adverse to the criticism, writing to Sutherland after the visit, 'Our press gets more and more reckless and mischievous... they based their conclusions that you were being 'considered'. The world is a village of glass houses through which phantasmagoria as well as men and women move' (the Duke of Sutherland, *Looking back. The autobiography of the fifth Duke of Sutherland* (London, 1957), cited p. 171).

133.Diary of Lady Lilian Spender, 1 July 1931 (PRONI, D/1633/2/33A).

134.Ball, *Parliament and politics*, p. 212.

135.Kershaw, *Making friends*, p. 17.

136.Sean O'Casey to E, 23 October 1931 (PRONI, D/3084/C/F/7/13). See *The Old Testament*, Judith, 13, ch. 1-10 for the episode of Judith who saved the city of Bethulia from the siege of Holofernes, general of the Assyrian king Nabucodonosor, by beheading him after a banquet and presenting his head to his fellow citizens.

137.Prof. F. A. Lindeman to E, 5 Nov. 1931 (PRONI, D/3099/3/2/479). Lindeman, later Lord Cherwell, became a scientific advisor to Churchill during the Second World War.

138.L. MacNeill Weir, *The tragedy of Ramsay Mac Donald* (London, 1938), p. 212.

139.Huw Benyon and Terry Austin, *Masters and servants. Class and patronage in the making of a labour organisation. The Durham miners and English political tradition* (London, 1994), cited p. 339. With a spiralling budget deficit, there were widespread concerns about uncontrolled taxation; in 1931 income tax increased from 4s in the pound to 4s6d and supertax also increased. By the end of 1931 unemployment stood at 2.7 million and exports had halved in value.

140.*The Times*, 19 Dec. 1930. In 1935 Horne told Edith that she was 'too good in my interests' (PRONI, D/3099/3/17/75).

141.Williamson, *National crisis*, pp 150-51.

142.PRONI, D/3099/3/2/487. Charley held the Garter from 1919.

143.MacDonald diary, 20 Jan. 1931 (PRO/30/69/1753/1).

144.MacDonald to E, 13 Feb. 1931 (Marquand, *Ramsay*, cited pp 495-96).

145.Ibid., 6 Nov. 1931, cited de Courcy, *Society's Queen*, p. 267.

146.MacDonald diary, 23 and 26 Aug. 1931 (PRO/30/69/1753/1). MacDonald announced that he would stand as National Government Prime Minister on 24 Aug. 1931.

147.E to Sir A. Godley, 8 Nov. 1931 (DRO, D/Lo/C251 (4)).

148.E, speech delivered at Newcastle, 24 Oct. 1934 (DRO, D/Lo/F615 (26)).

149.MacDonald to E, 24 Aug. 1931 (PRONI, D/3084/C/D/4/64-5).

150.Baldwin to E, 6 Nov. 1931 (PRONI, D/3099/3/15/17).

151.E, undated speech [c. 1934] (DRO, D/Lo/F615 (54)).

152.*North Mail*, 21 Oct. 1931.

153.*Evening World*, 26 Oct. 1931.

154.*North Mail*, 26 Oct. 1931.

155.Edith was hugely supportive and sympathetic to MacDonald, asking, for example, in mid 1931, 'What is it? I shall come and see you to-morrow morning - or what would you like me to do…I can not [sic] bear to think of you worried and wretched' (E to MacDonald, 2 May 1931 (PRO/30/69/753/291)).

156.MacDonald to E, 8 Sept. 1931 (PRONI, D/3084/C/D/4/66).

157.Ibid., 29 Sept. 1931 (PRONI, D/3084/C/D/4/71-3).

158.E to Charley, 30 Sept. 1931, cited Pauley, 'Edith', p. 319.

159.H. Montgomery Hyde, *British air policy between the wars, 1918-39* (London, 1976), p. 275 and Hyde, *Londonderrys*, p. 192. Stephen Gwynne wrote to Edith in congratulation on 29 Aug. 1931, 'I was glad to see your Lord in the new Government for other reasons and because I think you like to be in touch with running things' (DRO, D/Lo/C251 (2)). On Charley's performance in this post see Fleming, *The Marquess of Londonderry*, pp 141-76.

160.David Cannadine, *The decline and fall of the British aristocracy* (London, 1990), p. 600.

161.Charley to Lady Desborough, 25 Jan. 1931 (HALS, DIERV C2482/71). Charley met the Canadian premier, Bennett at an imperial conference of dominion prime ministers in London in 1930. Bennett subsequently asked the king if Londonderry would be interested in the position of Governor General. He refused as he wanted to pursue business interests and still hoped for office under a future Conservative administration and the king was understanding: 'G. G. of Canada, with practically all the powers gone which he used to have, I am sure would not appeal to you' (PRONI, D/3084/C/F/6/183).

162.MacDonald diary, 12 Oct. and 22 Nov. 1931 (PRO/30/69/1753/1).

163.E to MacDonald, 22 Dec. [c. 1931] (Rylands, RMD/1/13/27).

164.MacDonald to E, Nov./Dec. and 27 Dec. 1931 (Marquand, *Ramsay*, cited p. 690).

165.E to MacDonald, 29 Dec. 1931 (Rylands, RMD/1/13/9).

166.A. J. P. Taylor (ed.), *Lloyd George. A diary by Francis Stevenson* (London, 1971), p. 254.

167.*The Star*, 4 Dec. 1931.

168.*Evening Standard*, 1 Feb. 1932.

169.*Liverpool Post*, 16 Jan. 1932. On a smaller scale, but in a similar timeslot, Lucy Baldwin held weekly afternoon parties at 11 Downing Street in Feb. and Mar. 1932.

170.MacDonald diary, 22 Nov. 1932 (PRO/30/69/1753/1).

171.Hyde, *Londonderrys*, pp 193-94.

172.Edith to Beaverbrook, 22 Feb. 1932 (DRO, D/Lo/C251/3 (21)). Charley wrote to Beaverbrook in a similar vein.

173.E to MacDonald, 11 Nov. [1931] (PRO/30/69/3/114).

174.E to J. R. Bainbridge, 11 Aug. 1932 (DRO, D/Lo/C251 (8)).

175.E to Sir Percy Bates, editor of the *Morning Post*, 13 Aug. 1932 (DRO, D/Lo/C251 (8)).

176.Pugh, *Tories*, p. 45 and MacDonald to E, 23 May 1931 (Marquand, *Ramsay*, cited p. 496).

177.Cannadine, *Decline and fall*, p. 344; Charley to E, 14 Apr. 1932 (PRONI, D/3804/C/E/29) and her reply, 16 Apr. 1932, cited Pauley, 'Edith', p. 345. MacDonald was attending the League of Nations at Geneva. See also de Courcy, *Society's Queen*, p. 270.

178.Towards the end of his life MacDonald took steps to ensure that his diaries would not be misquoted or judged out of context by inserting the proviso that they were 'meant as notes to guide and revive the memory as regards happenings and must on no account be published as they are.' This was perhaps to be expected from a man who, certainly, in the latter stages of his career, felt many of his actions were taken out of context. See, for example, the diary of Ramsay MacDonald, with sporadic entries for 1910-35 (PRO/30/69/1753/1). He sounded another warning on 8 June 1933, 'These memoirs and recollection are becoming dangerous (though they are convenient) for the historian, for a great part of them is really unreliable' (PRO/30/69/1753/1). Approximately a hundred letters from Edith to MacDonald survive.

179.H. Montgomery Hyde, 'Mount Stewart and its owners', undated manuscript (PRONI, D/3084/C/F/6/287), p. 15. The censoring of letters amongst the upper classes was not uncommon, especially during the Victorian era.

180.E to MacDonald, 1 Apr. [1932] (PRO/30/69/754/639-40).

181.Tyrell sent this cutting to E on 28 Mar. 1931 (see PRONI, D/3099/3/15/88).

182.Tardieu to E, 27 and 30 Mar. 1932 (PRONI, D/3099/3/2/494-5). I am most grateful to Dr Ian McKeane for translating this French material. Tardieu was Président du Conseil (French Prime Minister) three times: Nov. 1929 to Feb. 1930; Mar. to Dec. 1930 and Feb. to May 1932. He left politics in 1936 with the arrival of the Popular Front under Léon Blum.

183.*Daily Telegraph*, 2 Apr. 1932.

184.E to MacDonald, 1 Apr. [1932] (PRO/30/69/754/639-40).

185.Tyrell to E, 21 Mar. 1932 (PRONI, D/3099/3/15/89).

186.John Andrews to E, 1 Apr. 1932 (PRONI, D/3099/3/15/4).

187.Gordon Martell (ed.), *The Times and appeasement. The journals of A. L. Kennedy, 1932-39* (Cambridge, 2000), p. 39.

188.Tardieu to E, 26 May 1932 (PRONI, D/3099/3/2/497).

189.*Yorkshire Evening Press*, 21 Nov. 1932.

190.MacDonald to E, 27 Mar. 1932 (Marquand, *Ramsay*, cited pp 690-91).

191.Hyde, *Londonderrys*, cited p. 199.

192.De Courcy, *Circe*, cited p. 228.

193.MacDonald to E, 21 May 1932 (Marquand, *Ramsay*, cited p. 691).

194.Ibid., 28 May 1932. MacDonald also kept Edith fully informed. For instance, he telephoned her and left a message with news of the Lausanne agreement in July 1932.

195.E to MacDonald, 21 June [1932] (PRO/30/69/754/643).

196.Ibid., 16 Sept. and 7 Oct. 1932 (Rylands, RMD/1/13/11 and 15). In a similar vein, Edith asked MacDonald if a decision had been taken regarding the Shakespeare Memorial Theatre in 1934.

197.Duke of Alba to E, 11 Apr. 1931 (PRONI, D/3099/3/7/4).

198.Edith recommended old friend, Col. MacAuley and long-time colliery and dock employee, Malcolm Dillon for honours, telling MacDonald, 'I know you won't mind me pushing this claim', E to MacDonald, Nov. 1934 (PRO/30/69/3/114).

199.See PRO/30/69/678/425-9 and E to MacDonald, 7 Apr. [1932] (PRO/30/69/754/637-8).

200.E to MacDonald, undated (Rylands, RMD/1/13/28).

201.E to Baldwin, 26 July 1932 (PRONI, D/3099/3/15/26).

202.Tyrell to E, 22 Apr. 1932 and Sankey to the same, 23 July 1932 (PRONI, D/3099/3/2/499 and 506).

203.E to MacDonald, 14 June [1932] (PRO/30/69/755/572-3).

204.*Belfast News-Letter* and *Daily Independent*, 9 Aug. 1932.

205.E to MacDonald, 20 Sept. 1932 (Rylands, RMD/1/13/12).

206.E to MacDonald, 21 Nov. 1932 (PRO/30/69/1177/189-92). She signed this letter formally as 'E. Londonderry' and enclosed a copy of her letter to Simon.

207.John Simon to E, 23 Nov. 1932 (PRONI, D/3099/3/2/515).

208.E to MacDonald, 21 Nov. 1932 (Rylands, RMD/1/13/26). This letter was signed 'C'. There were less society events in the 1930s and gradually government sponsored functions took over from private political events. The Londonderrys and their cousins, the Wimbornes were alone amongst the aristocracy in continuing to entertain en masse in this manner 1920s and 1930s. Lady Ettie Desborough was the last Whig hostess while Lady Craven and Lady Harcourt entertained for Asquith. Lady Sibyl Colefax's receptions were more artistic and literary with a reputation for courting celebrities and being the first to admit Americans into high society. Mrs. Greville and Lady Emerald Cunard's receptions, although attended by politicians such as Balfour, Churchill, Milner and Curzon, were both more artistic in composition. The Astors specialised in weekend parties at Cliveden and American Laura Corrigan entertained at Polesden Lacey but large society events were increasingly being held at hotels like the Savoy and Grosvenor House instead of at private houses. After renovating 'no. 10' in 1937 Anne Chamberlain held a series of luncheons but these were never on the scale of the Londonderrys' receptions.

209.Ibid., 16 and 20 Sept. 1932 (Rylands, RMD/1/13/11-12). See also his enigmatic diary entry that most probably refers to Edith: 'A friend has been very helpful and but for that I wonder whether I could have gone on' (Marquand, *Ramsay*, cited p. 692).

210.E to MacDonald, 8 Aug. 1933 (PRO/30/69/755/568-70).

211.MacDonald to E, 9 Oct. 1932 (Marquand, *Ramsay*, cited p. 692).

212.MacDonald diary, 16 Jan. 1933 cited ibid.

213.Nick Smart (ed.), *The diaries and letters of Robert Bernays, 1932-39. An insider's account of the House of Commons* (New York, 1996), p. 49.

214.*Northern Whig*, 7 Aug. 1933; *Daily Mirror*, 30 June 1933 and E to MacDonald, 12 Oct. 1933 (PRO/30/69/3/114).

215.Low's cartoon is reproduced in MacNeill Weir, *The tragedy of Ramsay MacDonald*, p. 313.

216.Walter Elliott to E, 22 May 1933 (PRONI, D/3099/3/2/524). Hailsham cited in de Courcy, *Circe*, p. 231.

217.MacDonald diary, 20 Nov. 1933 (PRO/30/69/1753/1).

218.E to MacDonald, 23 Mar. [1933] (Rylands, RMD/1/13/23) and his reply, 24 Mar. 1933 (Marquand, *Ramsay*, cited p. 692).

219.E to MacDonald, 13 Aug. 1933 (PRO/30/69/755/574-6).

220.Ibid., 21 Aug. [1933] (Rylands, RMD/1/13/21).

221.Ibid., 6 July 1933 (PRO/30/69/760/67-8).

222.MacDonald diary, 21 Jan. 1934 (PRO/30/69/1753/1).

223.Londonderry House party list, 20 Nov. 1933 (PRONI, D/3099/15/6).

224.MacDonald diary, 19 Feb. 1933 (PRO/30/69/1753/1).

225.Ibid., 28 Oct. and 2 Dec. 1934 (PRO/30/69/1753/1). MacDonald visited Mount Stewart on the way to Canada in July 1934.

226.E to MacDonald, 12 Oct. 1933 (Marquand, *Ramsay*, cited p. 689). In Aug. 1933 Mac-Donald discussed his political future with Londonderry and Hailsham, 'I gave them to understand that I did not wish to go on for a day longer than was essential' (MacDonald diary, 31 Aug. 1933 (PRO/30/69/1753/3)).

227.*New York World Telegram*, 14 June 1934.

228.Taylor, *Lloyd George*, cited p. 254 and p. 302.

229.James, *Chips*, p. 28.

230.E to MacDonald, 8 Jan. [1934] (PRO/30/69/683/166). Conservatives held 473 seats in the second National Government.

231.Charley to E, 19 Apr. 1935 (PRONI, D/3084/C/E/9) and Fleming, *The Marquess of Londonderry*, cited p. 167.

232.MacDonald to E, undated [May 1935] (PRO/30/69/114). Smart notes that Mac-Donald's last year in government was dogged by his 'appalling state of mental and physical health. His eyesight was declining, headaches and insomnia meant he could do little work' (Nick Smart, *The National Government, 1931-40* (Basingstoke, 1999), p. 92).

233.E to MacDonald, 18 July 1935 (PRO/30/69/760/55-56).

234.MacDonald diary, 24 and 26 Apr., 14 May and 2 June 1935 (PRO/30/69/1753/2).

235.Charley to MacDonald, 6 July 1935 (Rylands, RMD/1/13/5).

236.Keith Middlemas and John Barnes, *Baldwin. A biography* (London, 1969), cited p. 806.

237.Marquess of Londonderry, *Ourselves and Germany* (Harmondsworth, 1938), p. 68.

238.James, *Chips*, p. 35.

239.Londonderry, *Wings*, p. 144.

240.Lord Hailsham to E, 13 June 1935 (PRONI, D/3099/3/2/583).

241.H. Montgomery Hyde to Lady Mairi Bury, undated (PRONI, D/3084/C/F/6/180).

242.*Sunday News*, 12 Aug. 1979. Londonderry also lost the Lords' post and was replaced by Halifax.

243.Samuel Hoare to E, 21 Dec. 1935 (PRONI, D/3099/3/15/68).

244.*Morning Post*, 25 Nov. 1935. See also the Londonderry House party list which includes a handwritten note by Baldwin deeming the 1935 reception 'inopportune', 18 Nov. 1935 (PRONI, D/3099/15/6).

245.E to Neville Chamberlain, 2 May 1935 (Birmingham University Library, NC/11/28/30).Neville Chamberlain was the younger brother of the former Conservative leader, Austen Chamberlain. He was Chancellor of the Exchequer from 1931-37 and Baldwin's heir apparent. He served as Prime Minister from 1937-40.

246.Ibid., 21 May 1935 and his reply of the same day (Birmingham University Library, NC/11/28/33).

247.Neville Chamberlain to E, 28 July and 27 Oct. 1937 (PRONI, D/3099/3/15/44 and 46).

248.*Newcastle Journal*, 22 Oct. 1938.

249.Masters, *Great hostesses*, cited p. 47.

250.MacDonald diary, 3 Sept. 1933 (PRO/30/69/1753/3).

251.MacDonald to E, undated (PRONI, D/3084/C/D/4/5) and 26 Dec. 1933 (Marquand, *Ramsay*, cited p. 692).

252.MacDonald diary, 27 Dec. 1932 (PRO/30/69/1753/2).

253.E to MacDonald, undated (PRO/30/69/760/61).

254.MacNeill Weir, *The tragedy of Ramsay MacDonald*, pp 307-08 and pp 558-59.

255.E to MacDonald, 20 Sept. 1937 (PRO/30/69/759/624-6).

256.Ibid., 9 Oct. 1936 (PRO/30/69/758/593).

257.Williams, *Ladies*, cited p. 37.

258.A film based on the novel, directed by Ray Boulting and starring Michael Redgrave and Rosamund John, was produced by Boulting Brothers and Two Cities Film in 1947.

259.Marquand, *Ramsay*, p. 692.

260.James, *Chips*, p. 35.

261.Masters, *Great hostesses*, p. 51.

262.Cannadine, *Decline and fall,* pp 352-53.

263.Samuel Hoare to E, 22 Apr. 1936 (PRONI, D/3099/3/15/73).

264.E, typescript, 'Empire entertaining at Londonderry House', c. 1937 (PRONI, D/3099/15/11).

265.*Evening Standard*, 4 May 1937.

266.E to Hitler, 21 Feb. 1936 (PRONI, D/3099/3/35/2A).

267.MacDonald diary, 20 Nov. 1933 (PRO/30/69/1753/1).

268.Ribbentrop was an unofficial diplomat in London from Nov. 1933; special commissioner for disarmament from 1934; German Ambassador to Britain from Aug. 1936 and German Foreign Minister from 1938-45.

269.Charley to E, 30 Mar. 1936, cited Pauley, 'Edith', p. 363. Charley also joined the Anglo-German Association in 1929 but it is unclear how long he remained a member.

270.Londonderry, *Wings*, p. 158 and p. 160.

271.Kerhaw, *Making friends*, p. xvi. See also Cannadine, *Decline and fall,* pp 549-50. On Charley's relationship with Nazi Germany, see Fleming, *The Marquess of Londonderry*, pp 177-207.

272.Masters, *Great hostesses*, p. 179.

273.Londonderry, *Wings*, p. 108.

274.Kershaw, *Making friends*, p. 88.

275.*Birmingham Post*, 9 Aug. 1979.

276.Harold Macmillan, *Winds of change* (London, 1966), p. 399. Macmillan was Prime Minister from 1957-63.

277.Kershaw, *Making friends*, cited p. 134.

278.*Sunday Sun*, 3 May 1936.

279.E to Hilter, 21 Feb. 1936 (PRONI, D/3099/3/35/2A).

280.E to General der Fliegar, 21 Feb. 1936 (PRONI, D/3099/3/35/4).

281.Hoesch to E, 24 Mar. 1936 (PRONI, D/3099/3/35/8).

282.Nigel Nicolson (ed.), *Harold Nicolson. Diaries and letters, 1930-39* (London, 1966), p. 245.

283.MacDonald diary, 6 Mar. and 7 Apr. 1936 (PRO/30/69/1753/2).

284.Göring to E, 2 and 16 Apr. 1936 (PRONI, D/3099/3/35/10B and 16).

285.E to der Fliegar, 4 May 1936 (PRONI, D/3099/3/35/13A).

286.Ibid., undated (PRONI, D/3099/3/35/37).

287.See Kershaw, *Making friends*, pp 156-72 and Londonderry, *Wings*, pp 171-72. C. W. James and Sir William Milner later joined the Mount Stewart party.

288.Kershaw, *Making friends*, p. 156 and p. 162.

289.Göring to E, 3 July 1936 (PRONI, D/3099/3/35/24B).

290.The sixth Marquess and Marchioness were inaugurated as mayor and mayoress of Durham in 1910.

291.Londonderry House party list, 18 May 1937 (PRONI, D/3099/15/11).

292.Londonderry, *Ourselves*, pp 119-20 and p. 125.

293.Charley to Ribbentrop, 8 Dec. 1937 cited in Londonderry, *Ourselves*, pp 132-33.

294.Londonderry, *Retrospect*, p. 255.

295.Londonderry, *Ourselves*, p. 81.

296.E to Ribbentrop, 19 Mar. 1938 (PRONI, D/3099/3/35/33).

297.Göring to E, 22 Mar. 1938 and Ribbentrop to the same, 27 Apr. 1938 (PRONI, D/3099/3/35/34B and 35).

298.Kershaw, *Making friends*, cited p. 239.

299.*The Times*, 3 Oct. 1938.

300.Accompanied by Ward Price, Charley made another visit to Munich in 1938 to witness Chamberlain's meeting with Hitler. Charley also met with Göring and Ribbentrop.

301.Londonderry, *Wings*, pp 215-16.

302.E, notes for an article or speech, undated [c. 1945] (PRONI, D/3099/3/38/11).

303.Charley to Lady Milner, 11 Mar. 1937 (DRO, D/Lo/C237 (8)).

304.Charley to Hyde, 9 Oct. 1938 (PRONI, D/3084/C/E/3/211).

305.Londonderry, *Ourselves*, p. 138 and pp 142-45. Charley sent copies of the book to Hitler, Göring, Ribbentrop and von Papen. Hitler hoped the book would further understanding but the response from Göring and Von Papen was more muted. The latter deemed the book courageous but objected to likening Nazi policy towards Austria as akin to war (see PRONI, D/3084/C/C/6/36, 51 and 77). The book was well received in the British press and sold over 5,000 copies.

306.Copy of letters from Wallis Simpson to E, undated [c. 1936] and her reply, 8 Nov. 1936 (PRONI, D/3099/3/2/604B/1-2).

307.E to Neville Chamberlain, 7 Jan. 1940 (PRONI, D/3099/3/15/47). Chamberlain also failed to put forward her recommendation for the 1940 honours list.

308.*Daily Mail*, 9 Jan. 1940.

309.Charley to Lady Desborough, 21 Sept. 1947 (HALS, DIERV C2482/88).

310.Kershaw, *Making friends*, p. 330 and Christopher Sykes, *Nancy: the life of Lady Nancy Astor* (London, 1972), p. 481. Ribbentrop was hanged in October 1946.

311.Charley to Lady Desborough, 16 July 1945 (HALS, DIERV C2482/74).

312.Ibid., 21 Sept. 1947 and undated [1947] (HALS, DIERV C2482/88-9).

313.Londonderry, *Retrospect*, pp 224-25. Charley published *Wings of destiny* in 1943. In a spirit of self-vindication, he, the alleged friend of Hitler, made his position clear: 'We rightly condemn the Germans for their ruthlessness, their brutality and their negation of freedom…Hitler…aspired to muster the entire German-speaking race within frontiers of their own choosing, and not as intended by the conqueror at Versailles. [NP] Hitler was allowed to carry out these plans, without let or hindrance' (Londonderry, *Wings*, pp 2-3).

314.E to Hyde, undated [c. 1939] (PRONI, D/3084/C/E/6/100).

315.Stuart Ball (ed.), *Parliament and politics in the age of Churchill and Atlee. The Headlam diaries, 1935-51* (Cambridge, 1999), p. 145, p. 182 and p. 441.

316.Henry Rowlands to E, 1 June undated [c. 1940s] (PRONI, D/3099/3/2/951).

317.E to Hyde, 29 Dec. 1947 (PRONI, D/3084/C/E/2/10).

318.Andrew Barrow, *Gossip: A history of high society from 1920-70* (London, 1978), p. 196.

319.*Irish Times*, 17 Aug. 1957.

320.A memorial service was later held at St. Paul's in Knightsbridge.

321.*Daily Telegraph*, 21 Nov. 1933.

322.E to Charley, 1938, cited Pauley, 'Edith', p. 34. In the late 1930s Charley was remorseful and they discussed their relationship at length.

323.Ibid., 14 Oct. [1924], cited Pauley, 'Edith', p. 229.

324.Macmillan, *Winds*, p. 196.

325.*Sunday Graphic*, 15 Sept. 1935.

326.*Evening Standard*, 7 Feb. 1928 and James, *Chips*, p. 35.

327.Masters, *Great hostesses*, p. 7.

328.MacDonald to E, 17 Sept. 1931 (PRONI, D/3084/C/D/4/69-70).

329.Williams, *Ladies*, cited p. 26.

330.E to Charley, 26 Nov. 1939, cited Pauley, 'Edith', p. 406.

331.Ibid., 1927 and 17 Nov. 1931, p. 407.

332.Ibid., 26 May 1936. Edith's early feminism never left her. Much of her philanthropic work was directed towards improving women's lot and she often urged women to use their hard won rights responsibly. She was, for instance, president of the Girls' Realm Guild of Service and Good Fellowship that was founded to assist the deserving poor in 1900 and Pioneer Clubs for Girls that included Unionist instruction in its weekly meetings. She was a member of the Ulster Women and Children Committee that was formed to plan evacuation schemes if civil war in Ulster should occur in 1914. Post-World War One she was president of the Central Bureau for the Employment of Women and chair of the Ex-Service Women's Association dealing with the demobilisation, emigration and transferral of several thousand Women's Legion members into civilian occupations. She supported an array of hospitals for women and those dealing with specific diseases such as tuberculosis as well as district nursing as chair of the Queen's Institute of District Nurses in Northern Ireland, the rehabilitation of women prisoners, nursery schools, domestic servants (joining the Women's Advisory Committee on this issue in the 1920s), the Red Cross and hostels for women. She was a member of the Central National Service Committee (GB) and promoted linen and lacemaking in Co. Down where she ran an embroidery school. She also campaigned for additional female student accommodation at St. Hilda's, Oxford and a memorial scholarship at Bedford College for suffragist, Millicent Fawcett.

333.E, article 'Women in war', 12 May 1938 (PRONI, D/3099/3/38/6). Her opposition to suffragette activity in the earlier part of the century softened in the 1930s.

334.In 1948 Edith also accepted the presidency of Houghton-Le-Spring Ladies' Divisional Conservative Association in Durham. Lord Londonderry was president of the Conservative Association in the same constituency.

335.Londonderry, *Chaplin*, p. 2.

336.Londonderry, *Retrospect*, pp 251-54.

Conclusion

1. James, *Chips,* p. 28.

2. The ninth Marquess occupied one wing of Seaham Hall in the 1960s.

3. Hyde, *Londonderry House*, cited p. vi. The seventh Marquess returned to this theme in his 1943 publication, *Wings of destiny* when he remarked on the change in political society evident in the early 1930s: 'it was very different even in the days when I was a young man. Then politics were more or less confined to a small circle. This small group of party leaders used to meet and dine regularly at one another's houses and the discussions were wholly political. They were on terms of the greatest intimacy, and this also applied in their private dealings with their political rivals, except on rare occasions when party feelings ran unusually high. [NP] To-day…Ministers seldom meet each other officially, and rarely socially…most contacts are made by letters or messenger and the familiar departmental "box"' (Londonderry, *Wings*, pp 83-84). On the changing fortunes of the aristocracy, see Cannadine, *The decline and fall*.

4. *Evening News*, 9 Dec. 1924. Portland House, Holland House, Apsley House and Bridgewater House also survived. Visiting Londonderry House with his father in 1934, Wil-

liam Buchan reminisced that he witnessed 'something which, I perhaps half knew, I might not see again' (Buchan, *John Buchan*, p. 192).

5. *Belfast News-Letter*, 28 Jan. 1947.
6. Seaham Hall is now a spa hotel and Wynyard, a grade II listed mansion, is a conference centre. The latter went on sale with 768 of its acres for £8 million in 2003.
7. Davidoff, *Best circles*, p. 61.
8. Stuart, *Dear Duchess*, p. 115. See also PRONI, D/2846/3/11/1.
9. R. W. Sturgess, 'Landowners and coal in Co. Durham, 1815-50' in M. D. G. Wanklyn (ed.), *Landownership and power in the regions* (Wolverhampton, 1978), p. 96. The Vane-Tempest colliery finally closed in 1993.
10. Cornelius O'Leary, *The elimination of corrupt practices in British elections, 1868-1911* (Oxford, 1962), p. 233.
11. W. L. Guttsman, 'The changing social structure of the British political elite, 1886-1935' in *The British Journal of Sociology*, vol. 2, issue 2 (June 1951), p. 123 and *passim*. By 1955 only twelve sons of peers and baronets sat in the Commons. See also Davidoff, *Best circles*, p. 95.
12. John Mulhall to T, 23 Sept. 1917 (PRONI, D/2846/2/22/62) and *Lady's Pictorial*, 25 October 1919.
13. *Belfast Telegraph*, 18 June 1949.
14. Peeresses by succession were admitted to Lords in 1963 but no Marchioness of Londonderry ever sat in the upper house.
15. Nevill, *Reminiscences*, p. 121 and Mrs. George Cornwallis-West, *The reminiscences of Lady Randolph Churchill* (London, 1908), p. 39.
16. Arthur Ponsonby, *The decline of the aristocracy* (London, 1912), p. 16, p. 135, p. 138, p. 306 and p. 320.
17. Nevill, *Lady Dorothy Nevill*, p. 210.
18. See W. D. Rubinstein, *Elites and the wealthy in modern British history* (Sussex, 1987), p. 163 and p. 222. This increase and the practice of selling honours were remarked upon. For instance, Lord Selbourne complained to Lord Lansdowne about the sale of honours in 1912, suggesting that the practice should not only be discontinued but also renounced by the Conservative Party. Although Lansdowne sympathised he felt nothing could be done whilst the party remained in opposition (see Bonar Law correspondence, 15 May 1912 (Parliamentary Archives, HL/BL/26/3/21)).
19. *Northampton Evening Telegraph*, 22 June 1933.
20. See, for example, Reynolds, *Aristocratic women* where she claims that by the 1890s 'the political culture had altered to such an extent that the influence of the aristocratic political hostess was essentially redundant. ...The broadening of the franchise and the rise of a more plutocratic society both served to marginalise women in politics', p. 172 and p. 187.
21. E noted, for example, 'Few things have given me more satisfaction than when the women's Franchise Bill was passed' (E, 'Armistice Day').
22. *Scotsman*, 2 Feb. 1932.
23. *London Mail*, 12 Dec. 1924.
24. Garry O'Connor, *Sean O'Casey: A life* (New York, 1988), cited p. 244.
25. Londonderry, *Retrospect*, pp 251-53.

Bibliography

Primary sources
British Library
Robert Peel papers

Brotherton Collection, Leeds University Library
Edmund Gosse papers

Cambridge University Library
Stanley Baldwin papers

Centre for Kentish Studies, Maidstone
Earl of Camden papers

Durham County Record Office
Londonderry archive

Hertfordshire Archives and Local Studies
Lady Desborough papers

The National Archives, Kew
James Ramsay MacDonald papers

Parliamentary Archives, House of Lords
Andrew Bonar Law papers

John Rylands University Library, University of Manchester
James Ramsay MacDonald papers

Public Record Office of Northern Ireland
Antrim estate papers
Carson papers
Castlereagh papers
Court of Chancery papers
Craigavon papers
H. Montgomery Hyde papers

Lisburn Women's Unionist Association papers
Londonderry papers
Lurgan Women's Unionist Association papers
North Down Women's Unionist Association papers
Northern Ireland Ministry of Finance papers
Spender papers
Ulster Unionist Council papers
Ulster Women's Unionist Council papers

University of Birmingham
Neville Chamberlain papers

Newspapers and periodicals

Answers	*London Mail*
Belfast News-Letter	*London Illustrated News*
Belfast Telegraph	*Morning Post*
Birmingham Evening Dispatch	*Newcastle Journal*
Birmingham Post	*The New Times*
Cambridge Daily News	*New York Herald*
Church of Ireland Gazette	*New York World Telegram*
Country Life	*North Mail*
The Courier	*Northampton Evening Telegraph*
Court Journal	*Northern Whig*
Daily Chronicle	*Punch*
Daily Express	*The Queen*
Daily Herald	*Saturday Review*
Daily Independent	*The Scotsman*
Daily Mail	*The Sketch*
Daily Mirror	*The Sphere*
Daily Sketch	*The Standard*
Daily Telegraph	*The Star*
Darlington and Stockton Times	*Sunday Chronicle*
Evening Chronicle	*Sunday Graphic*
Evening News	*Sunday Herald*
Evening Standard	*Sunday News*
Evening World	*Sunday Referee*
Glasgow Herald	*Sunday Sun*
The Globe	*The Sunday Times*
The Graphic	*The Times*
Irish Independent	*TP's and Cassell's Weekly*
Irish Times	*Ulster Tatler*
Lady's Pictorial	*Vogue*
Le Cri de Paris	*Women's Pictorial*
Liverpool Daily Post and Mercury	*Yorkshire Evening Press*

Secondary sources

Adams, R. J. Q., *Bonar Law* (London, 1999).

Adonis, Andrew, *Making aristocracy work: the peerage and the political system in Britain, 1884-1914* (Oxford, 1993).

Airlie, Mabel, Countess of, *In Whig society, 1775-1818* (London, 1921).

Aldis, Janet, *Madame Geoffin. Her salon and times* (second ed., London, 1906).

Alison, Archibald, *Lives of Lord Castlereagh and Sir Charles Stewart* (3 vols., Edinburgh and London, 1861).

Almedingen, E. M., *The Emperor Alexander I* (London, 1964).

Altman, J. G., *Epistolarity: Approaches to a form* (Ohio, 1982).

Amory, Cleveland, *Who killed society?* (New York, 1960).

Antrim, Angela, *The Antrim McDonnells* (Belfast, 1977).

Apperley, N. W., *A hunting diary* (London, 1926).

Aspinall, A. (ed.), *The correspondence of George Arbuthnot* (third series, vol. 65, London, 1941).

---- *The correspondence of George, the Prince of Wales, 1770-1812* (8 vols., London, 1971).

---- *The letters of King George IV, 1812-30* (3 vols., Cambridge, 1938).

---- *Three early nineteenth-century diaries* (London, 1952).

Asquith, Cynthia, *Diaries, 1915-18* (London, 1968).

Asquith, Margot, *Off the record* (London, 1944).

---- *The autobiography of Margot Asquith* (London, 1920).

Atholl, Duchess of, *Women and politics* (London, 1931).

Bagot, Josceline (ed.), *George Canning and his friends containing hitherto unpublished letters, jeux d'esprit, etc.* (2 vols., London, 1909).

Balfour, Patrick, *Society racket. A critical survey of modern social life* (London, 1933).

Ball, Stuart (ed.), *Parliament and politics in the age of Baldwin and MacDonald. The Headlam diaries, 1923-35* (London, 1992).

---- *Parliament and politics in the age of Churchill and Atlee. The Headlam diaries, 1935-51* (Cambridge, 1999).

Bamford, Francis and Wellington, the Duke of (eds), *The journal of Mrs. Arbuthnot, 1820-32* (2 vols., London, 1950).

Banks, Olive, *The biographical dictionary of British feminists. A supplement, 1900-45* (vol. 2, Hemel Hempstead, 1990).

Barrow, Andrew, *Gossip: A history of high society from 1920-70* (London, 1978).

Bartlett, C. J., *Castlereagh* (London, 1966).

Bartley, Paula, *The changing role of women, 1814-1914* (London, 1996).

Bateman, John, *The great landowners of Great Britain and Ireland* (Leicester, 1971 reprint of 1876 ed.).

Beaverbrook, Lord, *The decline and fall of Lloyd George* (London, 1963).

Beckett, J. C., *The Anglo-Irish tradition* (Belfast, 1976).

Beckett, J. V., *The aristocracy in England, 1660-1914* (Oxford, 1986).

Bell, Peter, *Victorian women. An index to biographies and memoirs* (Edinburgh, 1989).

Bence-Jones, Mark, *Twilight of the ascendancy* (London, 1987).

---- and Massingberd, Hugh Montgomery, *The British aristocracy* (London, 1979).

Benson, A. C. and Esher, Viscount (eds), *The letters of Queen Victoria. A selection from her Majesty's correspondence between the years 1837-61* (first series, 3 vols., London, 1908).

Benson, E. F., *As we were. A Victorian peep-show* (London, 1971 reprint of 1930 ed.).

Benyon, Huw and Austin, Terry, *Masters and servants. Class and patronage in the making of a labour organisation. The Durham miners and English political tradition* (London, 1994).

Best, Geoffrey, *Mid Victorian Britain, 1851-75* (London, 1971).

Biddulph, Violet, *The three Ladies Waldergrave (and their mother)* (London, 1938).

Blake, Robert, *Disraeli* (London, 1966).

---- The unknown Prime Minister. The life and times of Andrew Bonar Law, 1858-1923 (London, 1955).

---- and Lewis, William Roger, Churchill (Oxford, 1993).

Bolitho, Victor (ed.), Further letters from Queen Victoria. From the archives of the house of Brandenburg-Prussia (London, 1938).

Bonham Carter, Violet, Winston Churchill as I knew him, volume one to 1916 (London, 1965).

Bott, Alan and Clephane, Irene (eds), Our mothers. A cavalcade in pictures, quotation and description of late Victorian women, 1870-1900 (London, 1932).

Bourne, J. M., Patronage and society in nineteenth-century England (London, 1986).

Bovill, E. W., English country life, 1780-1830 (Oxford, 1962).

Bradford, Sarah, Disraeli (London, 1982).

Bromhead, P. A., The House of Lords and contemporary politics, 1911-57 (London, 1958).

Brooks, David, The age of upheaval. Edwardian politics, 1899-1914 (Manchester and New York, 1995).

Brownlow, Emma, Countess of, The eve of Victorianism. Reminiscences of the years 1802 to 1834 (London, 1940).

William Buchan, John Buchan. A memoir (London, 1982).

Buckland, Patrick, Irish Unionism, 1885-1923. A documentary history (Belfast, 1973).

Buckle, George Earle (ed.), The letters of Queen Victoria. A selection from her Majesty's correspondence and journals between the years 1862 and 1878 (second series, 3 vols., London, 1926).

---- The letters of Queen Victoria. A selection from her Majesty's correspondence and journals between the years 1886 and 1901 (third series, 3 vols., London, 1930).

---- The life of Benjamin Disraeli, Earl of Beaconsfield, 1855-68 (vols. 4-6, London, 1916 and 1920).

Burke, J. B, The landed gentry of Ireland (London, 1858, 1899, 1904, 1912).

Bush, Julia, Edwardian ladies and imperial power (London and New York, 2000).

Callwell, C. E., Field-Marshall Sir Henry Wilson. His life and diaries (2 vols., London, 1927).

Cameron, Charles, Anecdotes and memories of a freeman of Dublin (Dublin, 1913).

Campbell, John, F. E. Smith. first Earl Birkenhead (London, 1985).

Cannadine, David, Aspects of aristocracy. Grandeur and decline in modern Britain (London, 1994).

---- Class in Britain (London, 1998).

---- The decline and fall of the British aristocracy (London, 1990).

Canning, Paul, British policy towards Ireland, 1921-41 (Oxford, 1985).

Chalkin, C. W. and Wordie, J. R. (eds), Town and countryside. The English landowner in the national economy, 1660-1860 (London, 1989).

Chamberlain, Austen, Down the years (London, 1935).

Chapman-Huston, Desmond (ed.), Daisy Princess Pless by herself (London, 1928).

Charteris, Evan, The life and letters of Sir Edmund Gosse (London, 1931).

Choiseul-Gouffier, Madam La Comtesse de, Historical memoirs of the Emperor Alexander I and the court of Russia (trans. by M. B. Patterson, London, 1904).

Christie, Christopher, The British country house in the eighteenth century (Manchester, 2000).

Churchill, Randolph S. and Gilbert, Martin (eds), Winston S. Churchill, 1874-1945 (7 vols., London, 1966-86).

Churchill, Winston S., The Second World War. The gathering storm (London, 1948).

Colchester, Lord (ed.), Lord Ellenborough. A practical diary, 1828-30 (2 vols., London, 1881).

Cole, Margaret (ed.), Beatrice Webb's diaries, 1912-32 (2 vols., London, 1952 and 1956).

Colley, Linda, Britons. Forging the nation, 1707-1837 (New Haven and London, 1992).

Colls, Robert, The pitmen of the northern coalfield. Work, culture, and protest, 1790-1850 (Manchester, 1987).

---- and Dodd, Philip (eds), *Englishness: culture and politics, 1880-1920* (New Hampshire, 1986).

Coogan, Tim Pat, *Michael Collins. A biography* (London, 1990).

Corelli, Marie, *Free opinions freely expressed on certain phases of modern social life and conduct* (London, 1905).

Cornwallis-West, George, *Edwardian hey-days. A little about a lot of things* (London, 1930).

Cornwallis-West, Mrs. George, *The reminiscences of Lady Randolph Churchill* (London, 1908).

Cosgrove, Art and McGuire, J. I. (eds), *Parliament and community. Historical Studies XIV* (Belfast, 1983).

Cowling, Maurice, *The impact of Labour, 1920-24* (Cambridge, 1971).

Davidoff, Leonore, *The best circles. Society, etiquette and the season* (London, 1973).

---- *Worlds between. Historical perspectives on gender and class* (Cambridge, 1995).

de Courcy, Anne, *Society's Queen. The life of Edith Marchioness of Londonderry* (London, 2004, originally published as *Circe. The life of Edith, Marchioness of Londonderry* (London, 1992)).

---- *The Viceroy's daughters. The lives of the Curzon sisters* (London, 2000).

---- *1939. The last season* (London, 1989).

de Vere White, Terence, *The Anglo-Irish* (London, 1972).

Derry, J. W., *Castlereagh* (London, 1976).

Disraeli, Benjamin, *Sybil or the two nations* (London, 1927 reprint of 1845 ed.).

Disraeli, Ralph (ed.), *Lord Beaconsfield's correspondence with his sister, 1832-52* (London, 1886).

---- *Home letters written by the late Earl of Beaconsfield in 1830 and 1831* (London, 1885).

Donner, Patrick, *Crusade* (London, 1984).

Dooley, Terence, *Sources for the history of the landed estates in Ireland* (Dublin, 2000).

Durham County Council, *The Londonderry papers. Catalogue of the documents deposited in the Durham County Record Office by the ninth Marquess of Londonderry* (Durham, 1969).

Dutton, David, *'His Majesty's Loyal Opposition'. The Unionist party in opposition, 1905-15* (Liverpool, 1992).

Dziewanowski, M. K., *Alexander I. Russia's mysterious tsar* (New York, 1990).

Elton, Godfrey, *The life of James Ramsay MacDonald (1866-1919)* (London, 1939).

Escott, T. H. S., *Society in London* (London, 1885).

Feuchtwanger, Edgar, *Disraeli* (London, 2000).

Fingall, Elizabeth, Countess of, *Seventy years young. Memoirs of Elizabeth, Countess of Fingall told to Pamela Hinkson* (Dublin, 1991 reprint of London, 1937 ed.).

Fitzroy, Almeric, *Memoirs* (2 vols., London, 1938).

Fleming, N. C., *The Marquess of Londonderry. Aristocracy, power and politics in Britain and Ireland* (London, 2005).

Foreman, Amanda, *Georgiana. Duchess of Devonshire* (London, 1998).

Fowler, Marian, *In a gilded cage. From heiress to duchess* (London, 1993).

Fraser, Flora, *The English gentlewoman* (London, 1987).

Garside, W. R., *The Durham miners, 1919-60* (London, 1971).

Gash, Norman *et al*, *The Conservatives. A history from their origins to 1965* (London, 1977).

Genet, Jacqueline (ed.), *The big house in Ireland. Reality and representation* (Dingle, 1991).

Girouard, Mark, *Life in the English country house. A social and architectural history* (New Haven and London, 1978).

Gleadle, K. and Richardson, S. (eds), *Women in British politics, 1760-1980. The power of the petticoat* (Hampshire, 2000).

Goldsmith, Annabel, *Annabel. An unconventional life* (London, 2004).

Gore, John (ed.), *Creevey's life and times. A further selection from the correspondence of Thomas Creevey (1768-1838)* (London, 1934).

Gunn, J. A. W., Matthews, John, Schurman, Donald S. and Wiebe, M. B. (eds), *Benjamin Disraeli's letters, 1813-37* (2 vols., Buffalo and London, 1982).

Hamilton, M. A., *J. Ramsay MacDonald* (London, 1929).

Hanham, H. J., *Elections and party management. Politics in the time of Disraeli and Gladstone* (Sussex, 1978 reprint of 1959 ed.).

Hardwick, Mollie, *Mrs. Dizzy: the life of Mary Anne Disraeli, Viscountess Beaconsfield* (London, 1972).

Harris, Jose, *Private lives, public spirit. A social history of Britain, 1870-1914* (Oxford, 1993).

Hartley, Janet A., *Alexander I* (London and New York, 1994).

Heesom, A. J., *Durham City and its MPs* (Durham, 1992).

Hendershot Park, Joseph, *British Prime Ministers in the nineteenth century. Policies and speeches* (New York, 1916).

Hibbert, Christopher, *Disraeli. A personal history* (London, 2004).

---- *Disraeli and his world* (London, 1978).

Hicks Beach, Victoria, *Life of Sir Michael Hicks Beach* (Earl St. Aldwyn) (vol. 2, London, 1932)

Holton, Sandra Stanley, *Suffrage days. Stories from the women's suffrage movement* (London and New York, 1996).

Hunt, Hugh, *Sean O'Casey* (Dublin, 1980).

Ilchester, Earl of (ed.), *Elizabeth, Lady Holland to her son, 1821-45* (London, 1946).

Jackman, S. W. (ed.), *Romanov relations. The private correspondence of the Tsars Alexander I, Nicolas I and the Grand Dukes Constantine and Michael with their sister Queen Anna Pavlovna, 1817-55* (London, 1969).

Jackson, T. A., *Colonel Edward Saunderson. Land and loyalty in Victorian Ireland* (Oxford, 1995).

Jalland, Patricia, *Women, marriage and politics, 1860-1914* (Oxford, 1986).

James, Robert Rhodes (ed.), *Chips. The diaries of Sir Henry Channon* (London, 1967).

---- *Memoirs of a Conservative. J. C. C. Davidson's memoirs and papers, 1910-37* (London, 1969).

Jenkins, Roy, *Baldwin* (London, 1987).

Jenkins, T. A., *Parliament, party and politics in Victorian Britain* (Manchester, 1996).

Jennings, Louis J., *The correspondence and diaries of the late Right Honourable John Wilson Croker* (3 vols., London, 1884).

Jersey, Dowager Countess of, *Fifty-one years of Victorian life* (London, 1922).

Jones, C. and Jones, D. L. (eds), *Peers, politics and power. The House of Lords, 1603-1911* (London, 1986).

Jones Parry, E. (ed.), *The correspondence of Lord Aberdeen and Princess Lieven, 1832-54* (2 vols., London, 1938).

Kchoe, Elizabeth, *Fortune's daughters. The extravagant lives of the Jerome sisters. Jennie Churchill, Clara Frewen and Leonie Leslie* (London, 2004).

Kendle, John, *Walter Long, Ireland, and the Union, 1905-20* (Montreal, London and Buffalo, 1992).

Kershaw, Ian, *Making friends with Hitler. Lord Londonderry and Britain's road to war* (London, 2004).

Klimenko, Michael, *Notes of Alexander I, Emperor of Russia* (New York, 1988).

Krause, David (ed.), *The letters of Sean O'Casey, 1910-41* (3 vols., London, 1975).

Kriegal, Abraham D. (ed.), *The Holland House diaries. The diary of Richard Vassall Fox, third Lord Holland* (London, 1977).

Lacey, Robert, *Aristocrats* (London, 1983).

Lambert, Angela, *Unquiet souls. The Indian summer of the British aristocracy, 1880-1918* (London, 1984).

Layard, George Soames (ed.), *Sir Thomas Lawrence's letter-bag* (London, 1906).

Le Strange, Guy (ed. and trans.), *Correspondence of Princess Lieven and Earl Grey, 1824-41* (3 vols., London, 1890).

Lees-Milne, James, *Harold Nicolson. A biography, 1886-1929* (London, 1980).

Legh, Thomas Wodehouse (Lord Newton), *Lord Lansdowne. A biography* (London, 1929).

Leigh, Ione, *Castlereagh* (London, 1951).

Leslie, Anita, *Edwardians in love* (London, 1972).

Lewis, Jane, *Women in England, 1870-1950* (London, 1984).

Lewis, Judith S., *In the family way. Childbearing in the British aristocracy, 1760-1860* (New Jersey, 1986).

---- *Sacred to female patriotism. Gender, class and politics in late Georgian Britain* (New York and London, 2003).

Lewis, Samuel, *A topographical dictionary of Ireland* (vol. 2, second ed., London, 1937).

Liddell, Adrian, *An illustrated history of Wynyard Estate through the passage of time* (Wolviston, 1989).

Lieven, Domonic, *The aristocracy in Europe, 1815-1914* (London, 1992).

List and Index Society, Public Record Office, *Ramsay MacDonald correspondence, 1890-1937* (vol. 199, London, 1983).

Littlejohn, David, *The fate of the English country house* (Oxford, 1997).

Londonderry, Theresa, sixth Marchioness of, *Robert Stewart. Viscount Castlereagh* (London, 1904).

Londonderry, Charles, seventh Marquess of, *Ourselves and Germany* (Harmondsworth, 1938).

---- *Wings of destiny* (London, 1943).

Londonderry, Edith, seventh Marchioness of, *Character and tradition* (London, 1934).

---- *Henry Chaplin. A memoir. Prepared by his daughter* (London, 1926).

---- *Retrospect* (London, 1938)

---- *The Land of the Living Heart* (privately printed, undated [1940s]).

---- *The life and times of Frances Anne Marchioness of Londonderry and her husband Charles third Marquess of Londonderry* (London and New York, 1958).

---- (ed.), *Letters from Benjamin Disraeli to France Anne Marchioness of Londonderry, 1837-61* (London, 1938).

---- and Montgomery Hyde, H. (eds), *The Russian journals of Martha and Catherine Wilmot, 1803-08* (London, 1934).

---- *More letters from Martha Wilmot: Impressions of Vienna, 1819-29* (London, 1935).

Londonderry, ninth Marquess of, *The Londonderry Album. Portraits from a great house in the 1890s* (London, 1978).

Long, Walter, *Memories* (London, 1923).

Luytens, Mary (ed.), *Lady Lytton's court diary, 1895-99* (London, 1961).

MacNeill Weir, L., *The tragedy of Ramsay MacDonald: a political biography* (London, 1938).

McConnell, Allen, *Tsar Alexander I. Paternalistic reformer* (Illinois, 1970).

McCoole, Sinead, *Hazel: A life of Lady Lavery* (Dublin, 1996).

Macbeth, George, *Dizzy's Women* (London, 1986).

Machin, Ian, *Disraeli* (New York and London, 1995).

Mackenzie, Norman (ed.), *The letters of Sidney and Beatrice Webb, 1873-1947* (3 vols., Cambridge, 1978).

---- and Mackenzie, Jeanne (eds), *The diary of Beatrice Webb, 1873-92. Glitter around darkness within* (vol. 1, London, 1982).

Mackintosh, John P., *British Prime Ministers in the twentieth century. Balfour to Chamberlain* (vol. 1, London, 1979).

Macmillan, Harold, *Winds of change, 1914-39* (London, 1966).

Maguire, G. E., *Conservative women: a history of women in the Conservative Party, 1874-1997* (Basingstoke, 1998).

Malcolmson, A. P. W., *The pursuit of the heiress: aristocratic marriage in Ireland, 1750-1820* (Belfast, 1982).

Malmesbury, Earl of, *Memoirs of an ex-minister. An autobiography* (2 vols., second ed., London, 1884).

Mandler, Peter, *The fall and rise of the stately home* (New Haven and London, 1997).

Marquand, David, *Ramsay MacDonald* (London, 1977).

Martel, Gordon (ed.), *The Times and appeasement. The journals of A. L. Kennedy, 1932-39* (Cambridge, 2000).

Martineau, Harriet, *Biographical sketches, 1852-62* (third ed., London, 1870).

Marwick, Arthur, *Women at war, 1914-18* (London, 1977).

Masters, Brian, *Great hostesses* (London, 1982).

---- *Wynyard Hall and the Londonderry family* (Teeside, 1973).

Maurois, Andre, *Disraeli: A picture of the Victorian age* (trans. by Hamish Miles, London, 1927).

Maxwell, Herbert, *The Creevy papers. A selection from the correspondence and diaries of the late Thomas Creevy, MP* (2 vols., London, 1904).

Middlemass, Keith (ed.), *Thomas Jones Whitehall diaries, 1916-30* (2 vols., London, 1969).

---- and Barnes, John, *Baldwin. A biography* (London, 1969).

Mitchell, Leslie, *Holland House* (London, 1980).

Monypenny, W. F. (ed.), *The life of Benjamin Disraeli, Earl of Beaconsfield, 1804-60* (2 vols., London, 1910 and 1912).

---- and Buckle, G. E. (eds), *The life of Benjamin Disraeli, Earl of Beaconsfield, 1846-55* (vol. 3, London, 1914).

Montgomery Hyde, H., *British air policy between the wars, 1918-39* (London, 1976).

---- *Londonderry House and its pictures* (London, 1937).

---- *Princess Lieven* (London, 1938).

---- *The Londonderrys. A family portrait* (London, 1979).

Morgan, Austen, *J. Ramsay MacDonald* (Manchester, 1987).

Nevill, Ralph (ed.), *Lady Dorothy Nevill. My own times* (London, 1912).

---- *Lady Dorothy Nevill. Under five reigns* (London, 1910).

---- *The life and letters of Lady Dorothy Nevill* (London, 1919).

---- *The reminiscences of Lady Dorothy Nevill* (London, 1906).

Nicolas, Grand Duke (ed.), *Scenes of Russian court life. Being the correspondence of Alexander I with his sister Catherine* (trans. by Henry Havelock, London, 1917).

Nicolson, N. (ed.), *A reflection of the other person. The letters of Virginia Wolfe* (vol. 4, London, 1978).

---- *Harold Nicolson. Diaries and letters, 1930-45* (2 vols., London, 1966-67).

Nossiter, N. J, *Influence, opinion and political idioms in reformed England. Case studies from the North-East, 1832-74* (Brighton, 1975).

O'Casey, Eileen, *Sean* (London, 1971).

O'Casey, Sean, *Rose and crown* (London, 1952).

O'Connor, Garry, *Sean O'Casey. A life* (New York, 1988).

O'Day, Alan, *Irish home rule, 1867-1921* (Manchester and New York, 1998).

O'Leary, Cornelius, *The elimination of corrupt practices in British elections, 1868-1911* (Oxford, 1962).

Oxford and Asquith, Margot, Countess of, *Myself when young by famous women of to-day* (London, 1938).

Palmer, Alan, *Alexander I. Tsar of war and peace* (London, 1974).

Parry, E, James (ed.), *The correspondence of Lord Aberdeen and Princess Lieven, 1832-54* (2 vols., London, 1938).

Perkin, Joan, *Women and marriage in nineteenth-century England* (London, 1989).

Pevsner, Nikolaus, *The buildings of England: Co. Durham* (London, 1983).

Phillips, Gregory D., *The Diehards. Aristocratic society and politics in Edwardian England* (Massachusetts and London, 1979).

Pimlott, Ben (ed.), *The political diary of Hugh Dalton, 1918-40, 1945-60* (London, 1986).

Pointon, Marcia, *Strategies for showing. Women, possession and representation in English visual culture, 1665-1800* (Oxford, 1997).

Ponsonby, A., *The decline of the aristocracy* (London, 1912).

Portland, Duke of, *Men, women and things. Memories of the Duke of Portland* (London, 1937).

Powis, Jonathan, *Aristocracy* (Oxford, 1984).

Pugh, Martin, *The Tories and the people, 1800-1935* (Oxford, 1985).

---- *Women and the women's movement in Britain, 1914-59* (Basingstoke, 1992).

Quennell, Peter (ed.), *Genius in the drawing room. The literary salon in the nineteenth and twentieth centuries* (London, 1980).

---- *The letters of Princess Lieven to Prince Metternich, 1820-26* (London, 1937).

Ramsden, John, *An appetite for power. A history of the Conservative Party since 1800* (London, 1998).

Rendall, Jane, *Equal or different. Women's politics, 1800-1914* (Oxford, 1987).

Reynolds, K. D., *Aristocratic women and political society in Victorian Britain* (Oxford, 1998).

Rhondda, Viscountess, *This was my world* (London, 1933).

Robb, J. H., *The Primrose League, 1883-1906* (New York, 1968).

Robinson, J. M., *The Wyatts: an architectural dynasty* (Oxford, 1979).

Rolo, P. J. V., *George Canning. Three biographical studies* (London, 1965).

Rubenstein, W. D., *Elites and the wealthy in modern British history* (Sussex, 1987).

---- *Men of property. The very wealthy in Britain since the industrial revolution* (London, 1981).

Sackville-West, Vita, *The Edwardians* (London, 1930).

Sadler, Thomas (ed.), *Diary, reminiscences and correspondence of Henry Crabb Robinson* (2 vols., London and New York, 1872).

Sanford, John Langton and Townsend, Meredith, *The great governing families of England* (vol. 1, Edinburgh and London, 1865).

Saunders, David, *Russia in the age of reaction and reform, 1801-81* (London and New York, 1992).

Seaman, W. A. L. and Sewell, J. R., *Russian journal of Lady Londonderry, 1836-37* (London, 1973).

Self, Robert C. (ed.), *The Austen Chamberlain diary letters. The correspondence of Sir Austen Chamberlain with his sisters Hilda and Ida, 1916-37* (Cambridge, 1995).

Shannon, Richard, *The age of Salisbury, 1881-1902: Unionism and empire* (London and New York, 1996).

Shiman, Lillian Lewis, *Women and leadership in nineteenth-century England* (Basingstoke, 1992).

Shoemaker, Robert B., *Gender in English society, 1650-1850: The emergence of separate spheres* (Essex, 1998).

Shkolnik, Esther Simon, *Leading ladies: a study of eight late Victorian and Edwardian political wives* (New York and London, 1987).

Smart, Nick (ed.), *The diaries and letters of Robert Bernays, 1932-39. An insider's account of the House of Commons* (New York, 1996).

---- *The National Government, 1931-41* (Basingstoke, 1999).

Smith, E. A., *The House of Lords in British politics and society, 1815-1911* (London and New York, 1992).

Smith, F. E., *Contemporary personalities* (London, 1924).

Smith, Jeremy, *The Tories and Ireland, 1910-14. Conservative Party politics and the Home Rule crisis* (Dublin, 2000).

Squibb, G. D., *Precedence in England and Wales* (Oxford, 1981).

St. Helier, Lady (Mary Jeune), *Memories of fifty years* (London, 1909).

Stacey, Margaret and Price, Marion, *Women, power and politics* (London and New York, 1981).

Stanley, L. (ed.), *The London season* (London, 1955).

Stewart, Robert, *The foundation of the Conservative Party, 1830-67* (London and New York, 1978).

Strakhovsky, Leonid I., *Alexander I of Russia* (London, 1949).

Stuart, Denis, *Dear Duchess. Millicent Duchess of Sutherland, 1867-1955* (London, 1982).

Sturgess, R. W., *Aristocrat in business. The third Marquis of Londonderry as coalowner and port-builder* (Durham, 1975).

Sudley, Lord (trans. and ed.), *The Lieven Palmerston correspondence, 1828-56* (London, 1943).

Sutherland, fifth Duke of, *Looking back. The autobiography of the Duke of Sutherland* (London, 1957).

Swartz, Helen M and Swartz, Martin (eds), *Disraeli's reminiscences* (London, 1975).

Sykes, Christopher, *Nancy: the life of Lady Nancy Astor* (London, 1972).

---- *Private palaces. Life in the great country houses* (London, 1985).

Taylor, A. J. P. (ed.), *Lloyd George. A diary by Frances Stevenson* (London, 1971).

Temperley, H. W. V, *Life of Canning* (London, 1905).

Thompson, F. L. M., *English landed society in the nineteenth century* (London and Toronto, 1963).

Thwaite, Anne, *Edmund Gosse: a literary landscape 1849-1928* (London, 1984).

Tillyard, Stella, *Aristocrats. Caroline, Emily, Louisa and Sarah Lennox, 1740-1832* (London, 1995).

Tiltman, H. Hessell, *James Ramsay MacDonald. Labour's man of destiny* (London, 1929).

Troyat, Henri, *Alexander of Russia: Napoleon's conqueror* (Sevenoaks, 1982).

Turberville, A. S., *The House of Lords in the age of reform, 1784-1837* (London, 1958).

Vickery, Amanda (ed.), *Women, privilege, and power. British politics, 1750 to the present* (Stanford, 2001).

Vincent, John (ed.), *The Crawford papers. The journals of David Lindsay twenty-seventh Earl of Crawford and tenth Earl of Balcarres, 1871-1940 during the years 1892 to 1940* (Manchester, 1984).

Walford, E., *County families in the United Kingdom* (London, 1918).

Warwick, Frances, Countess of, *Afterthoughts* (London, 1931).

Webb, Sidney, *The story of the Durham miners, 1662-1921* (London, 1921).

Weintraub, Stanley, *Disraeli. A biography* (London, 1993).

Wellington, Duke of (ed.), *Dispatches, correspondence and memoranda of Field Marshall Arthur Duke of Wellington* (vols. 1-2, London, 1867 and 1868).

---- *Dispatches, correspondence and memoranda of Field Marshall Arthur Duke of Wellington* (vols. 7 and 8, London, 1868 and 1880).

---- *Wellington and his friends. Letters to the first Duke of Wellington to the Rt. Hon. Charles and Mrs Arbuthnot, the Earl and Countess of Wilton, Princess Lieven and Miss Burdett-Coutts* (London, 1965).

Wheeler, Michael, *Death and the future life in Victorian literature and theology* (Cambridge, 1990).

Whittaker, Neville and Clark, Ursula, *Historic architecture of Co. Durham* (Newcastle, 1971).

Wiebe, M. B., Conacher, J. B., Matthews, John and Millar, Mary S. (eds), *Benjamin Disraeli's letters, 1838-47* (vols. 3 and 4, Buffalo and London, 1987 and 1989).

Williams, Susan A., *Ladies of influence. Women of the elite in interwar Britain* (London, 2001).

Williamson, Philip, *National crisis and national government: British politics, the economy and empire, 1926-32* (Cambridge, 1992).

Winterbotham, F. W., *The ultraspy. An autobiography* (London, 1989).

Woodward, Kathleen, *Queen Mary. A life and intimate study* (London, 1928).

Yonge, Charles Duke, *The life and administration of Robert Banks, second Earl of Liverpool* (3 vols., London, 1868).

Zetland, Marquis of (ed.), *Letters of Disraeli to Lady Bradford and Lady Chesterfield* (2 vols., London, 1929).

Articles and pamphlets

Arnstein, W. L., 'The survival of the Victorian aristocracy' in F. C. Jaher (ed.), *The rich, the well born and the powerful. Elites and upper classes in history* (Urbana, 1973), pp 203-57.

Blake, Robert, 'The rise of Disraeli' in H. R. Trevor-Roper (ed.), *Essays in British history presented to Sir Keith Feiling* (London, 1964), pp 219-46.

Colls, Robert, "Oh happy English children!': coal, class and education in the North-East' in *Past and Present*, no. 73 (Nov. 1976), pp 75-99.

Cooter, R. J., 'Lady Londonderry and the Irish Catholics of Seaham Harbour: 'No Popery' out of context' in *Recusant History*, vol. 13 (1976), pp 288-98.

Curtin, Michael, 'A question of manners: status and gender in etiquette and courtesy' in *Journal of Modern History*, vol. 57, no. 3 (Sept. 1985), pp 395-423.

Curtis, L. P., 'Anglo-Irish predicament' in *Twentieth Century Studies*, vol. 4 (Nov. 1970), pp 37-63.

de Vere White, Terence, 'Social life in Ireland, 1927-37' in *Studies*, vol. 54 (Spring, 1965), pp 74-82.

Guttsman, W. L., 'The changing social structure of the British political elite, 1886-1935' in *The British Journal of Sociology*, vol. 2, no. 2 (June 1951), pp 122-34.

Hanham, H. J., 'The sale of honours in late Victorian England' in *Victorian Studies*, vol. 3, no. 3 (Mar. 1960), pp 277-89.

Hannam, June, 'Women and politics' in June Purvis (ed.), *Women's history: Britain, 1850-1945* (London, 1995), pp 217-45.

Hardy, George, *A historical account of the Londonderry (Seaham and Sunderland) railway* (Durham, 2001).

Goodman, Dena, 'Public sphere and private life: Toward a synthesis of current historiographical approaches to the Old Regime' in *History and Theory*, vol. 31, no. 1 (Feb. 1992), pp 1-20.

Heesom. A. J., 'Entrepreneurial paternalism: the third Lord Londonderry (1778-1854) and the coal trade' in *Durham University Journal*, vol. 66 (1973-74), pp 238-56.

---- "Legitimate' versus 'Illegitimate' influences: aristocratic electioneering in mid-Victorian Britain' in *Parliamentary History*, vol. 7, part 2 (1988), pp 282-305.

---- 'Problems of church extension in a Victorian new town: the Londonderrys and Seaham Harbour' in *Northern History*, vol. 15 (1979), pp 138-55.

Irvine, Jimmy, 'Carnlough Harbour development scheme, 1854-64' in *The Glynns*, vol. 5 (1977), pp 20-30.

---- 'Glenarm soup kitchens' in *The Glynns*, vol. 2 (1974), pp 36-42.

---- 'Lady France Anne Vane's County Antrim estate' in *The Glynns*, vol. 3 (1975), pp 18-26.

Jackson, T. A., 'Unionist myths, 1912-85' in *Past and Present*, no. 136 (Aug. 1992), pp 164-85.

Jupp, P. J., 'Co. Down elections, 1783-1831' in *Irish Historical Studies*, vol. 18, no. 69 (1972), pp 177-206.

---- 'The roles of royal and aristocratic women in British politics, c. 1782-1832' in Mary O'Dowd and Sabine Wichert (eds), *Chattel, servant or citizen. Women's status in church, state and society* (Belfast, 1995), pp 103-113.

Large, David, 'The wealth of the greater Irish landowners, 1750-1815' in *Irish Historical Studies*, vol. XV, no. 57 (Mar. 1966), pp 21-45.

Lewis, Judith S., 'Maternal health in the English aristocracy: myths and realities, 1790-1840' in *Journal of Social History*, vol. 17 (Fall, 1983), pp 97-114.

Luddy, Maria, 'Women and politics in nineteenth-century Ireland' in Maryann Gialanella Valiulis and Mary O'Dowd (eds), *Women and Irish history. Essays in honour of Margaret MacCurtain* (Dublin, 1997), pp 89-108.

Lynn, Pauline, 'The impact of women. The shaping of political allegiance in County Durham 1918-45' in *The Local Historian*, vol. 28, no. 3 (Aug. 1998), pp 159-75.

McCahill, M. W., 'Peerage creations and the changing character of the British nobility, 1750-1850' in *English Historical Review*, vol. 96 (1981), pp 259-84.

Mackay, Jane and Thane, Pat, 'The Englishwoman' in Robert Colls and Philip Dodd, *Englishness: Culture and politics, 1880-1920* (London, 1986), pp 191-229.

Magnus, Philip, 'Disraeli' in Duff Cooper (ed.), *British Prime Ministers* (London, 1953), pp 108-22.

Martin, Peter, 'Dulce and decorum: Irish nobles and the great war, 1914-19' in A. Gregory and S. Paseta (eds), *Ireland and the Great War. 'A war to unite us all'?* (Manchester, 2002), pp 28-48.

Niall, Mrs. R., 'The political salon of today' in *The Lady's Realm*, vol. 26 (Oct. 1909), pp 150-7.

O'Gorman, Frank, 'Campaign rituals and ceremonies: the social meaning of elections in England, 1780-1860' in *Past and Present*, no. 135 (May 1992), pp 79-115.

---- 'Electoral deference in unreformed England: 1760-1831' in *Journal of Modern History*, vol. 56, no. 3 (Sept. 1984), pp 391-429.

Reynolds, K. D., 'Politics without feminism: the Victorian political hostess' in Clarissa Campbell Orr (ed.), *Wollstonecraft's daughters. Womanhood in England and France, 1780-1920* (Manchester, 1996), pp 94-108.

Rubenstein, W. D., 'British millionaires, 1809-1949' in *Bulletin of the Institute of Historical Research*, vol. XLVII, no. 47 (1974), pp 202-23.

---- 'The end of 'Old Corruption' in Britain, 1780-1860' in *Past and Present*, no. 101 (Nov. 1983), pp 55-86.

Spring, David, 'English landowners and nineteenth-century industrialism' in J. T. Ward and R. G. Wilson (eds), *Land and industry. The landed estate and the industrial revolution* (Newton Abbot, 1971), pp 16-62.

Sturgess, R. W., 'Aristocracy, social structure, and religion in the early Victorian period' in *Victorian Studies*, vol. 6 (Mar. 1963), pp 263-80.

---- 'Landowners and coal in Co. Durham, 1815-50' in M. D. G. Wanklyn (ed.), *Landownership and power in the regions* (Wolverhampton, 1978), pp 93-100.

---- 'The Londonderry trust, 1819-54' in *Archaelogia Aeliana*, 5th series, vol. 10 (1982), pp 1 79-92.

Taylor, A. J., 'The third Marquess of Londonderry and the north-eastern coal trade' in *Durham University Journal*, new series, vol. 17 (1955-55), pp 21-27.

Thomas, David, 'The social origins of marriage partners in the British peerage in the eighteenth and nineteenth centuries' in *Population Studies*, 26, no. 1 (Mar. 1972), pp 99-111.

Von den Steinen, Karl, 'The discovery of women in eighteenth-century political life' in Barbara Kanner (ed.), *The women of England from Anglo-Saxon times to the present* (London, 1980), pp 229-58.

Ward, J. T., 'Landowners and mining' in J. T. Ward and R. G. Wilson (eds), *Land and Industry. The landed estate and the industrial revolution* (Newton Abbott, 1971), pp 63-116.

Theses

Martin, Peter, 'Irish peers, 1909-24: the decline of an aristocratic class' (unpub. MA thesis, University College Dublin, 1998).

Pauley, Jennifer Anne, 'The social and political roles of Edith, Lady Londonderry, 1878-1959' (unpub. D.Phil. thesis, University of Ulster, 1994).

Walker, Linda E., 'The women's movement in England in the late nineteenth and early twentieth centuries' (unpub. PhD thesis, University of Manchester, 1984).

Index